A Celebration of Poets

Grades K-6
Spring 2015

A Celebration of Poets
Grades K-6
Spring 2015

An anthology compiled by Creative Communication, Inc.

Published by:

PO BOX 303 • SMITHFIELD, UTAH 84335
TEL. 435-713-4411 • WWW.POETICPOWER.COM

Authors are responsible for the originality of the writing submitted.

All rights reserved. No part of this book may be reproduced or transmitted in any form or by any means, electronic or mechanical without written permission of the author and publisher.

Copyright © 2015 by Creative Communication, Inc.
Printed in the United States of America

Thank you to our student artists whose work is featured on the cover:
Genevieve Wu - Grade 5, Laura Wang - Grade 6, Robert Hunter - Grade 8, Audrey Han - Grade 3, Nasim Dalirifar - Grade 9, Jacob Wong - Grade 12, Cassandra Fernandez de Aenlle - Grade 12, Haley Sellmeyer - Grade 2, Yihan Wu - Grade 9, Shiyi Huang - Grade 12, Landon Tinsley - Kindergarten, Pranav Sitaraman - Grade 3, and Xinyi Zhang - Grade 3.
To have your art considered for our next book cover, go to www.celebratingart.com.

ISBN: 978-1-60050-699-4

FOREWORD

Dear Reader:

Words are magical. Individually, a dictionary has all the words in the English language. Dictionaries contain words with denotative meanings that are void of any emotion. They simply state what the words mean. The magic of words comes in the combinations that are created from the emotional, connotative meaning that we associate with the words. Individually, words in the phrase "Two roads diverged in a yellow wood..." do not mean much, but combined in this order and you have a line from Frost's classic poem that has meaning to millions of people.

One of my favorite poems is by John Tobias, "Reflections on a Gift of Watermelon Pickle Received from a Friend Called Felicity." The first few lines are

> During that summer
> When unicorns were still possible;
> When the purpose of knees
> Was to be skinned;

These words take me back to a time of my childhood when unicorns were still possible. Through the magic of words, I reminisce and dream.

The words in this book are just that. Words. However, through the weaving of language, a uniqueness is created. A meaning is given that is individualized for each student. As you read the entries selected to be published, look for those words whose combination creates a synergy. A combination of words where the whole is greater than the sum of the parts and an image and meaning is made that sticks with you after the book has closed.

We are pleased to create this book and share these words. We thank the students for taking the risk of entering a contest and congratulate them on being selected to be published.

Sincerely,

Thomas Worthen, Ph.D.
Editor
Creative Communication

WRITING CONTESTS!

Enter our next POETRY contest!

Enter our next ESSAY contest!

Why should I enter?
Win prizes and get published! Each year thousands of dollars in prizes are awarded throughout North America. The top writers in each division receive a monetary award and a free book that includes their published poem or essay. Entries of merit are also selected to be published in our anthology.

Who may enter?
There are four divisions in the poetry contest. The poetry divisions are grades K-3, 4-6, 7-9, and 10-12. There are three divisions in the essay contest. The essay divisions are grades 4-6, 7-9, and 10-12.

What is needed to enter the contest?
To enter the poetry contest send in one original poem, 21 lines or less. To enter the essay contest send in one original non-fiction essay, 100-250 words, on any topic. Please submit each poem and essay with a title, and the following information clearly printed: the writer's name, current grade, home address (optional), school name, school address, teacher's name and teacher's email address (optional). Contact information will only be used to provide information about the contest. For complete contest information go to www.poeticpower.com.

How do I enter?

Enter a poem online at:
www.poeticpower.com
or
Mail your poem to:
  Poetry Contest
  PO Box 303
  Smithfield, UT 84335

Enter an essay online at:
www.poeticpower.com
or
Mail your essay to:
  Essay Contest
  PO Box 303
  Smithfield, UT 84335

When is the deadline?
Poetry contest deadlines are December 3rd, April 7th and August 18th. Essay contest deadlines are October 15th, February 18th, and July 14th. Students can enter one poem and one essay for each spring, summer, and fall contest deadline.

Are there benefits for my teacher?
Yes. Teachers with five or more students published receive a free anthology that includes their students' writing. Teachers may also earn points in our Classroom Rewards program to use towards supplies in their classroom.

For more information please go to our website at **www.poeticpower.com**, email us at editor@poeticpower.com or call 435-713-4411.

TABLE OF CONTENTS

POETIC ACHIEVEMENT HONOR SCHOOLS	1
TOP TEN WINNERS	7
GRADES 4-5-6 HIGH MERIT POEMS	15
GRADES K-1-2-3 HIGH MERIT POEMS	145
INDEX BY AUTHOR	181
INDEX BY SCHOOL	193

POEMS FROM CANADA ARE INCLUDED IN THIS EDITION
AS WELL AS POEMS FROM THE FOLLOWING STATES:

ARIZONA
COLORADO
PENNSYLVANIA
UTAH
VIRGINIA

Spring 2015
Poetic Achievement
Honor Schools

*Teachers who had fifteen or more poets accepted to be published

The following schools are recognized as receiving a "Poetic Achievement Award." This award is given to schools who have a large number of entries of which over fifty percent are accepted for publication. With hundreds of schools entering our contest, only a small percent of these schools are honored with this award. The purpose of this award is to recognize schools with excellent Language Arts programs. This award qualifies these schools to receive a complimentary copy of this anthology.

A J McLellan Elementary School
Surrey, BC
Twyla Koop
Cindy Zaklan*

Annieville Elementary School
Delta, BC
Jennifer Goodale*

Baker Central School
Fort Morgan, CO
Julie Frink*

Barratt Elementary School
American Fork, UT
Vickie Marrott*

Broadview Avenue Public School
Ottawa, ON
Katherine Cameron*

California Middle School
Coal Center, PA
Debbie Carnello*

Cheswick Christian Academy
Cheswick, PA
Sharon San Rocco*

Chickahominy Middle School
Mechanicsville, VA
Holly Angelidis*
Kimberly Harrell
Cynthia Sinanian

Colby Village Elementary School
Dartmouth, NS
Lynn Coolen
Mr. Cruddas*

Colorado Connections Academy
Englewood, CO
Jacob Clements
Olivia Cockey
Maureen Field
Fred Hudson
Nicole Jones
Jaclyn Lee
Benjamin Rohret
Jane Thomson
Laura Troy
Cassandra Vogel
Patty Wilson

Colwyn Elementary School
Colwyn, PA
Kevin Reilly*

East Stroudsburg Elementary School
East Stroudsburg, PA
James Parton*
Chris Tosh

Ecole elementaire Renaissance
Burlington, ON
Sandra Sevegny*

École Montessori de Montréal
LaSalle, QC
Mrs. Carlleen
Haroula Pilarinos*
Carleen Wrazen*

Ecole Montessori International Montreal
Montreal, QC
Lori Beauregard*
Kristin Gerchicoff*

Erie Elementary School
Erie, CO
Laurena Oliver*

Fishing Creek Elementary School
Lewisberry, PA
Clair E. Richcrick*

Foothill Elementary School
Boulder, CO
Molly Kirk
Aimée Newfield*
Frannie Parkinson

Forest Hill School – Senior Campus
St Lazare, QC
Grace Henderson*

George Washington Academy
Saint George, UT
Regina Kerr*
Valerie Sedgwick*
Kerri Wright

Jack Hulland Elementary School
Whitehorse, YT
Sara Tillett*

Jenkintown Elementary School
Jenkintown, PA
Leah Abdollahi*

Khalsa Montessori Elementary School
Phoenix, AZ
Lindsay Caglio*

Khalsa School - Old Yale Road Campus
Surrey, BC
Marlene Cruz
Indira Menon
Mr. Pascual*
Mrs. Thalagala

Klein Elementary School
Erie, PA
Elizabeth Brown*

Lancaster Mennonite School - Locust Grove
Lancaster, PA
Barbara Josephian
Pat Shelly*

Lfpa Charter School-Warner
Gilbert, AZ
Kimberly Marin*

Lincoln Elementary School
Pittsburgh, PA
Karen Flinter*

Lookout Mountain School
Phoenix, AZ
Grace Manno*

Luther Memorial Learning Center
Erie, PA
Julie Baldwin*

Poetic Achievement Honor Schools

Mary Blair Elementary School
Loveland, CO
    Tanya Brown
    Laura Saunders
    JoAnna Tripi*

Mary Walter Elementary School
Bealeton, VA
    Doreen Garvey*

McDowell Mountain Elementary School
Fountain Hills, AZ
    Lynette Gross
    Talia Houseal*
    Linda Ness*
    Anne Ruttler

Mifflin County Middle School
Lewistown, PA
    Mrs. Reese*

Mon Yough Catholic School
White Oak, PA
    Judith Butler*
    Marsha Giglio*

Monelison Middle School
Madison Heights, VA
    Lynette Smith*

Moravian Academy Middle School
Bethlehem, PA
    Cindy Siegfried*

Mount Nittany Middle School
State College, PA
    Scott W. Given*
    Katrina Lee*

Mountain View Elementary School
Broomfield, CO
    Tom Doyle*

Nazareth Area Intermediate School
Nazareth, PA
    Mrs. Fatzinger
    Karen Kammerdiener
    Maxine Marsh
    Lynn Post*
    Susan Young

Nevin Platt Middle School
Boulder, CO
    Michael Morrow*

Nottingham Elementary School
Arlington, VA
    Laura Hansen*

Oak Ridge Elementary School
Harleysville, PA
    Jill Schumacher*

Our Lady of Mount Carmel School
Doylestown, PA
    Dawn Brooks
    Paula Kin*
    Rosemary Miller

Paul L Dunbar Middle School for Innovation
Lynchburg, VA
    Brittany Clark-Slaughter
    Maria Galeone
    Contessa Johnson*

Peasley Middle School
Gloucester, VA
    Pearl Sadler
    LeeAnn VanVranken*

Penn-Kidder Campus
Albrightsville, PA
    Susan Becker
    Howard Gregory*
    Jason McElmoyle
    Kathryn McFadden*
    Angelina O'Rourke
    Mrs. Tirpak*

Providence Hall Elementary School
Herriman, UT
Kami Mecham*

Queen of All Saints Elementary School
Coquitlam, BC
Doug Graf*

Riverdale Elementary School
Thornton, CO
Jackie Woytek*

Robeson Elementary Center
Birdsboro, PA
Jean McCarney*

Roosevelt Edison Charter School
Colorado Springs, CO
Becky DeGarmo
Vickie Denman
Sharron Rutz

Rosemont Forest Elementary School
Virginia Beach, VA
Monica Garrison
Beverly Wooddell

Sagewood Middle School
Parker, CO
Agie Behounek
Carole Lively
Julie Shouldice

Saskatoon Christian School
Saskatoon, SK
Naomi Brecht
Christina McVittie
Tammy Parker*
Natasha Stonehouse*

Silver Stream Public School
Richmond Hill, ON
Mrs. Hilliar
Kelly Karalis*

Sol Feinstone Elementary School
Newtown, PA
Patricia Lipton*

St Jerome Elementary School
Philadelphia, PA
Luba Kwoczak*

St John Bosco Academy
Pittsburgh, PA
Mary Ellen O'Connell*

St John Neumann Academy
Blacksburg, VA
Rachael Beach
Katie Keyes
Jenny Mishoe
Niki Myles
Sarah Pickeral
Layla Staubus
Maggie Thomasson
Kara Thurman

St Peter Cathedral School
Erie, PA
Amy Parini*

Steamboat Springs Middle School
Steamboat Springs, CO
Mrs. Cathy Girard*

The Valleys Senior Public School
Mississauga, ON
Marina Fernandes*

Vernfield Elementary School
Telford, PA
Susan Mandia*

Villa Maria Academy Lower School
Immaculata, PA
MaryAnn Gratton
Maureen Wible*

White Pine Middle School
    Richmond, UT
        Jessie Datwyler
        Evelyn Meikle
        Wynnde Whittier

Top Ten Winners

List of Top Ten Winners for Spring 2015; listed alphabetically

Madeeha Alikhan	Grade 5	Fry Elementary School	IL
Tenesha Christiansen	Grade 6	Jack Hulland Elementary School	YT
Abbey Colbert	Grade 3	Northfield Elementary School	OH
Anais Coyne	Grade 5	Donna Shepard Intermediate School	TX
Deeya Datta	Grade 5	Brookwood Elementary School	GA
Kyla Geiger	Grade 3	Rushwood Elementary School	OH
Jack Kidnie	Grade 3	Ostmann Elementary School	MO
Jax Managan	Grade 6	Cross Classical Academy	TX
Siobhan Milton	Grade 2	The Montessori School	CT
Ava Moore	Grade 2	Duchesne Academy of the Sacred Heart	TX
Avery Munoz	Grade 3	Forest Ridge Elementary School	TX
Kanchan Naik	Grade 6	John M Gomes Elementary School	CA
Lea Prough	Grade 5	Laurence School	CA
Elliott Reaves	Grade 2	St Walter School	IL
Ella Rose	Grade 6	Oak Lawn School	RI
Ivyann Shen	Grade 3	Southgate School	NY
Shriya Sreeju	Grade 1	William Faria Elementary School	CA
Celina Stodder	Grade 3	Anneliese's Schools - Willowbrook	CA
Michelle Wilkinson	Grade 4	Fort Worth Country Day School	TX
Esther Woelfel	Grade 6	Northern Lights Private School	MO

All Top Ten Winners may also be seen at www.poeticpower.com

Ode to the Sky
Look up, see the glorious sky!
The sun arises, filling every view with warmth, lets everyone feel the company.

Chills when furious, he groans when the silver sword splits his horizon.
Admiration, he lures us with a big, welcoming sun, cloudless serene beauty.
"Let's go for a walk," or "Let's have a picnic" we say.

His tears of joy drizzle upon us, while his sorrow plop, plop, plops down heavily.
Coming down quickly, no two alike, delicate, as soft as a pillow,
melting on our tongues, 1,2,3, each snowflake falls after the other.

Evening: intense orange and red, light blue, pink, all at once make up the magnificent sunset.

His deep black never-ending cape covers with pride, glistening diamonds embedded,
inviting sleep with the dim light of the moon.

Madeeha Alikhan, Grade 5

Kory
I look down from the TV,
your legs splayed to the side
as you sit on the floor.
You push toy cars
up and down the ramps
I've built for you.

Your button nose
pokes out of your
blonde curtain of hair.
We slide down the brown carpet stairs
　　　　　　　bump
　　　　　　　　　bump
　　　　　　　　　　　bump.
You yell, "Piggyback!" over and over.

Then I see it,
the invisible wall
separating our ages,
the age of play and the age
of growing up.

Tenesha Christiansen, Grade 6

Always There
When children play alone and about,
　　A playmate that's never seen comes out,
Those that are lonely, seeking a friend,
　　Can play with him until the days end!

For when you lay awake in your bed,
　　He sends tons of thoughts into your head,
Some good, some bad, and all in between,
　　And some thoughts only your mind has seen.

It's he that makes your dolls become real,
　　And turns pretend food into a meal,
He makes your stick horse gallop away,
　　And loves to indulge in all you play,

And all the while he plays with you,
　　He's playing with other children too!
He's with children throughout creation,
　　He is known as Imagination!

Esther Woelfel, Grade 6

America the Beautiful

The seashores, full of population
A salt and sand station
An amazing vacation
You'll get at the shores

The forests' elevation
And their locations
Are worth fascination
To the foliated forests

If you could turn your attention
To the mountains' elevation
Our faith can move the destination
Of this God-glorifying monument

The rivers' situation
Is that it has no destination
Or starting location
Of these rushing, racing rivers

Use your imagination
This poem is to give you inspiration
Of what an amazing nation
We all dwell in today

Jax Managan, Grade 6

Water

Water gushes, roaring loud,
Over mossy slates of rock
Thinner, thinner it does grow
Until it trickles drop by drop
Reaching towards the glossy pond
Surface so serene
First drop reaches tranquil pool
Disrupting peaceful dreams
Ripples spread across the dream like creek
Upturning bubbles of foam
Reaching across in angry curls
An ashen fire grows
Milky droplets hit the edge
Its journey is finally at its end

Deeya Datta, Grade 5

Ripple

Ripple, ripple, rain or shine
Kissing stones, flowing fine
Always bustling, never calm
Still dancing in my palm
Catching sunlight, stealing blue
Always hiding its true hue
When all's quiet, it's still aquiver
Such is the beauty of the nearby river

Kanchan Naik, Grade 6

Where the Willow Hangs

Down by the creek where the willow hangs, a singer flies from her branch.
Her song is as sweet as the honey, which sways on the limbs of the tree.

Down by the creek where the honey sways, a weaver weaves his web.
His web is as intricate as the bark, which stays as still as stone.

Down by the creek where the bark stands still, a woodcarver whittles her wood.
Her pecking is as faint as the lines etched in the leaves, which fall silently to the bare ground.

Down by the creek where the willow's leaves fall, a racer takes a bound.
His leap is high as the tip of the willow, where the wind blows strong.

Down by the creek where the wind blows strong, an aviator takes flight.
Her wings are as clear as the creek, where the willow hangs.

Down by the creek where the willow hangs, a community there does live.
A miniature world, full of life.

Where the willow hangs.

Ella Rose, Grade 6

Words

My rosy pink lips
babble on endlessly
How must I make sense?
Should my sentences be
the nothingness in
this world?
Words that do make
sense ridicule me,
puncture me, tease me
As salty tears do
begin to form, I
conjoin my thoughts.
I look to the left,
and then to the right,
My words, which was
a sprinting stream,
finally found the
thought to say—
"This world is beautiful,
and so am I."

Anais Coyne, Grade 5

Ice

Scraped by rusty blades
Tap toe step, glide
Scuffed by white boots
Spiral spin
Crushed by jagged
Metal long thin lines
Etched in by clear
Intentions broken up
By jumps and
Music, giving instruction
Spraying snow with a stop
Smoothed by
New beginnings
Ready to take someone
Far, cold creeping
Through tights
Boxed in by walls
And boots eager to glide

Lea Prough, Grade 5

You Are You

A night reflection on the water,
sleek, white and shimmering
a flower blossom,
Beautiful, and full of passion
A deep blue ocean,
full of golden treasure.
A dream of hope,
Just slightly out of reach.
You are you!
A night reflection,
illuminating the dark.
A vision of light, hope, and peace.

Michelle Wilkinson, Grade 4

I Am a Lily Pad

I am a lily pad, swaying, swaying.
The frog jumps down,
The ducks swim past,
I make no sound,
With all the animals swimming around.

My flowers bloom, a dragonfly lands,
I wait and wait until the end.

Day and night pass,
The darkness looms avast,
A soul waiting in the dark,
A small beauty in a pond, at a park.
Celina Stodder, Grade 3

Wishes on a Winter Night

I gaze out the white sequin window
at the icing covered wonderland,
nothing like the secure place that grasps me.

Visions of snow angels and snowmen
dance in my head,
waking my will to grab my coat, snow pants, and mittens.

I observe a fluffy squirrel outside,
trembling even under its blanket of soft fur,
searching for just one puny acorn.
Instead it finds itself buried in the deep snow,
cold and hungry in the bitter world that traps him.

I shoot the creature one last stare of pity
before turning towards the cluster of
loving people sitting cozily in the arm chairs,
laughter as sweet as bells
as they dive into a pleasant conversation.

They sip their sticky hot cocoa,
the small fire crackling and blazing
beside our looming fir tree adorned in lights
under the stars in the Christmas air.
Ivyann Shen, Grade 3

World in My Eyes

Last night I had a dream,
It was so good I had to beam,
This is my dream that I tell to you,
Please enjoy it as I go on through.
I saw the world so glad,
Not a creature or person feeling sad,
I saw everyone being friends,
And I saw no more violence,
I saw everyone dancing in harmony,
And I saw no more cruelty,
I saw the water so crystal clear,
And I saw the fish swimming free,
I heard the rustling of leaves,
And I heard the buzzing of bees,
I heard the laughter of children,
And there was love everywhere!
If this dream had come true,
Then my heart would have leapt,
And I would have no longer felt blue,
The world would be better through and through!
Shriya Sreeju, Grade 1

Phoenix

I already feel the living legend
coming into my soul.
With it's swaying wings, it
makes the trees bend over
and touch the ground.
It flies with wings bigger than the sky can reach.
The beautiful Candid blue feathering erases
the blue within me.
Whenever life gives me trouble,
I think of one.
A Phoenix, rising and creating anew.
Kyla Geiger, Grade 3

Every Animal Is Unique

Every animal is unique.
A fish has fins and a duck has a beak.
A rhino has horns and a bear is brave,
and the nocturnal bats go to sleep in a cave.

The lions and leopards stalk their prey,
in the tall grass all night and day.
The dolphins skim the water, playful and alive,
and the bees collect pollen, then bring it to their hive.

The mice act cowardly, meek and wise.
The eagles soar above, using their watchful eyes.
Squirrels eat acorns and scurry up trees,
and dogs are obedient and like to please.

You see, all animals are unique, one way or another.
And I wrote this 'cause I want you to seek and discover,
that nature is not just nature—it's a glory.
And that is the end of my unique story.

Jack Kidnie, Grade 3

Happy Cars

Red, yellow, and blue,
there are so many things to do.

Fast and slow, dirty and clean,
there are many types of driving machines.

Smooth, rough, old and new,
lots of creations passing through.

One by one they are produced,
custom made just for you.

Peppy purrs, screeches and spurs.
Revving engines, winding curves.

On the move, sitting still.
Going places, what a thrill.

Charged to go, all night and day.
Happily humming along the way.

Elliott Reaves, Grade 2

A Heart's Life

A heart's life
is just happiness
filled with joy,
memories,
friendship,
but most of all
it's filled
with love
and peace
and family.

Avery Munoz, Grade 3

High Above the World

High above the world
High above the chimney tops
is my world
my home
my time
my life.
Level with the ground
sheltered by mountains
silent nights' stars
and living wild
living free!
Where do you belong?

Siobhan Milton, Grade 2

Winter

The wind whistles through the air calling me to come out to play
My nose is pressed up against the window and snowmen are smiling at me

People shoveling their driveways
Kids laughing

I can't wait any longer!
The crystal snow falls on my cheeks

The snow is as cold as ice floating in the ocean

I jump into the blanket of snow   Aaahh!
                                       I'm free!

Abbey Colbert, Grade 3

Deep in the Jungle
Deep in the jungle
the prey stay.
May the king sit on the highest spot.
Gazing down at his fellow subjects.
Spotted today's dinner, he did, descending
towards the water.

The foxes sipping water on the cool evening.
Returning home for dinner, before sunset.
They heard a crack, but nothing else.

Closer down he went making no sound.
He slouched down closest to the ground.
With his family close to home. Wanting
to provide a special dinner, he sprinted
towards the water.

Deep in the jungle.

Ava Moore, Grade 2

Grades 4-5-6
High Merit Poems

Black Steed
The noble steed glides,
Through the gloomy gray night,
His tail is flowing before him,
Like a black silvery flag,

Gliding like a eagle,
He gallops through the wind,
His hooves barely touch the earth,
His heart is pounding like a drum,

His ears are intent,
For he knows not what is ahead
Claire Gunther, Grade 5

Owls
Owls in the night
eyes shining so bright
changing direction swiftly softly

Tawny, snowy, great-horned
horned with no horns
white as snow
tawny watch them go

Nocturnal nighttime
cold and dark
hear them hooting in the still quiet night
Emma Hathaway, Grade 5

Ode to Pianos
My fingers glide across the keys
While I play the 7th symphony
Going an octave higher
To complete this famous song
Here's an ode to pianos
The one that has helped me learn
For a voice that doesn't sing
It has sung very well
It has helped me learn
Like a teacher in a school
It will help me learn
Until I graduate.
Audrey Southam, Grade 5

Me
I can be the stars,
I can be the sea.
I can be so unique,
Or without a thing to be.

I wish I were the earth,
I wish I were the sea.
I wish that I was so unique,
But all these things I wish I were,
was never meant to be.
Anna Currimbhoy, Grade 4

My Xbox 360
I play on my Xbox 360
I tap the keys
I drive cars
I earn money
I buy cars
I can fly planes
I put on masks
I can drive a tank
I love to play GTA5
Come play with me!
Ivan Arias, Grade 4

Graduation
G owns and caps
R eceiving a diploma
A speech is given
D rying our tears
U nforgetable memories
A rriving at the reception hall
T ime to eat
I will play the piano
O h no! Need to say goodbye
N ext year, new friends
Kristie Thai, Grade 6

Waving Hello
I sway and crash upon you.
I am gentle, yet dangerous too.
Home to many animals, I am.
In a storm, I crazily crash and slam.
Always, I brush the calming shore.
As soon as you see me, you'll want more.
Many people say I put on a show,
As I sway back and forth, waving hello.
Can you guess what I am?
The ocean
Audrey Kaufman, Grade 6

Life Is a Roller Coaster
Life is a roller coaster
Full of ups
And downs
You don't know
What to expect
Surprising…
Scary…
Spectacular…
Enjoy the ride
Life is a roller coaster
Patrick Dougherty, Grade 4

Bee
B uzz, buzz, buzz all day long
E xtraordinary pollinator
E ven though everyone is scared of them
Sophia Frank, Grade 6

The Test
A white paper gleams in the afternoon sun
It beholds the names of the Cho Dan Bo.
The Black Belt hopefuls
Who will soon train every day.

I am one of the few
I train day after day
I know the material
Like a child knows how to walk.
At one point, it was new to you
But now, it is habit.

And now the day has come.
I freeze during Combinations.
Drowning in my own sweat,
I fail to calm myself.
Desperately, I remind myself,
You know this.
You know you know this.

Months later
A new paper hangs in the lobby.
But this time it shows the Cho Dan.
And my name is proudly shining.
Vanessa Rainier, Grade 6

Don't Take Me Away
Don't take me away
Don't make this
My last day
Mama
Papa
Save me
Now

Don't take me away
Brother
Sister
Don't let this mister
Take me now
Don't take me away
Today

Don't take me away
Family
Please see
This choice is real
I will be here haunting

You let him take me away
Today
Sydney Topoleski, Grade 4

America's Pastime
I am soaring high like a bird
I wonder what a hot dog taste like
I hear the fantastic fans cheering
I see the webbing of a pitcher's glove
I want to be a fans souvenir
I am just a baseball
I pretend to be a booming homerun
I feel the bat hit my stitches
I touch the soft infield dirt
I worry about being a foul ball
I cry because
I am just a baseball
I understand I'm just a baseball
I say I want to be more
I dream of being more
I hope I can be more but
I am just a baseball
Bailey Hudgins, Grade 6

Where the Trees Once Grew
Here trees were,
Where they once grew.
With green-gold leaves,
Laden with dew.
They used to stand,
They were once new.
For here is where,
The trees once grew.

They fell from axe,
They got sliced right through.
They left no trace,
Not one small clue.
They were once here,
It is quite true.
I'm standing where,
The trees once grew.
Anika Davie, Grade 5

Watermelon
The sun's bright glare
forces me to blink.
I look down at the picnic table
and gaze
at your red luscious flesh,
as I imagine devouring you.
I begin to drool.
Temptation nudges me
to snatch you off my plate
and take a bite.
Desperate for your juicy flavor.
I wolf you down
and four seeds
chase your sweetness
down my throat.
Naoise Dempsey, Grade 6

The Asteroid
65 million years ago in the dinosaur's time
An asteroid hit the land.
Dust went up all over the world
It was made of ash, dirt, and sand.

The sun didn't shine through for months
The Earth was barren and dry.
No one could find enough food
And the dinosaurs started to die.

When those giant lizards started to die
The mammals went underground.
And so to this day
Those fellows are still around.
Brady Semtner, Grade 6

Hole in One
It's a bright morning,
at the first tee.

I hit the first ball,
and hope it will fly free.

195 yards it goes,
right on the green.

It's a hold in one,
and I shout with glee.

What a great day it is,
and golfing is where I like to be.
Thomas Betzner, Grade 4

Summer
Having fun in the summer sun,
My favorite time of year,
Some days seem as hot as fire,
Jumping into a pool as cold as ice,
So refreshing!
During the summer I can go to the beach,
I can stay at home,
Relaxing all day long.
I can catch lightning bugs,
Or watch fireworks at night,
I can eat some ice cream,
Or I can go on a roller coaster.
Being carefree is what it's all about,
I wish summer could last forever.
Emma Schultz, Grade 6

Grandfather
Billy likes to play with trucks.
They make him really happy.
But he'd trade them in a second,
To spend more time with his Pappy.
Alexandra Berish, Grade 4

Winter Is Coming
The wind blows softly
the ground is frosty

Little snowflakes fall
like feathers drifting
through air the sun is
hiding in the thick fog

Winter is coming,
the snow is falling

The cocoa is ready
in the cabinet, the
scarves are hung, the
Uggs are on

Winter is coming,
the snow is falling.
Maisie Wagner, Grade 6

Earth, Water, Sky
I am Sky
I wonder about the oceans
I hear the waves crash on the shore
I want to run along the plains
I am Sky

I pretend to run through lush forests
I feel the mist on my face
I touch the clouds in the sky
I worry the seas will flood me
I am Earth

I understand the oceans
I say I want to fly through clouds
I dream of running on grass
I try to count every star
I hope to be a tree
I am Water
Alec Daniel, Grade 6

The Blast
First I see the crowd
Then people all around me
I feel it's time to shine
And have a great competition
I see my target on the cardboard wall
And the people before me
Laying on the mats and ready to fire
BLAST! I hear a shot
Then it's my turn
BLAST! I am out of time
Trophies are behind me
I hear the crowd screaming
Because I am the champion
Mackenzie Johnson, Grade 6

Beach
Waves coming towards me crashing
I look down, then I get up and
look around

When I walk up and see the trees,
there's a beehive full of bees!

When I take a summer tan, it is so
hot that I need a fan.

When I see surfers on the beach
I can see them taking turns each.

It is cool to go to the beach today, because
I can have fun all day.
Jada Danquah, Grade 4

Teddy Bear
Teddy bear
Dreams of
A child's love.

Teddy bear
Knows of
The dusky attic.

Teddy bear
Wishes he
Could speak to the child.

Teddy bear
Promises
to always be by my side.
Alexandria Dobson, Grade 4

The Ocean
The ocean could be scary
It could pull you in
You can get swallowed
By a giant wave
You can try to hide
But it will always find you
Wash your dishes, it is there
Wash your hands, it is there
Go outside, it is there
One time I went too far out
I couldn't swim
If my dad wasn't there
I would have drowned there
Right there at the beach
Just make sure it doesn't
Swallow you.
Kai Davis, Grade 4

Nightmares
I like it when I'm asleep
Because I don't hear a peep.
The terrible words can't get to me,
It's really just a better place to be.
So calm, peaceful, and quiet,
No such thing as a riot.

But in your dreams,
The dark things scream.
They creep and crawl,
And squirm and sprawl.
One by one, ripping you apart,
Finally tearing at your heart.
Maybe there is no way to escape
The things we experience today.
Trinity R., Grade 6

I Can't Write a Poem
Forget it.
You must be kidding.
I have no paper.
My pencil is broken.
My brain is not working.
My hands are too dirty.
I am still asleep.
I just can't wake up.
Time is up?
Uh Oh!
All I have is a list of excuses.
You love it?
Really?
No kidding?
Would you like to see another one?
Max Yue Li, Grade 4

I Belong
I am a book about long lost adventures
I wonder if anyone will want me
I hear the bang of swords clashing
I see the ballrooms with laughing guests
I am like an ant to humans
I pretend to be a great king
I feel the sun on me
I touch the wind while I flap in the breeze
I worry I will never be read
I cry when rain pours down on me
I understand I can't walk
I say I will be great
I dream of a purpose
I try to forget I am not human
I hope I will be useful
I am happy with who I am
Skylar Tenan, Grade 6

Butterflies
Butterflies fly from here to there
Almost around everywhere

Their wings look like leaves in the trees
That sway in the breeze

When I see them
I try to catch them
But, they're too fast for me

Their colors are like rainbows that shine
Until they glow

You won't see them at night because,
The dark gives them a fright.
Victoria Baker, Grade 4

Mom
You can get cancer
Any minute
Like my mom
When I heard
I was scared
Like ice water down my back
She died from cancer
I wanted to be
A strong bull
You could hear
My tears whistle
As they fell to the ground
Crash, bang
I am a strong bull
You can get cancer any minute
Lainee Bernhardt, Grade 6

Black Jaguar
A shadow slinks through the trees,
Looking for a tasty snack.
Then like a frog he leaps,
And lands on a screaming monkey.

Done with his treat,
He sneaks
Into a midnight cave,
Then falls asleep.

He wakes,
Crawls out upon the jungle floor,
The rays of morning light is
Shining down on him
His eyes floating upon his domain,
Feeling like a king.
Lena Gibson, Grade 5

The Songs of Nature
Swish, Swoosh
The tree branches flow
Through the soft summer breeze

Splish, Splash
The river flows
Through the jagged edge rocks

Crik, Croak
The frog leaps
On top of the slimy but beautiful Lilies

Chip, Chirp
The bird sings
In the swaying trees

Softly, Singing
Nature flows
All around us softly singing, Nature flows
Emma Harris, Grade 6

Drops of Red Glitter
Drops of red glitter
circle down the drain.
Seems depression
is only a claim to fame.

Silver and diamonds
clatter on the floor.
She curls in a ball
and leans toward the door.

Slowly dying
but feels so alive.
It's finally done her over
can no longer thrive.

Sinking even deeper
to eternal sleep.
She takes her final breath
and dies without a peep.
Morgan Graham, Grade 6

Blue
Blue is the color of the sky.
Blue is the ocean at the beach.
Blue is a feeling of joy.
Blue is the fresh air.
Blue smells like a fresh meadow of flowers.
Blue tastes like blueberries.
Blue sounds like birds flying in the sky.
Blue looks like water.
Blue feels like a cool breeze.
Blue makes me want to go outside.
Blue is my favorite color.
Paige Misavage, Grade 4

Playing Basketball
I like to play sports
and be outside.
I ride my bike to the basketball courts
to play a game of horse.

When I play basketball,
I feel very relaxed.
When I win I feel like the king of the pack.

The sport itself is very fun,
we get a big woo-hoo when we are all done.
Aiden Gillespie, Grade 6

Imaginary Boy
I love Marco Green,
His smile lights up the night.
He isn't mean,
He's a delight.
I'm his queen,
He's my shining knight.
He's only thirteen,
I fell in love at first sight,
With his eyes of aquamarine.
We never had a fight,
Even though he can't be seen!
Maura Corkery, Grade 6

Friendship
Untouchable

Our friendship is real
But yet untouchable.
You can hear it
Yet you can't see it.
People think it is fake
Well that is a mistake.
It is real
Yet it's untouchable.
Our friendship is never ending.
Nicholas Dolan, Grade 6

Being Short
I stretched and stretched
But I'm still not tall at all

I jumped and jumped,
Not even close!

I was determined to grow
So I worked and I worked.

I was tall
One inch and all!
Briona Giles, Grade 4

Gone
I missed you oh so dear.
I love you even more.
Now that you are near,
I will be happy once more.
I've thought about you,
and about him too.
I've wondered if you changed,
and how much more he grew.
I will be the first of people
to see you when you come.
I am happy when you are here,
but sad when you are gone.
Bye-bye, farewell!
I don't want you to go.
I sat there watching you leave.
Farther, farther
up in the heavens you go.
I am happy when you are here,
but sad when you are gone.
And now you're gone.
Haley Allman, Grade 6

Drawing
Drawing is a
Circle
A Figure eight
On the ice
Drawing has no end
Everything's
Inside your head
Don't keep ideas
Trapped in your
Brain
Make sure
They pour out
Just like the rain
Drawing can be done
Anywhere
It starts right here
And it goes to there
Round and round
The ideas take shape
Drawing is a circle
Jenna French, Grade 4

Dragonfly
D ancing gracefully across the sky
R acing gently over the water
A lways looking beautiful in the sun
G iant eyes staring at you
O ften misconceived as beasts
N ever living very long
F earing humans all the time
L eaving one area every night
Y earning for a better day
Grace Sanborn, Grade 6

Grass
Grass
Walking with bare feet
Feeling like a summer day
Gentle on my skin
Katharine Pedroza, Grade 5

Polar Bear
Polar bear
Protecting their cubs
Catching their fish for dinner
Roaming in deep snow
Timothy Dudak, Grade 5

Big Rig
Tall, big, and strong
Roaring across the road
Sometimes scary but cool to observe
Eighteen wheeler
Christopher Kaatz, Grade 5

Egg Problems
I once saw an egg,
I cracked it on my head.
My mom was very mad,
But it really wasn't that bad.
Sarah Duetsch, Grade 4

Old Mold
All of our bread was very old,
And we ended up finding mold.
But we still decided to take a lick,
And then we all got very sick.
Sophia Mishoe, Grade 4

Bubbles
Soaring up
Tumbling down
Stopping then popping
Now they're gone
Rylee Nauffts, Grade 5

Mark
Maintainable
Artistic
Responsible
Kind
Mark Zern, Grade 4

Leaves
Leaves are falling
Colors everywhere
Spring is coming
Hurrah, hurrah
Rylan Coyne, Grade 4

Living in a Nightmare
I was 14 when it all started
I was living a normal life
I played piano, had friends, and a family
I was a normal kid
Then things started to change
I remember a man chose if he wanted us to die or go to the camps
I was sent to the camps
When we got there our heads were shaved, and a number was scratched into our wrists
Identities were lost
I remember going on a march
But it wasn't the kind of march you would think it was
We walked all day and night
But we didn't know where we were going
We couldn't rest or slow down the slightest bit
Or we would be dead
My best friend struggled to keep moving
I had to watch her die
I was so tired I wanted to stop
But I knew if I did
That would be the end for me
It was like living a nightmare
Olivia Dorko, Grade 6

The Wall of Blackness
I walked into the eerie filled night
The trees were staring and the lights were angrily flickering
But still I trudged on.
The blizzard pinched my face
Chills were creeping up my spine
The wind howled even louder
Yet, I could not stop now.
The snow was hurling down from the sky
My hands were frozen and my feet were yelling
Still I did not stop.
The road stretched itself further and my jacket got thinner
Home seemed a faraway word
I shuffled along.
The trees were laughing evilly
The birds stopped and stared
The wind let out a loud roar
My feet could not hold me up much longer.
Knowing that there would be a light at the end of a tunnel, I trudged on
The dark wall of blackness soon parted and I saw light.
I ran only to have my feet collapse under me
The night of misery and imagery was finally — over!
Renae Wipf, Grade 6

High Heels and Sneakers
High heels
High, beautiful
Walking, partying, pleasing
Stylish, different, colorful, fun
Running, dancing, playing
Flat, cool
Sneakers
Alexa Lafleur, Grade 6

Graduation
G rowing up
R eady for new challenges
A time to celebrate
D iplomas will be handed out
U nforgettable memories
A special time for everyone
T hrowing our caps in the air
I ndependence will be shown
O n this day gowns are worn
N ew beginning
Marco Luigi Sicoli, Grade 6

Friends
Friends
Can be
Anything
Friends
Can be
Milk and Cookies
Cuddly teddy bears
Beautiful butterflies
Friends can be that
And much more
Sara Perrigo, Grade 4

Graduation
G oodbye elementary, hello high school
R eady to start a new beginning
A cap and gown are worn at the ceremony
D iplomas are given
U nbelievable memories I will never forget
A special day for all of us
T ime to move on
I will miss my teachers and friends
O verwhelming emotions
N ew school here I come
Sabrina Guerin, Grade 6

Ode To Dirtbikes
Down goes the gate
Those engines roaring like a bear
Battling for the holeshot
Scrubbing up the jump
Whipping through the air
Soaring like an eagle
Landing like a jet
Battling for that first place spot
Looking for the best route
Cornering like a pro
Cole Duvall, Grade 5

Misty
Misty is active
This cat loves the toy laser
She runs, pounces, jumps
Marc-Olivier Pilon, Grade 4

About Me
I am different from everyone else,
I have blue eyes,
I have blonde hair,
and I am 11.

I love sports,
I like to play football, soccer,
basketball, and baseball.

I also love to play video games,
I have a game boy,
an Xbox 360,
and a PlayStation 2.

But the thing I love most is my family,
I live with my Aunt Lou Lou,
and my cousin Ashley.

And I can't forget my pets,
I have 4 cats,
and 1 hamster.

Well I guess that's all.
Brendon Deems-Warnick, Grade 6

Fields of Blue and Grey
A great field of battle,
Met on this here ground,
None like it, nor will there be ever,
So much death, so much sorrow,
Yet so much gain amongst the loss.

Trees cover the perimeter of the fields,
Cannons by their side,
The sounds of battle ringing in my mind,
Clashing of the rifles,
Booming of the cannons,
Clinging of the bayonets,

Now I am met here,
Among these fields,
Where the blue and the grey met,
I am one of them.

For I shall live as they did,
Shoot as they did,
And, sadly, kill as they did.
Also I shall die as they did,
In this here town of Gettysburg.
Xavier John Django Hons, Grade 6

Stars
Night time surprises,
Shine so bright, yet live so far,
Fade, but come again...
Karen Mendez, Grade 5

Oh Lovely Moon
Up in the licorice sky,
floating like a ghost.

Beneath the wispy clouds,
smiling as you look down.

Glittering as a large diamond,
shining brighter than a pearl.

Controller of the silent whistling,
singing a sad song through the branches.

Flying as a brilliant shimmering light
under the blanket of twinkling stars.

Queen of the night creepers
who lurk through the dark trees.

Appearing as a firefly,
better than the Sun.

Prouder than a waterfall,
showering a heavenly light
down upon the tender grasses,
bathing in the moonlight.

He, the Sun, may control the day.
You surpass him, oh lovely Moon.
You control the night.
NagaSriya Ramisetty, Grade 4

Seasons
Fall
Raindrops begin to plop
Autumn leaves start to drop
A warm fall comes here
Soon winter is near

Winter
Warm hot cocoa in my cup
School stops then starts back up
Animals start hibernating
Geese start Migrating

Spring
Flowers blooming
Their sweet scents fuming
It has been a beautiful Spring
I wonder what Summer will bring

Summer
Sun is shining
Children aren't whining
The waves are crashing
My sunburn is thrashing
Karsten Foster, Grade 6

The Dream

Whenever you are feeling bored or down,
Relax and close your eyes to be taken away.
When you arrive you'll see a red gate.
When you enter you'll see a town of candy.

All of the homes are made out of goodies.
Gingerbread and fondant for roads,
And also fudge for mountains.
To the left is a meadow with chocolate toads.

In the center there is a chocolate fountain,
Surrounded by flowers of lollipops.
Next to the center there is a theater,
Made of popcorn surrounded by gummy bunnies that hop.

The people look like Sour Patch Kids,
And the clouds are made of ice-cream.
The skyscrapers are giant Hershey bars.
And docks in the water are made of gum.

When I was in the bank,
I heard the sound of chimes.
The sound made me awaken,
And I realized it was a wonderful dream the whole time.
Evan Brewer, Grade 5

13

13
those harsh words stung like a hornet
hitting me hard in the face
knocking me to the ground like some sort of squashed fly

I stared at that lady
suddenly she looked venomous
became an it

her hair looked scraggled
like a rat's nest
her pleasant smile turned to a scowl

I couldn't go in
12
was my age

anger swept over me
I am *not* contaminated

my dreams promised
then snatched away
gone
never to come back
Cordelia-Marie Ceres, Grade 6

New York

Off to New York I flew
It was the best time I've had.
I did so many fun things
When I had to leave, I was not glad.

I swam on the shores of Jones Beach
And saw a Broadway show.
I went shopping at Bloomingdale's
And saw Times Square aglow.

I got a mani-pedi
And went to Central Park.
I ate pizza at Ray's
And heard lots of dogs bark.

I rode the Ferris Wheel at Toys R' Us
And shopped at the Disney store.
I rode the elevator in the Empire State Building,
Let me tell you, I was never bored!

I had so much fun,
I can't wait to go again!
Goodbye New York, Ta Ta for now
Until then.
Isabella Essler, Grade 5

Martin Luther King Jr.

It all started with the blacks.
They tried to get equal rights and didn't attack.
Then Martin Luther King Jr. came in
To fix how people looked at their skin.

He was born in Georgia on January 15, 1929.
He helped change their rights and put up a sign.
King is famous for his "I have a dream" speech
And would always stop to preach.

He led more than one boycott
And used nonviolence as he fought.
Martin used his Christian beliefs
To get equal rights and have relief.

Later, he won a Nobel Peace Prize
Because he fought for peace and was very wise.
Martin Luther King Jr. died because of an assassination.
Today, he is truly an amazing inspiration.

We celebrate him on the 3rd week in January every year,
And he will always give us a great cheer.
He is truly a great and amazing man
For helping African Americans find a plan.
Alexandra Harrington, Grade 5

High Merit Poems – Grades 4, 5, and 6

Black
Black
Is the color of a bison's fur coat
The dark night sky
A book is dark moleskine cover
Sounds like a bat flying through the sky
A black car driving in the night
A black helicopter flying to the rescue
Blackberries taste so sweet
Brownies so chewy in your mouth
Chocolate melts so softly on your tongue
Black scales under your fingers
Speed Stacks so smooth in my hands
Silk so slick through my fingers
Black can bring thought and peace
Jeremy Gerritsen, Grade 5

What Am I?
I have many different sizes

In the fall you rake me
I could be as far as you can see

I have many different colors

You can jump in piles of me
I fall off of a tree

I grow in the spring

I could be a bud on a tree
Then I grow and be free
Liam Roberts, Grade 4

The Take Over
Husky jacked-up corn stalks
Defending their land
Trees gasping for air
As the vines strangle them
Beware the fox holes
Dangerous tripping hazards
Evergreens dancing like hula dancers
Birds singing a high pitched opera
Leaves gliding
Like batman
The sun's rays
Beaming through the knitted branches
The wind howling like wolves
Autumn has taken over
Matthew Heffner, Grade 5

Summertime
Kids are running out of school.
They are waiting to go into their pool.
Sounds of kids beginning to cheer.
Summer is finally here.
Liam Mote, Grade 4

Snow Day
Waking up late to only see frost,
Already up to go play.
Reaching the door to see there was a cost,
Eat and go dress to spend a day out,
my mother declared challenging me.
Eating my bacon, running back up,
Buttoning my jacket,
Shoving my trousers,
Coming back down.
Running out feeling unfettered,
Grinning while eating a snow crystal.
No studying, no teachers.
My mind told me,
It was a great snow day for me and all.
Rosa Lee, Grade 6

The Seasons
When the autumn breeze goes away
and the fall leaves start to float astray
and when the birds start to fly askew
you know what's coming in your heart
WINTER
it freezes by day and snows by night
days are short and the nights are long
and what a perfect time to play
on a very snowy winter day

but when the snow starts to melt away
and children start to come out and play
and the sun starts to shine high above
the time for summer has begun
Beckett McVoy, Grade 5

Feelings of the Mountain
The mountain dreams about being with
other mountains.
 The mountain remembers being
a tiny rock.
 The mountain is a promise of
shade.
 The mountain knows about
all things.
 The mountain reminds me of a
triple layer cake.
 The mountain wishes that it
could move.
 The mountain shows us
about rock
Sam Hailey, Grade 4

Roses
Roses
romantic, lovely
colorful petals wave
beautiful, pretty
Kelli Hogarty, Grade 5

My Rescue Dog, Speedy
My little short-haired rescue dog
Fearless, fast, and strong
He was going to be killed
Though he did nothing wrong
His cape flows fast behind him
With a name that fits him fine
Speedy Gonzalez or Speedy G.
And now he is all mine.
Jessica Czekaj, Grade 4

Rain
Dripping and dropping all around
Gently, softly
Hitting the thirsty ground
Starting small
Then getting stronger
Drip…Drop…Drip…Drop
The rain is pouring
Louder and longer
Marisa Ferrari, Grade 4

Winter
Winter is cold when
The freezing air blows.
It sounds quiet like
A calm ocean on a summer day.
It moves like
A cloud soaring in the sky.
You can't control it.
But you can enjoy it!
Daniela Allegrini, Grade 5

Heart of Fire
I walk down the street
I see her on the other side
My heart burst on fire
Like an explosion in the forest

She leaves and I race after her
She disappeared into mid air
My heart goes out and turns cold
Jeffrey Smith, Grade 4

Lightning
Lightning looks like:
a flashing light!
Lightning sounds like
Fire crackling in
The sky!
Lightning comes before thunder!
And there I am in the sky
Listening to the sound!
Tiffany Tsang, Grade 5

Red Water Lilies
Such a calming flow,
while the water lilies blow.
Sun shining bright,
what a sight.
How red and beautiful they are.
Yet they seem so far.
Seeing the reflection,
and all its perfection.
Water, so blue.
Its beauty shines through.
Alicia Coleto, Grade 5

Unfair
Some Jews were shot.
Some Jews gassed.
But however they died.
It was a horrible death.
Every death was agonizing.
No mercy at all.
It was unfair for the Jews.
But the Nazis did not care.
All the Nazis wanted.
Was all the Jews gone.
Benjamin Pinel, Grade 6

Seem to Be
I seem to be a helpless boy,
But really I'm the ruler of everything.
I seem to be a starving man,
But really I give to the starving.
I seem to be tucked up scared,
But really I slayed the beasts.
I seem to be a slave of the devil,
But really I'm a son of angels.
I seem to be nothing,
But I am so much more.
Tragar O'Leary, Grade 5

Friendship
Friendship is not being lonely,
the trust that you have put in them,
the secrets that you have told,
the help if needed,
the company,
the shoulder to cry on,
the fun we had together
and no one can have
because friendship is
the most beautiful thing in this world.
Jasmeen Rai, Grade 6

Cookies
Soft, moist cookie dough
Into the oven they go
Fresh chocolate chip
Ailsa Campbell, Grade 4

If I Were a Pie
If I were a pie
I would be made from scratch
If I were a pie
I would smell like a fruity perfume
If I were a pie
I would feel like a fresh piece of leather
If I were a pie
I would bring family together
If I were a pie
Ella Brown, Grade 4

Love
Love, Love shining bright
In our hearts, binding tight
How can someone not know you?
Love only takes two

I can feel you day and night
Love, Love binding tight
I can feel you running through
I hope others feel you too
Thea Dardanis, Grade 6

Last Night
Last night I went to bed
I could have gone to get a sled

But instead
I went to bed
I said, "Mommy!
I have a fever."
She said,
"Go to bed!"
Vittoria Bentancor, Grade 4

Blue Jay
I am a blue jay
I glide in the wind like an oak
leaf on a fall day.
My back is a lovely blue.
I love to jump and land in oak trees.
My stomach is white like the
snow in the winter time.
When it rains, I shiver in the trees.
I am proud to be a beautiful blue jay
Ammiela Agayev, Grade 6

Ice and Fire
Ice
Snowy, frosty,
Freezing, snowing, warning
Snowstorm, frost, heat, humidity
Burning, heating, melting
Hot, burning
Fire
Mahad Jama, Grade 6

Spring's Here
The flowers grow,
The leaves turn green,
It's finally time,
The best time of year,
I pop out of bed,
I put on my clothes
And go outside and play,
I see the sun turn bright yellow,
And it's finally SPRING!
Evan Bidwell, Grade 5

Le Mystère de la Création
Nothing but darkness fills the Earth.
All alone in this empty world.
No friends, no family, nothing!
Filled with color but no place to spread it.
Lonely and scared, he trembles with fear.
No trees, no grass, no love to share.
Walking for hours and still sees nothing.
No reason to live, no reason to die.
But in his mind, he sees a bright blue sky.
Zachary Tremblay, Grade 5

Morning Bird
I saw a bird this morning
that had a purple head
it was the best of all
I made it look well fed
and then I let it go
my heart sank right below
the salty teardrops flow
I wish I'd never let it go
but if you love it, let it go
Ella Bartsch, Grade 5

Faces
As I look at the clock,
I see faces everywhere.
As they start to mock,
I can only just stare.

Why I'm seeing these faces,
I don't think I deserve this.
They're in so many places,
Just because I'm so nervous.
Aiden Lee, Grade 6

My Dog Finn
My dog Finn cuddles me,
while she usually scratches me.
My dog Finn never chews stuff up,
but she always chases the cat.
My dog Finn obeys me most of the time,
but... she bites me constantly.
I don't care how she acts, I still love her!
Declan Swarr, Grade 4

What Is Life Without You?
What is life without you?
You are up in the blue.
When I look up at you.
You look down on me too.

What is life without you?
You are the stars.
You seem so near.
When you really are so far.

What is life without you?
Will I see you again?
Even though I don't know when.
I know our love never ends.
Carolyn L. Greenwald, Grade 5

Hurricane
The wind rushes quickly
To whip through the trees
Suddenly the wind slows down
And everything is silent
Then the wind picks up and
Is horse playing again
Then the rain starts to
Slap to the ground
And all of the animals
Start to skip around to
Avoid not getting wet
Then everything stops
And the animals realize that
They are in the eye of the hurricane
Paige Riehl, Grade 5

Basketball
I love to play basketball.
We start practice in the fall.

When I make a hoop;
I let out a whoop.

Sometimes after I have run;
I think this is a lot of fun.

The referee had an unfair call.
All these girls seem pretty tall.

The end of the game is very near,
but I feel right at home, right here.
Emily Rosio, Grade 5

Puppy
Every day she gives me a lick,
Give her a treat and she'll do a trick,
I find it very exciting to play,
With my puppy night and day.
Megan Choromanski, Grade 4

Tsunami
Sitting in the water
Staring straight ahead
Paralyzed with fear at what's being said
The great wave is coming
And the countdown begins

Once they reach one
I run straight for the ladder
But it was too late
And the city came down with a clatter
Madison Poschner, Grade 6

Untitled
flying through the sky
the clouds in the way
wishing to stay
here today

wind blowing through its feathers
bright sun shining through the blue

the sky will never be gray
yet the sun will still go away
Samantha Lapointe, Grade 5

Revenge
Revenge is black,
Like burnt cookies.
It is piercingly metallic,
And is cold,
Like an ice cube.
Revenge is destructive,
And drives people mad,
Like losing the Indianapolis 500.

The world loves revenge ...
Hubert Starosta, Grade 5

Ocean Fun
The ocean, soft and breeze.
I see the seagull with beautiful wings.
The waves are big, slow and fun.
Kids laugh and play under the sun.
Fishing with dad near the lake.
Using all of the tasty bait.
Going on the boat to see the view.
The ocean seems happy and you can be too.
So come along to the beach.
If you enter, you'll think the same thing.
Peter Lee, Grade 4

Sunset
Lull of the Titan...
Blankets nature lovingly,
Ends with glowing rays.
Sarah Jacobs, Grade 5

Video Games
MINECRAFT
colorful, simple
Thinking, building, teaming
It is fun and exciting
Creative

TERRARIA
Big, open
Spawning, dying, raging
I create an Excalibur
Survival
Kaleb Martiny, Grade 6

A Camel
I play,
I even sleep in bed all day
I ride my sled
I hit my head on the bed

On my head is a bump
It is as big as a camel's hump
The noise the bump made was
Thump! Thump! Thump!
It is just like when you ride a camel
You go Bump! Bump! Bump!
Jacob Bradley, Grade 4

Spring
Spring is finally here
I've been waiting for this day all year
To play in puddles
And blow big bubbles
Oh yes, spring is here!

Spring is finally here
And no more snow to fear
Mother birds laying
And baby birds playing
Oh yes, spring is here!
Kaylee D'Amico, Grade 4

The Magical Wind
The unbelievable, strong, powerful wind
Blows the crispy brown leaves
Across the swaying grass,
Shivering dandelions
Trying to pull away
From the ground
To go on a nature adventure
Puffy white clouds
Slightly moving
So a bit of blue
Will shine through
Reese Pirtle, Grade 5

Bad Dream
tossing and turning
wrapped up in a thick blanket
getting trapped
sweating and breathing hard
unaware the dream is tricking you
into thinking it's real
only lasts for a couple minutes
it feels like forever
you jolt awake
don't go back to sleep
the dream will come back you say
but it never does
bad dreams are never the same
Meg Felsmann, Grade 6

The Dreamer
I bring you all my
dreams, my desires,
my life...
my love and hopes.

You put them on your highest shelf,
with other dreamers like myself.

You choose your path, I choose mine.
While we destroy what God creates,

the world will spin for me and you...
for us.
Hannah Garrett Vasquez, Grade 5

Spring to Summer
peaceful
powerful
mountains
with melted snow
making flowing rivers
far
far
away
a promise of a warm summer day
purple
yellow
red
flowers.
Ryann Durrett, Grade 4

Winter to Spring Transition
Snow
Cold, thick
Sparkling, freezing, coating
Precipitation that falls on the earth
Drizzling, misting, sprinkling
Soggy, wet
Rain
Abby D'Ambrosio, Grade 5

Children and Adults
Children
Fun, hyper
Obeying, smiling, laughing
Boy, girl, men, women
Boring, working, domineering
Important, grumpy
Adults
Aya Nizar, Grade 6

Sunrise and Sunset
Sunrise
Light, early,
Rising, awakening, beginning,
East, morning, evening, west,
Retreating, setting, ending,
Beautiful, colorful,
Sunset
Maya Wong-Fortin, Grade 6

It Could Be or Might Be
It could be dull or, it might be interesting
It could be fun or, it might be boring
It might be bright or, it could be dark
It might be big, or, it could be small
It could be fast or, it might be slow
Nobody knows only, time will tell
Francesca Worrall, Grade 5

Hitler
H is for hate that lingered in the air
I is for injured people that cried at nigh
T is for terrible things that happened
L is for love that was never there
E is for eager to kill
R is for the rejection of the Jews
Nathan Hildebrant, Grade 6

Beta
Swimming around so very gracefully
Blue, purple, and red,
Hear the water, hear the filter
Hear the silence in bed,
Smell the water, smell the fish food,
Taste the sweet air
Lane McFarland, Grade 4

Rain
Straight from the sky
Upon the floor
Drip, drip, dripping
Hitting my body even when I move
Saltiness and bitterness
I really love it
Ruby LeBaron, Grade 4

School
S tudents
C omputers
H omework
O bjective
O utstanding teacher
L earning
Anneliese Fenwick, Grade 4

Revenge
The colour of revenge is brown
It sounds like vengeance
It tastes bitter
It smells like stinky socks
It looks like hatred
It makes me alarmed
Rajnandini Ganguli, Grade 6

Pandas
Pandas are so beautiful
And of kindness, they are full
Black and white
And they are adorable, at your sight
So save them please
And you'll be pleased
Genevieve Karnis, Grade 4

Red
Red looks like apples and folders.
Red smells like ink.
Red taste like apples.
Red feels smooth.
Red sounds like your heart.
Red is twice as big as any other color.
Lucas Santise, Grade 4

Tigers
T ails wagging back and forth
I n the deep sleep of the jungles force
G etting ready to jump and bounce
E ating fiercefully
R oar!
S ilence walking
Giselle Ayala, Grade 4

A Funny Bunny
Bunny
There once was a fuzzy brown bunny,
He was known to be quite funny.
He danced all around,
Dug holes in the ground,
But mostly loved to eat honey.
Alex Jensen, Grade 6

Fan
Spinning cold air in circles.
Noises like tiny whispers,
escape from the slots.

Whoosh, dancing in the air.
Spinning, teasing hair.
Whirling as if the air was alive.
Clare Hoyt, Grade 4

Hunter vs Animal
Hunter
Alert, Eating
Aiming, Shooting, No talking
The hunter chases the animal
Dying, Running, Hiding
Sleepy, Fast
Animal
Brandon Ferstl, Grade 4

Spring
Spring is here
Spring is there
Spring is everywhere
Feeling the wonderful warm spring breezes
Saying goodbye to cold winter freezes
Seeing the colorful bright spring flowers
Being watered by the cool spring flowers
Susan Huang, Grade 4

Orcs and Elves
Orc
Ugly, evil
Killing, swarming, attacking
Weapons, caves, magic, bow and arrows
Defending, protecting, lurking
Proud, spirited
Elf
Samuel Deschenes, Grade 6

Sun and Moon
Sun
Bright, yellow
Boiling, burning, blinding
Day, hot, night, crater
Shining, changing, darkening,
White, cold
Moon
Chloé Byrne, Grade 6

Winning
Touchdown, home run, three-point, BOOM!
I just made a field goal, too.
All I do is never lose.
You might too, but not against me,
and you will never beat me.
Matt Trunzo, Grade 6

The Empty Cup
It's just sitting there...
Nothing, empty, blank, dry...
Just shaped glass sitting in a cupboard.
Waiting for the light from the lamp and that loud creak from the old cupboard door.
Anxious to hear those footsteps in the kitchen.
That hand to grab it, fill it, and drink out of it.
The sound of the water splashing against it's dry, spotless clear glass.
It's thinking: "I am a cup and I want to be filled."
Nicholas Booth, Grade 5

Gymnastics
Gymnastics is a way that shows who I am
With unbelievable flipping
Great technique, skills, the music, and lots more
You need confidence, strength, flexibility, and balance to take down challenges
The different events are bar, floor, vault, and beam
If I ever compete in competition I hope I'm ready,
Like in the Olympics!
Sa'Renity Burford, Grade 6

Skateboard
I spend most of my time sitting in the corner of the garage
I'm snatched from my resting place and go on an adventure
The kid stomps on my back and my wheels roll quickly down the hill
Oh no speed bump! Wee! That was fun
Slow down turn coming
My wheels constantly spinning makes me dizzy
I am a Skateboard
Drew Stephens, Grade 5

Come Home
Sojourner Truth's smile is glistening
I smile while listening
For I too was just like her
I called my master Sir
But now I am free
From this thing we call slavery

But I cannot always smile
Over there, for many miles
My family is there
Following directions from that bear
They could've gone with me
So they could be free

I hope they'll come soon
Free from that goon
We'll smile and laugh
I will give them a proper bath
Until then I will miss them so
But my chances of seeing them are very low
Maureen Kelly, Grade 6

Sunrising
The sunrise has wished for staying
as long as it remembers,

remembers
its first morning
on Earth.

The sunrise has shown us
the bright morning as if,
it was bursting into flames.

It keeps its promises
and promises us a new day
rising a new hope.

The sunrise is a reminder of
a big,
a beautiful,
bright
blaze.
Joshua Bustos, Grade 4

That First Tooth
That first tooth.
Oh, when it gets loose!
It makes all the gears spin,
like the wheels on a bulky train's caboose.

With bumps like a goose,
you take one final pull…
and that first tooth is no longer loose!
Makena Veitch, Grade 5

Hot Chocolate
After coming in from a big snow-
ball fight, I feel the warmth of the
indoors. On the table there's a
mug with hot steam coming
from the top. I sit down and
see all the marshmallows
melt away. I take a sip
for the delicious taste.
Alexi Plaitis-Levesque, Grade 5

Poems
Poems
They keep you alive.

They take you to another world
called rhyme.

I guess I could go there tonight.
What? You can go there anytime and fly?
Sam Louis, Grade 5

Dog and Cat
Dog
Skinny, fast
Eating, sitting, barking
My dog is so fast and my cat isn't.
Drinking, laying, meowing
Fat, slow
Cat
Ryland Bradnam, Grade 4

Sharks
Sharks
Deadly, powerful
Biting, eating, fascinating
Blue sea, dorsal fin, good sense, predatory
SHARKS!
Jada Mahmde, Grade 5

Worms
Worms
Unwanted for most
Extraordinary creatures
Crawling all around
Heather Herbott, Grade 5

Coming Home
Lacing up my combat boots
Hair tight in a bun
Getting my bag together
As I say goodbye to everyone
I see a tear stream down my mother's face
My dad says, "Be strong."
Before I leave I run up and hug them

Getting to the base was scary, surprising, and startling
It feels like there are butterflies in my stomach swirling around and around
Months later the base got a call
"We are going to war!"
Bang! Boom! Crash! The bombs explode
I fall to the ground
I see my parents crying at my hospital bed
I reach for their hands as they say, "You're coming home!"
Payton Pugh, Grade 6

What Happens to a Dream Deferred?*
What happens to a dream deferred?

Does it float out of your mind
Like a leaf falling out of a tree on a warm sunny day?
Or does it crash into a red brick wall
And then burst into flames?
Does it shiver on a freezing, snowy day?
Or does it crumble
like a bottle in the arms of a burning fire?

Maybe it just soars
like a plane disappearing into the sunlight?

Or does it flutter like eyelashes looking into the only light in a dark room?
Jake Wyatt, Grade 6
Inspired by Langston Hughes.

What Happens to a Dream Deferred?*
What happens to a dream deferred?

Does it smolder
like a fire in the dark of night?
Or does it shine bright like the morning sun
And then fade to make way for the moon?
Does it soar through the starry night like a shooting star?
Or does it crumble
like when you cut into a warm freshly baked cake?

Maybe it just clutters in your mind
like an attic full of unwanted toys.

Or does it wander in your head like a leaf being blown by the breezy wind?
Tilda Ellefson, Grade 6
Inspired by Langston Hughes.

The Marvelous Peacock

The peacock emerges in the springtime,
Reveals itself for all to see.
Emerald, violet and sapphire blue.
The colors are magical and vivid.
The peacock is proud, even arrogant.
He struts around to attract the peahen.
He gets noticed,
He feels proud and victorious.
Nadine Malak, Grade 4

A Friend

A friend is someone who you can trust
someone who does not tell a secret
someone who makes you happy
not sad
someone who does not bully you
a friend makes you laugh
hugs you when you cry
that is a friend
Myah Payne, Grade 4

My Animals

My animals have lots of fur,
They can out run you in a blur,
They drink a lot on hot days,
My animals may be strays,
My animals may blaze right by,
While my animals lay quietly,
No matter if the sun shines brightly,
My animals can do no matter if they're shy
Dale Morgan, Grade 6

Soccer Is

Soccer is getting past their defender
Soccer is shooting on the net
Soccer is passing
Soccer is tying games
Soccer is losing
Soccer is winning
Soccer is teamwork
Soccer is having fun
Sophie Van Berkel, Grade 5

A Day at the Beach

The waves crashing against the shore
The sight is a galore
The sand gets between my toes
And the water gets up my nose
I go surfing on the crashing waves
Now I can't walk for several days
That was my day at the beach
At least I didn't get a leach.
Sam Veinotte, Grade 5

Proud

Racing down the hill
So much speed and skill
Double back flip in the air
No backing out
No running scared

Win the race
Snab first place
Your spines tingling
Crowds so big
Almost sickening

You nail that first trick
The crowd is cheering
You are so slick

Feel proud
Take a bow

Shine a grin
Because
YOU WIN
Luna Casey, Grade 6

Here Our Moments Escalate — HOME

Oblivious in space,
Many things happen around,
Beyond the Universe,
And in Earth,
In this space,
Oblivious of outside,
To relax,
In this space,
Ready to explore,
In this room.

Where exploring the unknown starts,
Where lives are touched,
And lived...
New chapters,
New fights,
Opportunities,
No limits,
The starting line,
We are destroying home,
But there is a way,
There's always been a way.
Jenner Arriaga, Grade 5

Snow Day

Wake up
Fluffy as clouds
A blanket of white snow
I want to run outside and play
Freedom
Mr. Cruddas' 5th Grade Class

The Titanic

On the date of 1912
England was to be
Where the Titanic stood
Waiting by the sea

And all that no one knew
As all that watched that boat
That in some time soon
The big monster would not be afloat

What started with a happy dream
turned to a scary night
For that is when
Disaster struck, an iceberg came to sight

And for the unsinkable
Water rushed inside
Everyone realized
For men, women, and children began to cry

And for the few survivors
Can today tell their story
Of the ship of unsinkable
And how it ended with no glory.
John Cole McGee, Grade 5

My Piggy Bank

I looked in my piggy bank all afternoon
to find my hard earned cash.
It took me 'bout five minutes each day
to take out the trash.

I dumped the loose change out of it
and it shivered, rumbled, and growled.
My piggy bank almost smashed in two
and then something howled.

I took a wink at my piggy bank,
I wondered what was wrong.
I asked, "Who is speaking?"
It said, "It's me, ding dong!"

"Wow!" I said with much excitement,
this must be a nightmare!
This had to be a very bad dream,
it's worse than a ferocious bear!

I wondered what was happening,
a piggy bank that can speak?
I'll keep checking up on it,
I'll stare at it and peek.
Lucy Bickel, Grade 5

The Story of Rocks
Every rock
Tells a story
And it's name
Might be Norrie
It might be shiny
It might be tiny
It might be dull
It might be full
Every rock
Tells a story
And it's name
Might be Norrie
Caitlin Rogers, Grade 5

Piano
My fingers fly across the keys.
The music fills my ears.
Oh, that wonderful feeling
When I forget all my fears.
Walking up to the piano,
I take a deep breath and begin to play.
What in the world is better
Than feeling this way?
Piano is wonderful.
It always has an enchanting sound.
And if you ever can't find me,
You know where I can be found.
Gabrielle Mejalli, Grade 6

I Am Fearless
I am fearless,
I can do anything,
Anywhere I want.
I am fearless,
I can jump into the deepest waters,
And climb the steepest mountains.
I am fearless,
I can fight off the most vicious creatures,
And survive the most tragic accidents.
I am fearless,
I can be who I want,
Because I am myself.
Isabelle Chang, Grade 6

Happy
It was a happy day
When I was as happy as a birthday girl
Everybody is happy. I was full of joy.
I will sing and dance.
I love being happy.
I will laugh.
I will scream like there is no tomorrow.
Now I can have all I need.
That is as cool as I can be.
I can be as free as a bee.
Madison Prentice, Grade 5

School Day
Alarm, awake, eat
Awake, eat, shower
Eat, shower, uniform
Shower, uniform, shoes
Uniform, shoes, car
Shoes, car, wait
Car, wait, school
Wait, school, bell
School, bell, up
Bell, up, stairs
Up, stairs, work
Stairs, work, recess
Work, recess, inside
Recess, inside, up
Inside, up, stairs
Up, stairs, work
Stairs, work, snack
Work, snack, lunch
Snack, lunch, eat
Lunch, eat, recess
Eat, recess, work
Becky Mansfield, Grade 4

Life's Ride
We take on life's challenges,
Like scientists take on an analysis.
We shine like stars,
Even though we have scars.
Life is a wild ride,
With all us feeling like we've died inside.
There are ups and downs,
Smiles and frowns.
Twists and turns,
Scrapes and burns.
We've all been feeling blue,
We know that much is true.
But behind the strong faces,
Behind the filled spaces,
Everyone is fearful.
Know that you're not alone,
Know that you're not the only one.
Everyone takes on life's race,
No one is an ace.
So when you're feeling blue,
Know that someone else is facing it too.
Emily Miller, Grade 6

Summer and Fall
Summer
Warm, sunny
Blooming, growing, living
Nice, hot, colder, colorful
Blowing, falling, turning
Cold, autumn
Fall
Kaylee Chubak, Grade 4

About Me
Hi, my name is Nikki,
You should know I am not very picky.
I am a girl with blonde hair and blue eyes,
Smile as bright as all the stars in the sky.
Enjoy playing basketball and field hockey,
But I believe it is wrong to be cocky.
Bright as a new shiny button,
And as energetic as a child.
Strive for my goals and wishes,
While I always try to be ambitious.
Push myself to do the best I can.
A loyal and trustworthy person.
Look up to my sister and brother,
I have an amazing and loving father and mother.
As strong minded as a court full of lawyers
And as peaceful as flowers in a meadow.
Free as a bird flying through the sky.
I dream of always being joyful,
Living in a world where it is always peaceful.
Nikkole VanCamp, Grade 6

Cross Country
The whistle blows loud
The race begins
Nothing but pure muscle
is put into that hustle
We run up the hill,
Then fall down the slope,
All you can see is pure smoke.
The sweat pours down your face,
But you are going a steady pace.
You look at the sun that is fiery,
Will this race be inspiring?
Your heart pounds a steady beat,
Then you run through the creek
You take one breath,
Thinking you cannot breathe.
But then you think,
This race must end indeed.
You see the finish line,
Then think in your mind
You sprint and finish the race.
I finished and I did great.
Ava Dzurenda, Grade 6

Marshall
Marshall
Awesome, great
Running, building, wrestling
He is always awesome
Friendly, jumping, walking
Amazing, cool
Mr. Lane
Marshall Lane, Grade 4

Green and Blue
Green is for the grass growing in the valley.
Blue is for the sky shifting over our heads.
Green is for the cape of Mother Nature.
Blue is for the mountains you can see when you are driving by.
But when these colors meet each other,
They become the waters of Hawaii.

Jasmyn Guiffre, Grade 4

The Meadow
Green grass, yellow flowers, lightly sprinkled dew
Birds chirping and singing, the mountains in view
Cold springs are gurgling and bees are looming
Deer graze on the grass, flowers are blooming
This is the World's beauty
All in one meadow

Hayden Huckaby, Grade 5

Softball
Softball is a passion, not just a game…
I wish I could play it every day…
Fast pitch, slow pitch…
No matter what you play…
It may get a little rough but I love it anyway…
So always remember, softball is my passion, not just a game

Victoria Rose Tom, Grade 4

I Wonder Why?
I wonder why I plug my ears when I'm terrified
Is it because of too many scary movies?
Talk about scary things?
Reading scary things?
Experiencing scary things?
I wonder why I'm so terrified

Delia Stevens, Grade 6

My Family Is a Pair of Glasses
My family is a pair of glasses.
My Mother is the glue that holds us all together.
My Father is the frame always strong and powerful.
Surya is the lens always very delicate.
Skye my dog is the nose piece always sniffing us out.
And I'm the hinge keeping my family all moving.

Setia Joy, Grade 5

My Family Is a Cupcake
My family is cupcake.
Dad is the flour, one of the main ingredients, holding us all together.
Mum is the sugar, candied, kind, but firm.
My sister is the icing, wanting the attention, but still sweet.
Greg, our dog, is the wrapper, always around us and faithful to us.
And I am the sprinkles, full of colour, full of love!

Hannah Bier, Grade 6

Friends
I have a friend
She is always by my side
She knows when I'm sad or crying
She's the kind of friend you can always lean on
And for that I am grateful
Because friends are the siblings God forgot to give us

Falisity Speed, Grade 6

The Cry
When I found out the news, I knew it was coming
They teared up like a puddle after the rain
They came from my eye to my chin like a waterfall
I couldn't hold it back, how could I the feeling was to deep
Every time some went away, more came back
they expressed my feeling inside, sadness

Ariana Oduok, Grade 5

Angry T-Shirt
I peer into my closet,
And switch on the light,
And suddenly my favorite shirt wants to pick a fight.
It knocks me out unconscious,
And pulls at my hair,
Which makes me realize exactly what to wear!

Sagan Brinkert, Grade 5

Desert
A hot dry wasteland
The molten hot air is enough to kill
When you're in this desert it's like a furnace, there's icy tundra
The land itself is an icy battlefield and ice breaks underneath you
The water is so cold it feels like absolute zero
Antarctica

Matthew Windrem, Grade 6

Dreams
Dreams look like flowers blooming on a spring day
Dreams sounds like a choir of birds singing
Dreams smell like a garden of flowers
Dreams tastes like a fruit smoothie
Dreams feels like touching a soft bunny
Dreams make me feel like I am in heaven

Mahishajini Mohanathasan, Grade 6

Sleepover
A recipe book ready to be opened
Chicken stuffed pizza fresh out of the oven
A movie playing on the TV
A silky sleeping bag warming me
Creamy Oreo ice cream melting in my mouth
I'll do this tomorrow

Savannah LeGendre, Grade 4

Pugs
Snuggly, soft face
Playful pups in my front yard
Chubby, chunky rolls!
Leilani Shott, Grade 5

Swish
The colors so plain
Underwater joy fills them
Silent as night
Nickales App, Grade 5

Snow
Powder falls softly...
Flowers covered by blankets
Of glimmering snow
Madison Robison, Grade 5

Cherry Blossoms
In a bud you stay...
Petals! Petals! Growing fast
In a tree so high!
Cristal Mannrique, Grade 5

Sunlight
Shining down like rain
Shimmering on the water
Warming everyone
Aidan Riley, Grade 6

Nature
Birds tweeting loudly,
In the rising, morning sun,
Singing me a song!
Jersey Trout, Grade 5

Waterfall
Lovely waterfall,
Majestic, earsplitting, noise
Beautiful rainbow
Mykela Hansen, Grade 6

Summer
Burning wind whistles...
Hot, blistering, blazing, sun
Warming blades of grass.
Uriah Celestino, Grade 5

Fall
On a warm, fall day
Big dogs playing and running
Through the golden leaves...
Juan Lopez, Grade 5

Water
Swimming is a fun and competitive sport
I love to swim for fun
No losers...
No winners
For me it feels safe, sort of at home
It's a peaceful time
under water there is no noise
I would swim anywhere at anytime except for winter and in the ocean

For me, the water feels safe, or like I'm at home
Water is like my home away from home
I could swim in a pool for 4 hours and counting and not be hungry
I have a certain connection with water
When I'm around water, I feel something special
Gavin Michael Billett, Grade 6

The Sky Is Darkening
The sky is darkening turning red orange and purple
The deer and her fawn step out onto the cool lush grass
The creek gurgling quietly to itself
The trees sway in the gentle breeze
Two squirrels play together in the treetops
The stars twinkle onto the earth
When the moon is high in the sky the wind breathes one last time then is silent
The deer and her fawn are curled together behind a log
The squirrels are resting in a hollow tree
The forest is in a deep sleep
Until the moon hides behind the earth and the stars fade away
And the sun starts a new day
Valerie Jacobs, Grade 5

Macy
As my eyes are laid on you, every single day
I feel I can express myself in every single way
I can talk to you at any random times
And in this poem to you, no one cares about rhymes
So, here goes nothin'
Your eyes sparkle in the light like diamonds in the sky,
Your hair reflects the beautiful golden sunlight like a mirror atop a mountain,
Your smile is beautiful and makes me feel warm head to toe,
like a marshmallow over a fire,
And finally, last but not least, and all of those conclusions,
You are the best sister a brother could ever have
Thank you for being you
Carter Motichka, Grade 6

Sports
Whether it's from soccer, baseball, basketball there's are many more.
Always a team by your side.
When you play sports you play on a court.
Whether you play soccer or basketball you always got a blocker.
Any sport there's always a ball.
If you do track show no slack.
Teamwork makes Dreamworks.
You wanna stand tall, talk small, and play ball.
Devon McCalips, Grade 6

Friend
Friend
Loyal, loving
Talking, laughing, playing
Someone to talk to
Family
Nicholas Nielsen, Grade 6

Caribbean
Pretty blue water
Beautiful white sandy beach
Warm and sunny days
Bright and colorful fishies
Caribbean oh so nice
Leah Muirhead, Grade 4

The Annoying Tick
There once was a boy named Nick
Who was infected by a small little tick
So he started to scratch
But his nails were no match
For that tick continued to make him sick
Nick Johnson, Grade 5

Juice Liquid
Juice
Delicious, tasteful
Squeezing, pouring, flowing
Splashing in the glass
Liquid
Eden Evans, Grade 5

Skiing
Skiing
Cold, tricks
Cheering, competing, shredding
Spin it to win
Sport
Taylor Kellar, Grade 5

History
The past is history
the future is tomorrow's day
always unexpected
so the past was history
but the future is a mystery
Hunter Patterson, Grade 6

Bicycle for Two
You pedal, you pump
You bump on your rump
The other guy you cannot trust
It feels like you're going to bust
When you're riding a bicycle built for two
Daniel Lynch, Grade 4

If I Were in Charge of the World*
If I were in charge of the world!
I'd have food and water drop from the sky for everyone.
I'd make there be "NO" animal abuse.
Everyone would love each other and "no" one would fight.
If I were in charge of the world
There'd be no wars.
Ice cream, chocolate, Gummies, and lollipops would be everywhere.
One half of the world, would have veggies and the other half would be junk food.
If I were in charge of the world!
You wouldn't have to pay money for stuff
You wouldn't have homework
Or you wouldn't ever get sick
If I were in charge of the "WORLD!"

Madison Brasson, Grade 5
*Patterned after "If I Were in Charge of the World" by Judith Viorst

All About Me
I have big brown eyes and love french fries.
Generous and loyal, but not jealous or royal.
Super, silly, smart student who plays soccer at seven-thirty on Sundays.
Happy, healthy, hardworking, helpful girl who likes to hopscotch in the hot sun.
Kind, caring, creative, clever tween who loves to play cards with my cousins.
Proud as a peacock and pleased as punch when I perform perfectly on tests.
Sweet as a box of chocolates, busy as a bee.
Lucky as a leprechaun at the end of the rainbow.
Athletic as Abby Wambach and as fast as a cheetah.
Bright like a diamond; eyes are shining stars in the night sky.
I am sunshine on a warm summer day.
All of this and so much more.

Samantha Berish, Grade 6

Shower
Home is my shower,
　　pouring water flowing through it calmly,
squirting out like an elephant's trunk
　　fluently flowing like a deep blue ocean
　　　on a bright sunny day, flowing so delicately like a gushing river
　　　　sitting, raining, waiting for company to swim through it,
about to run out of water until
someone steps in and saves the day, solitary,
　　a dry, humid, and sometimes wet climate, peaceful
　　　as blue waves glide through it as if it were a stream,
　　　　calm unless you decide to turn it on all the way,
　　　　awake and vibrant always ready to go,
　　　makes you feel like you're the only one in the world, so elegant
　　　　like nice hot rain pouring from above, shower.

Jiana McDonald, Grade 4

A True Friend
Best friends always stick together.
A true best friend trusts each other no matter if they are apart or together.
Friends will always be there to cheer you up and be nice.
A true friend is the best of all!!

Lesly Chavez, Grade 5

The Wild
The spring comes
As the birds hum
Winds blow
As the rivers flow
When the animals are running
The trees are so stunning
Flowers are growing
Rocks are rolling
Mountains once covered in snow
As bright as a lightning bugs' glow
The sun goes away
As the moon comes to stay
Melissa Pjetrushi, Grade 6

The Wind, The Rain
The wind, the rain
The rain so hard
With the smell of a fresh storm
I feel the wind pushing me away
The rustling of the trees
The signs on the road
Even though they're metal
They still move like the wind
The rain pouring down
The power lines moving side to side
The damp soggy road
This wet gray December day
Emma Andrews, Grade 6

The Power of Love
Your heart,
is what really matters;
pain, sadness
will fade away,
with the power of
true love.

The sacrifice of one's true love
will save the princess;
although a fib,
will cause real pain,
in the hearts of Romeo and Juliet.
Raena Anderson, Grade 6

Volleyball
Volleyball isn't just a sport
It's a passion
You have tons of support
Your team is like family
One thing different, they're on a court
The net is like a guard for your team
It's like your very own fort
When the volleyball comes towards you
You have to get to it fast in some sort
Hoping that you hit it on time
Mikayla Murphy, Grade 6

Baseball
I hit a home run
Ran to the base
It went inside
And broke a vase

Mom came out
She got mad
Found the baseball
In the house

I went back out
To play some more
Sarah Brooks, Grade 4

Flutes
Flutes
In my opinion
Are
Magical
Turning breaths
Into sounds
Making music
From covered holes
Flutes
In my opinion
Are
Magical
Sophie Lentz, Grade 4

Floating House
There once was a floating house
like a boat on water
very small
no room to move
no place to go
moves so slow
like a turtle
the water
will take you
where every you go
a floating house
Swish, swish, swish.
Gracie Franklin, Grade 6

Dance
When I twirl through the air,
I feel so free,
While the wind blows through my hair.
I jump up and down just like a frog,
I pirouette through the fog.
I do my cartwheel round and round,
I land on the ground. "Boom! Pound!"
I do my dance.
I jump and prance.
I feel so free.
Jenna McFarland, Grade 5

Sleepy Babies
Piles of diapers
In the car
Watching the windshield wipers
Following the North Star

One boy, One girl
They're both asleep
Mom's head in a twirl
Dreaming of white sheep

Teagan and Gray
That's their names
Always trying to pray
Both going to the hall of fame

One boy, One girl
They're both asleep
Mom's head in a twirl
Dreaming of white sheep
Jacob Cox, Grade 6

Paradise
I see it in my head
I see it in the night
A wonderful paradise
Oh! what an unforgettable sight

Where everyone is rich
In family and friends
No person is forgotten
There no one ends

All sicknesses are gone
Every person is well
This is a paradise
That I can very much tell

Every problem with the world
Is fixed in this place
To learn and dream about it
Puts a smile on my face
Chloe Turman, Grade 5

The Seasons
The seasons are like a carousel,
They go round and round,
From the first bloom of Spring,
To the final blaze of Summer,
The seasons are a beautiful thing.

The seasons are like a carousel,
They go round and round,
From the first fallen leaf of Autumn,
To the final chill of Winter,
The seasons are a beautiful thing.
Lauren Poltorak, Grade 5

High Merit Poems – Grades 4, 5, and 6

Life: Is It What We Think It Is?
Life as we know,
Will always just flow
And when we fall down,
There will be no frown
Since there will be,
Someone to help us

There will be happiness,
And loneliness in the world
And we can't stop that,
For our chances to shine
May not seem so fine

Some might claim,
That life is just an old game
They say many souls have went through,
This deja vu
Others however disagree,
They assume that life is free
But is it really what we think it is?
Reshma Gudla, Grade 6

Wild, Wild Waters
In the place of the "wild, wild waters"
The true adventure awaits.
Trust me, this place is better,
Than any of the 50 states.
Rapid waters,
  with a slide.
You'll really want to
  go inside.
Did I mention that
they have free food, too?
That's something
you might want to do.
It has a sandy beach
  with free Wi-Fi,
For your phones and devices…
  Give it a try!
Water slides
are filling the air.
With amazing sights
to see everywhere!
Jared Haugen, Grade 5

A New Year
Making wishes for the year
Hearing lots of happy cheer
People coming from every town
Ready for the final countdown
Here it comes
Moving fast
Horns are blaring
It's a blast
Happy New Year!
Nicholas Tammaro, Grade 4

A Cloud in the Sky
I am in the sky.
I wonder why I was put in the sky.
I hear cars beep as if I was on Earth.
I see little people down below.
I want to walk on Earth like others.
I am hopeful.

I pretend to have legs and walk.
I feel the sun shine on my back.
I touch others like me as they drift by.
I worry that I will one day fade away.
I cry and my tears fall on the people below.
I am upset.

I understand I'm up here for a reason.
I say to myself that I've a purpose.
I dream about sunny days.
I try hard not to cry in the grey sky.
I hope I never fade.
I am a cloud.
Myra Keener, Grade 6

What Am I?
I am visited every day.
Some kids dread me.
Most kids dread me.
I start out early.
I end late.
I can be a place.
I can be a website.
Full of anxious children
Waiting to be set free
To be unchained
To have freedom
Like the patriots
But not the football team.
I am full of learning
Full of distraction
But the good kind.
What am I?
The world
Will never know.
Unless…
Marty Boyd, Grade 6

Unique
Little snowflake falling so,
Are you happy, being snow?
Tiny snowflake in the sky,
Do you feel as though you fly?

Yes, I'm happy being me.
I'm quite unique as you can see.
I do fly over all in sight,
Pity I'm afraid of heights.
Ava Lazar, Grade 5

Nightmare
Darkness,
Filled with fright, filled with dread.
All alone,
It's happening again,
She's standing in the corner,
Staring, yelling
HELP ME, HELP ME,
You want to run, but you can't.
Glued in place.
You can't escape her.
All you can do is watch her.
Watch her kill.
You must face your fears though.
And scare her away,
but it's hard.
Terror strikes,
your heart beats,
but you must fight it, before it's
too late.
Lilly Hasan, Grade 6

Greener as They Grow
Plants
  become greener
  as they grow

Ladybugs
  on leaves
  munching aphids
  helping plants
  become greener
  as they grow

Worms help soil
  be filled
  with nutrients
  for plant roots
  to absorb and
  help plants
  become greener
  as they grow
Larissa Williamson, Grade 4

My Treasure
Glittering gold shines
Through specks of silvery coins
In the treasure chest

Coins slip through fingers
While we grab as many coins
That fit in our pails

Crashing to the ground
Are sounds of clinking metal
A forgotten waste
Jenna Miltier, Grade 6

Imaginations

If I am sad, mad
Scared or bored,
I grab a paper and pencil
To start creating
I think a paper and pencil
As two peas in a pod
When I pick up my pencil and start writing,
Imagination is born.
Every time I draw, color, or write
It comes to life
Anything I created, was my thoughts
Every time I'm done
I won't be upset
I will always remember
My imaginations
Are my friends
I would never give up
What I like.
Katherine Hernandez, Grade 5

I Am

I am a loving boy.
I wonder what actors are doing now.
I hear a fairy flapping its wings.
I see a beautiful flower.
I want to fly.
I am a loving boy.
I pretend to fly and do flips in the sky.
I feel a fairy's wings.
I touch Barbie's hair.
I worry that I will get an F on math.
I cry about death.
I am a loving boy.
I understand that I am a good kid.
I say I love myself.
I dream I will become rich.
I try to do a back flip.
I hope to do theater in middle school.
I am a loving boy.
Max Fisher, Grade 5

Kidnapped

I was writing my essay,
and looking out the door,
Until my big brown eyes,
Saw kidnappers,
I knew it for sure!
They blind folded me,
and shoved me in a sack,
and wouldn't let me go,
but I had a big cramp in my back!
They drove faraway,
and threw me in a bay,
See my dear teacher?
That's why I wasn't in school yesterday.
Abigail MacAdams, Grade 5

When Spring Will Be Here

When spring will be here
We will let out a cheer
The trees will be pleased
Since they'll grow back their leaves

Spring makes the flowers bloom
So get out of your room
Go outside without a doubt
And go see the tulips sprout

Goldfinches come back
Then they eat seeds for a snack
Listen how well chickadees sing
To announce the arriving of spring!
Juliane Langlois, Grade 4

Spring Is Here

Spring is finally here
It's my favourite time of year
Winter is finally gone
We're going to have a green lawn!

Guess who's here? The Easter Bunny!
His Easter eggs are super yummy!
All the lovely flowers,
With their blooming powers.

We go on spring break
And swim at the lake
Winter is done
We get to feel the warmth of the sun!
Livjot Sivia, Grade 4

Veterans

Veterans are believers who serve,
They help save lives,
Anyone who serves as the nerve,
We show we are proud by giving
them high five's,
They stand up for our country and fight,
Family, friends, believers, strangers,
We are sorry for their plight,
They save us from dangers,
Whoosh! Went the plane
Flying like a bird in the sky,
Carrying their bodies aboard,
We give them a final bow,
We are sad to say goodbye.
Riley Butkovic, Grade 6

Pillow

A pillow is like
A million soft marshmallows
Caressing your chin
So comfy
Charles Henry Angleberger, Grade 5

Spring: You're Finally Here!

Finally, spring is here!
Animals are done hibernating!
The snow is melting,
The flowers are growing.

Children are riding their bikes,
And playing in the park.
They run around,
Climb some trees.

Leaves are growing on trees,
Birds are tweeting and flying.
Soon there will be blossoms.

Oh, how pretty a picture spring is!
With all the flowers and trees,
Making it even prettier.
It is a cherished season!
Elizabeth Richer, Grade 5

Into the Dark

It won't hurt you,
What do you say?
Just a wall, blocking your way

Into the dark
A journey waiting to embark

Hear the whisper in the shade
Why do you need, to be afraid?

Into the dark
like a walk through the park

Face your fear
Can something be so severe?

Into the dark
At last, you see the lighting spark
Lilly Nguyen, Grade 6

Fall into Winter

Howling wind,
Cools the air,
Leaves bright and colorful,
Drift to the ground.
Squirrels collect acorns,
And geese travel north,
For the bitter winter coming.

Shhh…winter is finally here.
Snow fills the air. As it falls,
Silence covers the earth.
The ground sparkles like crystals.
And shines like diamonds.
Madeleine Gerz, Grade 5

The Rainbow Lollipop
I am a rainbow lollipop
I wonder if kids love me like a pet
I hear a kid licking me viciously
I see the child's friends
I want to say "Hi"
I am a wet lollipop

I pretend I'm a spectacular spectrum
I feel the saliva splattering
I touch the child's tongue
I worry I will soon shrink
I cry that I may die
I am a small lollipop

I understand my time has come
I say that I am strong
I dream I will be an impenetrable fruit cake
I try not to wither away
I am a lollipop stick
Trent Fox, Grade 6

Why
Trees high and mighty
Mountains are large and are proud
This is Planet Earth

Oceans wide and deep
Lakes are fresh and so are streams
This is Planet Earth

Why do humans fight
When we could climb a mountain?
Why do we bully?

Why do we steal things
When we could swim in a lake?
We could avoid it.

Guess that's how it is
But I will always wonder
Can we change somehow?
Sawyer Tabor, Grade 6

Christopher
C ool
H umble
R esponsible
I ndependent
S mart
T hankful
O riginal
P roper
H elpful
E ager
R eliable
Christopher Chintalan, Grade 4

Beach
What is it like at a beach?
You're sitting on a huge pile of sand.
Down on the beach…
You might hear a little rock band.

People running everywhere
Hurrying to hear the waves,
They explore and discover
all the secret caves.

Scuba diving people
jumping off the boat,
sitting on my boogie board,
watching while I float.

People finding seashells
looking everywhere.
I love the crashing of the waves,
And how the wind feels in my hair.
Sophie Betcher, Grade 5

The Last Leaf
The last leaf of life
slowly floats away
swaying in the breeze
whispering softly
"goodbye my beloved tree"
a bird swoops by
"don't go," he cries
to the last leaf of life
for if it goes
so will
one's precious life
"farewell," whispers the
last leaf of life
the last leaf of life
gently lands atop a blue lake
stirring the water ever so slightly
"goodbye,"
the last leaf of life whispers
one last time
Barrett Bennett, Grade 5

The Offender
One of many offenders,
Prepare his team,
For an opponent,
That could cover,
The receivers,
And players,
Who were in that list.
But still he earned,
Sort of,
Spectacular mistakes,
Those two seasons.
Khulan Temuujin, Grade 5

Happiness
Happiness hops like a small bunny.
Happiness smells like fresh lemons.
Happiness tastes like sweet candy.
Happiness looks like a cheerful smile.
Happiness is warm and cool,
Like a breeze on a sunny day.
Happiness feels like the best day ever.
Happiness makes me want to squeal!
Mariana Gamboa, Grade 5

A Face in the Sky
He watches over me every night
He watches me with such delight
He shines so bright
With his magnificent white
Sometimes I watch him too
He watches all of us even you
While he shines with almost no hue
That wonderful face in the sky
Alex Hays, Grade 5

Ballroom
Masks of jewels
Painted walls
Unspoken tension
Rhythmic tapping
Whispers
White dresses
Red ties
Smiles…
Jessica Ly, Grade 6

Spring
There may be some calvaries
Of allergies!
Spring will ring
When you hear the birds sing.
The buzzing bees
Will sting you with ease
And they will seize your day!
Spring can bring anything.
Matthew Djordjevic, Grade 5

Koalas
Koalas, koalas, oh so fluffy
Their beautiful ears are so puffy
They climb up in the highest trees
Where they eat lots of leaves
They're up so high
In the sky
When they come down
They fool around
Morgan McHugh, Grade 4

Bullies
Dawn
Appease, cheerfulness, companionship
Sunset
Torture, depression, loneliness
Stay, go, come and leave
Friends who stick up for you
Bullies who tease and trick you
Homework
Whatever
Affection
Hatred
Home
Danger
Bullies
Tyler Metzel, Grade 6

Abby Wambach
Abby Wambach has a game
Soccer is its name.
Abby found her destiny
Not doing track, she could see.

Abby loves soccer and making goals
She was always in control.
She had trouble with her knee
It was just a minor injury.

She won gold medals twice
She and soccer are like sugar and spice.
Abby could always cheer
That's why she won player of the year.
Joey Gaglioti, Grade 5

Walt Disney
Walt Disney was a film maker,
But also was an inventor.
He invented Walt Disney World,
To go on rides that really swirled.

Walt Disney drew Oswald,
And I think he was very bald.
After that, he made Mickey Mouse,
Who lived in a club house.

He lost his right to Oswald,
But I still bet he hasn't bawled.
Walt Disney, Walt Disney, the cartoonist,
He will always be on our memorable list.
Christina Janowicz, Grade 5

Penguins
Black, white
Swimming, sliding, slipping
So cute when waddling,
Mammal
Isabella Martinez, Grade 4

Dreams
Candy, cake, and a pet,
a race car and a fighter jet!
I don't have to pick up messes
and there's plenty of pretty dresses!
Horses and swimming pools,
No rules! Fun schools!

Soccer fields and basketball courts,
lots of time to make forts.
Lots of dazzling flowers
and awesome superpowers!
I especially like my dog Fred
Then I sit up in my bed
What??? Fred? Fred?
Kiana Bowman, Grade 5

Recess
Called out for Recess
We go and play
This is the routine every day
We have fun with friends
And it never ends.
The whistle is blown,
While the teachers stand alone
They lure us in
Now it's time for gym
We run around
and make some sound
Then I wait and wait for recess to come
But I just remembered it will be back
In the snap of my finger and thumb!
Joanna Shorinde, Grade 5

Spring
Spring is the season
I love most
Winter's past,
School is toast!
Shorts and sports
All day long
Going to the beach
Having some fun
Now it's time to say goodbye
To a horrible winter,
We survived!
Welcoming spring in its glory
Watching a flower bloom its story
Colin Hulmes, Grade 6

Clockworks
Look at…
The hands spinning
They move smooth as silk
As the clock steadily ticks
Time flies
Zachary Thibault, Grade 5

My Little Family
My family might be crazy,
but I don't make a fuss.
My family might be lazy,
but they do so very much.

My grandpa likes movies,
he has three hundred or so.
He has a lot of Disney movies,
and he drinks a lot of Joe.

My mom is a nurse,
she works a lot through and through.
I think it is gross,
all of the surgeries she has to sit through.

My family might be crazy,
but I don't make a fuss.
my family might be lazy,
but I love them so very much.
Jaime Sprenger, Grade 6

Homework, I Love You
Homework, I love you
I think you are great
It's wonderful when
You keep me up late

I think you're the best
When I'm totally stressed
Preparing and cramming
All night for a test

Homework, I love you
I tell you it's true
There's nothing more fun
Or exciting to do

You're never a chore
For it's you I adore
I wish my teacher would
Hand you out more
Maryleeana Pellot, Grade 4

Sea Turtles
S wim in the sea
E xciting to see
A mazing

T errific
U nderwater life
R eptiles
T urtles
L ovely
E ndangered
S mart animals
Zoë Foose, Grade 5

High Merit Poems – Grades 4, 5, and 6

Cat
Sly kitten hiding
Under the bed stalking mice,
Watching carefully...
Nevaeha Paulsen, Grade 5

Big Bear
Fuzzy, furious
Waiting for its tired prey
Snack time has arrived!
Allen Cardona-Torres, Grade 5

Winter
Cold, snowy breezes
Dark clouds surround one color
Covering the sun...
Alicia Urias, Grade 5

Cougar
Furious, nasty
Waiting for its injured prey...
Dinnertime arrives!
Marco Mejia, Grade 5

Zoo
Walking through the zoo...
Almighty lions roaring,
Monkeys swing on vines!
Mario Bonilla, Grade 5

The Great Outdoors
Flowers bloom by streams
Kids play soccer in the spring
Animals roam free.
Kaiden Smith, Grade 5

Turtles
Eggs buried in sand
Waiting for the time to come
Hatching on their own...
Antonio Velazquez, Grade 5

Gorilla
Giant gorilla
Lies down in the cool green grass
While eating his pear...
Trent Templeton, Grade 5

Fire
Blazing flames of heat
Lights a burned path by itself
Smoke darkens your sight!
Torri Contreraz, Grade 5

Florida
Dragging my feet I walk in awe step by step out of the plane.
I smell the salty sunny air.
I ignore the weight of the suitcases as I sprint to my grandpa
waiting for me with arms spread out and a big smile.
I run into his arms nearly throwing him into the wall as I look at
the sleek ocean behind him.
In awe I have to let go of the beauty of the vast pool of water.
The moves of the waves like they were dancing to pieces
by Mozart knocks me out.
I wake up to the world running into my arms and kissing me on the cheek.
But I quickly dash to my room in the house and change into my
bathing suit in seconds, following after I am waiting anxiously
for the elevator to open.
When it does it was like the beginning of a race.
I sprint out like a cheetah, down the path, through the sand,
and into the water.
Now I think the true definition of Florida is the cool and glassy ocean.
Will Kerber, Grade 6

The Lake at Dawn
Waking up well before the sun, hiking on the trail by moonlight,
The chill of darkness wraps around, in the silence, every sound echos.

The cold stars shine so far above, here, in the thin air, I feel so high.
Yet the sky is still much higher, the vast black makes me feel so small.

I press on, the moon following, slowly, the sun creeps up on the night.
As I near my destination, the dark sky is tinged with faintest gold.

In the night, I travel swiftly. Soon, I arrive at the alpine lake.
The clear water is filled with stars, all are reflected, with no ripples.

As I gaze out the sky brightens. The sun peeks over the horizon.
A warm rosy gold glow seeps in. Soon, the sky is awash with color.

As the sun shines red and orange, the lake reflects, shining just as bright.
For fleeting, glorious moments, the lake glows with deep flaming colors.
Emily Mucchetti, Grade 6

Hidden
Hidden we thrive
Growing, expanding, underneath the seeking eye
Our culture, our gods, our language
Destroyed
For we trusted
The white-skinned man, not knowing
Of the evil spirits that dwelled in the darkness of the eye
And because of our trust, our descendants will never know our culture, our land
The feel of the earth, the kiss of the wind, the colors of the stars
Lost
Now only a soft lingering of the spirits within the eldest of our elders
Our ways lost, our land lost, our language that of the Spanish tongue
Yet we strain to hear, to thrive, to find our ancient ways
So that our children and their children will feel the kiss
Of the Native Culture
Devika Nair, Grade 6

Bullies

Bullies try to push you around,
With their mean words they will
 knock you down.
They'll break you like a twig, Snap!
Now you're trapped.
You try to find,
Some peace of mind.
You're feeling insecure,
Second guessing, not even sure.
The bullies think they have won,
But the game has just begun.
You stand back up, straight and tall,
Now you cannot fall!
Angela Sorbello, Grade 6

Electric Green and Gloomy Gray

Fridays I feel electric green.
Glowing with excitement!
Feeling lucky,
like a four leaf clover.

Mondays I feel gloomy gray.
Like a storm cloud,
 ready to burst!
Tired and careless.

Now I feel pool side blue,
relaxed and refreshed,
soaking up the summer sun.
Olivia Haun, Grade 6

Zoo Keeper

The monkeys swing and sway
While elephants stomp away.

Alligators are the king
Orangutans chill and swing

Giraffes stand tall
While canaries call

Can you guess who?
That's right!

I'm the keeper of the zoo!
Holden Orr, Grade 4

Titanic

Titanic sails across the sea
It is 882 1/2 feet long
Totally the best ship in its time
An iceberg struck it on April 14th, 1912
Now it is sinking
I stand on the sinking ship
Crack! It is over!
Levi Balzer, Grade 4

Frog Fish

F requently unseen
R eally may be mean
O utgoing, rather kind
G ulping down is fine

F riendly? I don't know
I t hides down deep below
S uperior little guy
H e gulped his meal — Good-bye!
Michaela Stillwell, Grade 5

School

It's the best
Friends with me
People by my side
Lunch is amazing
With awesome teachers
I love math
And the others too
School rocks
I hope it never ends.
Hope Rhodes, Grade 6

Buck

The winter winds chill my warm body.
I shake like there was no
summer or spring, just fall and winter.
My hooves are cold like
stepping in frozen water for two months.
It's hard to see with blizzard
winds in my face.
I have to be careful or I will
get shot by hunters.
Ethan Puscher, Grade 6

Mysterious Paint

Crazy swirls around the page
Polka dots over here
Wavy lines over there
Colors of the rainbow
Clear in my mind
My paintbrush going crazy
Painting left and right
The mysterious picture
No one knows
Mara Ginsberg, Grade 5

Penguin

I am a penguin
Black as the night
I waddle around the icy hills
I cuddle against you to keep warm
I can dive deep to catch my dinner
I can slide on my squishy belly
I am a penguin.
Sophia Goudy, Grade 6

Mexican Wolf

I am a Mexican wolf.
I like to eat a lot.
I will chase you,
Through the desert.
I will chase you,
Through the water.
And then,
When I catch you,
I would eat you up.
And my family,
Would want to,
Eat you up, too.
Brayan Cintron Berdeja, Grade 4

Minecraft

I'm playing Minecraft
Hitting angry creepers
While mining and crafting
I'm like an epic leaper
Jumping over lava
A creeper just exploded
I almost fell in lava
But my armor slot is loaded
With diamond armor
I'm unstoppable
The game just got harder
My TNT's unstable
Gregg Wenhold, Grade 4

Nature

Nature is more beautiful than gold.
The trees are green like emeralds,
And the sea is as blue as the sky.

Nature smells earthy and flowery.
When I touch the grass it feels moist.

Nature makes me feel calm.
Nature smells fresh, and
Nature is a place where,
I can speak with God.
Monica Perez-Ricaurte, Grade 5

Wanderer

Society is a wanderer,
Going here and there,
Sometimes it stops,
For a little while,
But hastily leaves again,
Here and there some people stay,
For years and years,
Others quickly leave,
Jumping for a next big thing,
Perhaps I stay, perhaps I leaves,
But I really don't care.
Albert Zhang, Grade 6

High Merit Poems – Grades 4, 5, and 6

Bullying
Mean words can make you sad
I haven't done anything bad.
You think being a bully is cool
Even though you're being such a fool.
Crying myself to sleep at night
It is such a sad sight.
I've wanted you to stop bullying me for years
All it has done is produce more tears.
Take the time and show that you care
so you can clear the air.
Carson Mendonca, Grade 6

Brainstorming
The storm, it is coming
The leaves are blowing like forming a tornado
Books, trees, folders and much more
spinning and, spinning
Those endless items start leaving this place
For those items are us
We were living in this storm
Living in this crowded place
Then landing on a sheet of paper
as ideas
Eshi Kohli, Grade 5

Not So Good Friend
Is she a friend if she tripped you in the hall?
Is she still your bff, just say "not at all!"
She talks behind your back, whispers to your friends,
To me that's not a friend at all, c'mon this has to end!
The inappropriate things she told you, admit it now it's wrong,
I think that if she keeps it up, we should just tell her mom.
Maybe her mom will ground her, or make her clean her room,
Possibly she'll have to sweep with the thing that goes vroom, vroom.
Maybe her mom will tell her to be nice and to stop,
Or make her say sorry; hey let's just call the cops!
Adrianne Rossman, Grade 6

Summer
The last day of school, is like the first day of summer.
There is so much to do, what should I do first?
Play hockey, go swimming, or even get a haircut?
Head down the shore there is even more to do.
Play in the sand or go in the water?
Ride the waves and watch the seagulls fly by?
Listen to the buzzing of their wings?
Playing in the sun, is so much fun.
There is so much for you to do in summer.
Summer is my favorite season of the year.
Liam Donaghy, Grade 6

Rafting
Rafting
Blaring, clamorous, deafening, cacophonous
As earsplitting as a volcano erupting
Sophia Henry, Grade 6

Spring
In spring all the animals have their cute babies.
The horses have foals.
The cows have calves.
The dogs have pups.
All the boys wash our orange carrots.
Also red, white, and yellow potatoes, too.
The little children play in the mud puddles
And made themselves muddy.
The prairie crocuses bloom in the spring.
The trees lose their red buds.
The grass grows green and the weeds, too.
That is where we play hide-and-seek.
Zach Gross, Grade 5

Meadow
The flowers danced along the meadow.
Spinning in the wind.
Running through the field.
The grass reached up.
Tickled my feet as I walked through the field.
I fell down and looked at the sky.
The grass rose up and hugged me.
As if to tell me something
with the grass hugging me.
The clouds watching over me.
The flowers dancing along the field.
I couldn't help but fall asleep with everything watching.
Aubrey Stuckey, Grade 6

Sarah Steckbeck
Daughter of Joy and Andrew
Who likes to jump, run, and play
Who brings to Locust Grove her smile
Lover of piano, laughing, and tacos
Who fears lightning, tornadoes, hurricanes
Who knows a lot about surfing
And desperately wants to surf more often
Who wouldn't be caught dead bungee jumping
Who hopes to one day be a professional singer
Who would be remembered for her laughter
Steckbeck
Sarah Steckbeck, Grade 5

A Flying Planet
Basketball is fun to play,
I could even play all day.
You learn to dribble and
  to shoot.
You sometimes take a
  straight route.
The basketball glides through the hoop,
like a star soaring through the sky and onto the moon.
The basketball is a flying planet,
It will never stop going,
to the end of time.
Sage McKay, Grade 6

The Creepy Lighthouse
Rocks crawl around the lighthouse
The water is sparkling
The lighthouse is huge
Xavier Rodriguez, Grade 4

The Lighthouse
A glowing lighthouse
I can see a city shine
The reflection shown
Jayden Ortiz, Grade 4

Fishing
A dark blue river
Light green beautiful tree
A person fishing
Elizabeth Coutts, Grade 4

Underwater
Ocean animals
Swimming through flowing water
Calm, cool open sea...
Bryonna Temple, Grade 5

Dogs
Playful friendly pets...
Bathe them, feed them, let them sleep!
Chubby little dogs
Kenneth Gonzalez, Grade 5

Flowers
Gorgeous flowers move
Roses blooming in the air
An amazing sight!
Anahi Toledo, Grade 5

Waterfalls
Waterfall floating
Gentle and innocent waves
Crashing down...Splish! Splash!
Amber Krehmeyer, Grade 5

Final Fantasy VII
This game is special
It means so so much to me
This game makes me cry
Benjamin Grégoire, Grade 4

Dolphins
Jumping and diving...
Dolphins using shovel snouts,
Eating chubby fish!
Brian Porras, Grade 5

The Tree
I am like a tower in the sky
I wonder when summer will come
I hear the birds singing to me, like a soft symphony
I see the construction truck stopping near me
I want to run away
I am very frightened
I pretend that I do not feel anything
I feel my bark coming loose
I touch my leaves to the ground; they do not even make any sound
I worry of what will become of me
I cry like a child who is afraid of the dark
I am crashing to the ground
I understand that I cannot live forever
I say to myself that time will fly
I dream of the summer that I will not see, the children lying under me
I try to stand tall
I hope that I will be created into something beautiful
I am a tree
Rachel Swain, Grade 6

Worrisome Lightning Bolt
I am a lightning bolt
I wonder when I will strike
I hear the thunder boom after I strike
I see people running for shelter
I want to strike, and hit something with all my might
I am a lightning bolt
I pretend I know when I will strike
I feel ready to strike
I touch the highest object around me
I worry that I might hit a pitiful person progressing towards shelter
I cry out when I hit something, worrying that it is a person
I am a lightning bolt
I understand I am feared
I say I am hotter than the sun
I dream to be thunder because they act like they are rolling through the hills
I try to make that boom, ear splitting sound when I hit the ground
I hope that one day I will be thunder, even though it's not going to happen
I am a lightning bolt
Josh Ipock, Grade 6

Love at First Sight
She was walking along the street,
And zoned out to look up at the sky,
When she bumped into a teenage boy.
They looked into each other's eyes,
And there was a shimmering sparkle that was brighter than the stars;
It was then they knew it was love at first sight.
They walked up to the top of the hill,
As they giggled and blushed,
While the various pink and orange streaks marked their places across the sky.
And the sun stood there,
In its setting position,
With the color even more radiant than gold.
So there they stood, hand in hand, his lips against hers.
Tara Gira, Grade 5

The Whale
He wades below the ocean blue
And comes up every hour
With two small eyes he watches through
Some krill that he'll devour

Two big gulps, the krill are gone
Behind the prison bars
He resumes his float which he is on
To the boat of ours

He jumps right up into the sky
And right before his crash,
He has a gift no one can deny
A big ginormous SPLASH!
Patrick Stoddard, Grade 5

Fall Wishbone
Corn stalks standing tall
Like soldiers waiting for an order
Arched brown trees
Looking for a new friend
Wind snapping tree branches
Like my sister and I
Fighting over a wishbone
After Thanksgiving
One lonely bird feather
Glimmering on top of glistening water
Newly trimmed grass
In bundles
Like heads of lettuce
At the grocery store
Tegan Farina, Grade 5

The Tiger
With eyes that watch
To seek it's prey,
He hopes to eat
That very day.

With fur that's orange
And stripes so black
Waiting camouflaged
He plans his attack.

Loves the water
Lurks at night
No matter who see him
They shriek with fright!
Jillian Schatz, Grade 5

Money
Money is like a fish.
It can slip out of your net.
It can make you set for life.
Or you could lose it all in a bet.
Jameel Anderson, Grade 6

The Beautiful Spring
Look at that beautiful rainbow!
With the blooming flowers,
And the fresh air.
Oh, look at the fluffy pollen,
And cute lady bug,
Flying all around.
Hmm, delicious ice cream,
Now that the snow has melted away,
The rain is coming,
Though I still love spring.
Yu Qi Zeng, Grade 4

A Poem for Veterans
Even in darkness,
you will shine bright.
For you have been brave,
and courage takes might.
You have been strong,
and strength helps with the fight.
You have been smart,
and knowledge is right.
Since all of these things give beautiful light,
even in darkness you will shine bright.
Froukje Schlingemann, Grade 5

Rain
The rain is falling outside the windows
The calm wind blows.
As you read your book and sip your tea
You stare at it calmly.
You finish your tea and put down your book
You stand and walk out of your little nook.
You grab your camera and smile
Your bare feet walk on the cold tile.
You step outside and forget all pain
You just dance in the rain.
Emily Jean Reardon, Grade 6

Graduation
G owns and caps are worn
R eading speeches
A time to celebrate
D iplomas are given
U nforgetable memories
A lot of new friends to be made
T ears of joy and sadness
I will miss my teachers
O utgrowing elementary school
N ew beginnings
Audrey Turgeon, Grade 6

Sharks
Eat seals, seagulls, fish
They are dangerous killers
Sharks swim rapidly
Joseph Coletta, Grade 4

Poetry
Poetry
Is a lump of clay
Molding
Shaping
What should I make?
What color will I use?
Deciding
Reshaping
What should it be about?
What emotion will it give?
Poetry
Is a lump of clay
Abby Green, Grade 4

Happy Spring
The lovely flowers
tulips, daisies, and daffodils.

Such a lovely time, the morning dew,
it's so delightful!

The grass is green
you can hear the birds chirp.

And that's why spring is happy!!

Happy spring!
Luke Sutton, Grade 4

A Lifestyle
Gymnastics can take a while,
It's not only a sport it's a lifestyle!
Vault, Bars, Beam and Floor
Aren't as easy as opening a door!
Gymnastics can make you sore,
You always want to do more!
The beam is thin and the bars are uneven,
It's like this sport came from heaven!
Gymnastics is a sport and that is true,
Not one where we worry about our hairdo!
Gymnastics is a sport from the heart,
It's #1 on the chart!
Caitlin Warburton, Grade 6

Sickness
My face is blue
Like the moon
My dog was green
Like a bean
I got chicken pox
Like polka dots
I thought I was a cat
Chasing a rat with a hat on a mat
My name is Pam
I like ham
Lucia Quinones, Grade 4

Squid
The majestic squid
Swims in the deep, dark ocean
Frightening others!
Owen Bruce, Grade 5

Waves
Rolling and crashing.
White foam spewing over top.
Lashing against the rocks.
Isaac Christensen, Grade 6

Leaves
Rustling in the wind
Falling from trees to the ground
different colors
Brinly Stapley, Grade 6

Storming Shore
Crashing foaming waves
Beat upon the rocky shore
Skies of thunder "BOOM"
Allison Langston, Grade 6

Blooming Summertime
Delightful flowers...
Beautiful rainbow colors...
Sweet smell fills the air!
Destiny Rojas, Grade 5

Rocky Mountains
Rough, beautiful, bold...
Massive Rocky Mountain peaks
Glisten white with snow!
Leevi McFarland, Grade 5

Llamas
Spitting in your face
Yucky, slimy, gooey spit
Stay away from them!
Briana Rose Gonzalez, Grade 5

Dance
Graceful, beautiful,
Dances for all the seasons,
Get moving all day.
Nyia Barrow, Grade 6

The Old Fisherman
Person in water
Green rapids hitting the rocks
Colorful leaves fall
Austin Tangora, Grade 4

Chatter Box
People call me a chatter box, for I talk and talk and talk a lot,
From Monday to Sunday 24/7 I'll probably be talking even in heaven,
From eating to drinking, to playing and snoring,
I'll have a tale on all of them, I'll be sprouting Latin root words and stems,
I talk so much that people think I don't breathe,
About cats and dogs, and zebras and hogs,
And soon I'll stop for a millisecond, but that will never happen I reckon,
I'll talk and talk and talk a lot, I'll talk and talk 24/7 nonstop!
About cars and planes, or poodles and great Danes,
About plates and spoons, or dawn and noon,
And soon I'll stop for a water break, but of course a second's all I'll take!
I will talk about pancakes and butter, the fire department or the streets clogged up gutter,
About mines and caves, or currents and waves,
Then I'll stop to eat a snack, but then, of course the talkative me will be back!
If you say silence in front of me, I'll just stop and stare then laugh with glee!
Then I'll talk about flowers and trees, or grasshoppers, butterflies and bees!
And while I sleep I'll talk about my dreams, mostly about me jumping laser beams!
I have to admit, although rather hard,
All I ever do is talk and talk and talk a LOT!
Sarah Qazi, Grade 5

Father
As I opened my eyes for the first time, a smile spread across you face.
I gazed up at your shining eyes, as you beamed back at me.
You gently lifted me up, as you took me in your arms.

During my days of joy, you dance and sing with me.
When life brings me happiness, you celebrate with me.

You comfort me when life feels like a grave of lost hopes.
When my path frightens me, you take my hand and lead me through.
When sorrow and misery strike me down, you raise me up
And shower me with love and joy.

You are always there, during the good and the bad,
During the sorrow and the joy, during the love and the pain,
You are always there.

So I thank you for those times, you are always there.
And I rejoice,
For you are a father beyond compare.
Carla Deetlefs, Grade 6

Popcorn
Fresh out of the bag feels smooth and rouge
The sound is tapping and dining when you drop the kernel
The popcorn goes ping pong when in the popper
It's like a fountain flow in the bowl
When it's falling down it looks like a white fluffy cloud
The popcorn smells like dinner cooking and so tempting to eat
Then the butter comes out and it's drizzling all over
The popcorn smells very juicy
When I put the popcorn in the palm of my hands it feels very squishy
Then the moment I put it in my mouth it melts quickly
That's my day with popcorn.
Addison McPherson, Grade 6

Graduation
G oodbye Montessori de Montreal
R eady to explore a new world
A good time to celebrate
D iplomas are handed out
U nforgetable memories of my friends
A ll caps are thrown up in the air
T ears of joy and tears of sadness
I will miss my favorite teacher Mrs. Haroula
O n June 19th, I'm graduating
N ow I'm moving on to high school
Marie-Helene Kozlova, Grade 6

If I Were a Rainbow
If I were a rainbow
I'd have lots of color
If I were a rainbow
I'd make someone's day
If I were a rainbow
I'd shine bright in front of the sun.
If I were a rainbow
I'd always be in the sky.
If I were a rainbow.
Riley Stutzman, Grade 4

Spring
Spring is coming
Birds are singing
It's time to plant flowers
For us to enjoy in summer

Maybe snow is gone
But when the wind isn't done
Even when the rain is falling
Children have fun splashing and playing!
Maíra Abran, Grade 4

Summer
Summer is the greatest season,
Yes, you know it's true.
It's the warmest time of year,
So much fun for me and you.

Summer is filled with heat and fun,
Swimming to keep you cool.
But maybe best of all,
Is that there is no school.
Quinn Erlandsen, Grade 4

Butterfly
It can be big, it can be small.
Can be colorful or dull.
Hang off the end of a branch.
They fly around in the warm sun.
Quiet as a mouse.
The pretty patterns flying through the air.
Kaley Sheehan, Grade 5

The Offensive End
Building up energy for the attack
When you reach the right spot
You shoot and score
Going back for the tap
Using your speed to catch the ball
You are running as quick as the wind
The ball is a rolling sphere
Going up and down the field
You play offense and defense
Getting to play with your eleven best friends
On that rectangular field
You call home
Julia Wilbekaitis, Grade 6

Nature
Nature is the best
The wind is like a whistle
Brushing thru the leaves
The grass is very soft under my feet
Some trees are as old as the Liberty Bell
Some are like newborn children
The animals are the best
They help nature grow
Nature shelters and protects them
Offering them food and water
Look around you
You can find nature everywhere.
Tyler Hoffman, Grade 6

Thunder and Lightning
Lightning strikes across
the sky. The bright light
Floods your eyes. It's
Crackling, I'm gasping
Wow! The sound screams
In your ear. My dog is
Howling as the thunder
Roars. It's crackling, I'm
Gasping wow! It's such a
Big racket, a riot in the sky,
A thud, a boom, a roar,
A hiss, it's gone, I sigh
Devyn Lalonde, Grade 5

My Life
I come from a town called Brownsville
My house is very grand
I play two sports
And I want to be in the band.

My favorite color is blue
I like pink and purple too
I have three friends
We have a Ninja squad
And we like to ride my quad.
Cheyenne Weld, Grade 6

Right Now
So much depends
on the life
of one girl

she not realizing
how very special
she is

and so much depends
on the life
of one boy

he not knowing
yet he is critical
to society

they are the last
the only ones left
what happened

what happened to joy
to smiles
to life

so much depends
on what we have
right now
Jazlyn Eskanos, Grade 6

My Home Is
Home is food, shelter
And water.

It is my bed,
And it holds my pets.

Home is light, relaxation,
And nutriance.

It is material, fun,
And my plant.

Home is health.

It is time,
And art.

Home is my bedroom, the couch,
And learning!

Home is:
Miraculous, affectionate, and warm,
It is kind, and amazing

Home is Life!
Jayne Bennett, Grade 4

Seminole Elementary
There once was a school back in the day,
where kids used to run and play.
It burned to the ground,
and is empty bound.
But you can still hear kids each May.
Jada Cooke, Grade 6

Pets
Puppy
Cute, cuddly,
Jumping, running, playing,
Loyal friend and pet,
Dog.
Bridget Cahill, Grade 4

Spring Blooms
Spring is in the air
flower smell sweet and nice
friends are playing outside
big smiles every where
Spring is everywhere!
Caitlin Humphreys, Grade 6

Spring Is All Around!
Flowers are blooming,
fruit is picked fresh,
the air is nice and warm,
butterflies are flying,
Spring is all around!
Gracie Humphreys, Grade 6

Panda
Panda
black, white, furry, big
climbing, eating, running
warm, fuzzy, cute, cuddly, Amazing
Big Panda
Dallis Mattson, Grade 6

Bunny
Bunny
fluffy, furry
jumping, thumping and hopping
likes to nibble carrots
pet
Syed Qasim, Grade 6

Wolfie
Wolf
beautiful, brave
howling, running, jumping
prize winning hunter
fluffy warrior
Reyna Mobney, Grade 5

Fear
I was happy before when things were the same. Now they are different.
I used to like playing with my friends and everything was ok.
I liked gardening with my mom and I like how every spring the seeds became
the most beautiful tulips you ever saw.
I liked listening to the birds chirp in the morning and the smell of fresh flap jacks
running up the stairs.

Now I fear all that stuff.
I fear that I will be next and I will never see my family or friends again.
I fear that I will never get to see the flowers I planted bloom.
I fear that the birds will be too sad to sing their songs and
I fear that I will never get to taste the delicious pancakes my family makes every
morning.
Most of all, I fear that I will never see happiness again.
I fear that we will never be the same.
What if I can't make it?
Will I fear this forever?
Fear.
Mackenna Kingsley, Grade 6

Midnight
Midnight,
Pitch black,
I can see nothing, I can do nothing.
So I think,
I think about today
I think about yesterday, and the day before, and the day before, and the one before that,
I think about all of the things I have done,
The good, the bad, and everything in between
As I think, I hope the good deeds out weight the bad,
But I do not know if they do,
Midnight,
Pitch black,
I can see nothing, I can do nothing,
But I realized it was time,
So to anyone and everyone,
Goodbye and Good night,
One more thing,
Remember to Think
Mary Grace Kelly, Grade 6

Rainbow
Red, stop. Yellow, slow. Just look around you, green to go.
Orange, taste. Blue's the sea, there's so many things that we don't see.
Kite, white, black as night, just listen with your eyes.
You say, "You, hey, keep it down." and this is my reply:
Rainbow! Can't you see it dancing in the air?
Rainbow! It's happiness is far beyond compare!
Rainbow! So follow me, let's dance around the square!
Rainbow! It's all just fun, no need to take a dare.
So just stand up, take a breath and show us all your smile,
So just calm down, laugh out loud, be happy for a while!
It's our rainbow! We got this, all under control
It's our rainbow! Yeah, we're a team, everybody knows!
Rainbow!
Megan Harris, Grade 5

The Shining Peaks
Mountains are purple
when the sun shines
on their peaks with little
pieces of snow everywhere
they know about being high
enough to touch the clouds
mountains show us about
keeping our heads up high
and believing in yourself
they love when people
look at them and call
them beautiful.
Caitlyn Biffle, Grade 4

In Love
Love is
something that happens
when you see someone you like

It builds up energy
so you don't grow apart

Your spirits will never leave each other
Night comes and you have to go home

You hesitate to say
goodbye
Suhana Mohammed, Grade 5

Noah
N oticeable
O utgoing
A wesome
H ero

Z any
E xtraordinary
R espectful
F riendly
O utstanding
S porty
S ensitive
Noah Zerfoss, Grade 4

Clearwater Beach
Only at the beach
Can you hear the seagulls screech
The palm trees clatter
See the fish all around, then scatter
Detect the pizza browning
View people laying on towels tanning
Strolling on the sand, feel the shells splinter
Not only in the summer, but also winter
Any time of year, it's always toasty
Go and swim, only on the coasty
Emma Yeager, Grade 6

My Sport
Great routines
"Yay" for gym
Meets
New skills
Awesome coaches
So much fun
Terrific tricks
Incredible classes
Chalk-covered hands
Strength
Martha Crawford, Grade 4

Basketball
Basketball is my favorite sport.
It doesn't matter if you're tall or short.
Every time I swish a three,
the whole crowd cheers for me.
Every time I go to shoot,
the crowd starts to hoot.
Even if I miss the shot,
the whole crowd cheers a lot.
Basketball is the best.
It is better than the rest.
Ronald Higinbotham, Grade 6

Hitler's Power
It was early 1930's
When everything was grim
No one could defeat him
No one could win
Hitler was powerful, they were not
All year round, cold or hot
German, Jewish, Asian and more
Didn't have a chance during the war
It was a very depressing time
Don't ever forget it.
Elle Podwats, Grade 6

The Bad Times
Their stories are told,
About the young and the old,
Their names are written in bold,
Hitler's heart was ice cold.

Hitler and his men kill,
While the others stayed still,
They tried to run away,
They tried to save the day,
But trying killed them anyway.
Alayna Weaver, Grade 6

A Perfect Day
The trees sway softly
Like waves on a calm bright day
The world is peaceful
Madalyn Hatfield, Grade 5

Reading
Flipping pages
One by one
Reading each
And every letter
Picturing fantasy
In our dreams
Or nightmares
In our minds
Carley Fauht, Grade 6

Autumn
Kind, funny, honest, weird
Sibling of Jaden, Taylor, Caleb, Dakota
Lover of dance and friends
Who fears heights
Who needs to have siblings
Who gives love to those who need it
Who would like to see her home again
Julseth
Autumn Julseth, Grade 5

Bright Sun
The sun so bright and big in the sky
The palm trees flowing with the air, so slow
A slight breeze, a little chilly
The fresh cold water waves, so low
Some kids swimming
Palm trees smell so good like...flowers
The sand so bumpy between my toes
I feel so happy.
Alexis Birch, Grade 4

Stormy Nights
Through the storms and dark nights
It waited, it held on tight
Waited for a change, any change at all
For the warmth to come greet it all
When the cold disappeared
And it was ready to come out
It fluttered away
Free once and for all
Keira Gagné, Grade 5

A Second Chance
Stars shining bright
Helping the bird with his sight
Flying through the sky
Now he has to try
He has a second chance
To take a new stance
He spreads his wings to soar
And fear he has no more
Cassie Reccord, Grade 5

Gold
Freezing Alaskan climate,
Turning on the bulldozer,
Stripping away the dirt,
Will there be gold?

Scooping up the rocks,
Dumping them into dump trucks,
Driving the rocks to the shaker,
Will there be gold?

Long weeks and lots of sweat,
Mud all over our clothes,
Cleaning out the sluice box,
WE FOUND GOLD!
Jackson Combs, Grade 4

Waters
Waters are:
Tranquil,
Silent,
Rippling,
Splashing,
Drinkable,
Stormy,
Rainy,
Rich,
Beautiful,
Liquids,
Seas,
Oceans,
Blue.
Toshan Jain, Grade 6

Shooting Stars
Shooting stars are white
Like the moon.
They are hot like
The burning sun.

Whenever I see one
I make a wish
But it never comes true.
They are just like a
Flying ball of light.

If you ever make a
Wish on a shooting star,
I hope your wish comes true!
Simone Shetty, Grade 5

Storms
Storms
Windy and creepy
Slow crawling, nasty dark clouds
Very dangerous
Christian DeFelice, Grade 5

Something About Life Itself
Isn't it exciting
to live life as it is
the tears
the laughs
the sorrow
the joy
for there is sunrise
after sunset
there are rainbows
after rain
and dreams
after darkness
Miles Wright, Grade 6

Where I'm From
I'm from Park Hills,
from the mountains and the plains.
The place a mile high,
in a fortress of stone and wood,
where no seas lay.
I eat strips of cheese and tomato,
and clumps of green,
with stems as thick as a broom pole,
dipped into pools of white.
I am from where I'm from,
and so are you,
and so are they.
Irving Wilson, Grade 4

What Makes Me Smile
She is orange and white.
She likes to roam at night.
She has a bunch of fur.
She's happy when she purrs.
She likes to cuddle with me.
She eats food from the sea.
She always lands on her feet.
She likes to steal your seat.
If you push her off your seat she will dive,
But don't worry this kitty has nine lives.
My cat Tiger makes me smile.
What makes you smile?
Clara Westcott, Grade 5

My Dog
Multi-colored
Straight fur
Loud howls
Medium beagle
Male dog
Five years
Named Sparky
Cat lover
Animal chaser
Really playful
Mariana Soto, Grade 4

Joshua
I have a baby brother,
who sometimes cries for his mother.

He's the youngest of four boys,
and he makes the most noise.

At night I give him a bedtime hug,
then mom makes sure he's nice and snug.

He is growing up so fast,
being a baby won't last.

He is lots of fun.
I can't wait till he runs.

He likes to play and play;
he does it every day.
Nathaniel Bonomo, Grade 5

Basketball
I have a basketball
it is old
I shoot for the hoop
I never miss.

It's orange and brown
with black strips
and words that you like
it's a circle with air.

And flies like a bird
but never like a bee
it bounces like a ball
and flattens like a pancake.

This is why I call
it my basketball.
Jaida Wright, Grade 6

Hope
Hope
Is the thing with a chirping
feathered heart
that perches in the great wide mind,
and always keeps on singing its lullaby
but never rests

The sweetest gale from the
kindest storm could kill that
little bird
that kept me warm even from
that growling wolf named fear.

But for all that, in exchange,
nothing, from me.
Cole Kokish, Grade 4

History
One day you'll see
who you can be,
who you are to me,
and although your name
will not go to fame,
have no shame
because to me, you will always be
in my heart,
part of my history.
Pearl Elizabeth Jean Torres, Grade 6

Feelings
Red is for anger
Orange is for sour
Yellow is for happiness
Green is for goofiness
Blue is for sadness
Purple is for playfulness
Gray is for guiltiness
Black is for darkness
Alicia Johnson, Grade 4

The Lonely Little Girl
Sitting on the bench alone,
The little girl sits unknown,
The people just keep walking by,
Nobody helps even when she does cry,
Sitting there for at least a day,
She just sits there and doesn't play,
So depressed from her parents' death,
It's so cold outside she can see her breath.
Alexandra DaRosa, Grade 6

Beach
The beach is great
You get away from school
You have fun
You go with family and friends
With the ocean breeze and sand
All the great fish and species
All the great food and treats
But most of all, the fun
Madalyn Hampton, Grade 6

Basketball
Meeting your opponent,
Staring eye to eye,
Defending the line.
Aggressive, quick,
Excitement fills your soul,
Dribble once,
Dribble twice,
Goal!
Lila Ehrlich, Grade 4

Cookies
Cookies
Warm and crunchy
Cookies
Soft and munchy
Cookies
Fresh out of the oven
Cookies
Like a glimpse of heaven
Cookies
They fill my mouth with delight
Cookies
I could eat them all night
Cookies
So delicious and yummy
Cookies
They feel good in my tummy
Cookies
They go munch, munch, munch
Cookies, I love them a bunch
Tyler Gaydos, Grade 6

On the Other Side of the River
On the other side
of the clear water river,
there is an ocean with a low tide,
free of oil spills and lost ships.

On the other side of the river
there is a world
where only peace thrives,
and hatred is hurled.

In the world over there,
the grasses grow tall,
and the food and water are rich and fair.
No one ends up too hungry.

People live happily,
without a shiver,
in what may be considered a dream world,
on the other side of the river.
Maya Birkenkamp, Grade 6

My Pencil
my pencil
helps me write ESSAYS
my pencil
has plenty of graphite
my pencil
as sharp as a skull piercing sword
my pencil
I use it all the time
my pencil
as bold as can be
my pencil
Alex Church, Grade 4

Happiness
There's a hole in my heart
When you're not there
But when you are in a place I can see
You fill a void in my soul
That I never could see
When you leave I feel like I'm dying
But when you're there
I feel happy and I feel alive
That's the HAPPINESS that I feel
When you're with me
Dayana Givner, Grade 5

Graduation
G oodbye elementary
R eady for high school
A lot of fun
D iplomas for us
U nforgetable memories
A wonderful surprise
T ears of joy and sadness
I will miss my teachers
O verwhelming emotions
N ever will we forget this day
Abigail Yohannes, Grade 6

Graduation
G owns and caps will be worn
R eciting jokes and speeches
A time to celebrate the end of grade six
D iplomas are given to students
U nforgetable memories
A special moment for families
T he feeling of accomplishment
I t's time to move on to high school
O utstanding way to finish elementary
N ew beginning starts
Adam Addona, Grade 6

Cruise
This cruise is something I'm going to do,
Even though it's not something new,
I know in my heart that it will be fun,
Even though I'll be sad when it's done,
This may be very foolish of me,
But I love being out on the deep blue sea,
Florida, Bermuda, Bahama, and more,
We'll even be getting tanned on the shore,
I know right now that it'll be fun,
Even though I'll be sad when it's done.
Joey Tiger, Grade 6

Cool
Great Wall of China
Giant pandas at the zoo
Wonders of the world
Frank Jiang, Grade 4

Life and Death
I am the darkest, death
I wonder when I will end
I hear unhappiness
I see misery
I want to stop
I am the loveliest life

I pretend not to care
I feel warmth
I touch, the bodies drop, thump
I worry if I will be too late
I cry sadness and darkness
I am joy and happiness

I understand what I do
I say the words of life
I dream of stopping
I try to do it right
I hope I could be normal one day
I am life, I am death
Colin O'Brien, Grade 6

Smiling with Joy
Spring, oh spring!
How beautiful you are,
with all your flowers blooming.
No more snow,
just rain and sunlight waiting.
Spring, oh spring!
With all your bees buzzing,
They are pollenating flowers too,
Making us delicious honey for toppings.
Spring, oh spring!
No more hibernation.
Animals walking around,
With no more tired heads.
All full of life and adventure!
Spring, oh spring!
People cycling around,
Swimming and playing in the pools,
With colourful suits.
Everybody is happy,
And smiling with joy.
Alexia Abou Nader, Grade 5

Wishing to Be Smaller
A canyon dreams
As if never going
To stop wishing
To be smaller
So he can
Finally fit in
Dreaming
As if never
Going to stop
Jayden Roberts, Grade 4

Yellow
Yellow is the color of my marker.
Yellow is the color of a pencil.
Yellow is the color of a candle.
Yellow is cheese.
Yellow is bright as the Sun.
Yellow smells like a golden s'more.
Yellow tastes like lemonade.
Yellow sounds like the Sun burning.
Yellow looks like Fall leaves.
Yellow feels like a soft pillow.
Yellow makes me feels happy.
Yellow is the color of a smiley face.
Ava Baker, Grade 4

Tubing the Yampa
As I lay in the sun
Away I go,

Into the distance
My resistance of jumping
Into the cold rapids crashing
Against the rocks

Laughter surrounds me
As I float the Yampa
The water glistens with glory
As I sit and listen to many stories
Rose Epstein, Grade 6

Penguin
Black and white blurs
Sliding down the mountain
Splash splash splash
Into the ice cold water they go
Glaciers float near
The snow starts to fall
Waddling out of the water
They start to go home
The yellow light fades
The day fades into night
The penguins are done
So is the day
Madeleine Barrus, Grade 5

Hold On
Hold on to your dreams.
Even if you get discouraged.
Hold on to hope.
Even if you fail.
Hold on to those that love you.
Even if they disappoint you.
Hold on to your passion.
Even if it is challenging.
Hold on to dance.
Even when nothing else matters.
Jade Garner, Grade 5

The Lifespan Friendship
Friendship is love,
Love as a friend.
Friends can borrow,
Borrow and lend.
Friendships are born.
Friendships shall be done.
When friends are gone,
Your heart weighs a ton.
When you choose a friend,
Oh, do be careful,
For there are people,
That are very disrespectful.
Friends are people to stick with.
Nice, gentle and fun to play with.
So climb aboard the friend ship,
And billions of friends you shall see.
You shall have a ton of friends,
And happy you shall be!
Juan David Lago Quijano, Grade 4

Good-Bye
I am leaving
forever
gone
good-bye

I am leaving
to a place
that no one
will ever know

I am leaving
miles and miles away
uncountable
unknown

I am leaving
and I wish
I could stay with you
Brick Dalsis, Grade 6

Love, Nora
The woman
wore clothes of lavender.
That woman
stands by me forever.
The woman
peered past the sorrow.
That woman
stepped up to the joy.
And when her name
was called out
from the heavens,
Mammaw waved,
and gone was she.
Ruthie Weeks, Grade 6

Education: Success
The endless possibilities,
The thirst for knowledge,
The amazing activities,
The path to college.

Reading, Writing, Science, Math,
Tests are on their way,
Surviving endless studying wrath,
Excited for each coming day.

My decisions,
Leading me in the right direction,
Evolving and changing my visions,
Striving towards perfection.

Striving to thrive,
Each step is a careful step,
Many more milestones to arrive,
For the future I prep.
Jivitesh Praveen, Grade 6

Fear
All the Jews felt fear
That they would be next
Taken from their homes
All day and night
Fear
Forced on trains to camps
Worked all day and night
If they stopped they died
Fear
Camps were too full but
Still they put more in
They killed old and young
Just to make room
Fear
We heard rumors
Camps were freed
U.S. soldiers rushed in
Saved us all
Hope
Scott Wright, Grade 6

Photo and Rose
I stand and wait
camera in hand
waiting for a beautiful scene
it soon dawns upon me
and guess what I see
a beautiful rose glimmering at me.
I blink, I stare
pretty as can be
because an amazing rose is waiting for me
and look on
to see my rose is finally gone.
Alison Righetti, Grade 6

Taylor Swift
Taylor was born in December
She is a girl we all remember,
She is a great inspiration
Everyone knows her in the nation.

Taylor has blonde hair and blue eyes
She went to the Grammys to win a prize,
The Dick Clark Award of Excellence
Gave her an awesome entrance.
Tori P., Grade 5

Car
I am a car.
I sometimes run through the street.
I wait for you for the next ride,
Through the street.
I sometimes hear the ambulances,
Going through the streets.
Sometimes I brake,
Or run out of gas.
I am a car.
Bryan Valverde, Grade 4

Cool Pool
Wet feet
Feeling drowsy
Looking down
Hair stands
People pushing
Starts countdown
And jumps
Slow m o t i o n (falling)
Belly flop
Vanderley Baltodano, Grade 5

A New Hope
To be threatened is a pain,
To be pained is a gain.
A gain that will change your life,
But the pain is like a knife,
So we must have a hope, as be,
And leave the past for one to see,
Pain is gain.
So leave the world and the sea,
And give a new world for all to see.
Jonathan Kong, Grade 4

Today
Day
Bright pretty
Burning fighting playing
Falling falling darker darker
black black lights
pitch black
Night
Benjamin Borsato, Grade 6

A Feather
I am a single feather
I wonder why the ground is coming closer
I hear the wind whipping around me
I see my owner flying away
I want to be with my friends
I am a single feather
I pretend to be in the crystal blue sky
I feel ashamed to be here
I touch the tall cut grass
I worry I will be here forever
I cry because my owner in out of sight
I am a single feather
I understand that I will never be found
I say I will be here forever
I dream that one day I will be found
I try to be seen like a neon light
I hope my owner will come back
I am a single feather
Andie Hartley, Grade 6

Earthquake
An earthquake is gray,
Like a gigantic rock.

It's hot like a,
Raging fire,
But cold like,
The arctic's water.

It echoes like,
A rumbling tummy,
And shifts like a,
Trembling branch.

It can yank you down,
And suck you in.

And there I am,
In the middle of a horrible dream.
Carissa Chow, Grade 5

Sailboat
S
ai
ling
on the
water, sun
beating down
canvas flapping in the
wi
nd
Strong, wooden body hard to face the waves
Fast cunning sailboat searching for a gust
Wind dies down, craft begins to slow
anchor down, go for a swim.
Jonathan Klein, Grade 6

Home

Home is where your family is, your feelings are,
your ideas are.
Home is where the heart is, your comforter,
your sweetener for your life.
Where life begins.
When you feel sad or alone your home is there for you.
Home is where the memories happen, the ones you look back on.
Where you gather and face new challenges.
Home is your protector. It is safety in good and in bad times.
Home always comes through.
Where you start and end.
Home makes your environment, your choices, your life,
your story.
Home is where it happens, it's Home.

Bailey Weaverling, Grade 6

Friends Recipe

Take a perfect loyal friend,
put moments to cherish.
Mix and stir peace, success, and power
until they amuse each other.
Gently add the chemistry.
Bake on a cool summer afternoon
at 350 degrees celsius until it's time for a sleepover.
It's obviously done when they "accidentally"
stay up all night.
Let it cool until they wake up at 10am sharp!
Sprinkle some mixed emotions
of good and bad times.
Serve with a glass of "always there when they need you."
Taste a perfect friend!!

Ryan Eyzaguirre, Grade 6

Colors

Red is the color of love.
White is the color of a dove.

Brown is the color of my hair.
The color royal blue is quite rare.

Black makes me go to sleep.
Yellow makes me think of an Easter peep.

Gold is the color of a brass band.
Light brown is the color holding my brother's hand.

Lime green is the color of my slushy.
And, pink makes me a little bit blushy.

Maximus Schlieper, Grade 5

My Dream World

My Dream World is a beautiful scene with all trees so green.
Flowers that are purple, yellow, and red.
Kids that are healthy, happy, and fed, they run and twirl.
That's what I dream when I dream of a Beautiful World.

Jovany Hernandez-Ramirez, Grade 6

My Time at the Beach

I hear the seagulls flying high
In the bright blue sky
The sand I step on is really hot
I don't even bother to sit in one spot
I lean over to pick up a shell
My face reflects on the waves and I hear ringing bells
I smell and taste the nasty ocean
For some reason, it tastes like sun tan lotion
When I see the waves on the sand it looks like mud
But next I think there's gonna be a flood
I run in the yellow hot sun
It was super fun
When I see the beach, sad
Then I say, "Don't worry, I'll come back!"

Jasmine Bugarin, Grade 4

A Tribulation Named Laptop

My school laptops are always slowed
They take hours and hours and hours to load
The keyboard is way too small
I can hardly see the screen at all

It takes forever to open a web page
The time it takes, no one can gauge
By the time I log in, the class is done
And I have to miss all the fun

If only it weren't so poky
And gets faster, I'd be so lucky
Still, it does help a lot
Turns out, it's not as bad as I thought

Diya Dinesh, Grade 5

Nature Spreading Across the Land

Bark shaped like camouflage
Roots twisting their way into benches
Curly Q branches
As if they were confetti
One wild strawberry
Sitting in a patch all alone
Wind picking up leaves like a colorful tornado
Little holes in the wall of a river bank
Look like insect hotels
Fluffy grass
Like bear fur
Vines twisting like cobras
Towards the sky
Filled with colors of a rainbow

Francie Flores, Grade 5

Love

L ifting your spirit from the beginning
O ne person is all you need
V ery positive, caring, and encouraging
E ven though you may fight, you'll always love.

Kennedy Gibson, Grade 6

Penguins and Polar Bears
Penguins
Adorable, precious
Sliding, dancing, swimming
Catching fish, searching for prey
Hunting, waiting, catching
Ferocious, awesome
Polar Bears
Noah Osborne, Grade 6

Summer vs Winter
Summer
Hot, Awesome
Surfing, Swimming, Sliding
Summer is hot but winter takes it over
Skiing, Building, Snowboarding
Cold, Amazing
Winter
Julia Kennedy, Grade 4

Africa vs Antarctica
Africa
Hot, Dry
Dansing, Mining, Eating
Lion, Sun, Ice, Snow
Freezing, Fishing, Hunting
Cold, White
Antarctica
Nathan Shearn, Grade 4

Loss
Losing something precious
Is a stream of sorrows
It's like a train of endless grief
Hitting you like a bullet
Memories disappear like ghosts
Spirits soar like rockets
Leaving behind hope for a new day.
Brandon Lam, Grade 4

Snow and Lava
Snow
Majestic, fluffy
Falling, shimmering, sparkling
Winter wonderland, flowing down fast
Racing, killing, bursting
Menacing, hot
Lava
Lydia Ramey, Grade 6

Beach
B eautiful
E njoying water
A ll people like it
C ool breezes
H ot sand
Bella Stillio, Grade 4

Earth and Friends
The vast and beautiful blue sky, like a blanket covering the Earth.
The bright and beaming sun, warmed the planet with it's scorching light.
wisps of cotton; clouds, they won't stay for eternity.

I wish it would stay for eternity, the magnificent sky.
Mystical clouds, they spread across the Earth,
with yellow gleaming lights that shine from the sun.

The brilliant sun wants to shine for eternity.
But sadly it cannot, one day there will be no light in the wide sky.
Just the big round earth, covered with puffs of white clouds.

They take over the planet; clouds, with no room for light.
Will they leave or stay for eternity?
Or maybe they'll be parted by the sun, in the endless sky, which covers the earth

It's in charge of a bright day; light, of course with assistance from the sun,
illuminating up the Earth. Now they are gone; clouds.
Hopefully they're gone for eternity, leaving a bright sky.

The wonderful Earth covered in clouds, with bursting colors in the sky.
If it would only be like this for eternity.
It looked beautiful with the sun, with beams of radiant light.

I wish that for all (eternity) that I could see the rise of the sun.
I wish that I could see the (clouds) that float on the Earth.
But for now, I can only see the (sky) lit up with streaming colors
Vivian Tran, Grade 5

The Garden of the Gods
What must exist
Then the magic grove that sparkles in the sun;
For, the water gurgles, the grass is green, that never ceases to shun.

In the middle of the earth
Embedded to the root, sprouts an apple tree
So serenely, in peace with thee, Tremor may walk this realm but never evade to pollute.

Tis' this not a magical tree? That strong will never die…
Growing golden apples; The apples of dolor and youth.
And many a theft has but try…try…try.

A wish to pick a golden apple
Watering mouths within; To live forever is great prosperity.
Is this not a special garden? Making a plucked apple a sin?

Hear it not the voices of singing eternal dames?
They lurk within the tree protecting it from harm
Beautiful as they are, but dangerous as rams.

And when the sun dips
And all heaven breaks lose, remember the garden
The grass so green; The secret garden of the gods that will continue to produce.
Reese Sprister, Grade 6

Holocaust

1933 was when it started,
When Adolf Hitler introduced hate to the world,
Concentration camps started opening,
People's cries kept getting louder and louder,
Families getting taken away from each other,
While Hitler's plan kept progressing,
But people had hope and that's all they needed,
They started to resist at ghetto Warsaw,
Then an uprising came,
Allies kept coming and coming to help the Jews,
While Danies rescued 7,200 Jews,
The day finally came,
The Nazis finally surrendered,
And hate was finally gone,
But hope still lived in the people of the Holocaust,
And it will stay there forever.

Branden Doherty, Grade 6

Nature's Lullaby

Twitters and tweets fill the air
Glistening dew hanging on the last strawberry
Moss padding vines
Allowing chipmunks to scale them
Leaves grazing my hand
Summer has left
Fall is here
Frigid dew slipping to Earth
Unknown paw prints make stepping stones
I'm pulled into a beautiful clearing
I'm peacefully sitting
In an emerald colored world
With beautiful rows of flowers
I'm falling asleep
Listening to
Nature's Lullaby

Carleigh Carmody, Grade 5

The Butterflies

The butterflies
There they are
They always accompany me to the ice
The announcer's voice in my ears
I'm on
One deep breath and they double in quantity
A sudden frenzy of calm
Frozen into position
Then I'm awoken by the music
A twirl
Then a jump
The wind in my ears
Faster and faster
My butterflies slowing down
Then silence
My butterflies fly away with the sound of applause

Natasha Curzon, Grade 6

The Life of a Dog

I am a dog and I live in a house,
Atop the hill of where me and my spouse,
pull together and make a living
growing and selling are hard works of giving.
My life is simple and
Non complex
but I reflect the true meaning of life
Life is not to be
Wasted
but to cherish
The pages of life we turn every day.
I am cared for by my people
known as the glue who hold me together.
Just like you and your parent or lover.
We as living things,
Need appreciation.

Julia Keating, Grade 6

My Dad

My dad, John, was the best father in the world,
He cared for me and my brother all the time.
He always went out of his way to teach us well.
My dad was smarter than a rocket scientist,
He could learn anything.
Though my dad is gone,
My life is still going on.
I know my dad is very proud of me.
When I get sad, I might cry out a sea.
I know that for sure,
My dad is always here.
My dad's love for me is very pure.
My dad loved me very much,
He was the best.
I was always there for him,
Especially when he was laid to rest.

Joseph Richardson, Grade 6

Mary Jane

(To be read quickly, in as little breaths as possible)

I fly down the mountain, the wind in my hair
I go even faster as my face hits the air.
The snow's flying up like a rocket has crashed it,
slides under my skis with a swisedy-swash-it

Now here comes the moguls, the hardest part
Going down without crashing is some sort of art.
I hit the first bump, and my knees start to buckle
My skis make a sound like crunchety-crunchl

I regain my footing, but almost tumble
The snow slides down the mountain with a very loud rumble.
I reach the end of the run and I sigh with content
And then I look down and my skis are all bent.

Quinn Hirschland, Grade 6

High Merit Poems – Grades 4, 5, and 6

Little Sister
Sister,
Shy, loving,
Learning, playing, imitating,
Almost always watching,
Sibling.
Maria Adamow, Grade 4

Sun Star
Sun
Beautiful, golden
Blinding, shining, amazing
Yellow rays of warmth
Star
Ella Farnell, Grade 5

An Eagle
Eagle.
Wise, majestic.
Screeching, piercing, soaring.
Darting through the sky.
Stalker.
Karim Alomar, Grade 6

Ocean
Ocean
Cold, refreshing,
Swaying, splashing, soaring.
Broken seashells under water.
Water
Shane Haggerty, Grade 5

The Fire
Blankets catching fire
Smoke rising to the ceiling
Cinder and ashes
Flames dangerously dancing
Terrifying empty screams
Emma Ferguson, Grade 6

Tacos
Tacos
meaty, juicy,
loud, crunching, soft.
Tacos are meaty delicious
food!
Edward Weaver, Grade 5

You
Because of you
I opened my eyes
I open my heart for other people
You help me understand what love is
Because of you
Avery Lockwood, Grade 6

Love
Love is a bright gleaming glistening firework on the fourth of July.
Love is a loving warm hug from my wonderful mom when she tucks me into bed.
Love is spending fun times with my loving dad when we watch "Dark Shadows" together.
Love is being loved by my awesome grandpa when we go to the North Pole together.
Love is my aunts when we swirl around in the tea cups laughing heavenly.
Love is my grandma's sweet voice coming down from heaven saying I'm protecting you.
Love is my family's big red heart that grows every time we hug.
Love is my toys that my parents buy for me.
Love is a big warm blanket that covers me from freezing in the night.
Gillian Estes, Grade 4

All of Me!
I like to sing,
I like to dance,
When the audience wants a glance.
I pop and drop and show everybody who I am.

I dance like fire for being so great,
And I let my body flow like a river and lake.
When I sing I see a star like the one in my dad's jar.
The star represents my shine. I know this because the spotlight is all mine.
Shameka Fletcher, Grade 6

The Knight
There was a man who loved to write
He was a knight who had no fright
And then one night
He rode toward the battle to fight
In front of the castle there was a big hassle
About the big battle
And then the knight who loved to write spoke to the king about the fight
And then they said good night
Tristan Brocklehurst, Grade 5

Light Blue
Light blue is the colour of a calm ice rink, and a new born baby boy baby's clothes.
Light blue is the colour of a smooth running river, and the summer sky.
Light blue is the colour of relaxing, and family
Light blue is the colour of good feelings and comfort.
Light blue is the colour of my mom's eyes and warm bubble baths.
Light blue is the colour of my bed sheets, and the colour of some of my stuffed animals.
Light blue is one of the colours of my favourite Selena Gomez cd and my skis
Light blue is the colour of peace
Abra Glover, Grade 5

Fairy's Closet
What's in a fairy's closet?
An old button that did nuttin' but sit.
There might be some leaf dresses that have gone out of style.
A pile of paperclips all rusted and brown.
A top from an acorn which has molded a little more than when it was found.
Some spare pixie dust all golden-brown.
And probably some ribbon all tattered and torn.
Lost things found and used again.
Kailee Thompson, Grade 5

Summer
Oh how I miss summer.
I wish it would come back soon.
It being gone is a bummer.
School seems so filled with gloom.
Snow is fun,
But I can't wait till it's done.
It's okay when it's icy and cold,
But I'd rather have ice cream to hold.
Oh how I miss summer.
Caleb Ruby, Grade 6

My Cat
My cat is my best buddy,
He's furry, cute and fuzzy.
We like to play outside together,
And we don't care about the weather.

He also likes to play with toys,
And those toys make a lot of noise.
He usually hides under the bed,
That's where he naps after he's fed.
Alexandre Howard, Grade 5

Dogs
Dogs are amazing.
Dogs are funny.
I have two dogs.
They cost a lot of money.

Dogs are as sweet as pie
And as sour as a lemon.
But they are the apply of my eye.
I love them so much!
Lily Park, Grade 4

Music
This enjoyable sound
Makes you jump around.
Until it goes away
And you say, "No way!"

Music has a lot of meanings.
It can express your feelings,
It could also describe
Along with a nice sense of vibe.
Maika Saw, Grade 4

Night
The night is velvet
The stars are bright shining pearls
And I am at peace

The nighttime wakes up
The sunny day goes to sleep
What a pretty sight
Tiffany Iraheta, Grade 6

Cats on Sunday Morning
I stand perched
Upon your headboard
And leap down
And rest my haunches
On your stomach
My paws drag
Across your eyelids
Oh, you're up?
Feed me.
Elizabeth Rosenblatt, Grade 5

Spring
Spring feels like a light breeze,
On a wonderful day, it looks like a
Meadow of bright colours and beautiful
Rays of sunshine, I love spring
Because Easter is in spring, and
Of all the bright colours, spring is
One of my favourite seasons,
And I hope it is one of your favorite
Seasons.
Olivia Iorio, Grade 5

A Special Place
Tropical fruit, thin air
Oh that special place
Where the sun is bright
And at night the moon glows
The clear water and sky
I would love to go there
The palm trees sway in the wind
The strong smell, it's like heaven
Oh that special place
Alexandria Hause, Grade 6

The Puppy
Carefully crawling as it goes,
smelling along with it's little nose.
Pouncing on it's prey with might
while his tale goes left, right.

When he runs to the park
he goes bark! bark! bark!
He has energy like the sun
because he is having fun.
Porter Anderson, Grade 5

Science
S ets my focus
C oncentrates on the task
I gneous is made when magma cools
E very time is something new
N ever bored
C lear cutting is bad
E very class is fun
Tony Yao, Grade 4

The Wonder of Spring
Spring is here!
There hops the little hare.
The sun is up, the flowers are blooming,
This woke up the big brown bear.
The warmth of spring is in the air,
The children come out to play,
A little squirrel woke up from his sleep,
To search for an acorn along the way.
The birds eggs have finally hatched,
And spread their featherless wings.
They hopped on a branch,
Close to their mom,
To see the wonder of spring.
Dalia Jaafar, Grade 6

The Warmth of Sun
I love the warmth of the sun.
It wakes me up every day.
It makes me play.
It keeps me warm.
It keeps me safe.
It reminds me of my family.
It helps me when I'm lost.
It helps me when I'm sad.
It keeps me going.
It makes me stop.
The warmth feels nice.
Or sometimes cold.
I love the warmth of the sun.
Caleb Clarke, Grade 4

Door
I am just a door
Nothing more
Some can be new
Some can be old
At least that's what I have been told
I am just a door
Nothing more

Maybe, just maybe
There is more
Maybe I am not just a door
There could be more to me to explore
Maybe, just maybe
Mackey Munion, Grade 5

Spiders
spiders spiders crawling up your back
they crawl up and down
they bite you in the back
they are so fast
you can't get them of
they will never let go of that
itchy itchy big bite
Kaleb Demill, Grade 4

Forward
There are wonderful places,
And beautiful things,
All just out there waiting to be seen.

Don't look behind you,
Don't turn around,
Or what you're looking for,
Will never be found.

Don't tell me the limit's the sky,
When I've seen people walk the moon,
Don't tell me I can't make a difference,
When all I have to do is try.

If you keep going,
If you keep trying,
You will see wonderful things,
Flowers more colorful than a sky full of rainbows,
Stars that shine brighter than the most beautiful diamonds,
And mountains that will pierce through the clouds.

It may be a small world,
But if you keep going,
If you keep trying,
You will realize that it is a good one.
Breck Dunbar, Grade 6

I Am
I am the weird one nobody knows.
I am different. I am the one many people don't like.
Sometimes I think that I'm not brilliant.

Don't listen to them. In my mind you're a gem;
You are amazing,
Your spirit and soul are blazing.

I am the one that some people know.
I am out of the ordinary. I am the one that some people like.
Sometimes I feel solitary.

Don't listen to them. In my mind you're a gem;
You are amazing,
Your spirit and soul are blazing.

I am the happy one a lot of people know.
I am unique. I am the one many people like.
I don't care about their critique.

Don't listen to them.
I am a gem.
I am amazing.
My spirit and soul are blazing.
I am.
Maria-José Lema, Grade 6

Untitled
A butterfly waiting to be free.
Saying to itself "How will the big world be?"
Butterflies soon going to fly.
Winter is over time for me to fly.
Now I know how to fly high in the bright sky.
Maya Keirl, Grade 5

Knitting a Family
My family knitting; all strung out!
My dad is the needles, that bonds us together.
My mom is yarn, that loops around sharing her love and hugs.
My sister is the knot, holding us all firmly together.
And me the excess yarn that keeps us all going, moving and playing.
Jessica Andrews, Grade 6

Homerun Hitter
Sliding over home plate
Pitcher Throwing wicked curve balls
That should be a home run
Outfield can't even catch that ball
Batter hitting every ball, no need for a catcher
Sheridan Maines, Grade 6

Happiness
Happiness
Looking at stars, oh what shape they make
Banana bread perfect, ready to bake
Admiring all of the bright, colorful, shining lights on a lake
Happiness is magic at midnight just waiting to happen.
Korben Long, Grade 6

Football Game
The crowd cheering for the home team.
Freshly popped popcorn as I open the bag.
Catching the football as it's kicked into the stands.
Sugary goodness of cotton candy.
This is the best game ever.
Mikey Endrizzi, Grade 4

Parades
The floats are driving by.
The candy that the floats throw tastes delicious.
The gas from the floats smells bad.
The candy is very smooth.
The parade is now over.
Blake Taylor, Grade 4

When Is 4th of July
When sparkling fireworks crackle
And happy barbecues smell delicious
When loud parades are marching
And my lovely mother makes delicious candy to eat
Then it's 4th of July
Maleah Neiport, Grade 6

Food
I love turkey rolls, they are so yummy
Turkey rolls are so yummy in my tummy.
Chips and candy are good to eat
Even chocolate is a treat!
Pizza, pancakes and pumpkin pie
This food is so good
Would you like to try?
Megan Waldner, Grade 4

The Art of Dance
Ballet
Beautiful, graceful
Spinning, twirling, moving
Dance, pirouette, tap, beat
Stomping, pounding, moving
Edgy, exciting
Jazz
Jordan Groves, Grade 5

Summer Fun
Baseball
Glove, bat
Catching, swinging, running
Net, ball, grass, players
Running, kicking, scoring
White, green
Soccer
Carter Behm, Grade 5

Winter Day
The ice cracks like an egg hatching
so quiet just barely hearing the breeze
the trees grow
while the river freezes
sitting there under God
the mountains as beautiful as gold
it makes you feel happy inside.
Trent Stephenson, Grade 4

Orbits
Sun
Hot, bright,
Rising, shining, setting,
Star, gas, rock, satellite,
Glowing, orbiting, rotating,
Dark, round
Moon
Jason Wolstenholme, Grade 4

Dessert
Dessert
It is so good!
It gives you energy
You can have ice cream with it
YUMMY!!!!!!!!!
Makara Gawryluk, Grade 4

Track
I stepped onto the track
the nervousness ran through me like runners speeding down the lane
I lined up
my legs shook uncontrollably fast
every second I got more and more nervous
then, BANG!
the gun fired
I jolted forward the hardest I ever could
I could barely control it
second after second I ran
then, it was over
the nervousness finally ended
I felt thrill instead
which was the new place of the nervousness
it was so quick and quiet I could barely believe I did it
I caught my breath
I couldn't believe it
I won!
Colton Dash, Grade 6

All for Nothing
We barrel onstage,
waving wildly,
smiles glued to our faces.
"Give 120%!" my teammates remind each other ...as if that's possible.
We perform; we must be perfect to win.
Excitement builds up inside of us, as we sit at the awards ceremony,
in a circle, heads down, holding hands, praying
for our team to be called, followed by "1st place!"
We listen intently, and it hits us like a great — big — bag of bricks.
120% will never be good enough in the world we live in.
We wish for the day when we could be just as good as everyone else.
We stand and clap for the team in 1st place.
Fake smiles.
Tears in our eyes.
Where they are, is what we have always worked for.
All of our practices,
all the pain,
all for nothing.
Mikayla Irvin, Grade 6

The Apple Tree
My yellows and reds are now falling like the leaves of most trees.
It's fall.
It's cold.
It's time for you to start taking all my apples till I have no more.
I sit like a person in a chair swaying from side to side,
waiting for summer.
People drink hot tea, coffee, and hot chocolate in a warm house, while I
sit in the cold getting nothing
but what the air provides for me.
When the summer is here again, most people will think it's extremely
hot but I'll think it's
just perfect.
Trinity Walker, Grade 6

About Me
I live near Coal Center.
I live near Grange Road.
I live in the country.
Not in a town.

My favorite sport is soccer.
I play center midfield.
I have played since I was 3.
I still remember getting my first trophy.

I like Under Armour.
I like to be outside.
I like to ride quads.
I also like dirt bikes.

My favorite subject is math.
I also like science.
That is all I got to say.
I also like to jump over hay.
Donny Ross, Grade 6

Fireworks
Fireworks flying to the sky
　Peeeew!!
　Boooom!!
　Crackle!!
The fire sparkles
　Slowly
　Disappears
　Suddenly
　Peeeew!!
　Boooom!!
　Crackle!!
Another one but
This time it's
　Blue
Pew pew pew pew
Wow 4 go flying to the sky
Boom boom boom boom
Crackle crackle crackle crackle.
Leticia de la Zerda, Grade 6

Cross
Why are you the symbol?
I know
that JESUS touched you.
But now he's gone.
I don't believe that.
Do you feel darkness?
Do you feel happiness?
What do you feel?
　Grace
　Thankfulness
　Sadness
　Hopefulness
Tyan Archer, Grade 4

A Day at the Beach
On a sunny day I went to the
beach with my family
I ran with my brother
with great excitement into the
salty, blue water.
Something pinched my foot
Looking down into the dark
murky water there was
a red crab running away
Trying to kick him, he escaped
I swam away to my brother
We splashed each other
The salty water went into my
mouth
It was gross
Overall, my day at the beach
was fun
I hope to return
Kyle Mack, Grade 4

You Come Too
You come too, with me
To a land of stories and dreams
A land where our imaginations
Run
Free

You come too, with me
On a journey
Free
Exciting
Together

My sister, My sister
Travel
Seek
And Discover
You come too
With me
Posy Skov, Grade 6

Our Record
We all have our own record.
Some are short, some are long,
But in the end we all have a song.

Every song is different in its own way.
But the sad part,
Not all of them come to stay.

We all have our own record.
Some are short, some are long,
But the sad part,
There's always an end,
to every song.
Kaiden Bubash, Grade 6

Ocean
You better watch out for the
dangerous ocean.

You will think it's beautiful, because
it's so wide and so open.

But there are evil creatures out there,
sharks, whales and rays everywhere.

You say the beach is peaceful, but it
harms a lot of people.

If you don't believe me, see it
for yourself.

You will be saying, "I want the ocean
to disappear."

Because there's evil creatures trying
to hunt you out there.
Chaka Mishoe II, Grade 4

Good Bye
I see you lay across the hospital bed
You're as still as a tree
Your pale face is now yellow
Your soft skinny skin is now hard and fat
Your eyes are closed in deep sleep
Your breathing slows down
Your heart slows down
You move your legs
You move your lips and whisper
I come closer and hug you
I whisper in your ear I love you
My dad starts pacing
The monitor suddenly starts beeping
You stop breathing
And the room suddenly goes quiet
They cover your face
Everyone starts crying but me
You'll still be remembered
In our hearts
Good bye
Talia Khatib, Grade 6

Ode to Books
Oh Books!
I loved when it was just you.
No Kindles nor iPads nor Nooks.
One way to read, not three or two.
As you speak your story,
I begin to act like it's mine.
I share your adventures, and all your glory.
To me, you will always shine.
Oh Books!
Sara Hess, Grade 6

We All Fall
As we struggle through the days
we should look and ask can I get through this
Of course there's kids that you think don't have these problems
But we all do
But some can handle it better than others
don't judge by how they look
because we all fall
Just some take harder hits than others
we are all different and, if you ask me, that's good
that's why each new year is new
because we find different friends and different enemies
but if we were the same, New Year's wouldn't be new
that's why we should take advantage of now
because when one falls really, a part of us does too.
Stevie Guthoff, Grade 6

Christmas with My Family
On Christmas Day everyone is happy,
Cheers and laughter are heard down the streets.
See the presents under the Christmas tree,
With some boxes full of treats.

You can smell the yummy turkey,
So impatient to see Santa eat the cookies.
Gathering at the table with my family,
Siting near the fireplace and watching movies.

Wait seven more days for New Year,
All the streets are filled with snow.
This Christmas will end in good cheer,
With all the lights that glow.
Marie-Hélène Kozlov-Shishkina, Grade 6

Spring
Spring time is finally here
And the grass dances wildly in the wind
That turns to a warm spring breeze
As it wakes up the trees and they bloom their blossoms

The sun shines brighter than ever
Showing the land to sprout their little pink buds
That will soon turn into exquisite flowers

Rain falls so sudden and ends so soon
The birds flutter out and sing their sweet song
And animals scurry from their hiding places
To hear the sweet music and taste the fresh green leaves
Finally spring is here
Bailey Arellano, Grade 4

Rain Drop
Slowly, floating up to the sky combining with others to make a huge structure
Then gently falls back down to the ground then, POP!
It explodes on the ground
Austin Sumerlin, Grade 5

Noises (A Moment in Time)
Click, clack
Tiny fingers on piano keys
Buzz, buzz
The song of humming bees

Creak, creak
Tiptoeing at midnight
Thump, thump
Your heart when you know something is right

Tick, tock
A clock counting minutes one by one
Swish, swish
The wind blowing away our fun

Pitter, patter
Rain ruining the day
Tap, tap,
Someone clicking their heels to while the time away

And you kind of like the sound
For a moment, just one moment, in time
Annie Roe, Grade 6

It Was a Bad Time
It was a bad time
There were tons of camps
There were death marches
There was no identity

It was a bad time
When you were in a camp there was no escape
Not a lot of food
If caught escaping, you got killed

It was a bad time
In a death march if you walked too slow you got killed
If you couldn't keep up you got killed
If you stopped walking you got killed

It was a bad time
In a camp your hair was shaved off
People couldn't tell if you were girl or boy
You didn't know who your parents were
You didn't know who your brothers or sisters were

It was a bad time
Amber Buskirk, Grade 6

Apple Pie
Smells like a fresh rose.
Looks like the sun smiling up at you.
Tastes like you're flying for the first time.
Feels like a warm fireplace during the winter.
Apple pie is the greatest dessert.
Gwendolyn Holt, Grade 4

The Race*

A battered old dogsled sits patiently at the Alaska State Museum,
Waiting to tell its stories of riding through stormy nights and frigid days.
Underneath it is a plaque that reads:

In the town, disease is spreading,
An outbreak the world is dreading,
But the medicine is gone,
So a team of dogs is heading out into the storm.

The dogs will run and run
But their race is not done,
They have nearly 500 miles to go, so
In fact, their race has just begun.
They battle through the cold weather bravely
Although messengers bring news gravely
Of the pandemic epidemic raging,
They would have to put the patients in caging.

When they got to the roadside hospital,
They got a box a meter wide.
"Will it be enough?" they said and sighed.
It was enough and when they got back
A race was annually held in their track.

Corinna Healey, Grade 5
*This poem is talking about the 1000 mile diptheria serum run of 1925 or the "Great Race of Mercy," in Nome Alaska.

Used to be True

I planted that seed when I was so young.
Only around 3, I believe.
I remember the day as clear as a piece of broken glass on the heartless cement sidewalk.
It was so sunny, and the sky was as blue as the flowers petals, the color of my aunts vivid eyes.

I saw the clouds not as what they were, but as what they could have been if they had only just tried. I saw a pirate ship and princess crown and unicorn and sand castle. I saw a dragon breathing fire into the soul of my flower.

My flower, oh my flower. She helped me plant and raise it like it was her own child.
It grew forever young, like a petite, proud evergreen.

It grew every day with water and the sunlight that sprouted from her caring eyes. Then the winter came. I was 11. It never occurred to me that something a gentle and small as a snowflake could hurt that flower as bold and daring as dragon that was watching.

My aunt was the sun, my uncle the water. I was only the love.
But I figured out that sun and water can't live together. The hard way.
The sun was gone, everything dark.

Drip, Drip went the water. Trying to be what he once was.
That flower had seeds of that once happy life. It didn't surprise me
when they blew away on a gust of wind, the day my aunt and uncle parted.

The flower bowed by the brick fence under that strong, strong snowflake.
That life with those special people died.

Ella Chapman, Grade 6

The Lake

The lake is calm, peaceful and hushed
as ducks and geese swim through.
Fish slip by while being unnoticed,
with dragonflies buzzing too.

A rink in the winter, a nursery in summer,
with plants sprouting in spring.
Perhaps for shade, perhaps for protection,
or food some may want to bring.

On a quiet day, the lake is hidden
beneath the cover of the trees.
Only a few animals get by:
the birds, bunnies, and bees.

So if you ever pass by the lake,
take a moment to pause and look.
For the wonders of nature are in front of you,
something you can't get from a book!

James Yu, Grade 6

Home

My home is great
The TV in the dining room and all,
but in my eyes,
There's only one place
that takes the prize
My study room with a chessboard
and few electric outlets
My laptop on the table sitting with the charger in
My desk stands in a corner,
papers spread everywhere
My books on the desk,
papers stained and ripped
The window open, a shallow breeze fills the room
The bulletin board full holding all my notes
Relaxation my only feeling
sitting on the beanbag reading a book
When someone says home I think of this place
My favorite place to be is here,
Home.

Aagam Prakash, Grade 4

We Have Power

We have the power to change the world
Make a difference and help people while we're doing it.
We have the power to create the environment
We want to live in,
The world we choose.

We have the power to change the future.
We are the future.
We have the power to be unique and ourselves
In every which way
We have the power.

Maddy Smith, Grade 5

King of the Field

I am faster than cars
I wonder if I will ever get to touch the goals netting
I hear wow, awesome, great job
I see the goalie get in his stance
I want to zip right past him
I am as colorful as a rainbow
I pretend I go faster than planes
I feel sad when I'm flat
I touch sharp pointy cleats
I worry when a team lacks confidence
I cry when I slam into the hard ground
I am the king of the field
I understand when I am alone
I say I am the best
I dream to get into the goal
I try to avoid dogs
I hope to fly so I could get across the field faster
I am a soccer ball

Samuel Briscoe, Grade 6

A Stray Puppy

I am a stray puppy
I wonder if I will ever have a home
I hear the roar of a truck nearby
I see a sign that reads 804-872-4065 on the side closest me
I want to run but
I am frozen with fear
I pretend I am not scared but
I feel my heart beat thump thud thud
I touch my chest
I worry I am going to have a heart attack
I cry out as I am seized from behind
I am being kidnapped, I don't believe it
I understand now that the man was only trying to help me
I say my new dream over and over in my head
I dream of a palace now
I try to hide all of my excitement as my owner comes into the house
I hope she buys a palace but in reality
I am as happy as a smiley face

Trevor Johnston, Grade 6

Dogs

Dogs are cute, fluffy and energetic.
They are never lazy logs!
They are as cute as a button.
But when they make things go CRASH,
   they make you go crazy.
When they run, trying to catch something,
   they are like gold-medalist athletes!
They are as protective as a bodyguard.
Maybe even better!
Dogs are the most loyal of all animals.
You can always count on them to make you smile.
Dogs are the best of friends.
You love them until the end!

Elizabeth Stampone, Grade 6

Seasons
Winter
Frozen, white
Sparkling, snowing, playing
Ice, sled, beach, sun
Scorched, traveled, canoed
Break, fun
Summer
Norine Rensberger, Grade 5

Devil Angel
Devil
Red, mysterious
Flaming, horned, horrifying
Mischievous, demon, grand, beautiful
Welcoming, loved, rising
Wonderful, guardian
Angel
Alexandra Ramey, Grade 5

Over the Moon
As the cow jumps over the moon
A loon
Pops a balloon
In an empty, empty room
It goes boom
And to its doom
As the cow jumps over the moon.
Luke Fritsche, Grade 5

Sun and Moon
Sun
Orange, Day
Burning, Turning, Exploding
The sun makes light but the moon does not
Freezing, Floating, Craters
White, Night
Moon
Mackenzie Rabeau, Grade 4

Hornet and Wasp
Hornet
Long, ugly
Buzzing, scaring, flying
Hornets and wasps make people soar
Stinging, drinking, eating
Short, mean
Wasp
Ibrahim Telili, Grade 4

Good Books
Sounds like a person reading their book
Looks like adventure to walk through
Tastes like words that hide in the book
Smells like plain old words
Feels like I can't stop reading
Jack Johnson, Grade 4

Garden
I sink my tools into the earth
moving the soil, tossing it around,
making a cavern for life
creating a home for a beauty to be found.

Gently placing the flowers in the hole,
covering the roots with soil
sit back and relax,
waiting for the sun to boil.

Filling my pot with water,
water falls out the spout
racing to meet the flower
now it's time for the seeds to sprout!

Growing larger every day,
photosynthesis taking its toll
a beautiful creature is all made
now it's time for life's role.

Now that there is no garden
all that remains is and vacant spot,
thoughts are swirling in my head
thinking what to do with this empty lot.
Bridget O'Brien, Grade 6

Home
Many things are home to me,

Home to me is a good book,
that I can read all day.
The smell of the pages,
the feeling of the cover,
and the words it holds inside.
Every bit of that good book,
is home to me.
The turn of every page,
takes me deeper into the story.
I'm part of the characters,
riding along in their minds.
I share the feelings they have,
and the secrets they hide inside.
Every good book is home to me.

My friends make any place,
a home where I can be happy.
The way they laugh,
the way they smile,
make a hard life worth living.

Many things are home to me.
Samantha Andres, Grade 5

Bulling Is Not Okay
I'm sad and scared
what if they come back?
It hurts when they kick me
and hit me and when they call
me names
why does nobody help me?
what's wrong with them?
can't they see me getting hurt?
do they not care?
am I even loved?
this is not okay,
they should stop this
don't they know this is
bulling?
Brooklynn Levy, Grade 6

Under the Willow Tree
under the willow,
she lays down,
spreads her arms out,
yawns,
hair sprawled against the
hard, grassy meadow,
slowly stands up,
laughs,
sways in the moonlight,
sighs,
lays back down,
shuts her eyes,
and dreams all night,
in her own beautiful world
Mckenzie Shea, Grade 5

Swimming
I like to swim
Deep down in the water.
Nothing else down there,
No one to bother.

Sometimes I relax,
I float on the top.
Sometimes I jump in,
I do a belly flop.

Swimming is fun
In every way.
Even if you just sit there,
You can do it all day.
Brody Conner, Grade 6

Flowers
Flowers
Growing and blooming
Beautiful shining colors
Petals so lovely
Emma Connors, Grade 5

The Holocaust

Horrible screams rock the air
Blood darkens the river's clear flow.
The Holocaust, the Holocaust,
The Nazis use their horrible stare
Never forget their bow,
To the one known as Adolf Hitler,
The Holocaust, the Holocaust,
Silence will sweep over the land
By Hitler's merciless hand,
The Holocaust, the Holocaust,
"To the camps!" they said, but the Jews knew,
They would be gone before this war flew,
World War II, World War II
People dying, children crying,
No mercy came except for a few,
Who locked Jews to save the race,
Finally over, finally over,
World War II, World War II

Julia Lynch, Grade 6

Nature Is Great

Today is a day of happiness and joy,
Someone is playing with his toy.
However, he does not know the wonders of outdoors,
Here come the winds, they blow and blow,
Into the woods they go.
The trees are as still as the rocks in the lake,
Up in the hills,
The snake awakes.
Next to the city,
There is a park.
The flowers bloom,
They are so pretty!
The thunder roars out loud,
BAM! across the sky.
You chose this destiny,
Now follow the melody.
These are the many wonders you see outdoors,
Next time, open your doors, and go outside!

Ruben Aguilar, Grade 6

Greeting

Dark and happy colors fill my eyes.
Bright colors fill my heart with joy and happiness.
Sad colors hurt my heart with death.

Arrows from all directions, small and long.
In one city there's brightness and laughter, but in
another there's death and danger.
Arrow in the blue tries to sneak away, ones dressed
in red stop his way.

Flames of laughter darkness of death.
The arrows became friends and each day
they would meet at the dry river banks.

Aliyah Maximo, Grade 5

Home Is My Chair

Brown and old, worn and soft.
Comfortable and loving, I'll never get off.

Tall and big, its arms are high.
Like three walls, the perfect size.

Under the windows, basking in the sun.
I get the best light, more than anyone.

I bring my drink, and my book.
I start to read, my own little nook.

I watch TV, my favorite shows.
What the time becomes, no one knows.

Looking out the windows, or down at my homework.
Sitting there for hours, watching the shadows lurk.

Everything I want, right then and there.
All I could need, right in my chair.

It's always in the same place, waiting for me.
Never going anywhere, as comfy as can be.

Drawing a picture, or playing a game.
Or just listening, to the piano being played.

Comfortable and worn to the bone
It is mine and it is my own.

My chair is my home.

Soph Balliet, Grade 6

The Lost Hope

His hope was all lost,
His hope was all gone.
He finds this out on a very new dawn.
He won't live again
To see the same life
Its time for him to make a sacrifice

Knife in one hand, nothing in the other
At least he thought like this, unlike his brother
His brother was gone, taken with his hope
His whole life is going down the slope

His knife found the chest of a fate
The fate disappeared,
And it was goodbye with his fears,
He stepped forward and everything started to change—
His chest opened
And his soul scorched back in from his empty hand.
His brother was back, and his hope was returned.
The two brothers smiled, with fates trust they've earned.
What a destiny, what a journey, that the world must learn.

Jordan Seigel, Grade 4

The Experience

I stare down at the floor, fog surrounding me.
I say nothing, because I am scared, but at peace.
I hear the silent patter of feet.
I know he is watching me.
I glance at the wall then back at the floor.
I cringe to that old feeling, that Mr. Hitler is behind me.
I know what he is thinking in his mind when he sees me:
You're a Jew, a disgusting Jew.
I've seen the newspapers.
They have their own name for this:
The Holocaust.
There is no sun where we are,
It is dark and cold.
Just like that man.
I've heard others say that there's hope, but I don't think so.
If I ever had children, I would say
"Run and leave your mother behind."
I wouldn't want to, but I would have to.
I hate this experience.
I hate the Holocaust.

Katie Berry, Grade 6

Hope

Why is Hitler doing this?
Why does he hate us?
Why is he taking people away?
I don't want to be taken away.
Don't worry, something will get better.
All we can do is hope.
I've been waiting for something to get better, nothing has.
Hitler has gotten worse and worse.
My family is next.
What can we do?
I'm scared from my head to my toes.
I don't want to lose my family.
All we can do is hope.
Hitler will take us away to the camps.
We will never survive, we will never make it.
We could make it, if we stick together.
What if they take us away, what if they take me away from you.
I don't want to leave you.
Forget about that, we are together, we don't have to worry.
All we can do is hope.

Alyson DeMarco, Grade 6

O Turtle in the Soil

O turtle in the soil, why are you so slow?
O turtle in the soil, why don't you go, go, go?
O turtle in the soil, why in the water are you fast?
O turtle in the soil, in the race you ran why did you not get last?

My child, my child, I am very tired.
Unlike you, I am not very wired.
I let the stream carry me at a rather fast pace.
The Hare was over self-confident, so I won the race.

Joey Pettinger, Grade 5

The Magic of Spring

The mystical white wonderland is gone,
The blooming glory of harmonized beauty is back!
Back from their vacation, they come to their station.
Down from their rainbow, to make this spring glow!
The fairies are here,
And they will do it today!
They bloom the flowers,
And color the petals; from green, to white.
The colors are bright!
With their trumpets and flutes,
They wake up the animals.
Flying with the butterflies,
Running with the mice,
They dance in the festival,
Once or twice!
The night falls,
And the lights shine bright.
They all celebrate,
The magic of spring!!!

Eliana Salloum, Grade 6

Sleep

Sleep, sleep,
Sleep all night long.
If you can't sleep, I'll read you this bedtime song.
Dream, dream,
Dream the best you can.
If you can't dream I'll surely make a plan.
Before you go to bed I'll give you something to eat.
Should it be milk or a really small treat?
Now now dear, can you please go to sleep,
if you can't sleep just count the fluffy sheep.
After all the things, you've done in the day,
I'm sure when you dream, things will go your way.
Now go lay down, I'll tuck you in bed.
If you just can't, maybe read A to Zed.
One final thing, I'll give you a kiss.
Now go to sleep, you'll dream of only bliss.
Sleep, sleep,
Sleep all night long.
If you can't sleep I'll read you this bedtime song!

Abbas Raza, Grade 6

Holocaust

Hitler destroyed many peoples lives
He tortured them and many never survived
He made them walk for miles and miles
The dead were stacked up in piles and piles
And the only reason is one reason why
All because they were different
And all because of Hitler, the man full of hate
We shall always remember what happened
We shall never, ever forget
And there is one more thing to remember
There is nothing wrong with being different

Adam Fatebene, Grade 6

The Titanic

It started as a wonder, but it turned onto a terror.
The air went cold and the night suddenly felt barer.

Deep into the night, our party was interrupted by a jolt.
But they just said "the unsinkable ship" so we put this aside and continued in our holt.

Soon it was clear as the boat was starting to tip,
but wasn't it queer that Dismay was nowhere? That he was abandoning his own ship?

The water kept flooding in and the ship began to tip.
We cried for help, and our hold on the bars began to slip.

The people in third class had to be held back, they were poor and they hadn't paid for the deck.
Soon it was clear that everyone was showing their colors and most of us might soon be part of a wreck.

The screams of terror were chilling and drowning.
In the midst there was a one man alone in a boat, not letting anyone in, just frowning.

The water kept flooding in and the ship began to tip.
We cried for help, and our hold on the bars began to slip.

People floating in water, some limp, some struggling.
But Dismay, that man, just sat frowning as if the whole thing was a bad act of juggling.

"I can't look," he said " I can't see her go down."
So he looked away and frowned, Dismay knew that everyone wanted him to drown.

And that tragedy lives on, if we ever forget it won't be quick.
We all get over things to prevent other things, but we can never forget the Titanic.

Samuel Woolley, Grade 6

Remember

Remember the Nazis who killed thousands of Jews,
because they thought of them as ugly mushrooms.
Remember,
Remember Hitler who sent all the captured Jews to Camps
where they were either gassed, burned, or starved. They didn't have a chance.
Remember.
Remember the Bystanders who watched the Nazis and stood idly by
as those Jews being captured looked them right in the eye.
They thought if they ignored it, it would go away, but things just got worse day by day.
Remember.
Remember the victims who suffered the Nazi's horrible acts
but also those who were saved by others heroic acts.
Remember.
Remember the Rescuers who were the real Holocaust heroes.
They risked their lives day by day, just to save the day.
Remember.
Remember the Holocaust and all the Nazis and ask yourself why?
Why did so many have to die?
Remember.
Remember the Holocaust and all of the Nazis and bystanders.
But most importantly, remember the victims and those that were rescued.
Remember.

Kyle Morris, Grade 6

Hidden
through the pouring rain we walk
sympathetic looks but the yellow star speaks for itself
our bags filled with clothes and books

to daddy's building we hide three stories high
how long are we here? and how will we get by?

behind bookshelves and doors
quiet footsteps and many a closed window
one messenger save our fear of hunger
our small voices sing, "bravo"

to daddy's building we hide three stories high
how long are we here? and how do we get by?

Many nights the sound of war kept us awake
each bomb dropped seemed to get closer
jumping all night to every gunshot
the sound of war is just like an angry composer

peacefully sitting, reading one day
but the door opened with a "bang"
eagerly waiting
"they found us," I sang

to daddy's building we hide three stories high
how long are we here? and how do we get by?
Riley Jones, Grade 6

The Never-Lasting Song
The beautiful blue jay sang her song
Serene and proud, loud and strong
Sing she must with all her might
For her song is ending soon

With a single tear drop
She flew across the bright blue sky
Stopping wars with her tune
Making feuds as she wept
Bringing spring with her dance

But one day as her song relentlessly came to a stop
She flew up to the mountain
She made a river with her tears
All was sad and gloomy

The raindrops made a pitter patter
The waterfall sang and roared
The trees made a whisper
And once more, the song was heard

The blue came back to the sky
The green came back to the grass
The yellow came back to the sun
And the blue jay was happy at last
Machenzie Wernsman, Grade 6

Setting Sun
Red as blood and bright as hope,
Yellow like the singing goldfinch in the trees,
Orange as the flesh of a sweet tangerine.
Looking peacefully upon all who dwell here,
Saying goodbye to another day of life.
Staring into the purity of people's hearts
And loving our earth of good and evil.

Watching over our loved ones alike,
Shining the reflection of bold kindness.
Like a prism it glows the compassion of our hearts,
Warming our faces with beautiful rays.
Becoming one with the good souls and air,
Creating just a second of long tranquility,
Gifting a second of rest and assurance to all.

Sinking slowly to awaken life again.
A day of sweet memory and trust,
A day of friendship and meaning,
A day of delayed triumph.
All from one short moment
When we stop to see the setting sun.
Samantha Cake, Grade 5

Under a Rainy Sky
Plip, Plip, Plop
Droplets of bleached blue
skydiving from the clouds
reach out to tap my the roof of my house
with soft fingers like the petals of a rose
calling me out to play

Splish, Splish, Splash
Shimmering beauty is a pity
when upon hitting solid earth
they shatter with a cry

Drip, Drip, Drop
So small and mellow
but the feeling of rain against my face are like soft tears
so kind and warm, yet so cold and harsh

But above the heavens, the gray sky weeps
so hard, that I must ponder...
What makes the clouds cry?
What makes the sky
so sad?
Angela Chung, Grade 6

Little Mouse
There once was a mouse
Who lived in a house.
He saw a little chip
attached to a clip.
Now the little mouse no longer lives in my house!
Addison Vaught, Grade 5

I Am Selah

I am shy but outgoing.
I wonder if I could ever be a hip hop dancer.
I hear an applause of an audience after I'm done performing at a talent show.
I see lights on a Broadway stage.
I want to be a wonderful hip hop dancer.
I am shy but outgoing.
I pretend to be on a dance team.
I feel invisible and left out like a girl's ghost that doesn't know she's dead.
I touch the rose stem my parents give me.
I worry about being bullied again like in fourth grade.
I cry when I hear a depressing song because it reminds me of how much I miss my older brother.
I am shy but outgoing.
I understand people judge people.
I say you just have to love yourself.
I dream about making millions just by dancing on a gigantic stage by myself.
I try to dance with my friends as much as possible.
I hope I will succeed at making my dreams come true by practicing and making my own dances.
I am shy but outgoing.

Selah Hilyard, Grade 6

Soccer

Soccer, soccer what a wonderful word so many ways to say it!
Futball for Spanish, futebal for the Portuguese, soccer for the English, fotboll for the Swedish, Sakka for the Japanese.
But for all the languages and all the continents there is one "goal," the one goal that every kid Dreams about running down the field seeing just the goalie and the goal.
Lining up the shot and hearing the crowd roar and the announcer booming "GOAL, GOAL."
After the game ESPN comes and says, "You and your national team are going to the World Cup!"
You did so much to get to this spot—now you can claim it as being yours.
But there are many more challenges ahead, better players from all around the world coming together for one goal
—the World Cup Trophy.
You're at the opening game looking Lionel Messi and the Argentina national team in the face.
Your heart and thoughts going a hundred miles an hour.
Then the whistle blows and the race of the greats starts, scoring goal after goal.
You get to the finals tied two to two against the reigning champs—one minute left and you get past the opposing defenders, your heart beating fast and you kick and when you kick all you see is the goalie and you shut your eyes and the announcer yells something and you don't know what he said. Then your teammates come running up to you and lift you up and you know you just scored the winning goal!
Your life's biggest "goal" has finally been accomplished.
You've got the cup trophy in your hand—you can finally say "I'm one of the best!"

Trent Shade, Grade 6

Flowers

Roses, sunflowers
Daffodils, orchids, lotus
All grow in nature

Marianne Crowe, Grade 4

Music

I play violin
I love it very much
So much fun!

Abby Craw, Grade 4

It's Your Birthday

It's your birthday
Not a workday
Have fun and relax
Just don't push yourself to the max
Eat candy, ice cream and cake
Just don't try all day to bake
Listen to the latest hits
While opening your wonderful gifts
Celebrate with friends and relatives
Just make sure none of them are negative
Have a great day
And listen to people say Happy Birthday!

Hayley Corson, Grade 6

Summer

Summer has now come
Red roses blooming on earth
Feel the gentle breeze

Rachel Sweeny, Grade 5

Plant Growth

Tiny green stalks sprout softly,
Rise into the leafy canopy,
Emerald leaves emerge.

Walker Jennings, Grade 5

What Happens to a Dream Deferred?*
What happens to a dream deferred?

Does it exasperate its jealous comrades
like a rude character unhappy with his possessions?
Or does it turn into a nightmare
And then haunt you on eerie nights?
Does it torture others who long for dreams of pleasure to be reality?
Or is it scorched by a fire of large proportions
like a dead man condemned to Hades?

Maybe it just loses itself
like a child in a deserted forest of tall dead trees.

Or does it become the death that will one day consume us all?
David Hunt, Grade 6
*Inspired by Langston Hughes.

My Alien
An alien's spaceship landed in my yard
He was all weird and slimy like old rotten lard
He was also very green like fresh picked limes
But the silliest thing was that he couldn't tell time
If I remember correctly, his name was Bob
And when he couldn't find Mom he began to sob
So I told him, Don't cry, it will all be all right
He replied back, "But it's almost night"
I took him inside for a warm cup of tea
And he said politely, "More sugar please"
We enjoyed time together, it was very fun
When he left he said, My time here is done
We said our goodbyes and he went back to Mars
The last thing he said was, "I love chocolate bars!"
Jillian Klopp, Grade 4

It's Far Beyond Imagination
It's far beyond imagination.
Ribbons of colors
are woven into the sky,
one after another.

They fly away into the distance
in silky, long strands
shining in the milky, white sun,
beckoning for the wind to follow.

At last, they join to become something;
something that seems like a fantasy;
something that words nor poems can tell;
something that will be etched forever in our soul.
Keertana Yalamanchili, Grade 5

Black
Black is the sorrow in my heart.
Black is the terror in the woods.
Black is the color that cloaks me from the light.
Naomi Gesler, Grade 4

About Me
My legs are so quick,
people think I am a trick

I am Ryan,
But my spirit isn't dying

Very athletic,
Because I'm energetic

Not that strong,
But I do belong

Much fun as a barrel of monkeys

As caring and outgoing as Maniac Magee

My arms are so big,
They're as strong as God's power and justice

Legs move so fast like a cheetah on an energy drink

I am an imaginative, inspired, intelligent, and interested kid

Ryan's reindeer rapidly ran 'round he room

Made my miraculous muffins that make me go Mmm.

I am a dove,
Following God's rules
Ryan Englebreth, Grade 6

Never Perfect
I've tried to be perfect
And I've tried to fit in
I've never failed a class
Or cheated
Or harmed someone dear
And still they judge
And harm
And criticize

I'll never be perfect
Like the other girls
And I'll never be with one of those perfect boys
I've tried, and tried
But why do I care
This is who I am

So why do they tear me apart
And act like they care
Even when they don't
Just add it to the list
Of things I fail
Because I'll never be perfect
But who will
Maddie Hanscom, Grade 6

Life

Life is a treat, we need to cherish
Our existence

While we can,

Our life story doesn't last long,
It goes back and forth
From page to page

And when life's candies go sour
We need to hold our noses
And swallow the bitter taste.
When our candy goes sweet,
We savor every bite

Our journey is a adventure
Waiting for you to fulfill

Life is something to enjoy
Not ruin.
To share among the world
Not hide in the shadows of despair

Living is for the living,
Cherish
Every page, Every bite, Every quest.
Life.
Kaylee Prince, Grade 6

Rain

Clear drops falling,
The rain is calling,
"Come out to me,
Come out to me"

My siblings and I...
We can't help ourselves
The wet plants are sparkling
Dancing like elves

Smiling, laughing,
Have some fun,
Splashing in puddles
Together we run

Back to the house
For we are cold and wet
But the fun is not over
For us you can bet

Because while sipping hot chocolate,
Outside we can see
The rain is calling
"Come back to me"
Emily Colbert, Grade 5

Homework

homework, homework
I hate homework I'd rather
eat paper bags
homework, homework
I hate homework I'd rather
swim in lava
homework
when I see you
I want
to stomp
on you
Hunter Stewart, Grade 4

Imagine

When I imagine I wish I could go to space
But I can't and that's just a waste.

When I imagine I wish I could fly
But I can't and that makes me cry.

When I imagine I am glad
But imagining sometimes makes me sad.

When I imagine time goes fast
And sometimes it can be a blast.
Elise Levison, Grade 5

Butterflies

B eautiful colors
U nbelievable
T ale of miraculous new beginnings
T ruly amazing creatures
E legant and free
R oaming freely over gardens
F lying over flower beds
L ovely designs on their wings
I ncredibly graceful
E very one is different
S ipping sweet nectar from flowers
Claudia Santoro-Hernandez, Grade 6

Revenge

Take one bowl of rage,
Two cups of jealousy,
One spoon of wickedness.
Mix in a cup of madness.
Pour everything into a basin
And beat in three spoons of bitterness.
Bake in an oven at 900 degrees Celsius
Until the smell of hatred fills the air.
Chop into vengeful pieces.
Pour some betrayal on top of it,
Taste revenge!
Melanie Nguyen, Grade 6

Only Human

I'm only human
with imperfections.
I'm not senseless, I have reactions.
My soul is pure; a heart so solid
that refuses to be broken.

I'm only human.
I make mistakes:
I get in trouble; I have bad days.
I can get hurt; I can feel pain.
I do worry, but I'm still sane.

I'm only human,
not Superman;
but I shall save you if I can.
I will not fall, for I will stand.
Float on sea, walk on land.

I'm only human;
the fact is true. The things I say,
the stuff I do; it's not abnormal,
just take the clue. I'm only human,
and so are you.
Hannah Chestnut, Grade 6

The Colour Black

Black is the colour of despair,
and staying wide awake at night.

Black is the colour of darkness,
and getting a cold shiver when you see it.

Black is the colour of horror,
and a dark void that will never end.

Black is the colour of sinister,
and the feeling of fear.

Black is the colour of chaos,
and hiding away from it.

Black is the colour of death,
and being under a midnight sky.

Black is the colour of sadness,
and the feeling of running away.

Black is the colour of loneliness.
Norielle Ukisu, Grade 6

Dirt Bike

Colorful, fast
Popping wheelies, throwing dirt
Loud, vibrates, awesome, pure joy
Motorcycle
Andre Bousserghine, Grade 5

Oceans

Ocean ocean is that an ocean?
They make a motion with such a commotion
With their waves bumping ashore
Make some room for some more
With some nice white gritty sand
Which is so grand
Some eyes the color of the ocean
Some have such a devotion
As I say goodbye to the ocean

Jenna Rhoads, Grade 6

Wanted

Someone to put the dishes away,
Must have a strong grip.
Must be good at organizing.
Mustn't care about having their time wasted,
Just like I do.
If you are good,
And if you don't complain,
You might get a quarter
From my mom.

Leilani Krady, Grade 6

Home

Xavior
Son of Joel
Likes Halo, Legos, P.C.
Feels brave, shy, cool
Needs Xbox One, PS4, Destiny
Fears death, people, and guns
Like to see Destiny, Evil Within, Dead Space 4
Resident of Lancaster
Figueroa.

Xavior Figueroa, Grade 6

The Butterfly

A butterfly flies over the hills
As the gentle breeze blows.
Its wings, softly, steadily beating
Keeping it above the melting snow.
It then soars high, near the thick white clouds
Where the threat of a storm is looming.
However, the butterfly does not fear
It knows, the flowers will soon be blooming.

Angela Chen, Grade 6

Tornadoes

They whirl around like kids on a merry go round
They are the color when you mix all the colors of the rainbow together
They ruin houses, stores, and can injure many people
Then it starts to go away, but don't be fooled, it may start again
You hear *cracks* and *booms* and lots of *shrieks*
everyone is running for shelter
Then it is calm, it is over.

Kate Lefever, Grade 5

The Life of a Jew*

How terrible it was
They made them march day after day
Shooting, killing, he never cared
They forced them to live in ghettos
Until they came and killed them all
Some were taken to concentration camps
Where they worked day after day
No food, No family, No friends
The life of a Jew

Brandon Pieper, Grade 6

*The poem is incomplete to show how their lives were incomplete

Spring

When spring has sprung,
Most animals have their young.
The spotted cows their cute calves,
The Shetland mares, their newborn foals,
Bluebirds return from the tropical south,
Purple crocuses are all about,
Poplar trees and grassy meadows start turning green,
In some places daffodils can be seen,
When the sky is blue and clear,
I love the smell and sounds of spring I hear.

Susan Gross, Grade 5

Good Dog, Bad Dog

My dog is very quiet,
as he eats his food.
When he's done he jumps up on my lap without me knowing
scratching up the leather couch
getting yelled at by my mom because he cries all day long.
We play with him,
we pet him,
but he just won't stop!
I love him anyway,
'cause everything turns out A-okay.

Jack Reed, Grade 4

Spring

Play on the steep hill.
Lush green grass growing on the steep hill.
Pretty flowers popping up everywhere,
Red, green, orange, and yellow.
Playing with my fluffy, little kitten.
Running, laughing, and playing hide-and-seek.
Having a picnic in the warm sunshine.
Spring is the most exotic season of all.

Johanna Gross, Grade 4

Music

Music, art that's one of a kind
Tunes that are emotional and unique
It moves you, makes you feel things and think things
Lyrics from the heart
People's personalities

Vanessa Dick, Grade 6

The Life of a Jersey
I am a jersey
I wonder when I'm ever going to get washed
I hear the muscles flexing
I see the shaking motion of running
I want to always let the wind blow in my face
I am a jersey
I pretend that I'm catching the ball
I feel people hit me
I touch the hearts of my fans
I worry that I might rip
I cry because I'm smelly and dirty
I am a jersey
I understand I'm only a jersey but I have pride
I say I'm not some shirt people wear
I dream of the clank clanking of the lockers
I try to make people happy
I hope I don't get thrown away
I am a jersey
Cameron Gunther, Grade 6

One Baseball's Story
I am a baseball
I wonder why I get thrown around
I hear a sharp "CRACK" when a bat hits me
I see all the people running below me
I want to zoom back to the ground
I am an airplane soaring through the sky
I pretend I crush the bat instead of it crushing me
I feel a tear when I get hit
I touch the infield dirt going a thousand miles an hour
I worry I will not be used again
I cry when I am put in the dugout
I am a torn baseball
I understand why they don't use me anymore
I say "don't rip me," but they do it anyway
I dream I get put back together
I try to stay away from the people who ripped me
I hope I can be used again
I am the rubber in a baseball
Douglas Pruim, Grade 6

Happy Place
Collapsing prickle bushes
Leaves crinkling
As the wind blows
The clouds
As puffy as cotton candy
The wind causing the colorful leaves to be discombobulated
Catching my attention
As they try to hold on to the thick branches
Tiny bugs crawling up my legs
From the abandoned birdhouse
Covered with
Long vines
Like chocolate long Twizzlers
Reiley Bell Knize, Grade 5

I Am a Wonderful Thing
I am a wonderful thing
I wonder how you feel when you see my awesomeness
I hear all the sounds of the weather, rumble
I see everything
I want to see a dry land
I am a wonderful thing
I pretend to be colorful
I feel nothing except for the wind
I touch striking, silky, smooth water
I worry about not seeing you for a long time
I cry myself to death before I leave
I am a wonderful thing
I understand all the wonderful colors
I say nothing for I cannot speak so I just wonder
I dream to one day see you again
I try to be there for you on a rainy day
I hope to see you
I am a rainbow
Mikie Lawson, Grade 6

Ivan and Ruby
I am a silverback, a mighty gorilla
I wonder what's beyond this glass
I hear the screams of kids frightened by lions
I see the sticky cotton candy mess on the floor
I want to feel the crisp air on my fur
I am Ivan, a gorilla without a roar
I pretend not to care
I feel the cold hard floor
I touch my small stuffed gorilla
I worry for Ruby, the baby elephant
I cry when she is hurt
I am Ivan, Ruby's only friend
I understand why she is sad
I say please feel better
I dream of us in a meadow visiting peace
I try to break free
I hope this new place will be nice
I am Ivan this is Ruby and POOF now we are free
Eden Smith, Grade 6

Dancing
Dancing is so much fun to do
You should try it one day or two
Dancing turns a bad day upside down
It turns a frown right around
There are lots of different dances like Tango or Tap
You can dance to anything like Ballet or Rap
Dancing is as fun as a playground
There are all kinds of moves like kicks or spinning around
You can do it at any time or any place
All you have to do is move at your own pace
Dancing is great
Take it from me
I love to dance as you can probably see
Brooke Graham, Grade 6

The Train
I am a train zooming around the country
I wonder if I am adored when I approach the station
I hear laughter and whispers while I am chugging along
I see daffodils swaying in the wind like they're at a concert
I want to pop all of the rain drops on a rainy day
I am a train zooming around the country
I pretend that my smoke is what makes clouds
I feel the cool breeze on a summer day
I touch the train tracks with a heavy force
I worry that my engine will break
I cry when my seats are empty
I am a train zooming around the country
I understand my life will soon come to an end
I say I am the best train around
I dream of one day when I have a great family
I try not to go so fast that I flip off the tracks
I hope everyone will remember me
I am a train zooming around the country
Gracie King, Grade 6

A Tree with a Dream
I am a tree
I wonder if I will be cut down
I hear birds chirping
I see many other trees like me
I want to be the tallest and sturdiest tree
I am a tree
I pretend I can see past the clouds
I feel like I can't be cut down
I touch the ground and feel like I'm invincible
I worry that my wish will not come true
I cry like rain falls from the sky
I am a tree
I understand that wish may not come true
I say not to worry, like how water does not go BANG!
I dream that I'm an air balloon in the sky
I try my best to get taller and sturdier
I hope one day my wish will come true
I am a tree
Ryan Riordan, Grade 6

Aaah, Scared, Frightened
Aaah, scared, frightened
Clink
Clank
Clink
Clank
Flash, BOOM, kids running
Like the animals outside
Flash
Flash
Flash
Flash
The wind roars like a lion
The clouds are as dark as the inside of the house
Flick
The candles shine like the sun
And talks like the wind
There's a big flick and boom
The lights magically appear
Sarah Lapp, Grade 5

Just Another Puddle
I am a puddle
I wonder who will notice me
I hear splitter, splatter, and splash
I see big feet like dirty clouds above me
I want people to notice me
I am unnoticed
I pretend people don't run me dry
I feel destroyed
I touch the burning concrete after a rain shower
I worry that one day I will run out
I cry when children don't jump in me
I am a puddle
I understand I am just a puddle
I say people don't need me
I dream that one day I will fall again and form what I am now
I try to enjoy being a puddle before I leave
I hope people remember me
I am important, confident, a puddle
Madison Los, Grade 6

Seth
Seth
The writer
Son of Tim and Maria
Who likes to swim, fish, ride four wheeler
Who brings to Locust Grove his knowledge
Lover of ice cream, cake, fishing
Who fears drowning, snapping turtles, and falling off the bunker
Who knows a lot about farming
And desperately wants to buy a fishing boat
Who wouldn't be caught dead eating coffee ice cream
Who hopes to one day water ski
Who hopes to be remembered for his helpfulness
Forry
Seth Forry, Grade 5

Friendship
Take two best friends.
Put in Kindness, Delight, and Love.
Add in some cheer.
In a pan blend with a mixer until
You start to see some laughter.
Pour in some joy, and fun.
Bake in an oven at 350,
Until it's crisp
You can tell it's done when you smell excellence.
Let cool until you see loyalty.
Sprinkle on happiness.
Slice and serve with secrets.
Taste pure friendship!
Ketaki Thatte, Grade 6

I Like Myself the Way I Am
I don't have a pretty smile
But I like myself the way I am
I stumble and fall a lot
But I like myself the way I am
I watch geeky shows
But I like myself the way I am
I still play with dolls
But I like myself the way I am
I still need a light at night
But I like my self the way I am
No matter how much people tease me about my flaws
I always tell myself I am
Katelyn Shand, Grade 4

Did It Really Happen?
Did cavemen roam the Earth?
Did they ride Dinosaurs?
Did Thomas Edison really invent electricity?
Did Alexander Bell really invent the telephone?
Did Charles Jenkins really invent the television?
Did any of these things really, happen at all?
Did the Civil war even happen?
Did the south even have slaves?
Did the United States always have states?
Did the 13 colonies really boycott English goods?
Did Indians really exist?
Did any of these things really happen at all?
Leesha Shilling, Grade 6

Summer
I love the sweet summer breeze
But sometimes it makes me want to sneeze!
The sun is always up in the sky,
But when it's too hot my mom often says, Oh my God!!

I love to take long walks on the beach,
My garden is full of fruits, like a peach!
Swimming in the sparkly ocean,
Or resting and putting on sunscreen lotion.

In the summer we see a beautiful dove,
This is the season we love!
Kamilia Shome, Grade 4

When You Are Downcast
When you are downcast, look to the sky
Can you see a bird flying high?
Imagine yourself as that bird with those wings
Aren't they just glorious things?
Now imagine yourself soaring high,
With joy in your heart, air, and sky
Now look down at those wondrous things
The buildings, the forests, the land and the seas
Now remember how beautiful all things are
And remember, they'll still be like that tomorrow
Sarah Bjornstad, Grade 6

What Is Blue?
What is blue?
Blue is the colour of the sky,
Without a cloud.
Cool, distant, beautiful and proud.
Blue is the quiet sea
And the eyes of some people
And many agree
As they grow older and older
Blue is the scarf spring wears on her shoulder
Blue is twilight
Shadows on snow
Blue is a feeling way down low.
Eunice Tolujo, Grade 6

The Sun
The sun is hot like a stove on full power
It's pretty like a dandelion flower.
It is bright like a star shining in the night,
Oh, how amazing is the sight!
Red, yellow, and orange, the sun is multicolored
It looks beautiful when it is uncovered.
You better watch out! The sun is really hot,
I should wear the sunscreen that my mom bought.
Dancing in the sky during the day,
But it goes down after a long day of play
With the sun we never go cold
God gave it to us to cherish and behold.
Jessica Araiza, Grade 5

I Don't Understand Friends
I don't understand friends
They get mad over such little things
When you tell them to do something and they don't
When they don't pick up after themselves
But most of all
When they get into fights
When they don't listen to you
When they copy you
What I understand most is
They trust you
They hang out when you need them most
They need a friend, too.
Michelle Martens, Grade 6

When Is Christmas?
When joyful boys and girls open presents
And excited adults prepare Christmas dinner

When happy people celebrate the birth of Jesus
And we all remember the great miracle of Jesus' birth

When children of every age decorate a tree
And lay out milk and cookies for a very special guy

Then It's Christmas!
Brandon Karafilis, Grade 6

High Merit Poems – Grades 4, 5, and 6

The Star Wars Family
My brothers obsessed
with Star Wars, you see

His light saber is near
His mask is on
He's ready to slice off your arm
[Preferably Luke's]

When he isn't fighting
He's calling us names

I earned
Obi-Wan Kenobi
and my mom
Queen Padme'

My dad is Luke,
he is
Anakin or Darth
[Which confuses me.
He grows up fast!]

My brother has named us
The Star Wars Family
whether we like it
or not
Malia Steel, Grade 4

The Ocean
Waves crash
Winds lash
I am on the beach

The sand is soft
I'm aloft
My spirit floating in the gentle breeze

A wave chases me up to land
On the sand
I chase it back

Home to many
Full and plenty
The ocean gives more than it receives

Beautiful water
Shells galore
Fish and seaweed
And lots more

But what do we do
We make it suffer

We throw trash into it without a care
It's not fair
Grace Long, Grade 6

Book
I am lost,
Everywhere at once,
Within a different world,
One created by
the words on the page,
This world is mine,
My will to go and travel,
My body still here,
Mind gone in space,
Thinking wonderful
THOUGHTS

It tells of happiness
and sorrow,
A place in time,
Where you can find
whatever you are looking for,

And I am forever lost,
Everywhere at once,
between the pages of a
BOOK
Zoe Bennett-Manke, Grade 6

Game Day
It's game day
Everyone is rushing,
Players are practicing

Take a sniff,
smell the sweat
of the players,
listen,
as the bat hit the ball
ring, ring

As the baseball soars
it dreams
that one day it will glide
over the radiant green fence

Baseball remembers
being caught
with a big thwack!
Baseball will promise you
a lot of
excitement.
Elliott Tripi, Grade 4

Mother
Mother
Kind, helpful
Caring, loving, sharing
A special person in my life
Friendly
Olivia Hache, Grade 4

Presenting
Up in front
Tongue so dry
With a twitch in my eye

Stomach in knots
Heels on point
Straightening out every joint

Standing tall
Ready to fall

Paper in hand
I need a fan

Sweat on my brow
Almost ready now

Taking a breath
Cool breeze on my neck

Making eye contact
Ready for combat
Olivia Roschat, Grade 6

Who I Am
Hi, my name is Tim,

I'm as swift as a fox,
While wearing my red socks

Like to smile,
Cause I have great style

Busy as a bee,
Never free

I'm a shark,
Swimming in the light and the dark

People say I'm funny,
And I have a lot of money

Sleeping soundly, silently in my bed
With happy dreams filling my head,

Last, but not least, I am shoe size seven,
And I am eleven.
Timothy Mehlmann, Grade 6

Robert E. Lee
Robert
Appomattox
He surrendered his troops
Surrendered to Ulysses S.
E. Lee
Lauryn Pardee, Grade 4

Sunset

I look up at the sky and what do I see?
A beautiful red and orange sky shining through the clouds.

I sit on a hill looking out to the horizon,
The breeze of the wind blows through the trees.

I hear the rustling of the trees and leaves,
and the blowing of the wind
then it all stops.

I wait for the sun to go down
and the moon to go up.

I watch the sky and think,
How can something so beautiful
and bright
end so quickly?

Chloe Elie, Grade 6

I Am a Ball

I am a ball
I wonder what it would be like to jump all the time
I hear loud boom noises from footsteps and laughter from kids
I see wonderful children
I want to play and have fun
I am a ball
I pretend to be a stick and twist through the air
I feel like a cloud in the sky
I touch soft grass
I worry my life will come to an end
I cry for friends
I am a ball
I understand why I sometimes deflate
I say nothing and enjoy the silence
I dream about flying in the clouds
I try to bounce on my own
I hope to be more colorful I am a ball

Carolina Masiak, Grade 6

My Soul Is a Beautiful Thing

My soul is a hungry lion
Easily upset
Always searching for the fruit of knowledge
Yet it is a deer
Shy, always calm
It floats on a summer breeze
Impossible to catch, beautiful and peaceful
And a summer breeze can turn around
A winter storm
Raging without mercy
My soul is a wonder within wonders
A bright, blinding light
A bank full of opposites
It is soft, like the flower petals blown onto your shoulder
Or hard, like the nuts thrown by squirrels
A young, spongy star
Soaking up a universe of knowledge

Isabella Lee, Grade 5

A Shining Star

I am a star in the sky.
I wonder why no one notices me.
I hear the sun calling to the moon.
I see them work together like grass and rain.
I want to be like them.
I am looking for a purpose.
I pretend I am the Sun glowing bright.
I feel the loneliness grow inside.
I touch the dark skies.
I worry about the earth.
I cry for the future.
I understand why I am not noticed.
I say that there are billions of stars like me.
I dream of the slightly silly, Daisies.
I try to be like the Daisies, being silly.
I hope this will help my loneliness shrink
I am a shining star in the sky hoping to be something else.

Lanazia Whalen, Grade 6

The Liveliest Tone

The Bird who tweetles may be a secret to a great life.
Not that anything else is worse, but the bird's hum is gracious.
When the bird's tweetle is shared,
The whole world will sing, shining like a glare.
And no, this won't happen elsewhere.
It almost feels magical, like everyone's lives had changed.
No longer bad, here comes good.
Isn't the world great this way?
No scars in hearts, no tears in eyes.
No one will have to say goodbyes.
The bird's tweetle changes people,
The bird's tweetle changes things.
This tweetle can change everything.
No blood on skin, no bruises on bones.
The bird's tweetle is the liveliest tone.

Catherine Noelle Brown, Grade 6

Being a Pitcher

As soon as I step on the mound
It's like I've been lost and then I was found
I take a deep breath
I don't think of death
I start to windmill with a flick of the wrist
The batter is out; it starts to mist
The inning is over; I step back on the mound
The ball became slippery so I frowned
The best batter is up, her name is Holly Seth
I think I should take my biggest breath
The ball flies past the plate,
   that's strike three on the list
Holly gets mad, so she makes a fist
The game is over; I step off the mound
I feel like I have just been crowned

Madison Kerns, Grade 6

High Merit Poems – Grades 4, 5, and 6

Hearts
Red hearts
They are lovely
They come in all sizes
Happy, sad, confused, delicate
Red hearts
Shevelle L. Shelp, Grade 5

Snow
Snow
Cold, soft
Falling, glistening, freezing
Very cold during winter
Beautiful
Benita Bernard, Grade 5

Snowflakes
Snowflakes
Cold, beautiful
Falling, freezing, dazzling
One of a kind
Unique
Cassidy Fischer, Grade 5

Hockey Player
Hockey player
Smelly, strong
Skating, hitting, scoring
A sport that we play
Hard hitter
Logan Lanagan-Blanc, Grade 6

Bears
B ears are cool animals
E at meat
A re ferocious predators
R un fast
S uper deadly
Ebar Amir, Grade 4

Gymnastics
Gymnastics is life
I work hard
I sweat hard
I fall and flip
But that's part of the sport
Julia Simpson, Grade 6

Don't Judge
Don't judge that I'm black
Don't judge the way I act
I know we aren't the same
But who is that to blame
Don't judge that I'm black
Alayna Byes, Grade 6

I Am Elise
I am a girl who doesn't feel good around her family.
I wonder if I will ever stop seeing my parent's conflict.
I hear constant strong voices and negative words.
I see tears down my face when I can't control my crying anymore.
I want to have the fighting to stop.
I am a girl who doesn't feel good around her family.

I pretend to have the best family in the world.
I feel a sense of relief when the house is silent.
I touch my emotions when I am upset when the fighting gets insane.
I worry if I could be taken away from my family.
I cry when the fighting gets out of control.
I am a girl who doesn't feel good around her family.

I understand people fight and it's not healthy for them.
I say you must make the best choice for yourself.
I dream that one day people will not struggle.
I try not to hear or see my parents fight.
I hope the arguing will soon stop.
I am a girl who doesn't feel good around her family.
Elise Hernandez, Grade 6

I Am Chaziyah
I am a caring and unique girl.
I wonder why the government prints money and doesn't give it to people in need.
I hear sounds of joy and happiness when I eat junk food.
I see people getting along with friends.
I want to visit the Eiffel Tower in Paris.
I am a caring and unique girl.
I pretend to be famous sometimes.
I feel happy that I can do things in gymnastics such as cartwheels,
    bridges, backbends, round-offs even backbend stand-ups.
I touch my goals of being the best.
I worry about natural disasters.
I cry when people are mean to me.
I am a caring and unique girl.
I understand that some things are going to be hard for me.
I can try again.
I say there should be no more war and just compromise.
I dream of being an actress.
I try my best to understand things in math.
I hope to meet Zendaya Coleman.
I am a caring and unique girl.
Chaziyah Claggett, Grade 6

Holocaust
H itler was a bad man killing all the Jews.
O nly leaving few.
L etting Jews die at camps.
O bsessed with power.
C oncentration Camps hold Jews prisoned.
A cting really mean to all, except his brethren.
U ltimately killing almost every Jew.
S ilently taking women and children from their home at night, taking men at last.
T aking freedom from the Jews was what the Nazis did fast.
Armaan Pandher, Grade 6

Go Inside the Ocean

Go inside the ocean,
It's blue like the summer sky,
It smells like seaweed
And tastes very salty.

Inside its really hard to breath,
You don't hear a thing,
And you can't see the bottom.

You might see a shark,
Or a group of jellyfish
Swimming to sting you.
It would be the most
Horrible challenge of your life.

But the worst part is
You never know what will
Happen next!
Vanessa Amoroso, Grade 5

I Am

I am unique in my own way
I wonder why she is doing this
I hear her voice
I see what he doesn't
I want her to stop
I am unique in my own way
I pretend to stand up for myself
I feel the pain
I touch my heart when I think of her
I worry about what she thinks
I cry when I think of her
I am unique in my own way
I understand what you're going through
I say the wrong thing
I dream about things I shouldn't
I try to hold it in
I hope she will come back
I am unique in my own way
Alyson Nabozniak, Grade 5

Pink

my shoes
my coat
my room
ink
mink
stink
link
a cherry
a beautiful burst in my mouth
a warm sunny day
a day at the beach
watching the sun set
make you happy
Miranda Harmston, Grade 5

The Frowning Clown

The clown with brown eyes
Went downtown
To the pound
To find his hound
He heard a sound
And fell to the ground
Because of a mound

The sound was a grand old man
In a band
With a great hand movement
Playing the drum
With some sort of hum
That sound,
Was what he was hearing
But still don't have his problems solved
He never found his hound
Vanessa Lucio, Grade 5

I Am

I am creative with my character
I wonder what will happen
I hear their voices
I see their faces
I want to be surrounded by them
I am creative with my character
I feel their encouragement
I touch them when I can't reach
I worry it won't happen
I cry that he dies
I am creative with my character
I understand how he thinks
I say it's okay
I dream of a time it will happen
I try to understand
I hope I'm right
I am creative with my character
Cassandra Christensen, Grade 6

Wesley Fletcher

W ell at chess
E ats a lot
S uper awesome at baseball
L oves cats so much
E ducated at Locust Grove
Y earns to become a mechanic

F inds cool things to build with
L aughs a lot
E ncouraging to other people
T akes apart stuff
C aring for other people
H as a good sense of humor
E nergetic indoors and out
R eally dislikes bugs
Wesley Fletcher, Grade 6

The River

"Swish, swish, swish!"
the water tumbles
down to me.

It flows
like the
tail of
the squirrel
rushing into
his tree.

"Where are you?" "How are you?"
the river whispers in my ear.

Freedom, it must feel
for rushing wild and
free.
Angela Yu, Grade 4

The Colors of the Wind

The wind
Oh, the wind,
Blew my laugh
 away.
My laugh
 is the
 wind.
It never stopped
to say hello.
My laugh is
the wind.
My day is
 gray.
And it always got
in my way.
My laugh is
the wind.
Presleigh Goodwin, Grade 4

Basketball

I can barely describe it,
But I can describe happiness.
Happiness to me is
Hearing the basketball
Going through the hoop
And hearing the "Swoosh" sound
Bending your knees
Release
Hit, Squeak, Crash
Then finally, "Swoosh."
It makes me feel
Like a million bucks!
It's NOT just a game,
It's a lifestyle.
Basketball
Alexis Hitchens, Grade 5

Love and Hate

Love
Romantic, unique
Caring, adoring, pleasing
Feelings, union, rival, agony
Disgusting, horrifying, denying
Unattractive, dark
Hate
Emilie Grosser, Grade 6

Fall

Fall is striking orange.
It sounds like squirrels chattering.
It tastes like delicious apple pie.
It smells like fresh cinnamon rolls.
It looks like bright and colourful leaves,
    falling swiftly from the trees.
Fall makes me feel relaxed.
Luca Pozderka, Grade 6

Bear and Cat

Bear
Big, Dangerous
Hibernating, Eating, Hunting
Bears are ugly and cats are cute
Nibbling, Playing, Chasing
Small, Nice
Cat
Ashley MacLean, Grade 4

Cake

Tasty, delicious, amazing!
Cake is loved by many,
    disliked by few.
Cake is baked with love,
    cut with knowledge,
    and eaten with passion.
Cake.
Stefan Rosenboom, Grade 6

Life

Life
Fun, sad
Happy, great, mad
Sometimes it's good, sometimes it's bad
Always be glad
It's there
End
Trevor Ferreira, Grade 6

Penguins

Penguins are so cool.
Watch them fly through the water
Chasing a small fish,
So their children can have dinner,
And survive the freezing cold.
Mac McKittrick, Grade 6

Hurricanes

It comes with anger destroying everything in its way.
It brings heavy rains to ruin everyone's day.
The winds are strong making everything blow away.
All I can do is pray, pray, pray.

The floods keep rising.
Trees knocked down are not surprising.
Stay indoors a newscaster keeps advising.
I get on my knees to pray, pray, pray.

The roaring waves I see off the Chesapeake Bay,
makes me want to stay inside and play.
Will the sun come out today?
Maybe I should pray, pray, pray.

Hours and days pass without a ray of sun.
Thank goodness my TV and Xbox still run.
I won't let this hurricane ruin my fun.
I still have time to pray, pray, pray.

Sun is out,
Flood dies down.
I go out to check out the town.

Family, friends, and neighbors lending a hand to pick debris each and every day.
God is smiling because we all held hands to pray, pray, pray.
Parker Cruz, Grade 4

Lassoed Heart

Footsteps imprinted in the dirt,
Her heart had turned cold and dull,
She left without a word,
Brushing away any trace that followed her,
My heart was left frail,
Trust had been broken beyond repair,
Yet for some ludicrous reason,
She crept back not knowing what she did.

The hole in my heart had been tied together,
Not once did it cross my mind,
About the pain she had strangled me with,
All felt calm as our thoughts were being exchanged,
The lasso around my heart had snapped,
She had emerged from a white canvas to be concealed by black acrylic.

A final time after tears had been shed,
Her picture daunted me through the brightness,
My fingers twitched as tears traced my face,
Photographs of memories started to burn,
Hurdled into a barrel of flames,
Ink from the glossy paper flaked off,
One question still haunts my unforgiving mind, Why?
Kayleigh Texter, Grade 6

Math
Why can't you solve your own problems?
We can't solve them all for you.
Dear Math,
Your life is a mess
Kids just want to be free
Want to live in peace!
Dear Math,
I can't sleep, you're unstoppable!
This is getting out of hand,
This is so annoying!
Dear Math,
Please, I'm begging you
I'm not putting up with this
All my friends seem to be getting it.
Why not me?
Why…how…when?
OKAY MATH — You win.
I'll solve all your problems for you,
But just know
I'll get you back for this
Math, you made my life worse, but smarter.
Nicole Amoroso, Grade 5

Have Fun in Spring
Spring starts
Flowers grow
Just like trees.

It is the season,
when children play outside.
Pollen flies through
the sky and the plains.

Animals start waking up.
The birds fly north.
Children play outside,
with joy and energy.

The sky is blue.
The grass is green,
Spring is here,
So have some fun,
Before it is too...
Late.
Ryan Tran, Grade 6

Falling
Slowly falling
Falling down
Into darkness
Very deep
h
e
l
p
Alex Horn, Grade 5

Confidence
Inside or out
sun or snow
stop or go
your confidence you cannot doubt
Whether surviving drought
or drawing back a bow
even catching someone's throw
you must have confidence no doubt
In many situations
this will come
confidence is key
to many operations
even when having fun
confidence is key
Kaden Du, Grade 6

The Best Actors and Actresses
The best actors and actresses,
Aren't seen on a screen.

They don't star in movies,
and they don't sing.

They laugh with their friends,
Until the day ends.

Then they go home and lie on their bed.
They cry, and weep, and down is their head.

They are doing what they do best,
Acting.
Quincy Caldwell, Grade 6

Nature
Nature is a beautiful thing
I love when it rains in the forest
Because the leaves drip off the trees
It sounds like this
Drip
Drop
Drip
Drop
As the trees get wet
They say "I'm getting wet,
I'm getting wet"
Then the rain and wind start
Whipping the trees and plants all around
Then it slows down and stops
Madison Wissler, Grade 5

River
River
Colorful and calm
Beautiful gleaming waters
Flowing gracefully
Daphne Camacho, Grade 5

Amber
kind, caring, hard working, join clubs
Sibling of Ethan and Peyton
lover of kittens and family
Who fears thunder storms
Who needs to be loved
who gives time
Who would like to see her aunties.
Trzaska
Amber Trzaska, Grade 5

Paper
I am paper.
They write on me.
They draw on me.
They make notes on me to remember,
About stuff, I have a,
Friend named pen.
He writes on me and we are,
Family.
Adrian Salayandia Moran, Grade 4

The Monster of My Dream
The moment is here
And the monster is near
We fight until night
The sun rises when
The battle was done
We had some fun
But when day came
I realized it was a dream
Ayden Beach, Grade 4

Friendship
Friendship is helping each other
when you fall over
Friendship is never being
mean to one another
Friendship is having
fun together and hanging out
Friendship is staying together
and never leaving each other
Adam Johnson, Grade 6

Pencil
It's waiting to be sharpened.
So someone can pick it up and use it.
It can't wait to make something nice.
On a big piece of paper.
When someone picks it up.
It will cross the paper.
Making a beautiful picture or…
A nice piece of writing.
Emilly Rodger, Grade 5

High Merit Poems – Grades 4, 5, and 6

Dancing
Dancing is a fun thing to do,
It's my favorite sport and that is true.
I love the slosh, when I glide on the ground,
To me that is the most satisfying sound.
Some people don't think dance is a sport,
I'm just saying, not every sport is played on a court.
Dancing is like football in a way,
They both have you jump, kick and sway.
Dancing can make you feel like you're,
   flying in the sky,
It's very exciting like eating a pie.
Ma'a Neba, Grade 6

Basketball
It is my favorite sport.
I love the rush of the game.
Dribbling the ball down the court makes me feel in control.
Every move in sync.
The cheer of the crowd makes me feel alive.
Play upon play, pass upon pass, basket upon basket, we are a team.
The team wins the game not one person.
We help each other in every way.
We cheer for each other.
On and off the court, we are a family.
Basketball is amazing!
Brianna Pasternak, Grade 6

Hope and Faith
Hope and faith,
Joy, love,
brings the family together from the heart.
It's caring love that makes the star shine so bright,
or maybe the moon glowing tonight.
With the American flag flying left and right,
hearing our freedom cry every night.
And seeing the sight of a baby being held tight,
makes me feel smart and bright.
Joy, love,
Hope and Faith.
Sam Roccograndi, Grade 4

How to Make a Mom!
Take appreciation, happiness and empowerment.
Put a hint of children and frustration,
In a pan shaped like a person.
Mix love, peace and respect.
Blend with care.
Add a unique couple.
Until you see a brave, determined lady.
Let it stand until you see success and empathy.
Add a terrific amount of work and mini helpers.
Serve with a slice of dignity.
Enjoy an awesome Mother!
Rahul Marwaha, Grade 6

Twister
A twister is like a strawberry Twisler.
It tastes like sand from the beach.
It is cold like a midnight breeze,
It is hot like the blazing sun.
A twister is very scary.
I hope I never see this scary monster as I can't out run it.
I get nightmares about twisters.
It sounds like a hissing snake.
If I ever saw a twister I would twist into a ball and roll
Away. That's why I don't live in southern USA.
I love my cold province where there are no twisters
Onai Murevesi, Grade 5

Many Changes Happen in Spring
Flowers will burst open,
Bears will come out from their hut,
In spring, all sorts of thing can happen.
Squirrels will finish their storage of nuts,
Birds will finally get a chance to spread their wings,
Kids will be joyfully playing outside,
Winter is coming to an end, eventually stopping.
School will almost be over,
You will also see more people walking, boy and girl, men or women,
So here we come summer,
Let's just wait until the changes in spring happen!
Vincent Dinh Vien Duong, Grade 5

Nature's Summer
As I sit, and relax in the fresh green grass,
I think of warmth as it beats down onto me.
I feel the refreshing air being absorbed,
I hear children laughing and swimming,
as they play games in the pool.
I see the birds gracefully flying through the rays of sun,
I smell the flowers when they bloom.
As I fall in love with the nature,
I feel as if I was in paradise.
I think to myself,
What a wonderful gift God has given me...
Carmen M., Grade 6

Matthew
Matthew
Energetic, funny, friendly, talkative
Relative of David
Lover of hot rod's, dog's, popcorn
Who feel's happy, cool, mad
Who needs friends, music, running
Who fears the dark, bees, loud noises
Who gives sympathy, love, support
Who would like to see forests, mountains, blue sea
Resident of Earth
Achenbach
Matthew Achenbach, Grade 6

Holocaust
H orrible things
O ur country was ruined
L ives were taken over
O ne man started it all
C rying children
A dolf Hitler started it all
U nderground people hid
S cared people everywhere
T errible noises
Sydney DeFranco, Grade 6

Holocaust
H is for the Horrible things hitler did
O is for the jews being Ostracized
L is for the Liquidation of people
O is for the Outrageous punishments
C is for the Concentration camps
A is for the Allies who fought the nazis
U is for Understanding this tragedy
S is for all of the Survivors
T is for the Trains children were sent on
Sean Daly, Grade 6

Holocaust
H itler is the beast that started this.
O h the horror he brought.
L ay low and you might survive his wrath.
O n this night there is no sleep to be found.
C an't take any more of this.
A time of darkness is here.
U nder water would be better than here.
S top this madness from happening.
T his is the end, goodbye.
Connor McGaughran, Grade 6

Spring
When the winter goes away
A new season will come that day
Lovely flowers will grow
There will be no more snow

Many bright different colours
Of pretty beautiful flowers
But now that the winter is gone
I could relax on my green lawn
Maya Stoica, Grade 4

Gone
The windows are closed
He's gone tonight
I wish I held him closer last night
Although I'm upset
I will not fear
Because I know
He's right here
Sarah Rovnanik, Grade 6

Home
Pets make up a
huge part of
my home,
my pet is a cat,
pets are very kind.
They are extremely cute,
my cat can be very
funny and he is always
friendly!
My cat's name is Buster.

Family is most important
at my home,
my brothers, cousins,
and parents
are the most
awesome people I know
they all play games
with me,
we have loads of fun.
Family is
life when I'm at home.
Ian Collison, Grade 4

If It Is Sweet
Bitter beyond the delightful honey
Sweet syrup invites all in
Into The Meadows of Summer
Verdant valleys
Crawling the vines behind the window
Shy be the wind though the breeze is happy
Song singers singing a joyful melody
which brings all together
The river
It sings
A pleasant song
In night it glides along
to the lake and far beyond
And if this happy is to break
All joy be at stake
And through the night
And To thus day
Far from home adventures thrive
And through the night And to thus day
The honey will drip
For all to Taste
Jaron Barrett, Grade 4

Spring Has Sprung
S pring is fun and winter is done
P repare some food
R ain comes most of the time but it's fun
I n spring go out to see the snow melting
N o pressure is put on you
G oing to cool places is fun in spring
Damandeep Singh Jabbal, Grade 4

Everyone Is Different
You are you,
I am me,
We are completely different,
Can't you see?
You are blonde,
I am brunette,
We are completely different,
You want to bet?
You like soccer,
I like dance,
You will never be me,
We even have different pants.
You are you,
I am me,
We are completely different,
And we will always be.
Ava Iatesta, Grade 6

Ode to Music
Music, my life
My favorite thing
Like a friend by my side
Makes me happy when sad
So very peaceful.

Melody as incredible as can be
like an angel it plays.
Melody, gentle, calm I describe.
Loud and rock sometimes.
I like the calm sounds.

I wish I were music
So gently it plays
Can express myself
Through its lovely tunes.
Britnee Jackman, Grade 5

Hitler
Full of hatred,
Has no soul.
Used to be sad and dull.
Then got angry at the Jews
Machine guns fire while bombs blew.
He killed the Jews one by one.
Hoping that his work was done.
Anger, hatred, discrimination
Pain and so much desperation
Rebels rose up from the ashes
Living in arrogance
As his empire crashes
Full of hatred
Has no soul
Hitler died sad and dull.
Natalie Eberly, Grade 6

High Merit Poems – Grades 4, 5, and 6

My Life
So much depends upon
my life
with all it's laughs
and all it's love
without it
I would be nothing
Carl Raitano, Grade 4

Candle
Candle
slight warmth
melting its wax
a glow through each dark hall
a light to lonely travelers
shares hope
Charlotta Truscott, Grade 6

Ocean
The Ocean is blue.
It tastes like saltwater.
It sounds like crashing waves.
It smells like fresh air.
It looks like a blue sky.
It makes me feel free.
Maya Nichols, Grade 4

Flowers
Flowers are multi-colored
They taste like broccoli
They sound like grass swaying
They smell like pollen
They look like a rainbow
Flowers make me feel fresh as a daisy
Alexis Zalevsky, Grade 4

Ice-Skating Rink
Glittery shoes with silver blades dance
Hot chocolate cups filled to the rim
Hair whipping against the cold wind
Numb fingers grip metal railings
Peppermint sticks fill sore mouths
I think I'll stay forever
Alyssa Newton, Grade 4

The End of Spring
Tic, Toc, the clock goes off
Because today is the day
When I say: "Yay! It's May!"
Today, it's time to throw away the gray
Today, we can plug the rain away
Because today, it's finally May!
Hudson Macdonald, Grade 5

Journey Home
As you are on your way homeward, desolate and alone
The dull black sky reflects sorrow
And darkness clutches you as tears sting your eyes
The scorching wind shouts and screams your name,
Sending piercing snowflakes cutting their way to you
The silence behind the wind and the snow is deafening as you force yourself on.
You look up, seeking hope among the stars,
But they hide their face from you,
Having sought and found refuge behind clouds
It seems that all your joy is sapped from you.
Icicles hang from an old forgotten little farmhouse
Showing the way its heart looks towards you
An unfriendly bit of light escapes from the frowning moon
Glaring off the icicles.
Nothing seems to show compassion or sympathy
The unfriendly trees seem to stare at you
Showing their most mischievous faces
Grim expressions surround you.
A little warm light shines from a lone, afar cottage
Joy leaps within the depths of your heart as you glance at it
Encouragement sends you on your way.
Tamar Waldner, Grade 6

I Am Natalie
I am an enduring, hopeful dancer.
I wonder if bullying will ever stop.
I hear voices calling me crude, hurtful names at night.
I see myself reliving the time I almost died when I was 5.
I want people all over the world to look up to me
because, it would make me feel accomplished.
I am an enduring, hopeful dancer.

I pretend to be a famous dancer and You Tuber at times.
I feel like dance lets me express myself in a way nothing else can.
I touch the night stars when I move my body to a piece of soft music.
I worry if bullying will chase me my whole life.
I cry when I see no hope because, it shows people that will not try.
I am an enduring, hopeful dancer.

I understand the world has hurtful people who make us feel worthless.
I say, prove them wrong.
I dream of being on "Dancing with the Stars."
I try to make the best out of every day.
I hope I will inspire young dancers to push forward during hard times.
I am an enduring, hopeful dancer.
Natalie Cardenas, Grade 6

Nature's Beauty
Raindrops fall down glistening, nourishing the open mouths of hungry beggars.
The sweet fragrance of roses fill the air, blowing away the gas of pollution,
which was killing thousands around the world.
The crystal moonlight shines down, lighting the path of hurrying feet.
A rainbow shimmers in the sky, bringing hope to desperate hearts.
The true meaning of beauty is helping those in need.
Nothing is more beautiful than nature.
Medha Gaddam, Grade 5

Dogs
Dogs
fluffy, furry
running, jumping, playing
I love my dog!
Golden Retriever
Camryn Rogers, Grade 4

Rain
Rain
Thunder claps
Beating, soothing, crying
Brings back sad memories
Tears
Emma Myers, Grade 5

Lena's Adventure
Lena
Went on her first outdoor adventure
After receiving her first cat harness
Walked around our newly landscaped yard
To explore the great outdoors.
Ethan LeCuyer, Grade 4

Toothless
You fly so high
In the sky
Never look down
Beyond the ground
Never look down
Faith McGowan, Grade 4

Rainbow, Illusion
Rainbow
Beautiful, colorful
Arching, stretching, gleaming
An inspiration to all
Illusion
Mariana Jaramillo, Grade 5

Pennsylvania Keystone
Pennsylvania
Mountainous, beautiful
Inspiring, amazing, eye-catching
American history lives here
Keystone
Thomas Smith, Grade 5

Ohio
Ohio
Beautiful, gorgeous
Dreaming, entertaining, inspiring
Amazing places to visit
State
James Costlow, Grade 5

Trust
Trust is like the Twin Towers
they took years to build but seconds to destroy
The importance is trust is simple
you feel better when you know someone has your back
It feels like a newborn puppy sitting on your lap comforting you
Trust is the sky,
 you can depend on it every day.
It smells like a batch of gooey brownies just coming out of the oven Mmmmmm
It is as extraordinary as finding out about a trip to your favored place.
You find it in a true friend
one you truly cherish
one you can rely on
one you treasure
one who you feel good around
who brings out the best in you
Eve Koester, Grade 5

What Happens to a Dream Deferred?*
What happens to a dream deferred?

Does it sob
like a little girl getting surprised by her mom or dad from the military?
Or does it slam like a basketball getting dribbled down the court
And then it shoots out of your mind?
Does it feel lost like when you move to a new place?
Or feel abandoned
like a house that villains might go into in a movie?

Maybe it just disappears
like an assistant in a magic act.

Or does it just fly away?
Hannah Gilmartin, Grade 6
*Inspired by Langston Hughes.

Day at the Beach
I walked on the hot, sandy, beach,
and I smelled the salt water.
I dashed into the ocean water,
and was swept off my feet.
The waves crashed down on everyone there.
Once the waves tired me out, I sat on the sand.
I reached out for my sandwich than,
a seagull swooped down and vanished into the sky with my sandwich.
Than, a crab crawled past me and
the water washed the crab away forever.
Patrick Bennie, Grade 6

Purple
Purple sounds like butterfly's flapping their wings and thunder rumbling
Purple tastes like grapes and grape juice
Purple looks like morning glory's opening up and storm clouds rolling in
Purple feels like rain falling from the sky and your purple ink pen
Purple smells like grape flavoring and the violets in your front yard
Purple is joyful
Madelyn Holland, Grade 4

High Merit Poems – Grades 4, 5, and 6

Flowers
Different sized shapes
Delicate fragrance in spring
Colorful petals
Jorge Torres, Grade 5

Immense Brook
Mossy, humid woods
Smaller than rocky rivers
But bigger than streams!
Lexys Siebrands, Grade 5

Ice
Slippery, frigid
Rapidly falling downward
Transparent and clear
Riley Pastor, Grade 5

Storm
Rain falling to earth
Thunder booming in the sky
Dark clouds hoarding light...
Dacey Pliley, Grade 5

Spring
Springtime begins now,
Joy overflows in my mind,
A warm breeze calms me.
Kaylee Helton, Grade 5

January
At the cold window
The snow leaves a white sleet on
The cold icy ground
Natalie Hartman, Grade 5

Plants
Beautiful objects,
All with astonishing scents,
Surround the vast world!
Anthony Ha, Grade 5

Spring
Lukewarm night weather
Rain falling while the sun sets
No need for blankets!
Steven Martinez, Grade 5

Summer Breeze
warm and blowing wind
sweet citrus smelling grasses
fresh blooming flowers
Destiny Friday, Grade 5

Cold and Creamy
I am cold and creamy
I wonder what warmth is
I hear the lips smacking
I see small children
I am cold, creamy, and now nervous
I pretend to be warm
I feel as cold as ice
I touch the cold metal
I worry I will be eaten
I cry when I'm licked
I am cold, creamy, nervous, and now wet
I understand what is happening
I say goodbye cold freezer
I dream that it will be warm
I try to stay frozen
I hope I do not melt
I am no longer cold, yet I am still creamy, but I am no longer ice cream
Austin Glockner, Grade 6

Animal
What is it?
This riddle poem if you're a whiz
Will tell you what this creature is
It stands about 38 cm tall
If it waddles it won't fall
They communicate by a series of chirps and peeps
Their peeps are subtle to a human ear so they can creep
They are found in northern Canada
In the black hills of North Dakota
They mate in the mid-summer, this behavior happened when males start hooting
They are going down to 3,000,000 adults in the wild because of shooting
The average time they live is not that long
So sad but the average is only 3 years strong
They eat bugs and berries for a main meal,
Doesn't that sound gross?
If you have not guessed I will have to tell you
For it's a ruffled grouse.
Brinley Huddleston, Grade 5

The Death Call
I am watching TV.
when the phone rings.
You answer
and the colour drains
from your face.

The pain seeps in,
and your tears become a river.
Shock pulses through me.
You muster the words,
"Your grandmother died."

Your sentence hangs in the air
as more tears drizzle down your face.
My heart echoes your pain.
Angus Lau, Grade 6

Books
All the paperback books
Open them up and smell the page
The best books are hardback
Lucia Frezza, Grade 6

Winter
The cold bitter air
snowflakes are like falling stars
winter is snowflakes
Ashleigh Richards, Grade 4

God Is
God is awesome
Jesus is God over me
Jesus is the BEST in the whole world
Jesus
Samuel Van Agteren, Grade 4

Kasi
K asi
A wesome
S porty
I ntelligent
Kasi Arneaud, Grade 4

Carrie Kyle Cory Cat
Carrie Kyle Cory Cat
Didn't know where her sock was at.
She had put it on the night before,
It turned out it was in her drawer.
Ella Semtner, Grade 4

Skies
The skies crystal like a diamond.
They're as alert as a siren.
As the sun switches places with the moon,
We will see it again tomorrow, soon.
Edrea Burgwin, Grade 4

Horse
I am a horse.
People ride on my back.
My owners give me hay to eat.
Sometimes I lay on the ground in the sun.
Karina Calixto Rodriguez, Grade 4

Friends
Friends share loyalty
They always trust each other
Friends are family
Bryan Langevin, Grade 4

Beach
Swimming at the beach
Hot sand in between my toes
Building sand castles.
Alice Hong, Grade 5

Falcons
Speedy black falcons,
With huge razor sharp talons,
Grasp birds in midair.
Arohan Prasai, Grade 5

Best Friend
Someone who loves you,
Someone who likes you,
Someone who's kind and very polite to you

Someone that smiles when they see you—
Someone that will take a bullet for you

Someone who doesn't laugh when you fall or trip,
Someone that supports you and you support them

Someone that you stand up for—
Someone that you'll reassure

A person that when they knock,
you'll never close the door

A person that would give you their umbrella—
At the lightest sprinkle of rain

A person that treats you with the most utmost respect,
A person that will give you the shirt of their back

A person that keeps their word,
And their word is worth wanting—

Someone that you will never embarrass— Or be embarrassed of,

A person that will ALWAYS have you in their heart—
In a corner of their mind— And would travel around the world any day—
Just to find— You
Kenza Amaris Scott, Grade 6

The Cat
The cat, the cat dances!
The cat, the cat prances
around the house at night.
Her fur as black as the shadows she lurks in,
she creeps quietly to my
my poor Mother! Oh dear! There she goes!
Waking her up at night.

At three in the mourning hour the cat scratches and claws and bites!
Each time she meows the same loud tune of
"Wake up my Nana! Come on, let us play!"
My mother sighs and reaches for her only savior,
the spray bottle that sits close by.

And there yet again, goes the prancing black cat,
galloping her way by, by my room as
she zooms from my mother's.
Oh and yet the poor beloved pet,
as she prances away,
but now
is
soaking wet.
Dakota Marshall, Grade 6

High Merit Poems – Grades 4, 5, and 6

The Holocaust
The Holocaust was a terrible time that burned into memories of people who survived, who were hidden when young or old by good people in the Nazis.

The thousands of Jews that were caught, arrived, haggard, weak, deprived of their belongings, and were lucky to still be alive. Some were so sadly killed on arrival.

Everyone from the young to the old was picked off one by one and separated from their families.

The men were taken away to work while the women and children were so sadly gassed.

The man we know as Hitler, was the man who was responsible for all the deaths and this terrible time.

Thousands of Jews died in that terrible time until the man finally came to a stop in 1945.

Amber Allen, Grade 6

Sleep
Mommy mommy hold me tight so I can sleep tonight.
Nightmare, nightmare, daddy help me this is not healthy.
Sleep walk, sleep walk, up and down up and down someone help me cause I'm going all around.
Honey go to sleep right now because mommy's tired of running around.

Brennan McLaughlin, Grade 5

The Word Poetry
The word poetry means to express yourself.
To write your thoughts and feelings, to let your mind go free in books or just a piece of paper.
The word poetry means to be yourself with your words and not let anyone tell you differently.
The word poetry means to inspire words into poetry.

Hermasia Law-Jackson, Grade 6

Years and Years
Years and years of running to school doing excruciating homework
Years and years of learning dreaded math and the beautiful subject of reading
Years and years of testing the same old rustic skills
Seven more years and I will be on my own path taking those old rustic skills and turning them into my life

Sawyer Prince, Grade 5

Poetry Days
My teacher wants us to write a poem
I do not like to write poems
The rhyming is fine but it takes to much time
I do not like to write poems

My teacher wants us to write a poem
I do not like to write poems
The wording is done and it just wasn't fun
I do not like to write poems

My teacher wants us to write a poem
I do not like to write poems
The paper is glued and I'm just so confused
I do not like to write poems

My teacher wants us to share our poems
I do not like to share poems
The people are watching I cannot start talking
I do not like to share poems

I take a deep breath and start to read
Hey that wasn't so bad
I say with glee

Shira Linkow, Grade 5

Home
Home means my hideout
To shut humanity out
Home is my favorite place to be
Where I get to be free

Home is outback
Where I get to play
Outback we get to party and dance
Or swim all day

Home is where I get to be with my family
And play games with them gleefully
Home can be concrete or abstract
For example my house is my home
But with my family that is my real home.

I can be quiet or possibly alone
As long as I have my house and my home
Home is my family
When I am with them
I am home even in the alleyways cowering due to fear
I would be home
As long as I have my family right by my side

Kellen Newsome, Grade 5

Turtle Time!!
Shells hard as boulders
Slow as an iron anvil
Swimming quietly...
Skyler A. Wood, Grade 5

Boy and the Blue Sky
Dark blue sky glowing
A boy with a telescope
Searching the gray moon
Cherif Diarra, Grade 4

Beginning of Spring
Flowers bloom in spring
As birds fly back to their home
And soar to the sky
Reagan Bui, Grade 6

Winter
Snowflakes fill the air
Children's hands are frost-bitten
The First Frost has come
Michaela White, Grade 6

Lily Pads
Frogs...growing, thriving
Leafs, vines, green water forests
Living beams of light!
Damien Carrera, Grade 5

Artic Animals
Lives in snow and cold,
Eats fish out of the ocean...
Slow, wild polar bears!
Khadro Abdi, Grade 5

Bunnies
Rabbits roam slowly
Running briskly at nighttime
Such a pretty sight!
Jennifer Watson, Grade 5

Bees
Flying through the air
Eating pollen...helping plants
Stinging to protect!
Faith Flores, Grade 5

Soccer Goal
Playing games right now
Kick the ball into the box
Chanting all day long!
Bryan Quinteros, Grade 5

The Worst Day Ever
One day, as I sat at home relaxing, I heard the phone ringing
I picked it up slowly; it was my mom
She told me the day I had dreaded, had finally come
I started crying, I knew it would hurt; but I didn't know how much
It felt like a thousand needles poking at my brain
I didn't know what to think or do or feel

My uncle came to get me, and we drove to the hospital
He tried to talk to me. I was silent
When we got there I ran to the room on the third floor
It was good, but mainly bad at the same time
He had stopped suffering, but was gone now
The person I loved most — my Dad — was laying dead on a hospital bed

At that moment I knew my life would never be the same
My baby one year old cousin was there
She kind of cheered me up,
But nothing would make me feel completely better
I wasn't entirely sure what I was feeling
All I knew was that it was negative

That was the worst day of my life
Nico Castleman, Grade 5

I Have a Little Friend
I have a little friend,
He seems to follow me,
When I look over, he's there right beside me.
I have a little friend,
He can be quite strange,
This is because his height has changed.
I have a little friend,
He really likes a certain color,
Because he is always the color black; when he's bigger or he's smaller.
I have a little friend,
But he has no key,
Because when I go inside he seems to flee.
I have a little friend,
Who plays a good game,
Because whatever I do, he seems to do the same.
I have a little friend,
Who must love the sun,
Because he most often comes when the sun is out and fun.
I have a little friend,
He is very shy,
He doesn't talk at all, not even a whisper to a fly.
Olivia Peterson, Grade 6

Weaving
Weaving my thoughts right to your heart
Sewing the blue ocean right onto the orange horizon
Stitching the green grass onto the dark and hopeless sky
Painting the cliffs of sharp mountain peaks with the teeth of dragons
Knit the mighty peaks of Everest to the depths of the Mariana Trench
Color the dazzling wildfire to the obscurity of Son Doong
Brayden Salankey, Grade 4

The Horse in the Meadow
The horse in the meadow
runs so fast
clicking his black hooves
and kicking up the grass
smelling the flowers
on the sunny days
exploring through the forest
just like a maze
eating the apples
right from the trees
letting his mane flow
in the breeze
falling asleep
as the sun goes down
dreaming about the meadow
without a sound
Lilianna Chitambar, Grade 5

Gymnastics
Gymnastics
It makes me feel as free
as a bird flying in the air.
When I stretch,
I feel loose as the air.
When I do a flip,
I feel as light as a mouse.
When I fly,
I feel like a butterfly.
Twisting and twisting down the floor
I feel so nice
Vaulting, jumping, hitting,
Landing down,
Gripping on the bar.
Turn, turn on the beam
Dismount landing on my feet.
Haley Dobich, Grade 5

Rolling Ocean Peace
The ocean is deep and blue
turning into waves rolling
bigger and bigger.

The ocean is a promise
of surfing with gentle
dolphins.

The oceans LOVE is
spread across the land
and the islands of rock
will swim forever.

The ocean is its own
land by space, not by
wretched, ugly rocks.
Arianna Hubley, Grade 4

I Used to Be…
I used to be…
small
young
mini
limited
little
youthful
a minute
cramped
miniature
modest
brief
bare
shorthanded
Tydan Campbell, Grade 6

Freedom
As I stand there
   I think
As I look up and see
     the thing that makes
me free,
   Freedom isn't a word,
it's an emotion
     Freedom is our fathers
that died to save our flag
       Freedom is
you,
   Freedom is me,
      Freedom is all of
us.
Ashley Little, Grade 4

Hurricanes
The wind is howling
Like a ghost,
The water's crashing
On the coast

A flood is coming,
As quick as light,
We need to leave,
Leave, take flight

When the wind dies down,
We will return,
For now our home,
We'll have to yearn
Lillian Keith, Grade 5

Winter
Winter smells like a burst of wind.
Winter looks like an iceberg.
Winter feels like a nice cool breeze.
Winter tastes like ice cream.
Samuel Ley, Grade 4

Happiness
Happiness is a warm feeling,
a special delight in your heart.
It warms you like you are sitting by a fire.
Like soup in your stomach in the winter.
The exhilaration in your body.
The well-being of the world.
The brisk breeze flowing through your hair.
The adrenaline rushing down your spine.
Happiness is so divine.
Wyatt Eppolito, Grade 4

Bugs Bunny
Bugs Bunny is a tall bunny
And sometimes he is really funny,
Bugs Bunny has grey hair
And sometimes he is quite unfair.

Carrots are his most favorite snack
If you get too close he'll attack,
He has buck teeth and long ears
And he absolutely has no fears.
Abigail Todd, Grade 5

A Good Friend
I love a friend,
One like you,
One that loves me,
just like I do.

If I fall down,
You would catch me.
You help me through everything,
You're the other half of me.
Timea Johnson, Grade 5

Shirley Temple
Shirley Temple is a beauty,
She also is a television cutie.
She is honored with a drink,
And her favorite color is pink.

She has a lot of talent,
Her voice has a perfect balance.
Brown eyes, red hair,
She is remembered everywhere.
Olivia Currie, Grade 5

Pokemon
P owerful strikers
O ur favorite game
K arate chop says Hitmonchan
E ther is a potion
M an they're awesome
O ver the top our Pokemon go
N o, no, no … we do not suck!
Oliver Morrow, Grade 4

Beauty

In life there are directions uncounted; lefts, rights, ups and downs
So the only way to get through is to move forward and since the beginning,
People see life as a chance to make their moment count.

That moment that feels like years and counting.
You forget. You get bombarded by beauty,
Because beauty is a symptom of pain, and because beauty is pain,

Weakness isn't weak. It doesn't flicker in you soul like a dying candle.
It makes a pathway. A pathway to your greatest strength.
Beauty to pain. Pain to weakness. Weakness to strength. Strength to beauty.
This incredible cycle of hope prepared the tightropes frozen over for the balancing act called life.
Making every step important. Every lesson learned.
People say life is a book, Everyone is a word. A word used to describe what you valued.
What you made of pain, what you gained from strength.
What you need to learn from your weaknesses. All of this in one word.
Where does one find such a word? It all begins with a name

Your name is you, nobody has it the same
Nobody carries themselves with such love than you.
And in a book full of names how do you read?

You remember. The ones before with beauty untapped
Pain unresolved. Strength of unmatched amounts. And keep your beauty

A reminder of you — a beautiful amazing you.

Mags Hornsby, Grade 6

Home

Your home is where your family is.
It's where important things happen and where memories are made.
It's where you say your first word...
...where you take your first step.
It's where you put your tooth under your pillow or leave out cookies and milk for Santa.

Home is freedom.
It is where you dance silly in your pajamas...
and turn your music up really loud...
It is where you can chew with your mouth open or lay on the couch for hours and nobody minds.

Home is love.
It's the place where you get hugs and kisses, and good advice.
It's the place where you swap stories, cry your eyes out,
and laugh your head off...
It's where you can be you, and be as proud as a peacock, without being judged.

Your home is everything you need: your food, your shelter, your family, your memories.

Your home is the best place to be, right now.
It is the place where you find love, laughter, tears and joy.
Your home is not your house; it's the love that surrounds it.
Your house may change, but your home remains the same
because your home is where your heart is...
...and hopefully where it will stay.

Desiree Wong, Grade 5

Friendship Is Forever
The friendship we have is rare to find,
We hate to see each other in a bind.
We made each other laugh so hard we've cried
We feel each other's pain if we are hurt inside.
We can always find the right words to say,
To help us get through any dreadful day.
We have told our darkest secrets, with feeling no shame,
We tell each other the truth even if we are to blame.
Thinking of you not being here makes me feel so sad,
We will have to look back at our memories to make us glad.
The miles between us can't keep us apart,
because we will keep each other close at heart.

Isabella Bonanno, Grade 6

Hurricane
The wind is howling like a swirling storm.
The eye is coming towards us.
Hiding in the basement.
Now, we are hearing the rain right above us.
Splat! Splat!
Silence!
Everything is still.
Is it over?
We walk around and suddenly the wind starts,
Yelling and screaming again.
That's when we notice we were in the,
Eye of the hurricane.

Erin Good, Grade 5

A Firefighter's Job
My dad is a firefighter, who saves people's lives.
He always needs his co-workers to help.
He is one of the highest ranks of a firefighter.
He has saved a baby in a big fire.
He has fought a four-alarm fire before.
He has got an award from the Mayor.
He is the best firefighter I think that is in Baltimore.
When he is firefighting he gets to work with some friends.
He is always getting back to work to help people.
Also, he is kind to his workers and cares for them.
He always gets to fight the fires at night.
That is what my dad does.

Nicholas Beebe, Grade 6

My Sister
My sister is a crazy one all right
She dyed her hair rainbow
So now she looks insane
We had to go to the doctor to make sure she was all right
Even though she was to crazy to go
But we new she was fine
So that's my lunatic sister
A really really demented one today
Oh wait I remember now that wasn't my sister
IT WAS ME

Oakley Barney, Grade 5

Inca Walls
The stars shine above sweaty workers.
They chisel everything into place.
The stones fit together perfectly
No cement only strength.
All the slaves work very hard.
Get beaten if they don't.
They create forts, temples, dwellings
Some walls used to worship the sun.
Other walls part of everyday life.

Hundreds of years they have not fallen.
Inca walls still standing.
Standing through earthquakes and floods
Hardly touched by the ravages of time.
The walls are now history.
People come to touch them
Some think they are magic and want their power
Others only want a photograph
Something to remember,
The wonderful walls that still stand proud
The Inca rocks which endure.

Ella Brubaker, Grade 6

Nature
Nature, my love
Woosh — a gentle breeze blows
blows by. Shady trees, green grass,
and pretty bushes. Shining sun, glowing moon,
bright stars, tailed comets streak by.
Shining meteoroids burn from
in the sky tonight!
Peaceful nights,
Busy days
Warm spring,
hot summer,
Fruitful autumn
and angry
winter.
Storm clouds create
Rain, snow, sleet, and hail,
Shining lightning and BOOM —
Thunderclaps! Animals all shapes
and sizes. From whales to bugs and eleph
ants to mice. Dogs and cats, birds and fish.

Robert Barkley, Grade 4

Trips
My adventure is out there
Not for you, just me
so what if I'm alone I'm still free
I ended up at home but I still tried
so you're across America I tried to find you
but remember through the rocky hills
and amazing thrills you're in my thoughts and in my heart.

Haley Luffman, Grade 4

I Am Ava

I am a girl who has survived bullying and depression.
I wonder if somebody will ever love me for who I am.
I hear my dad's best friend's voice in the distance, telling me to stay strong and overcome my fears and doubts.
I see him everywhere, all the time.
I want to meet my best friend Hailey in South Carolina who helped me through all of this.
I am a girl who survived bullying and depression.
I pretend I'm stronger than I really am so that my friends can use me as a shoulder to cry on.
I feel his presence in every room I walk in.
I touch pictures and timeless memories that remind me of why I'm still here and healthy.
I worry that the depression will start again, and that I won't be strong enough to overcome it this time.
I cry when I remember the past and how it has changed my entire life, as well as my families.
I am a girl who survived bullying and depression.
I understand I'm not completely normal.
I say it doesn't change who I am and what I stand for.
I dream that all the bullying will stop one day, and that I can talk of my past without bringing myself to tears.
I hope my younger brother doesn't have to go through this, because It sucks all the happiness and joy out of your life.
I am a girl who survived bullying and depression.

Ava Sluka, Grade 6

The Bully Cycle

As I went by, a tree of a leg was out, but I'm not one to criticize. I fell like a baby, everyone laughed, I wished I'd stayed home that day. Now it is a new day, still I want it to end as soon as it began. But, I still had to go to whatever else? School. I walked by the same place, same time, and same people. Not one person touched me nor stuck out a leg, some even became my friends. This is the bully cycle, embarrass people and laugh. Once people stop this cycle, the world would be a better place.

I'm too shy to speak, and when I do, my words get twisted and sound different. People call me names and I can't stick up for myself. One person doesn't tease, but instead comes over and says, "It is all right, its good to be different." We soon became friends and I wasn't bullied anymore. In fact, more people came and said hi. I soon loved the new school I was even glad I didn't fit in!

I'm stuck in a wheelchair and everybody acts like its a contagious disease. Everyone gives me a wide berth. Another kid comes soon after and hangs out with me, he is a pretty cool guy. His friends stare at him like, "Are you crazy?" But he doesn't mind. The world is little by little improving it's bully cycle, we ourselves need to perfect it.

I follow the rules and help others. But some call me names that are not mine such as, tattletale, kiss-up, parents pet and so on. Soon they realize that I just follow the rules and try to help others follow the rules also and then my life becomes better; and instead of getting picked on, I get defended.

Shaylee Johnsen, Grade 6

Sunny Day Sunflowers

The sunflower field swishes from the wind. Sunny yellow is reflecting off the sun into my dark brown squinting eyes. Tall amazing sunflowers outside in nature, growing higher and higher above the dark green grass.
The light is reflecting off the sunflowers while pitch black shadows form next to them on the ground. The light is as bright as a gleaming shooting star
The sounds of blowing wind and leaves crunching under my feet filled with air. A few people are talking it is very peaceful outside with the amazing sunflowers.
These flowers can make you feel beautiful on the inside and out.
Tall amazing sunflowers,
Tall amazing sunflowers,
Tall amazing sunflowers growing higher and higher above the dark green grass.

Isabelle Milani, Grade 4

Serve and Protect

As I stare into the gates of hell every day I go on fighting in dangerous places for my family and friends. I fight so than they don't have to. I will fight until my days are done and when I lay in that casket I want only two words with me in my casket: Serve and Protect.

Ryder Hendry, Grade 6

Wrestling

Wrestling, my favorite sport fun to play, fun to do, wrestling is the best sport.
States, Nationals even your little tournaments I love it.
Team Tournaments are best hanging with friends doing what we do best.
Take down TWO the crowd goes wild, every fan cheering for me.
The feeling when you go out on the mat is amazing, just you and your opponent.
If you lose nobody to blame but yourself.
Work harder and harder every night at practice for that one golden moment to wow the crowd,
that one shot to complete everything you ever wanted in your life.
That one opportunity to reach life's goals.
You and nobody else determines your fate on the mat.
That moment you hear the referee slap the mat and you pinned that amazing kid.
Wrestling friends off the mat, enemy on the mat; the most serious sport in the world.
All other sports you play, not wrestling, you always wrestle your hardest on the mat.
The moment you win States is the most incredible feeling in the world.
The moment you look into the crowd, see your mom with tears of joy in her eyes.
The moment you run into the corner and jump into your coaches arms.
The moment you walk off the mat and you see your dad like you've never seen him before,
in tears he feels like the happiest dad on earth, he is so proud of you.
You love it so much you cry too.
But remember if you're not having the time of your life don't do it.
The best experience ever. Wrestling, I love it.

Nicholas Allison, Grade 6

It Wasn't Good

Hitler thought that all Jews were bad which created the Holocaust.
  It wasn't good.
  Hitler rose the Nazi party since he thought all Jews were bad which created the Holocaust.
  It still wasn't good.
  Hitler created Nazification when the Holocaust started after he rose the Nazi part since he thought all Jews were bad which created the Holocaust.
  It still wasn't good.
  Hitler confined Jews to Ghettos when he created Nazification when the Holocaust started after he rose the Nazi party since he thought all Jews were bad which created the Holocaust.
  It still wasn't good.
  Hitler held the Jews in concentration camps in addition to confining the Jews to Ghettos when he created Nazification when the Holocaust started after he rose the Nazi party since he thought all Jews were bad which created the Holocaust.
  It still wasn't good.
  The Jews resisted Hitler since he held them in concentration camps in addition to confining the Jews in Ghettos when he created Nazification when the Holocaust started after he rose the Nazi party since he thought all Jews were bad which created the Holocaust.
  It still wasn't good.
  Alas, the war is over and Hitler died because the Jews resisted him since he held the Jews in concentration camps in addition to confining the Jews to Ghettos when he created Nazification when the Holocaust started after he rose the Nazi party since he thought all Jews were bad which created the Holocaust.
  Finally, it was good.

Austin Bentzinger, Grade 6

Weave

Weave your sadness through a deserted ocean, full of emotions and thoughts.
Sew the long grass of a field, swaying in the wind against a framework of mountains.
Paint the sun like a clump of lemon juice in the congested sky of clouds.
Color the horizon with a blazing hot sun, scorching like a fiery, vivid wildfire.
Knit the waves and the sand together, into a blanket of a harbor.
Stitch brave and confident into a pocket of intelligence, glowing with aptitude, gleaming with pride.

Reilly Landis, Grade 4

My Friend
Good
Awesome
Really nice
Runs well
ncrediblE
Trusting
inTeresting
Gabriel Lunsford, Grade 4

Brother and Sister
Brother
Lovable, honest
Caring, helping, excited
Funny, trustworthy, polite, sweet
Play, joking, laughed
Clumsy, awesome
Sister
Victoria Jaime, Grade 5

Ocean Happiness
The ocean is calm
I hear the seagulls squawking
I see the people swim
I feel the warm sand on my toes
I smell the salty water
I taste the tasty hot dogs
My feelings are joyful.
Gabrielle Truong, Grade 4

Water and Fire
Water
Wet, life giving
Swimming, splashing, sprinkling
Lake, ocean, ashes, flames
Burning, dancing, scorching
Bright, pretty
Fire
Catherine Shewchuk, Grade 5

Puppy to Dog
Puppy
Tiny, cute
Eating, sleeping, playing
Soft, sweet; furry, toys
Barking, running, fetching
Big, tired
Dog
Eric Hardgrove, Grade 5

At the Horror Movie
My family and I went to dine
We all were having a good time.
We picked a horror film to see,
Until my mom said, "Stop touching me,"
We then realized the hand wasn't mine.
Michael Ellison, Grade 4

My Brother 12/12/13
His eyes are brighter than the sun.
The father is taking care of him.
Who is he? Where is he?
He's in heaven. He passed away in my mom's belly yesterday.
He's my little brother and he's growing like a weed.
He is one year old and tomorrow he will be.
Today he is young and my little man, now he will grow just like a weed.
His eyes are like the stars.
So tiny and bright he is one of the stars in Gods light.
It's hard to be strong because he is gone.
My little brother Dy'mere I will always be near.
He is my prayer, thank you Dy'mere Brandon Snuffer, whom will never suffer!
Alexis Robinson, Grade 5

Hockey
You know hockey has begun
When the first period is on the run.
My favorite team the Anaheim Ducks battle the rubber puck.
The right winger stickhandles across the blue line.
They shoot, they pass, they are so fast,
And they pass some more and shoot some more.
As Nashville Predators try hard to keep the puck and their zone,
but each Nashville player can't defend themselves alone.
Down come the Anaheim Ducks centerman with a good deal of pressure.
He gets that puck and shoots at the net and guess what?
They score and the roaring crowd goes wild!
Tim Gross, Grade 6

Aidan
Son of Todd and Stephanie
Who likes to run, swim, play
Who brings to Locust Grove his brain
Lover of dogs, food, and sleep
Who fears second graders, Daleks and Smaug
Who knows a lot about dogs, sharks, and slimes
And desperately wants to get an Xbox, to Texas and get a push mower
Who wouldn't be caught dead jumping out a window
Who hopes to one day go bungee jumping
Who would like to be remembered for his personality
Grambau
Aidan Grambau, Grade 5

Friends
Friends are very nice, plus they give great advice.
Friends are like the sun, they show you the way and are always fun.
Friends are always there, even if you are attached by a bear.
Friends always have your back, but would still love a snack.
Friends will make you happy, even when you're feeling sappy.
Friends always make you smile, not just once in a while.
Friends will be there when you cry, you will never catch them in a lie.
Friends will always put you first, even when they feel their worst.
Friends are like an ice cream sundae, when you're with them it's always a fun day.
Friends are never a bummer, when you're with them every day feels like summer.
Friends are hard to find, that why I am glad to have mine.
Emma Fahey, Grade 6

Gold and Black and Pink
On happy days I see Gold to show that this day is golden.
On days that are not going right I see Black to show I can't see.
Right now I see Pink to show a normal day.
These are my colors to show my day: Gold, Black, and Pink.
Days can be tie-dye, or just one Color,
Still I see Pink,
What do you see?
Janet Rogers, Grade 6

Bees vs Wasps
Bees
Nice, healthy
Flying, buzzing, protecting
Bees fly all day and wasps sting more than once
Stinging, building, going
Mean, poisonous
Wasps
Nicolas Grondin, Grade 4

Animals and Humans
Animals
Fast, Cute
Running, Attacking, Devouring
Animals can be enemies of humans and humans love animals.
Sitting, Protecting, Caring
Slow, Beautiful
Humans
Mathieu Delorme, Grade 4

Hockey
First, do face off then fake and fall.
Then, slide, shoot and save, then score.
Pass the puck, play harder and get a penalty.
Then trip and trample, and chase the puck.
Boom!! In with a breakaway,
Finish with a flashy fake and make the fans wild!!!
Jesse Waldner, Grade 6

I
I put my foot down
I push off with a blast
I take a quick look
I know I won't be last
I gain more speed, as I go down hills
Gosh! Riding skateboards sure gives me thrills!
Trevor Hudson, Grade 4

Zoo
Hear the lions roar, watch the birds soar
Flying through the air, without a care
Monkeys swinging from vine to vine, all of the elephants in a line
The bunnies hopping here and there, animals everywhere
Finally day turns to night, children go home with a great delight
The animals are now asleep too, after a long day at the zoo
Zoë Law, Grade 5

Colour
Yellow is the colour of lemonade,
And is the colour of lemon-meringue pies

Yellow is the colour of sunlight,
And a cheetah running fiercely in the wild

Yellow is the colour of summer,
And is the colour of warmth

Yellow is the colour of gold in the mines,
And cheese on cheeseburgers

Yellow is the colour of happiness,
And the colour of souls around the world

Yellow is the colour of the sun in the sky,
And is my favourite coloured crayon

Yellow is the colour of a lion, king of the Savannahs,
And is the colour of candy

Yellow is the colour of relaxation,
And the colour of my thoughts

Yellow is BRIGHT!
Eric Mei, Grade 6

Home to Me
What is home to me?
Well it is easy to see.
My bed,
Where thoughts swirl in my big head.
And my book,
I read it in my little nook.

In my bed I dream,
Of what seems, it beams.
When I wake up I read,
Not quite sure what happened previously.

Sometime times I look,
At my big books
And then I stop,
And I rock,
Myself to sleep
Where I creep
Up into my dreams.

And then I wake up.
And I'm calm,
Hearing songs.

My home isn't only, home to ME, but also my FAMILY
Lily Terpstra, Grade 4

My Underwater Journey
I sink down
letting the water grasp me
I see bubbles floating above me
that have emerged from my mouth
I put my hands through the wet sand
leaving a mark
I feel as though that I am
not in control of my life anymore
I lay down and look up at the light
shining through the water
then I realize
who I really am
I see my life
surrounding
me
Ruth Pechersky, Grade 5

Ode to Kittens
Ode to Kittens
So cute and small
Oh, I want them all

Ode to Kittens
How bad they can be
Just find their sweetness, then you'll see

Ode to Kittens
For cuddling at night
I hold them with all my might

Ode to Kittens
For when the day is over, no need to sorrow
Just wait until tomorrow
Madison Buhaly, Grade 6

My Old Friend
My old friend,
We have been through so much.
I'll never forget your ongoing smile,
Upon your happy face.
I feel like you are still here,
But you are not.
And every time I close my eyes,
I see you,
Not with me.
I'll have to bid you farewell,
Until we meet again.
And I will get to see that smile again,
But for now,
I will say,
"See you later forever friend."
Emma Loop, Grade 6

Nature's Battle
Wind hissing at whoever trespasses
Corn stalks
Guarding their territory
Leaves trapping the ground
From being free
Fall waiting
For the ambush of winter
The woods thriving to keep their land
The river frigidly freezing into ice
Falls kingdom is falling
Soon to be taken over by winter
Pricker's hope they survive
Leaves dropping
Like storming torpedoes
Fall going in quick retreat
Winter has won
Antonio Linberger, Grade 5

Hockey
When I play road hockey
It's sometimes rocky
And also foggy
But it reminds me
Of Bobby Orr
Number Four

My coach
Has a good approach
Because he is positive
And competitive

I like playing hockey with my friend Ben
He is ten
He is tall
I am small
Colin Sloan, Grade 5

Basketball
Ball bouncing
shooting threes
playing defense
making shots
sad losses
trying your best
being a sport
all stars
fouling out
time out
biffing
awesome plays
good passes
dunking the ball
win streak
buzzer blowing
Riley Hoben, Grade 4

The Swaying Water
The water sways
against the shore.
The birds sing
on the rocks.
The mist rises
as the water falls.
The peaceful wind blows
through the trees.
You are going in
the cool water.
That feels
so relaxing.
Nolan Stricker, Grade 4

Bear
Ahh!
That was a long winter,
And now it's spring,
After getting out of my cave,
I go and eat some berries.
Until I am full and ready,
Then I go and take a walk,
And then I thought,
I am going to eat some salmon,
After getting full I go to bed,
And say to myself, "goodnight"
This is how a bear's life goes.
Isabel Al-haddad, Grade 4

The Reign of Winter
The reign of winter ends.
Winter winds never stop.
Always blowing here and there,
Isolated in a frozen desert,
Locked in an eternal cage with snow.
No chains.
Still can't move,
Little hope still lives.
From the abyss, the spring will emerge.
Dark clouds come and go,
When they go,
Happiness will come.
Kevin Phan, Grade 6

Sing!
You can be young or old,
shy or bold,
singing is something fun,
even if you aren't number one.
You can be in peace,
or you can let your voice be released.
Even if you are a bore,
you should let your voice soar.
Why don't you sing a song?
Don't worry, I'll sing along.
Raquel Rhoads, Grade 6

High Merit Poems – Grades 4, 5, and 6

Figaro
Brown, spiky, and slow
Eats worms, lettuce, raspberries
A Bearded Dragon
Paul Alexandre Mejia, Grade 4

Spring
The sun is shining,
Birds are singing and chirping,
Spring is on the rise.
Bryce Keating, Grade 6

Midnight Breeze
Gleaming stars shining...
A cool breeze through the night air
When the clock strikes twelve.
Nadiah Maurer, Grade 5

The Third Season
Winter snow-filled days...
Kids longing to see Santa
On those Christmas nights!
Jenni Faudoa, Grade 5

Daylight
Breezy afternoon
Lonely flowers in the wind
Dancing side to side!
Mario Madrid Jr., Grade 5

Leaves
Autumn winds blow strong
Gently floating to the ground
Slow to disappear
Emma Spath, Grade 5

Marsupials
Koalas on trees
Eating leaves from the branches
Feel the breezy air...
Jose Garcia, Grade 5

Electric Sky
Lightning striking now!
A huge bolt struck before me,
Flashing in my eyes!
Allie Lauck, Grade 5

Wolf
Hunts during the night
Howling to call its own kind
Gray, fierce, fighting dog!
Jesus Argoth, Grade 5

Ode to Family
Oh, family
We enjoy so many things together,
Like a stroll in the park with red, yellow and orange trees
Or a swim at the beach.
Oh, family
We taste, smell and see
The very same things.
We feel the excitement when going shopping, getting a new dress or outfit.
We taste the tangy flavors of Rumbi's, our favorite restaurant
We see the stars and moon when getting ready for bed.
Oh, family
What would I do without you?
You are my heroes.
You are the one's there for me
Every step of the way like a pack of wolves,
Never leaving each other's side
Oh, family
How I love you!
You do frustrate me from time to time
But, oh family, how I love you!

Katie Heitmann, Grade 6

Spider's Web
Sunbeams dance across the sky, illuminating an old, forgotten corner
powdered with the dust of time
Threads of silver shine with hidden, brilliant fire
An endless pattern
stretching into infinity, eternity
curving, twisting, spiraling
on and on and on, forever
Stars shimmer, caught in the silvery net of dreams, the tapestry of awe…
Yet there is darkness in this spellbinding picture of luminance
Poison, death, hate, desire and sin
A shadow sneaking up on you, slowly, slowly
Can you see now, the torture awaiting you on that glimmering, shimmering net?
Can you see now, the pain you will face on what looks to be the mirror of your dreams?
Writhe in agony, now,
regret what you should not have done, although it won't help you
not anymore
Think back on the mistakes you made
and wonder
how did a dream turn into a nightmare?

Sara Xiao, Grade 6

A Change Is Upon Us
It started out perfect all nice and untouched, brand new, right out of the box.
But sometime today it will change it will change into something that can create.
This thing will help you when you don't know what to do.
I used a simple machine to give it a shape.
You may have multiples of these or many different kinds.
But on the other end of it is a creation destroyer.
Your work will be destroyed.
Can you guess what it is?

Answer: a pencil

Laya Phillips, Grade 5

War

War is bad, it must be stopped.
War is unliked in this world.
War is known for its destruction.
War is a terrible experience in life.
War is life changing.
Mehrbod Rostami, Grade 4

Potato, Vegetable

Potato
Tough, hard
Planting, sun burning, harvesting
Growing starts with itself
Vegetable
Victoria Ress, Grade 5

Horses of Night

Horses
Big, graceful
Galloping into the dark night
Riding into the navy sky, running
Darkness.
Molly Hedlund, Grade 6

Salty Sea Memories

Ocean
Sunny, Cloudy
Fishing, Surfing, Swimming
Waves crashing on the beach
Seashore
Nyah Petrakis, Grade 5

Paint

I love to paint
Rainbow of colors to see
You need paint, brushes, and paper
when you have all of this
you can start…
Kimberly Padgett, Grade 6

Paper Wasps

Paper wasps black, brown, or red.
Making nests atop high buildings.
Eating delicious fat caterpillars.
Aggressive, fast, powerful.
Watch out!
Jake Sobiech, Grade 6

Lady Bug

Oh little tiny lady bug.
Who eats on some leaves with a tug,
Your dots so cute on your back.
They are always on tack.
Their personality is so special like a hug.
Krysta Nichols, Grade 6

Albinism

Why are these people so mistreated?
They are nice to us, but are simply cheated
Why do we think they are evil creatures,
Only because they have different features?

Albino and stupid, synonyms in the same trash talk
We should get to know these wonderful people instead of just mock
If you are born with this condition, you are considered by some as an unequal
They only have white skin, they aren't crazy people

Should it be considered a disorder or a personality trait?
Chanel Côté, Grade 5

Lightning

I am the rain transformed I travel with amazing speed
I am bright, I am quick, and I am loud I do the world around me proud
Do not look for the sun when I am here for that is when he will disappear
Even the moon not dare challenge me in the air
Yes I am beautiful but to be truthful
To be near me when I strike would not be something you'd like
I truly am dangerous my touch would make you ageless
I strike without warning I will be gone before morning
I cannot be snatched I cannot be matched
You cannot trap me I am forever free
I am beautiful and frightening. I am Lightning
Onkar Singh Bajwa, Grade 5

The Best Time of Year

Winter has come, the flowers have gone.
Where is the pollen? Where are those lovely creatures?
Dead vines, dead leaves, not even bushes not even trees!
The fresh smell has left, the bitter winter is here.
The stems have shriveled…OH MY!
I miss the fresh smell of the petals…Why can't the summer sun come faster?
I miss the sound of the bee's buzz and the feeling of dandelion fuzz.
Summer has come, happiness is spreading…what is better than this?!
I am so thankful that summer even exists on this planet.
I am going to cry when fall season comes around…again.
Shaye Rohrer, Grade 5

Truth

ItfeltlikeIlivedinaroomwithnowallsnoboundariesjustrules.
IwassurroundedwithnothingbutDeepfights,Darknights,andDangerouseyesstaringat
me.ClawmarksinmybrainthatcannotberemovedfromthescreamsandthreatsShes
madetosendmeaway.LastyearItriedtostandupbutIgotknockeddown,eventhoughIam
usedtoit,itstillhurtswhenIamcallednames.IhavebeenonthisearthforIIyearsandallI
haveheardisfighting,screaming,yelling,shaking,andapologies,thatnowmeannothing
becauseIhaveheardthemsomanytimes.Neverthinkapersoniswhotheyreallyareuntil
youmeettheirparents.
Rayvin Houtz, Grade 6

Asleep Forever

As I walk past my father sleeping, I see him stir
I Stop and turn around, watching the gentle breeze swing him and his noose,
Attached to the gallows.
Marcus Orlando, Grade 6

Slender Man
Have you heard of Slendy?
He loves the fog covered streets
He loves the dark woods
So easy to watch the children

When little boys and girls
Tell mommy and daddy about the man
In the suit
Long arms and legs
That grow and wrap around
And pull into darkness
They laugh and say, "Go to sleep."
But he is waiting in the dark
A dark shadow, faceless
Watching us sleep
I know so soon it will come inside
And take us.
Nicky Messick, Grade 6

Rain Drops
Why so sad?
I find it quite peaceful
The constant
Drip, drop, drip, drop
It's just so…
Relaxing.

It may be cold and grey,
But it's so soft against my face,
So cool to the touch,
So gentle,
Yet so harsh.

But I must ponder…
Why does the sky weep?
What makes the clouds
So sad?
Paige Raymond, Grade 6

Little Pup
Little tiny pup
Golden as the sun
Thinking of sleeping
All day long

Little tiny pup
Dreaming of swimming
As his legs are
Doggie paddling

Little tiny pup
Waking up
Jumps in the sea
Where he may swim
Like his dream
Brooklyn Ewert, Grade 4

Fire
Fire is a burglar
Sneaking
Stealing
Taking away
Precious belongings
And hurting others
Alexis Muller, Grade 4

Red
Red is the feeling of anger
Red is the color of love
Red is the blood buried deep in your skin
Red is the color of an apple
Red is the burning sun
Red
Tommy Tafoya, Grade 4

A Storm of Wolves
Wolves are storms
Howling winds on a stormy night
Like a sad song with splashing tears
Soon the packs come to battle
Thundering growls tremble the earth
And ends with a pitter patter of rain
Jordana Kamenitz, Grade 4

The Baseball Game
Baseballs coming at me
Loud cheers from the stands
A baseball bat hitting the ball
Hot and ready chips and nacho cheese
Water when I drink it
I think I'll keep playing.
Tatum Packer, Grade 4

Ocean Fun
Here I am
At the beach
Riding the waves
Enjoying the sun
Having good times
With my family
Robbie Wood, Grade 4

Hockey
Hockey is the sport that I like best.
I like it better than all the rest.
I run really fast down the dek.
If I catch you, I'll give you a check.
I try to put the ball in the net.
If I try very hard, I can score, I bet.
Luc Normandy, Grade 4

Pittsburgh Pirates
Ode to Pirates Baseball,
For the emotional wins,
And the heartbreaking losses.
Ode to Pirates Baseball,
For raising the Jolly Roger,
And disliking the team.
Ode to Pirates Baseball,
For the 2013 Wild Card win,
And the terrible 2014 Wild Card loss.
Ode to Pirates Baseball,
For all the bad calls,
Especially the curse of Sid Bream.
Ode to Pirates Baseball,
For the twenty bad seasons,
And the last two great seasons.
Ode to Pirates Baseball,
We love our Bucs,
So beat 'em Bucs.
Philip Osborn, Grade 6

Fall Is Calling
Breathing in fresh
Crisp fall air
The dark bark
Forming majestic Brown waves
Thin, loose branches
Holding on
By the thread of a needle
Fallen leaves
Yelling "OW!" as I step
Vines squeezing
The color out of the trees
Like a snake suffocating its prey
Winding vines forming
All kinds of marvelous creations
Like a sparkling crescent moon
The wonderful sight
Of fresh grown corn
Hoping to live just one more day
Katie Dalton, Grade 5

Tree
The tree is so cool to
look at, it reminds me of
my grandfather, all old and
gnarled and when I look at
the other trees and they're all
full and young and the one all
gnarled up is happy.

For being there, from lifting
weights of snow and the roots
like feet holding them in
from the horrible wind
that whooshed against the tree.
Morgan Suit, Grade 4

The View of a Patriot

Please listen to what I have to say for I wish to have independence one day,
Cruel King George, leader of Redcoats, we don't want him ruler and that's our vote.
The Sons of Liberty, leaders of us, we trust what they say, we make no fuss
We hate you King "for imposing taxes on us without our consent"
For all the acts, yes, we knew what it meant
Your country was in debt from the French and Indian War
But why are you making us suffer?
Because of your taxes, upon you we have closed the door
For what I mean to say is we will not tolerate your tax on everything we need
Especially the Quartering Act, which was worst of all,
It took all our items, but trust me, soon time will come to King's downfall
We all know the King has pushed our limits, which is why all these battles are arising minute after minute
We 13 colonies will stand together, the King's acts and battles for power will not last forever
Fighting, dying, we must do whatever to gain our freedom and independence together
Our victory at Concord was a plus point for us,
We need to fight harder, without any fuss
Please consider what I had to say for I wish to have independence one day

Parnika Saxena, Grade 6

Letting Go

Letting go of a loved one is like a little kid letting go of a balloon.
You think life stinks and you want to scream and cry about what happened.
But then you think about holding on and that makes you think about letting go.
And you do.
We don't realize how lucky we are until we have something horrible happen.
Then we thank everyone for everything and think about
what would've happened if we didn't.
I thought about how easy it might be to move on and just forget about it and think the past is the past.
Everyone can move on it is just the most dreaded thing in life.
Until we move on.
We can do it if we just don't think about all of the
bad things but think about all of the good things like Sunday night ice
cream cones and watching Barbie Life in the Dream House until we
were 11 years old.
We can LET GO.

Kelsey Keenan, Grade 4

Disparity of Aspect

I have always seen the world differently
You call it strange and unnatural
I will not be blinded by colors' short-sighted impressions
I dive beneath the surface to the true meaning of why colors are colors
I plunge through the outer layer of hues as you know it, through a blurring, misleading haze
But puzzling only to you
I float on a breath of sincere, colorless wind
I soar through steps of precise gray and black
Here I let go of all the deceptive emotions that shallow colors deliver me
I see what you couldn't possibly dream in my world of colorless clarity
Yet you call it strange and unnatural
You see the dull surface of me
But I see your deceiving, colorful heart
I am colorblind.

Zoe Deems, Grade 6

Holocaust

Remember the Jews, and how they were tortured for no reason?
Did you hear the cries from the women and children?
Do you know how much it would hurt to lose your loved ones because of
stereotypes or get torn apart from your family?
Did you see the fear in their eyes?
Hitler killing the Jews one by one for being different.
Hitler convinced the Germans to kill Jews for bad things and their racism.
People ran far away from home, trying not to be seen trying not to be caught by the Nazis.
It did not matter how fast they ran or how small they were the Nazis were going to get them, capturing innocent Jews.
Thanks to all the freedom we have today or the world would still be cruel.

Sara Purtle, Grade 6

I Remember

I remember everyone screaming help.
I remember people saying don't go outside.
I remember all the lives that were taken.
I remember all of the outrageous screaming.
I remember seeing people get chased down the street while I hid from the Germans.
I remember seeing all the people burned and their ashes.
I remember seeing the Germans march down the street trying to find us.
I remember the horror when they found me.
I remember the thrashing pain shooting down my body when they put me into the gas chamber.
This is something I will always Remember.

Rivers Edwards, Grade 6

An Eagle Soars

One early morning a big brown bald eagle was gliding gently in the breezy wind.
It was searching and circling for its dinner; it spotted a small animal with its amazing eyesight.
The light was like diamonds in the sky sparkling against the bald eagles wings; it soared in the warm sun on a summer day.
A miraculous perfect echo of the eagle's call rang through the air.
I just wonder how the eagle performs its beautiful call.
The eagle made me feel amazed as I watched it soar through the sky, circling like an airplane about to land.
The light was like diamonds,
The light was like diamonds,
The light was like diamonds as I watched the eagle soar.

Austin Hilyard, Grade 4

Sand-dollar

Lying on the sandy beach, cradled in the warm, golden sunlight, a sand-dollar dreamed of better times when it was bathed in the ocean.
The tide lapped at the edge of the sand-dollar's body coaxing it to come back in to the water, but the sand-dollar could barely move.
The water suddenly washed away its' agony and the sand-dollar's hopes swelled, but the tide came again and washed the sand-dollar farther on to the rough beach.
Just as the sand-dollar thought its' future would collide with its' past, the tide commenced up on the beach again sliding the sand-dollar into the water.
With its' future unraveled part of the way, the sand-dollar went on with its' life, happy and satisfied.

Miranda Jones, Grade 5

Lost and Alone with No Hope

Tears aching your heart, silencing your depressed soul. Sadness, heartache, and fear fill you body with emptiness. The sounds of your cry, fills the night with loneliness. Where the tears were cold and wet. The millions of stars reflect the sorrow in your eyes. The clouds cry tears of regret. The sun slides behind the clouds in shame, leaving me all alone in the darkness. The moon melts from all the heated sadness. Here I am all alone forever lost nobody and nothing. Just me, once again, alone and lost. No hope. No future.

Maggie Mastrangelo, Grade 5

To Be a Canadian
To be a friend
To wipe a tear
To change the world
To show no fear

To be kind
To sing real loud
To share a smile
To show you're proud

To have courage
To be brave
To say goodbye
With a wave

To always oppose
Discrimination
To spread peace
Across the nation

To stand strong
Hand in hand
To have hope
For this great land

To be a Canadian
Sophie Wilhelm, Grade 6

In the Sky
As I glide across the sky
I realize
I no longer can see my home
for I have flown too high.

I don't understand how I got up here
but I refuse to have any fear.
Perhaps the universe wants to show
how my family loves me so.

Sometimes I fear the world around me
but that's no reason to run away
for Earth's magnificent atmosphere
will not make me stay.

I have always known my family adored me
but actually, more than I thought.
For when I looked down from the heavens
they were crying an awful lot.

I realized right then and there
I did not want to be in the sky again.
I figured out that sometimes
you must know your limits.
Lilyana Crawley, Grade 6

It's Spring
The rain you hear
Flowers blooming
You hear bees buzzing

You smell the BBQ
that your dad is grilling
It smells good

Can you smell it
it's the best
but it's not ready

so I wait
I keep smelling
the BBQ

The roses smell
the flowers grow
it smells flowery awesome
It's spring now

Quiet as a Ninja
you can't hear anything
but rain
Elisabeth "Elise" Adams, Grade 6

Pug Life
I am a pug
snorting away.
Give me attention,
I want to play!

From my curlicue tail,
to my pushed-in nose,
I'm as cute as a button,
maybe even a rose!

Where are you going?
Can I come too?
Oh, your eating,
Let me join you!

Now throw this toy,
It's driving me crazy!
But don't throw it so far,
You know I'm quite lazy

Lets cuddle I will nap
uncomfortably on top of you
I don't care if you can't move
It's not like you have things to do.
Elaina Nicholson, Grade 6

Nature's Beauty
The water is as gentle
as a feather
f
a
l
l
i
n
g
into an ocean
of darkness

at times the water rushing so hard
it looks like clouds

smelling the woods
with wet bark and leaves
birds chirping
autumn is coming in!

On a damp cold morning.
Anna Kash, Grade 4

The Journey of a Shy boy
This boy
who had no friends
became a loner
only to realize that
it was because he was shy.
His tears drip out to the sky
he prayed and prayed
all night long.
God please send me
some friends along
so my days won't be
long. 'Cause he stayed
strong God sent a friend
along, although still shy
they built a connection
ten times strong
now he's not that
turtle no more
a social butterfly
beginning his journey
filled with adventures.
Yakeir Madison, Grade 6

Blue Balloon
Blowing, blowing
Not to pop
A long string
To make it stop
Oops let it go
There it goes
Away from home.
Clara Robinson, Grade 6

They Didn't Even Come Close
From time to time,
That's a nice thing to think of.
Playing again.
It's a satisfying image.

Thursday was a night for such thoughts,
For memories of history.
Familiar faces, video montages made the days.
When the fiercest and the fearsome play.

Feel as if they had lasted forever.
A real long time period.
You're looking at a short, intense moment.
When you have a strong feeling,
cherish it.

But that's the thing,
About those days,
They didn't last forever,
They didn't even come close.
Caitlin Zielinski, Grade 5

My Hero
M usic is his passion.
A ny challenge that comes his way, he will get through.
R ap is extraordinarily important to him.
S lim shady is one of his great nicknames.
H ailie Mathers, his daughter, is his favorite person in the world.
A ll of his songs make me happy.
L ove The Way You Lie, is one of them.
L uca Bella is his biggest fan. (That's me!)

M y favorite person in the world is him.
A ny time one of his songs come on, I get excited.
T he Real Slim Shady, is one of my favorites.
H e would do anything for his daughters.
E minem is the best person ever created.
R est in peace Proof.
S urrounded by fans at his concerts.

I pray for him every night.
I want to be just like him.
I want him to live life to the fullest. Thanks Eminem!
Lucabella Macri, Grade 6

Colors
Sometimes I am sunshine yellow
ready to make everyone happy
and like other times I am on top of the world!
like a squeezed lemon, so very sour!
Other days I am stormy gray
sorrowful and furious,
useless and locked up,
stressed and worn out.
But today I am as happy as a lemon!
Cenya Jacobson, Grade 6

Shimmering Shining Stars
I am a shimmering star shining brightly in the night sky
I wonder what it feels like to be on Earth
I hear sounds of love and kindness
I see the World's fear
I want to be near
I am like fire in the darkness
I pretend to be as cool as the night
I feel the ocean breeze
I touch swirling clouds around me
I worry if I touch the ocean floor
I cry when the days pass on
I am a heart warming star that never burns out
I understand my journey will end
I say that the fear of never letting go is still inside me
I dream that one day I'll be with all my friends
I try to surf in the wind, whoosh
I hope to never die out
I am a star that goes on forever
Avery Cady, Grade 6

I Am Old
I am thick
I wonder why I am not very liked
I hear them talk about the others
I see smiling faces all around
I want to be liked
I am a million years old
I pretend to be new but they see through me
I feel lonely
I touch the shelf nothing else
I worry I will be thrown out
I cry when they close me with a big bang
I am alone as I always will be
I understand that I am old
I say a lot
I dream that I will be famous
I try very hard to be noticed
I hope that it all changes
I am a book
Lily Duncan, Grade 6

Heaven
Heaven where our lost loved ones go
when they have gone into an eternal sleep

Heaven, where my soul longs to go when
it has graduated from only being human

Heaven, every human being
has their own version of it

Heaven, A magnificent place
to go the place I want to go
Haley Quillen, Samantha Carpenter, and Leyna Dockter, Grade 4

Live in the Now
Adults don't remember the changes we are going through now
They only think about the past and the future
I will remember them
I don't know why but I will
People only remember the past
Think about the future
But why not think about the now
Why not
This past will stay were it is
The future is a mystery
But the now is well…now
So forget the past
Don't think about the future
Live in the now

Janie Tyree, Grade 6

Soccer
All I could hear was my breath
I had to set aside the yells all around me
The wind blew in my face as I ran
Watching every move the opponent took
Like a lion with their prey

My mind trailed off to the first soccer game I'd ever played
Then I remembered that it's different now
I'm here at this game, I thought
I looked at the clock with just 30 seconds left
We were down 4-2, there was no chance

The buzzer went off
We were out

Evelyn Ryan, Grade 6

Flowers
Flowers, oh my flowers
You can grow as tall as towers.
We plant your seeds
Then we pull your weeds.

We will then watch you grow
But never in snow.
You start to grow in spring
As pretty as a ring.

And when it starts getting fun
There is a disappearance of the sun.
That's when we start heading home
So you could be a flower, oh my flower again.

Sarah Bielawski, Grade 6

Fear
Curled up in a ball
Screaming at the top of your lungs
Shiver, sweat, paranoid
Fear is flying on an airplane a week after 9/11

Dylan Perlow, Grade 6

Elvis Presley
Elvis Presley loved rock "n" roll
Helping people he had a heart and soul
He made it on the silver screen
Also, he had a very big dream.

After leaving the Army he resumed his career
Singing and dancing he never had fear
He played the guitar
And he was a famous star.

He had blue eyes and suede shoes
And he never liked to lose
His hair was black
And he sang on a eight track.

Sophia Busciacco, Grade 5

Baseball
Baseball is a lot of fun,
We play outside in the sun.
Sometimes it is a hard sport,
That's why the games aren't so short.
Sometimes baseball's as slow as a snail,
If we start hitting we will never fail.
While we play baseball we never sit,
Unless we're waiting to get up and hit.
The baseball goes speeding out of the pitcher's hand,
In the catchers glove it should land.
We love it when we have to run,
Baseball is so much fun.
Baseball is an exciting game,
It puts all of the other sports to shame!

Luke Elitz, Grade 6

The Wonderland of Mysterious Plants
I can feel the flower petals on its stem
while the mountains are guarding the flowers
that are dancing silently in the wind.

The sun is envious watching the valley of flowers
below having the best time of their lives.

I can smell the wonderful mint in the exquisite
glowing green leaves.

The delightful colored plants are swaying
joyfully in the cool wind.

I can taste the sweet pollen in the terrific flowers.

Payton Rechkemmer, Grade 4

Spring
The flowers are blooming, the trees are budding.
The grass is growing, the wind is blowing.
Our spirits are rising, the willows are crying.
The rain is pouring, it's finally Spring.

Elijah Maxson, Grade 6

Farming

Farming is a fun thing to do
It is a lot of responsibility to do
You feed them twice a day
You don't have any days off

Farming is a fun thing to do
You can make a lot of money
By selling your cows

You can get money for selling your star cows
It is also a lot of fun to raise them
They can be mean they can be nice

Farming is a fun thing to do
It is a lot of responsibility to do
You feed them twice a day
You don't have any days off

Dustin Hesser, Grade 6

Turning into Spring

Spring here starts cold, the snow on the mountains,
Snow on our rooftops, our noses have stuff,
We blow them every day. Snotty fountains,
We sneeze a whole lot, we go huff and puff.

You catch the cold and slip on icy ice,
You can also get a dreadful disease.
In your garage, there might be hidden mice,
The pretty bloomed flowers will start to freeze.

However, the weather will become warm,
There will be many blossoms flourishing.
The awful weather will quickly transform,
Animal mothers will start nourishing.

Spring will be cold then turn to something warm,
Cold will change to warmth as seasons take form.

Yvonne Kim, Grade 5

The Weather Comes and Goes

The weather comes and goes,
it rains and hails and snows.
The wind is a wolf, hidden from sight,
creeping and howling all through the night.
The summer sun pats the sand
with his warm, gentle hand.
The rain is like a clown,
dancing and falling to the ground.
The snowflakes are little ballerinas,
falling in Anchorage and in southern Argentina.
The hail is falling all around, pounding
on the frozen ground.
I like the weather an awful lot,
you enjoy it, too, it's the only weather
you've got.

Kade Sanderson, Grade 6

Pond Deep

You bark and wag your tail
at the sight of your blue leash.
I hook it to your collar
and grab your favorite green tennis ball.

I throw the chewed ball
And it lands in the clear blue water.
You can see its blurry reflection.
You fetch it.
It's so shallow you don't even have to swim.
You retrieve it
and drop the saliva soaked sphere at my feet.
I throw it farther
and you chase it mid-way.
You stop.
I urge you onward.
Stubborn, you refuse.

I went swimming that cold summer day.
At least I know my love for you
is pond deep.

Annabelle Salvin, Grade 6

My Comfortable Bed

My comfortable bed,
The layers that cover me freshen my soul
Sinking in the mattress on those
Stormy, thundering nights
The springs singing loudly
A terrible song
But to my memory singing a lullaby
Snuggled up tight giving a big hug
A warm hug that makes me comfortable
It's the boat that protects me from the sea
The train that keeps me safe on the ground
And the log that keeps me away from the lava
My bed gifts me a puff of fluff
That supports my mind full of dreams
Jumping and bouncing
On the old screeching springs
And that is where other fun begins
Falling down onto my bed
Always there to catch me when I fall
And finally at the end locks my thoughts up tight in my head
My comfortable bed

Maria Reyna, Grade 4

Flowers

F luent colors that shine from the sun
L ush petals that bend gracefully on the ground
O rnate hues that brighten your backyard
W et, soft stems that support the flowers
E cstatic, lively shades that sparkle on the grass
R apturing scents that show beauty in the flower
S weet and smooth parts like in a rose or tulip

Neha Skandan, Grade 6

Why Can't We Have Freedom
Why can't we have freedom like the birds flying so high?
Why can't we have freedom like the children running by
Why can't we have freedom like the clouds in the sky?
Why can't we have freedom like the grass swaying high?
Why? Why? Why?
Why can't we have freedom like the fish swimming by?
Why can't we have freedom like the trees up so high?
Why can't we have FREEDOM?

Emma Hickey, Grade 5

Lies
Lies.
Lies are tearing the world apart.
Lies, we know they are wrong but we still tell them.
We can't help but hear them.
Why do lies keep us from telling the truth?
Lies can grow from something small to something big.
Lies.
Lies.

Danielle Murriell, Grade 6

Freedom
Freedom
Smells like a cherry with a hint of strawberry
Tastes like sweet fluffy cake
Sounds like something breaking through the atmosphere
Feels like life in a time of the world
Feels like hope in the world
Feels like freedom coming soon
Freedom

Bayla Furmanek, Grade 6

Low-tide of Morning and High-tide of Night
It was low-tide of morning and high-tide of night
the massive round ball returning
it ascends with such certainty but also with grace.
Such providing an end for the dim
the people gaze up with hope at the sky
to guide them out of the darkness
but hope is futile, the people know this
darkness will happen again.

Preston Pitzer, Grade 6

Angry
Angry
Smells like annoyance
Tastes like stale, burnt popcorn
Sounds like screaming at the top of our lungs
Feels like salt in the wound
Feels like dead flowers in the winter
Feels like confusion
Angry

Jessica Zajac, Grade 6

The Secret Garden
In the chill autumn air
You spot a gazebo standing there
All the orange leaves
of the big oak trees
are falling to the ground
The small brook whispering to the wind
The sun shines onto the serene secret garden
you are finally home

Charley Holt, Grade 6

Baseball
Baseball, the most famous game on dirt.
Also the best game on earth.

The sound of wooden bats cracking,
then the crowed starts clapping.

The ball player walks off the field with bragging rights
and a good night.

Jacob Thomas, Grade 6

Leaves Boil Off the Oak Tree
Leaves boil off the oak tree
Mice flee out of their holes, and play in the leaves
Crunch squeak squeak!
Sun changes color to purple, it's a beautiful sunset
It looks like a flock of purple and red birds
Ducks fly over my head quack quack quack
I guess they're going to their nest
It reminds me that I should go to my own nest

Regan Thomas, Grade 5

Lady Bug
L ovely to look at
A ngels of the insect world
D ots all over their back
Y ellow, pink, red, or orange

B eautiful when it lands on my shoulder
U sually found near plants
G ardens are one of their favorite places, too!

Margeaux Donchez, Grade 6

Skiing
Slipping down the silver slopes
Gliding like a bird
When you fly up the bump
Then down you go
As if the wind was taking you to a faraway land...
With the howl of wolves in the crisp dark night
Makes you shiver with all your might
As you ski on

Ian Haddad, Grade 5

Fishing

Fishing is fun
Sitting in the sun

Our ride is grandpa's boat
We can sit all day and float

I get out my rod and put on a hook
And I think of all the fish my mom will cook

If the fish aren't biting we sometimes troll
But I better hold on to my pole

We head back to the shore
With more than just four

I fill up my dish
With all my Jackfish

Toby Siemens, Grade 4

Holocaust

They wait in camps, wait, wait.
Only to meet their fate.
Children watched their parents shot and fall into pits.
Others watched them get chopped up, bit by bits.
The Nazis went on a killing spree.
These heartless, unholy beasts.
These Nazis gave no remorse.
They slay the Jews with brutal force.
Meanwhile Hitler sits and feasts.
He is the deranged one.
He is the beast.
Nazis were his evil slaves.
They killed and filled the graves.
Many Jews died in pain.
Many Jews died in vain.
This was his joy. His win. His time.
Our Holocaust.

Trevor Howell, Grade 6

Music

I am music.
You know me for the sweet sounds you hear.
My mother is melody.
My father is rhythm.
I was born in a band.
I live in your ears.
My best friend is dance.
We like to give kids performances.
My enemy is silence.
Because it always tries to stop me from singing.
I fear that everyone will forget about me.
Because silence will take over the world.
I love it when people nod their heads to my sound.
Because it shows that they appreciate my effort.
I wish that one day everyone will be able to create me.

Eileen Chen, Grade 6

Dancing Irish

One thing I love to do,
Is dancing like you never knew.

I love when the music goes on,
It's always such a lovely song.

The music always soothes me, It relaxes me so much.
It holds me like a infant, with a mothers gentle touch.

I step onto the dance floor,
I just can't seem to get much more.

It can be very stressful, yes indeed.
But to be the best, hard work is what you need.

Irish Dancing really moves me, I love to dance a lot,
It's just like an ice cold drink, on a summer day that's hot.

Brianna Kane, Grade 6

Land of the Blue

When you enter my land you see two doors
One leads to friendship and another to bores.

I choose the friends door for I know the way
To all the friends I see each and every day.

When you enter the door you hear a sweet song
That just keeps you moving along and along.

There are animals galore and smiles see you through.
All the love and danger in the Land of the Blue.

How do I get to, this land of great love?
Well, you look in your mind at a land way above.

When you see what I mean, it will make it quite clear,
That the land you are seeking is really quite near.

Neely Burns, Grade 5

About Me

I am a caring, kind person, I'm silly and smart, but not very serious.
As happy as a little kid on Christmas,
Friendly as a puppy,
My hair is blonde like the ocean sand,
I am not musically talented and do not play in the band,
My eyes are stars in the sky,
Although I can be loud, I'm pretty shy,
My hands are as warm as my heart,
My favorite subject in school is art,
My smile is as big as the state,
I never like to be late,
I'm as knowledgeable as a teacher,
I'm as fun as a roller coaster,
When I'm bored I like to swing from trees,
This is me.

Reilly Cahill, Grade 6

Where Are the Words?

Into my mind, the words will fly,
Twirling into the sky,
Traveling near and far,
Away into the stars…

Swimming in the deep,
Ready to leap,
Out into the air,
With so much flair

Ready to pounce,
Springing up with a bounce,
Fully projected,
All so connected

As the words flow,
They move so slow,
Coming towards me,
They are the key…

They are the words,
Tweeting like birds,
The ones I need…
For my poem!

Simren Jayaraman, Grade 6

Earthquake

An earthquake is not a feeling of fear,
It's a feeling of death.

An
earthquake
devours

the buildings and cars around you,
every person in sight.

Earthquakes
feel alive
around
you

as the cold surrounds you.

Earthquakes
are as fatal as bombs,

And as it shakes,

Everybody
is in fear.

Sophia Caleca, Grade 5

Heroes

I am not a hero.
But, I don't need to be.
Because, I'm in my own world.
And that's okay with me.

Because, when I'm alone.
There's someone always there.
A word I like to call family.
No matter when no matter where.

Hey, take my advice.
Family is your hero.
They will always be there.

I am who I am.
Because, that's who I want to be.
And like I said.
No matter when no matter where.
That's okay with me.

Ca'Mari Walden, Grade 6

Cat

Pointed ears up,
Eyes revealed, green as emeralds.
Dirt colored pelt twitching
As she trods from
Her
Silk lined bed.
Sharp teeth shown
As her gaping mouth
Forms a yawn.
Whiskers like frozen tree
Branches straighten, losing
Their shakiness. Ears
Move uncontrollably. Pink
Pads feeling the rough
Ground return to
Their rightful place
In the soft fabric, twirl
Two times, and a head is
Rested.

Jezebel Posey-Risberg, Grade 4

Seagull

I stretch my frosty wings
for a morning glide.
The sun peaks out like a mouse
cautiously coming out of its hole,
then darts back behind the clouds.
I flap and swoop down
like a maple leaf ruffled by the wind.
I elusively dart between the reeds,
enjoying the coolness of the breeze.
I fly with grace, no one can compare.
With my wings I glide swiftly in the air.

Shelby Carter, Grade 6

A Morning in the Rainforest

Among the weeds
and grasses tall,
a gentle humming begins
to throb.

A speck of light
comes in the door,
the animals at rest
no more.

The drenching rain
washed the sun's face
the monkeys swing from trees
with grace.

A drop of water
here and there.
Thus passes morning
all the year.

Alyssa Vorobey, Grade 5

To Write a Poem

As white as snow
As light as a feather
As bright as the sun
Can't wait for another!

Like a twig
Like a quill
Like a paintbrush
With art as its will.

My part is clear
My feelings are true
The words are there
And they flew.

There are many ways
Like days of a year
To write a poem
So give a cheer!

Ananya Rao, Grade 6

Pink

Pink is the color of the sunset.
Pink is a field of blooming flowers.
Pink is a kitten's soft, wet nose.
Pink is the petals on a rose.
Pink smells like a warm summer day.
Pink tastes like watermelon popsicles.
Pink sounds like a harp.
Pink looks like Valentine's Day.
Pink feels like sticky Laffy Taffy.
Pink makes me want to ride a roller coaster.
Pink is my favorite color.

Norah Scott, Grade 4

Dogs
Long, fantastic ears...
Obedient and proudly
Standing at the park!
Jessie Campa, Grade 5

Sunlight
Sunlight peeking through
trees big and colorful with
birds around singing.
Isabella Verhage, Grade 5

Animals in Rain
Rain is pouring down
As animals seek refuge...
Peacefully sheltered.
Emmanuel Cendejas, Grade 5

Spring
Raining all the time
Growing season is starting
Summer's on the way!
Daniel Serna, Grade 5

Spiders
Quickly trapping prey
Creepy, crawling arachnids
Blend into the ground!
Raymundo Garfio Quezada, Grade 5

Nature
Golden, crunching leaves
Wilderness flowers popping
Endless brisk outdoors...
Amber Shaver, Grade 5

Frogs!
Looking for water,
Jumping across lily pads...
Love to swim around!
Patrick Strauch, Grade 5

Springtime
Fields of prancing deer,
Rabbits hopping all around...
Birds glide through the air!
Joshua Robertson, Grade 5

Spiders
Eight long, pointy legs
Tiny, skinny, grey body
Stringy, sticky webs!
Joshua Ormsbee, Grade 5

A Home, House and My Home
A home is a home:
Always welcoming you and its dwellers,
Alive with the voices and laughter of a lively family
Customized with interior decorations,
Safe with a family watchdog and alarm.
A house is a house:
Unwelcoming and shoving you past, leaving you with chills,
Dying and yearning for someone to buy that poor soul,
Boring, empty with molting wallpaper and dusty carpets,
Dangerous with rickety floorboards and a broken roof.
Your home is your home:
Calling you in to join again,
Wild and reckless when you imagine it's something else,
Special with your favorite designs and decor,
Secure, a haven and resting from any problem or thief.
A home is a home and is not yours to judge
A house is a house but not yours to keep
Your home is your home to:
Have, enjoy, work, rest, protect, love, and BE ANYTHING YOU WANT TO BE!
Lily Banks, Grade 4

Unwanted Rose
I am a rose, deep red, like blood
I wonder about the world around me that I may never be able to explore
I hear the light rain around me start falling, harder and harder, with each drip drop
I see the pounding raindrops, slowly settling on my petals
I want to be seen as one of them, one of the other beautiful flowers
I am a rose
I pretend that I am as tall, as pretty, and as strong as all the others
I feel my petals suddenly pull against me, withering in the strong wind
I touch the sky but soon the wind just pulls me down once again
I worry as I wish to grow powerful and strong
I cry when I realize how fast time is flying by
I am a rose that is running out of time
I understand, now, that I will never be like the others
I say to myself that it is okay to be different
I dream to be a queen, pretty and amazing
I try to accomplish that dream
I hope that one day I can do that, but for now it's all right
I am a rose, unique and like no other
Ella Poulson, Grade 6

Free Willow
First I was simple, within a little shell,
But then I grew roots, for I needed water well.
Next came the stem, then branches and a vine.
To get out and breathe air I found quite divine.
I lived a few years, and had became so tall,
That the ducks that I once thought were huge now seemed very small.
But when I was almost full grown, just by a few leaves,
There was an earthquake that uprooted me with several great heaves.
Yes, I know, I should be very sad.
But instead I am happy, very, very glad!
Even though I didn't become a full grown Willow Tree,
With my roots out of the ground, I've never been so free.
Alaina Douglas, Grade 5

Home to Me Is a Secure Warm Cottage
Home to me is a secure warm cottage
that cozy chair by the warming fire.

A place where I can feel safe and sound
like a bird maturing in its nest.

A comfortable isolated bed
friendly and inviting with a book on its sheets.

Home to me is an enchanted place
a place to learn and grow.

Home is somewhere I can play
using imagination from time to time.

Home is always where family is
keeping you happy and safe.

Alone in a chair every now and again
chasing small worries away.

Home to me is a place where furry friends live
four-legged, two-clawed, or even no-legged.

peaceful in the presence of the woods
this old cottage stands.

Home is place where I get to know myself
relaxed as a butterfly on wind.
Hannah Story, Grade 5

Gone
I'm called many names
But only two are nice,
The thoughts in my head can be abnormal
Demonic and chaotic are some words to explain,
That's why I'm gone

To be normal you have to have a key
But what about us without keys
Are we without sense if we don't have a key,
Is that why I'm gone

Gone to the point of no return
Nerves of steel breaking a little more each day
My emotions are complicated,
That's why I'm gone

Now past the point of no return I wonder:
What if there was no diversity or creativity,
Would the world be a better place,
Why live in fear people when some care about you,
I chose my destiny,
But now I'm rewriting it,
That's why I'm here
Sage Kinnison, Grade 6

Best Friends
They always have your back
Won't cut me any slack
But that's okay
When we listen to music together they click replay
We tell each other secrets
When it an important one I sit there speechless
Emily, Rylee, Brook, Rylee, Ashley, and Olivia
Maybe someday we'll go on a trip to Virginia
But as long as we're together
No matter the weather
We are invincible
If you break one of our hearts you better run
For we will come after you
For if you mess with one of us, you mess with all of us.
Anna Curry, Grade 6

Spring Time
Spring time is a wonderful time of the year
It brings me happiness and cheer

Enough of this winter air
The weather is never fair

I want to go outside wearing a sweater
Not bundled from head to toe I had my fun in the snow

But now it's all ice
Winter is not very nice

Spring is the one just enough sun
To have lots of fun!!!
Haley Zehr, Grade 5

I Am Creative
I am very creative.
I love to play.
I make up my own games.
I don't mind if someone plays.

My brother usually plays.
But sometimes he doesn't like my game.
And I just say okay.
Sometimes he likes the game and sometimes he says no.

So as you can see I am creative.
I don't mind if I play alone.
But if you want to play.
I will let you, and say okay.
Jacob Wilson, Grade 6

A Friend
A friend is there to mend all broken hearts,
A friend is nice to you right from the start,
So if you do not have one go out and ask,
You don't really know you might make a friendship that lasts
Selena Bauder, Grade 4

Spring Is Happiness

Spring is back,
Birds are here too.
Birds are singing their songs peacefully.
We finally see the animals peek out.
The animals are playing around,
All of them are out to explore.
All day long,
They are making new discoveries.
The animals look up to the night sky,
Imagining how the future will be.
The world is full of happiness.

Brian Ly, Grade 4

Candy

Chocolate bars
Minty mints
Crunchy Kit-Kats
Sweet jellybeans
Hershey Kisses
Tangy SweeTARTS
Sour candy
Striped canes
Peppermint patties
Colorful lollipops

Rusel Steele, Grade 4

Fast Kitten

Fluffy kitten
Chasing toys
Doing flips
Running fast
Eating food
Pawing you
Meowing constantly
Snuggle snuggle
Purr purr
Very shy

William Harrison, Grade 4

One Moment

Let's take this one moment
To give our thanks to those we love
And most of all give thanks… to God
He keeps us safe
All night and day,
So let's keep our love and faith in God

Lexi Dingwell, Grade 5

Poetry

Poetry is short, it is long.
Poetry is stacked, it's in lines.
Poetry is rhyme, it is plain.
Poetry is sad, it is happy.
Poetry can be anything,
anything at all.

Kennedy Jewell, Grade 4

Ode to Nature

Willow tree, willow tree
Won't you listen to my plea?
Please stand boldly over me
As I sing my song to thee.

Butterfly, butterfly
Gliding through the bright blue sky
Please bring comfort when I cry.
You will make me happy nigh.

Brave blue jay, brave blue jay
Listen to me as I pray.
Under bright blue skies I lay.
Make me smile when skies are gray.

Blowing breeze, blowing breeze
Making music in the trees.
Blow away the buzzing bees.
You can make me laugh with ease.

Nature's sound, nature's sound
You make beauty all around.
I can feel your love surround.
Free my spirit when I'm bound.

Ashleigh Patterson, Grade 6

The Hummingbird

His eyes are trained on his work
No time to stop and smirk,
He needs to go
For the oppressing foe
Is his growing hunger.

His wings not there,
A strip of hair
Is for his beak of yellow.
Just a fool,
Made of jewel
Sipping nice, sweet nectar.

He hovers on the flower buds,
Buzzing like a bee,
His beak descends
Into the well,
Forever it does seem.

Jittered up and down a while
Until he saw me there,
We shared a look
And then —
 He shot straight through the air.

Caleb Leach, Grade 5

Punxsutawney Phil

He said we'll have 6 more weeks of winter
I was happy for the snowmen I could mold
But, sadly, it is the end of March
And it is still freezing cold

It is after Saint Patrick's Day
And it snows, snows, snows
Hats, gloves, scarves, coats
Wind blows, blows, blows

We cannot go outside for recess
Sun is now just a dream
We all huddle 'round the heater
If we can't go outside, I'll scream

Now I am sulking in a corner
Wait a sec, look! The sun is glowing
It is like 65 degrees out!
And it has stopped snowing!

I run outside and have fun
I skip and shout and roll down a hill
I bask in the sunlight and climb a tree
Thanks for nothing, Punxsutawney Phil!

Nora Betts, Grade 5

Winter Is Over

The warm weather is finally here
I've been waiting for it for almost a year
It's time to take off our winter coats
And maybe go ride a motor boat

Even though in winter there is a cold breeze
That makes you sniffle, cough, and sneeze
I'll really miss that beautiful white snow
That is the opposite colour of a crow!

Melina Pittarelli-Papadeas, Grade 4

Sports

I love all sports,
If it is scoring a touchdown,
Or fumbling it,
If it is making a try,
Or being in a scrum,
If it is hitting a home run,
Or being struck out,
If it is throwing a strike,
Or throwing a gutter ball,
If it is shooting a basket,
Or getting a foul,
If it is scoring a goal,
Or going to the penalty box,
If it is pinning someone,
Or being pinned,
I love all sports no matter what.

Brandon Yoder, Grade 6

Mrs. Walker
Mrs. Walker is so sweet
Every time I get to see her is a treat.
She cares for me like her own child
Her personality is gentle, soothing and mild.

We really enjoy shopping
For pigs and Muppets—No stopping!
We shop at lots of stores
Even when our feet get tired and sore.

We go to church on Christmas Eve
She is the one who influences me to believe.
We put on our pj's to take a picture by the tree
We have been doing this ever since I was three.

Our relationship is very dear to me
I hope it will always be.
I really want her to see...
How much I love her and how dear she is to me!
Paige Edwards, Grade 6

Who Am I
I am an object
I wonder what it feels like to be wrapped in me
I hear people breathing
I see happy faces
I want to keep people warm
I am a cuddly object
I pretend to be a pillow
I feel human bodies
I touch warm skin
I worry about being forgotten
I cry when I feel lonely
I am a cuddly and sometimes lonely object
I understand that in the summer I'm pretty useless
I say "I'm sorry I was made."
I dream of being used again
I try to be helpful
I hope that one day I will be loved again
I am a blanket
A'nya Strazdins, Grade 6

Carter
Carter,
Son of William, Amy.
Who likes to play games, video games and go water skiing.
Who brings to Locust Grove his smarts.
Lover of dogs, sports, and bumper ripstick.
Who fears big spiders, horror movies and my older brother.
Who knows a lot about sports.
And desperately wants to be a millionaire.
Who wouldn't be caught dead singing in the shower.
Who hopes to one day become famous.
Who would like to be remembered for his awesomeness.
Cameron.
Carter Cameron, Grade 5

Unmasked
I am as free-minded as the wind,
a gentle breeze just rippling the water,
yet a tempest, making ten-foot waves

Unstoppable, that's me,
roaming freely as a wild cat,
but fiercely holding my stubborn ground

I persist like fire 'til the edge of time,
a gentle flame in the hearth, warming a winter home,
but still a blazing inferno, destroying five trees at a time

Racing through the deep, dense woods,
I'm seeking refuge,
yet I'm as open as a stranger standing naked in a crowd

The raging wind and surging sea
could never start to budge one that's as stubborn as myself,
but neither could a quick, small mouse
slip past me yet unnoticed

Unmasked, my secret lies within
Aidan O'Brien-Turner, Grade 6

Home
Home is magnificent
The place where I relax
Play
and sleep like a hibernated bear
In this cottage I play many sports
On the green grass yard like a grass plain.
Like baseball or football
Home is the place where I relax on my couch
like lying on a pile of soft cotton
The place where I sleep on a very cozy bed
like sleeping on a large fluffy pillow

At home I like to do many things
like playing and drawing
When I draw, I am an artist

At home I play baseball
and hit the baseball hard
like an airplane soaring through the air
catch the baseball well
throw the baseball well
 Home
Tyler Fales, Grade 4

The Appalachian Trail
The Appalachian Trail is the place to be,
 let's take a walk so you can see!

We will start in the south and walk to the north,
 put on your shoes and "Let's Go Forth!"
Halle Vidil, Grade 5

Winter

I love playing in the snow,
The sun makes it shine and glow.

It's Christmas time, we're kind and jolly,
Put up the mistletoe and holly.

Outside everything is white,
Trying not to get frostbite.

Making snowballs, going sledding,
The holiday cheer sure is spreading.

It's very cold, you get the chills,
Tobogganing down through the hills.

You have red cheeks on your face,
so you warm up by the fireplace.

The chilly air in the wind that blows,
there are icicles running off your nose.

All the trees outside are bare
Not the evergreen, which stands alone out there.

The snow then melts, the grass grows tall,
To the winter, I say "goodbye" to it all.
Abbie Morgan, Grade 5

Ode to Dreaming

Sitting on the couch watching TV
When a movie comes on
As I stare for hours
Until it ends

I walk up to my bed like a zombie
Half asleep
I get ready to go to sleep

As I slowly fall asleep when I touch the cloud pillow I start to dream
I felt like the most tired girl in the world
The dream starts to began

I dream about my dog
Woof, Woof
Giving me kisses then I awake

I go back to sleep I dream again
I dream the mountains roaring
What a dream

Another dream dreams the dream everyone dreams
Flash, Flash goes the cameras
Ahh, Ahh go the fans as I walk down the red carpet
Er, Er, Er goes the...wait that's my clock
Ode to dreaming
Kasia Puc, Grade 6

Remember

Remember the Holocaust,
The ones that were lost.
Remember the days of Hitler's rule,
The days that the Jews were treated so cruel.
Remember the cries all day and all night,
The Jews all wished Allies would stand up and fight.
Remember the fear in the face of the Jews,
The Jews all thought of what they might lose.
Remember the hate that Hitler had,
The things that he did were way worse than bad.
Remember the things that Hitler said,
The things that he said were filled with such dread.
Remember the gas chambers, poisons, and fire,
The fences that were covered in barbed wire.
Remember the soldiers and all their hate,
The Jews would just wonder what is their fate.
Remember the Holocaust,
The ones that were lost
Remember the Holocaust
Nathan Schmidt, Grade 6

Michael Jordan

Michael Jordan is famous for basketball
Some people think he knew it all
Inducted into the National Memorial Basketball Hall of Fame
He was probably the best at the game.

At the 1992 Olympics he won gold
Three NBA Championships he holds
Most decorated player in the NBA
Then his father passed away.

He retired from basketball
Then he started a career in minor league baseball
After a while he came to play
And was back to stay.

Retired from the game he loves
Now his dad watches from above
Known as the best basketball player
He will inspire me forever.
Madison Frank, Grade 5

Best Friend

Wind yourself up to start the day.
Don't waste your time, don't delay.
The clock ticks, reminds you why.
Why you don't have the time to cry.
"You...need...some help?" I begun to say,
"No thanks I got what I need to make the day."
"I know that's not true, stop being so blue."
The bear did say, "Yes, but what will you do?"
Then I reply, "I'll be your friend, from dawn til the end."
The bear then smiles back at me.
"Oh what a day this will be!"
Kamryn Greenland, Grade 6

Dreams

Once upon a time I was asked why I have so many dreams,
Looking at that now, it seems like some kind of scheme.
Giving up on creativity,
Would be living in a world of captivity.
Without my dreams I would slowly crumble,
And my sleeping visions would slowly tumble.
I have dreams of imagination,
Any of them, there is no recreation.
All of the magic of my nighttime slumbers,
Take away the scariest thunders.
Any season of dreams will do,
As long as I dream with all of you.
Glimpses of all of my hopes flash in those times,
Of nighttime hallucinations every night.
Now why don't you proceed,
In asking about all of my dreams?
I have all of these dreams each and every night,
Because it chases away the nightmares with their light.

Annie Regenhard, Grade 5

I Was Free

A light breeze whisks me from the chains of Earth,
soaring sunward, reaching for something not even I know,
I drift through the clouds, letting gusts of air sweep me about,
I am free from the terrors of things far below me,
up here I am a bird, soaring near and far.

But suddenly my wide awake dream is interrupted,
howling wind, freezing rain, pounding on me,
and I wish I was back where I came from, where I belong,
back with everything I know,
and everything I love.

But the rain keeps pounding, crashing, pouring,
And I'm falling down, down into a deep abyss of color,
All the while the rain keeps pelting,
As I leave this to fate, I have one last comforting thought,
I was free.

Becky Rasmussen, Grade 6

Haunted by the Thought

Walking, tripping, crying, night.
Searching and hoping for the light.

Tossing, turning, lost in thought.
Forgetting things that I've been taught.

Full of sick feelings, like I'm fighting in war.
Wishing for the life I had before.

Listening, waiting, loud and clear,
Wishing for some hope to hear.

Imagining and living through the thought's ignite,
I am going to die tonight.

Mari Tobo, Grade 6

The Baseball Game

The sound of the crowd cheering,
the crack of the bat just as it leaves the pitcher's hand,
the cloud of dust as the player runs the bases,
it all comes together at a baseball game.
The delectable, smooth, creamy ice cream,
during the unbearable heat,
it all comes together at a baseball game.
The sweet smell of fresh cut grass,
the loud over-powering music,
I wish I could see a baseball game every day.

Gracie Giordina, Grade 6

My Two Purples and My Blue

When I think of a bright grape purple
I am both happy and excited for one beautiful heart racing day
I have energy building up inside of me, just waiting to get out
making me hop and jump about all around my little town
But sometimes life's not so swell and I think of a lilac purple
I feel shy and weak, and not myself
It's as if nothing's possible and all's gone wrong
I do not speak I only think, inside my head I lazily dream
Now I feel Seaside classic blue
Calm, but ready for action

Savanah Bang, Grade 6

Little Red Fox

O little red fox why are you so still?
Aren't you getting quite a chill?
Why are you so posed toward the ground?
Do you see a little hound?

I am waiting for the right thing to eat.
My bright red coat will keep me warm and on my feet.
I hear my prey under the deep, deep snow.
I think it's a mouse, which is my foe.

Grant Walker, Grade 5

Why Does Friendship Matter?

Friendship is the sprinkles on my doughnut,
The strength in my back,
The light in my heart,
The freedom in my life,
The truth in my words,
The laughter in my head,
The respect in my help,
The care in my hug,
Friendship is all of the above!

Zoey Jones, Grade 6

Walking Through the Battle

Gun shots being fired every second of every minute
People in need to see their friends and family
Pain, grief and regret are on the battlefield
Blood stains across many uniforms
Citizens hoping and praying for peace

Jordan Caron, Grade 5

High Merit Poems – Grades 4, 5, and 6

I Am Richard
I am brilliant and joyous.
I wonder what's in the dark, deep universe.
I hear my college professors teaching math.
I see my interested fellow students.
I want 50 years of delicious Kentucky Fried Chicken.
I am brilliant and joyous.

I pretend I am a college student.
I feel proud of my academic achievements.
I touch my shining Nobel Prize in math.
I worry that I will get killed.
I cry when someone close to me dies.
I am brilliant and joyous.

I understand a lot of mathematics.
I say learning is something you should starve for.
I dream of getting a Master's Degree in math.
I try to study all academics, like language arts.
I hope to invent something brilliant.
I am brilliant and joyous.

Richard Claytemple, Grade 6

I Am Kylonna
I am a beautiful, singing island girl.
I wonder what life is really about.
I hear my voice, singing the National Anthem in a baseball stadium.
I see my beautiful island of Dominica from a small airplane.
I want to meet a person who loves me for who I am.
I am a beautiful, singing island girl.

I pretend to be on a stage every time I sing.
I feel my voice grow in clarity as I age.
I touch my soft, curly hair and smile.
I worry about failing in school because the expectations are high.
I cry because I long for a father to be there.
I am a beautiful, singing island girl.

I understand the strong love of friendship.
I say that love is equal and meant for everyone.
I dream about meeting a loving, sensitive person to marry.
I do my best to inspire others.
I hope that my life will be worth it.
I am a beautiful, singing island girl.

Kylonna Leevy, Grade 6

I Am Scottie
I am a girl who misses her dad.
I wonder when I will see him again.
I hear his laughter and hilarious jokes in my head.
I see his face making funny faces and singing random songs.
I want to have him back more and more each day.
I am a girl who misses her dad.
I pretend that I'm all right with him not being here.
I feel like my heart breaks each day without him.
I touch old memories and pictures of him and
my eyes begin to water.
I worry that he won't come back or he will forget me.
I cry when I remember that he has been gone for more
than three years.
I am a girl who misses her dad.
I understand that he loves me.
I say I need to be strong.
I dream for him to come back.
I hope that he will come home still loving me and my
sister and that he won't leave again.
I am a girl who misses her dad.

Scottie Atkins, Grade 6

Batter Up
It was my turn to bat
It was the bottom of the sixth
The pitch was slow
So I swung like no tomorrow
I did it! I did it!
I started to run until I realized...
I missed the ball.

It was my turn again in the bottom of the ninth
The pitch was curved so I thought I should swerve
Instead I stood tall
CRACK!
Right over the wall.

I finally did it, my first home run.
It was great. It was a miracle
How could it be true?
Beep! Beep! Beep!
How was I asleep?
Too bad it was a dream!

Carson Svidron, Grade 4

Crayon
Crayons
Coloring our world
Red, orange, yellow, green, and blue
There are so many creative things
That you can do
A swirl here, a swirl there
Use your imagination if you dare
You're in charge, so have some fun
The world will be brighter when you're done

Kelsey McGrath, Grade 4

Butterfly
B eautiful wing patterns
U nreal transformation
T ropical climate is where most live
T hought-provoking self-defense
E xtremely small eggs
R egal in flight
F astest butterfly can fly 30 miles per hour
L ifespan from 1 week to 1 year
Y oung spend most of their life as a caterpillar

Caroline Davis, Grade 6

Footprints
We were kids,
Laughing, playing
Until one day they were saying
You're not good,
Go away.

On these wagons they did take us.
Guns in arms, ready to break us,
Shot and beaten, taken, gassed,
What is left?
No one asks.

No one talks,
No one listens.
Not a whimper,
Not a whisper.

Silent screams, silent pain.
Silent worries, silent names

Numbers scratched on our arms,
Living hell, we're on a farm,
All of us have been mistreated

We're walking in footprints, of those defeated.
MeiLi Van Hise, Grade 6

A Hometown Hero
Swish! Now we are down by two.
Fifteen seconds left the coach calls a time out.
"We are going for the win!"
He tells our shooting guard to set a screen.
"Get the ball to Gold," he says.
The shooting guard sets the screen.
10, 9, 8, 7, 6, 5, 4, 3, 2, 1, Gold gets the three pointer off,
but he misses. But wait there is a foul, three shots.
Swish there is the first swish, and the second and
for the win he sinks it. Swish! The whole town cheers
A Hometown Hero.
Drake Schaeffer, Grade 6

Last Day of School
Every student everywhere
Is counting down right now
Waiting for that one last day
Where their frowns turn around
Their pencils small
Their erasers gone
Their memories are forever
Finally that one last bell that signals that it's over
School is done
Summer is here
Now the year's complete
Stephanie Williams, Grade 6

Here and There
I like to go running
I like to play
I like to have fun all through the day.

I like to yell and scream at my bestie,
But I hope that our friendship doesn't get fiesty.

I like to jump and jump in the wind,
Until next thing I know, I've been pinned!
It was my older brother, I should've known
Obviously, I wasn't blown!

I got him off me, and slapped him in the face
Then I started running,
I was clearly in a haste!
I outran him, finally that's over,
Then I look down, and saw a four leaf clover!

I just knew I was lucky,
Then before I knew it, I saw a little ducky!

I just looked and said, "Whoa!"
After that, turned and saw my brother,
I could only say one thing,
and that was, "NO!"
Amira Kines, Grade 4

Mom
As beautiful as a flower,
The sun when she's happy.
My mom is the most loving person in the world.

She is as energetic as a mountain lion chasing its prey.
She is the best photographer ever.
Her smile could light up the whole world.

I love when she takes me to Keystone pond and we feed the ducks.
My mom is full with laughter, she is the funniest person I know.
I have no clue what I would do without her.
Claudia Hicks, Grade 6

Home Run!!!
I grabbed my bat and headed for the plate,
it was a tied game
the pitcher threw the ball
STRIKE ONE!!!
I backed out the box and looked at all the fans around me
then I stepped back in the box and the second pitch flew at me
STRIKE TWO!!!
I focused on the ball as it floated in toward me.
I swung my bat
HOME RUN!!!
We won the game that night.
Miranda Sprouse, Grade 6

The Waldo Canyon Fire

Standing stiffly like towering giants
Protecting the people below
The city bathes in their shadow of defiance
Gazing at them, shimmering in the snow
Home of the aspens, the spruces, the pines
That sway with the wind's icy breeze
With a majestic dance, the tall trees climb
Approaching summer with ease
Then one fateful day, and no one knows how
A flame begins to grow
The people look up, filled with fear now
As the sea of orange devours their homes
Spreading over the mountainside
Like the tide washing over the shore
Stretching forever, miles wide
Sweet memories engulfed by the horror
All that is left of the once beautiful figures
Is a barren form, full of shame
A fragile monument, shattered into shards
Will it ever again be the same?

Kate Nelson, Grade 6

Summer

Summer is here!
Listen with your ear,
The sound of seagulls squawking,
Coming from over the bay while you are walking.
Look around with your eyes,
At the sunset in the skies,
Before going off into dreamlands.
Touch with your hands,
Rough and bumpy seashells,
While putting them away on shelves.
Take in a deep breath,
Of air salty and fresh.
Taste with our tongue,
A fresh hot dog bun,
Sitting by the stand,
Or while sitting in the sand.
Think with your mind,
"Hey, it's Summertime!
I can run around, dance, and play,
Without another school day!"

Maura Nolan, Grade 5

Paris

Paris stars are as bright as the blinding lights from the city, the shimmering landmarks are Paris' precious gems, the sweet aroma of the fresh croissants is like the smell of my mother's Christmas cookies, Paris is a grazing swan, all the amazing fashion is like one huge store, the city is one gigantic museum, the art is like a painting come to life, all of Paris' beauty is a wonderful book just waiting to be explored by millions of people

Mackenna Pierson, Grade 4

Rain and Water

Rain falls down
on an unfamiliar town.
It's a really grey day.
Nobody is out to play.

But rain is not all that sad.
It's not all that bad.
Yes rivers overflow,
but it helps crops grow!

The flowers need water just like you and me.
They use their roots to suck it up.
They're underground where you can't see!
They carry water up through their stem.
It fuels every part of them!

The rain falls into dried up rivers and seas.
It fills them to the brim for all the little fishies!
Then animals and humans eat the fish so they can grow.
So when you see rain and water, let it flow!

Hailey Rowe, Grade 5

The Secret Song

The secret song is where I lay,
Its sound against my skin in midmorning day,
The music so capturing my mind wanders off,
To the place the tunes take me so I can do stuff,
Like run and jump and fly in the air,
For I would love to take you, but that would not be fair,
Because you have your own secret song stuck up under your hair,
Just dig a little deeper, you'll find it soon,
And once you do, your secret song will be you.

Emma Bessey, Grade 6

Lake Erie

The elegant sun sparkles on the water
like glitter on a girl's shirt.
Cold nights freeze the water like fresh water on an ice rink.
Spring's warm days bring sunlight that melts the bitter ice
like ice cubes disappearing in lemonade on a lovely summer day.
The waves rush as fast as a roller coaster at an amusement park.
The serene water is as still as dew on my lawn in the morning.
Many rocks pile up on the lake's bottom like
6th graders trying to stampede into the lunch room.

Marielle Parks, Grade 6

Ode to Michael Jackson
Ode to Michael Jackson
your music makes me smile.
Ode to Michael Jackson,
your music's also worthwhile.
Ode to Michael Jackson,
you encourage people to heal the world.
Ode to Michael Jackson,
Oh and how I loved it, when you twirled
Ode to Michael Jackson,
Some people say you prance,
Oh man, but how I loved to watch you dance.
Ode to Michael Jackson,
People may say you're dead,
but Hee-Hee you're still alive in my head.
Ode to Michael Jackson,
the Beatles might have thought they had the world won,
but in actuality you're the only number one.
Ode to Michael Jackson,
I loved when you talked.
Ode to Michael Jackson,
now let's do the moon walk!

Maya Poziviak, Grade 6

My Home
My home is a beautiful and happy place
it is very bright and colorful
if you ever go there it is a nice and bright place
It's a place where I let my imagination run free
even my imagination has a giant world of its own
in my home is where I spend my long days and sleepy nights
My friends are where my home is
my memories house there too
I love my nice colorful and cozy home
because it's where my family and my friends are
This home this wonderful wonderful home
that is where my daily chores are accomplished
my home could be anywhere
My home where I live could even be yours too
It could be inside your large backyard
even if I know so little about it
it is still so much knowledge
all I know is this home is strong safe and bright
this is what my home is
it could also be yours
but that is what I call my home

Mina Vining, Grade 4

My Dearest
I knew from the moment I met you,
You made me laugh, you made me smile,
There was so many things we used to do,
We played and played for a long while
You gave me cute kisses,
We walked along the shore,
I tried to give you my best tour,
For the world isn't entirely pure
Some nights I cry,
But then I hear your feet pitter patter,
As my tears slowly splatter,
To my rescue you fly, with you I'll never die
We took silly photographs,
We stayed hidden from the aftermaths,
Aftermaths of the bad times, when things weren't okay
I'm ever so sorry,
You always rescued me,
But this time I couldn't rescue you,
I watched your eyes slowly close,
As I held you, on your last dying breath,
Rest in peace my dear pug.

Maddie Sweeney, Grade 6

Unknown Magic
I've heard the legions,
I've heard the stories,
But they all seem pretty boring,

But right now I'm here to shout,
While telling you what they are all about,

They all have kings,
They all have queens,
But that's not what I really mean,

From the smallest creature,
To the largest of them all,
The spell from the wizard will continue to revolve,

The magic that passes is throughout the air,
Casting a spell on those unprepared,

But something so powerful,
And something so rare,
A kiss must be dealt to those in despair!

Kloie Teague, Grade 5

Babies
Babies are a gift from God.
They are sweet, tender, and soft.
Always smiling and making funny faces,
making gurgle sounds when they are happy.
Always making a mess when eating.
Sometimes smelly diapers, too.
I love babysitting babies.

Leah Gross, Grade 6

Mountain
Mountain:
Dreams some adventurous prospectors mining in it
Remembers mines drilling into its back
Knows about ore
Reminds me of the beautiful Colorado and its gold
Wishes he could sell his ores
Is as wealthy with his minerals as Bill Gates

Kayne Hayden, Grade 4

A Building in the Sky

I am a building gazing over the busy city night
I wonder if the people that walk the streets are all right
I hear people chatting and cars rushing
I see the stop lights blinking
I am a building gazing over the busy city night
I pretend that I'm taller than the clouds
I feel the moon getting bigger each night
I touch as high as the stars
I worry about them destroying me one day
I cry when people leave me at night
I am a building gazing over the busy city night
I understand that I'm not that tall
I say that I'm the best ever
I dream of being restored
I try to wave to the planes passing by
I hope to be as tall as the Eiffel tower
I am a building gazing over the busy city night

Matthew Shackelford, Grade 6

Darkness

Darkness…
The hardest thing to escape in life
It is a disease that is drenched on us all
From our first breath, to our last
Some get the beautiful sky…
Yet, some get the storm
It affects us all mentally
And physically
It determines the path we take in life
Even the best get it, so don't be afraid
Some think it is impossible to face
And I say, "You just haven't found the solution to it."
Yet…
Someday you will find light
But use it wisely…
Because if you don't…
It will leave you stranded

Mark Argiro, Grade 6

My Home

What is a home to me?
well it's quite easy you see,
it's my room.
A place where I go every day
after school.
My bed.
where I think in my head
My rug.
as long as the earth and
is black and white just like a zebra
and how lays on the wooden floor.
The baby blue wall is as blue as
could be.
My soft as a cloud
sheets are spread out on my bed.
I dream of all the most wonderful I could ever
think.

Ariana Dominguez, Grade 4

My Friends, Braided Across the Page

I like how words are braided across pages wavily,
Like Haley's hair.
I like how grass blows mischievously,
like Sophie's smile.
I like Madison's encouragement,
always in despair.
I like Clara's songs,
topped with lots of flair;
Leah's enthusiasm,
with a side of sympathetic care;
Campbell's ideas,
creative and rare;
Natalie's entertainment,
with a silver sliver of dare;
Carly, kind and fair.
All the styles mixed together,
braided across the page.

Dana Douglas, Grade 4

Snow

The cold star slashing on my face in the stinging cold night.
I should have gone home earlier.
Mom will be worried.
I will be grounded for at least a week.
In the morning it will be glorious.
Ready for snowball fights and sledding,
Even if I can't play in it now.
The beauty will be incredible, sparkling.
Maybe Mom will forgive me.
She will see the need to go out there.
Snow angels.
Igloos.
Fun!
In the morning it will be glorious.
But now I wish it was gone.

Evander Deorsay, Grade 5

Look at Me

Yes, that's me
Look and you'll see
My hair as black as the night sky
My eyes as brown as dark chocolate
My arms as warm as a fire
My hands as soft as a warm blanket
My heart is a safe that could hold enough love for the world
I'm here to be your friend
I never would leave a friend alone
My friends think I'm nice, friendly, loving and kind
I live to make friends to all
I hope to be the greatest teacher ever
I dream that war would never exist again
It's all clear as can be.
That's positively, absolutely me.

Louisse Occena, Grade 5

Gymnastics
It makes me feel happy.
It makes me feel sad.
Here's a hint: when you fall
you're definitely not glad.
Don't get mad if you don't
qualify. There's always
a chance that you
may modify.
You're never
wrong when you
pick your song. Just
remember you're strong and
that you can do this.
Believe believe that's all you
have to do. Someday you'll be on
that podium and everyone will
be proud of you.
Chloe Kruslicky, Grade 4

Land in Rhode Island
The land in Rhode Island is low,
Water travels wherever you go.
But if you like to climb,
Then go for a ride,
To Jerimoth Hill which has snow.

Rhode Island is surrounded by water,
Sometimes it couldn't be hotter.
If you swim in a lake,
Avoid the mistake,
Of waking the brown, fat otters.

The state is short and quite small,
By Alaska it's nothing at all,
Yet, there's lots of people,
But not as much to triple
Arkansas's people who tend to say y'all.
Jerron Barker, Grade 5

The Animal
This is an odd animal
but very interesting.
It hops from tree to tree
and from rock to rock looking
for that animal it wants to eat.
It finally finds that animal
it wants to eat it. It pounces
and jumps on the animal.
It keeps running through
the desert looking for that special
animal it wants to eat.
Running through the night like a Ninja,
it hunts until bright.
You will not know this animal until
it snatches you.
Isac Filler, Grade 6

To Me Home Means Family
To me home means family.
my family can be very exciting.
I really dislike it,
when I hear them fighting.
on my couch is where I lay,
waiting to get my energy back,
so I can go outside and play.
My friends are waiting for me,
today will be a good day.
I should be on my way.
I give trust to my dad
to keep a roof over my head.
I give trust to mom
to get me into my bed.
my home is a safe place.
it is not prejudice
and welcomes any race.
I love my home.
And you should be grateful of yours, too!
because if you love it,
it will thank you!
Ava Smiley, Grade 5

Snowy Weather
Snowy weather is
White like feathers
Falling from the
Sky, and is soft like
A cloud that moves
From town to town.

Snowy weather is
Peaceful like an
Empty forest.

But is cold like
An ice cube in
The refrigerator.

Snowy weather is
A perfect time to
Play in the snow!
But here I am
Inside drinking
Hot chocolate!
So-Won Park, Grade 5

Imagine
Imagine a world
Where everyone is treated fair
Where we can all play together
Imagine a world
Where you can make the change
And you can stand up
Imagine a world where all is peaceful
Sarah Jane MacKenzie, Grade 5

I Am Me
I am me,
you are you.
Don't be someone you're not,
it explains a lot.

Don't try to fit in,
it shows who you are.
Do what you like,
who cares if they dislike.

They'll like you for you,
and that's good enough.
Don't be ashamed,
we're all the same.

I am me,
you are you.
We're all alike,
but different too.
Julie Barron, Grade 6

Ode to Cheetahs
They see food
And wait
A stilled tree
Unmoving

Representing patience
They know a foe
Like their very self
Concealed in the reaching grass

They pounce
A streak of spotted fur
They are patient
Until the right moment

No more patience
They have found an antidote
To hunger
Now they can eat
Ethan Streeter, Grade 5

Great Green
Green is the color of grass.
Green is the stem of a flower.
Green is a big ogre named Shrek.
Green is a huge, ripe watermelon.
Green smells like fresh mowed grass.
Green tastes like lime Gatorade.
Green sounds like the rustling of leaves.
Green looks like a spring day.
Green feels like a slimy frog.
Green makes me go outside.
Green is my favorite color.
Melanie Hahn, Grade 4

The Baseball
I am a baseball
I wonder what it is like to be in a glove
I hear the crowd yell, Whooo! Whooo!
I see the world for less than a second
I want to live in the world
I am a baseball

I pretend to be a bird
I feel the wind against my stitches
I touch the cold, hard wood for a long second
I worry I will get hurt
I cry when I get caught
I am a baseball

I understand that my stitches may fall
I say I am as old as a dinosaur
I dream of being the star of the team
I hope I never leave
I am a baseball
Seth Case, Grade 6

The Distraught Thistle
My beloved neighbors are tugged
out of the rich garden soil.
I believed our pointy spikes would protect us,
but the gardeners are relentless
with gloves as thick as my fear.
How I will yearn
for the rush of water traveling through my roots.
I dread the hour
of my departure
into a forested grave.
No longer will my roots thrive in the brisk fall air,
but I am determined
to continue my legacy
from seeds I leave in the ground.
Though my dread is as great
as the grains of sand
on all of earth's beaches
I will live on
through my descendants.
Rylie Baldwin, Grade 6

Link's Life
Oh how the arrows fly and the sword slashes
He beats the monster then dashes
His name is Link
He doesn't think
He get rupees and monstrous items
This is Link's life
He isn't high in height
He rides a horse
To get to dungeons faster
He gains experience to fight his nemesis
This is Link's life, he saves the world!
Dalton Paige, Grade 6

All About Me!
I am healthy, happy, warm hearted, and a hard worker
Have a pool and OLMC is my school

As wise as an owl and as quick as a cheetah
And as you all know, my middle name is Rita

Pretty, imperfect, and positively precious
As graceful as the waves on the beach

You might not know I love the snow
But not as much as I love the spring

Sometimes I'm sad, like ice cream without the cone
Other times I'm happy, like a dog with his bone

To conclude this poem there is one thing to say
And that is May 3rd is my birthday!
Nicole Steinbach, Grade 6

The Magical World
Tall trees that look like monsters
Birds whistling peacefully
Bees buzzing crazily
Happy white flowers
That look like angels
Vines knitting themselves
Thru the branches
Roots dangling
Out of the rough ground
Ivy swarming up trees
Corn stalks waving
Trying to say hello
Wind is cold yet calm
I feel like rocking
In a soft hammock
I know this is the place I belong
Madison Waehner, Grade 5

Believe
If a door is closed,
Open it!
If there's a decision,
Make it!
If you have a question,
Ask it!
If you need something,
Get it!
If there's an opportunity,
Take it!
Always have the courage to make your choice.
Follow your heart and believe in yourself.
You will know what the right choice is
once you have made it.
You know what the right choice is for yourself.
Always believe and trust in yourself.
Jaclyn Bauerle, Grade 6

Mechanical Pencil
I am a mechanical pencil
I wonder what I will write today
I hear other pencils scraping against paper
I see the paper in front of me
I want to write a long story
I am a mechanical pencil
I pretend to dance across the paper
I feel my led crack
I touch the bare desk
I worry that I will be thrown away
I cry out to the spare led across the desk
I am a mechanical pencil
I understand that I'm not like every other pencil
I say I will be abandoned soon
I dream of being reused
I try to stay together
I hope to be used forever
I am a mechanical pencil
Ayla Liles-Crayton, Grade 6

Pretty Trees in the Forest
I am a baby tree that has started to grow
I wonder if I will ever grow
I hear birds and monkeys on my branches
I see waterfalls around me
I want to be as big as the other trees in the forest
I am a baby tree that has started to grow
I pretend that I am the king of the kings of the trees
I feel the wind blowing in my leaves
I touch my branches and leaves
I worry if I am going to lose all of my leaves in the winter
I cry if I'll die
I am a baby tree that has started to grow
I understand why I am so small
I say hello to everything that lives in the forest
I dream that I'll have the most beautiful leaves
I try to be a good help to my universe
I hope to be the biggest tree ever to live
I am a baby tree that has started to grow
Emmylee Crockett, Grade 6

Cat and Mouse
CAT: I am a majestic feline.
I wonder what I will eat tonight.
I hear a small mouse pitter-pattering.
I see the mouse stealing from a trash can.
I want to eat the mouse, but I don't want to hurt it.
I am going to starve tonight.
MOUSE: I pretend the cat cannot consume me.
I feel as scared as a child at dawn.
I touch the rotten food in the trash.
I worry about eating tonight.
I cry that I might die tonight.
I am a tiny mouse.
BOTH: I understand the cat needs to eat.
I say I will not eat the mouse.
I dream the cat will disappear.
I try to find another mouse.
I hope the cat will leave.
I am the hungriest cat in the world.
Logan Hall, Grade 6

Flowers
No flowers grow on the path of normal,
For it is already paved,
Flowers do grow on your path,
The path of you,
The path that really matters.
Flowers grow on the path of friendship,
The path that is the hardest,
But has the best outcome.
New found friendships,
New found interests,
Flowers grow on the path of love,
Lucky for you if you walk along it.
No flowers grow on the path of burdens,
For it scares them away.
Flowers do grow on the path of forgiveness,
Because forgiveness is the best kind of giving,
You won't pick these flowers,
They shall pick you.
Annie Castagnero, Grade 6

What's a Tree?
A huge enormous woody plant.
A big use for resources.
Shelter for many animals.
Gives oxygen away.
Lives more than 7 years.
Barky on the outside,
Hairy in the inside.
and also makes food by itself.
Has so much weakness,
But always stays strong.
The problem is that we are losing tons of them,
So let's start protecting them.
That's a tree!
Sean Kim, Grade 6

Yellow!
When I think of yellow, I think of daffodils so gay,
when the wind blows I like to see them sway.

When I think of yellow, I think of bees collecting yellow pollen
I see and hear them buzz, oh, look at their yellow fuzz!

When I think of yellow, I think of the sun so bright and so lively!
When the sun comes out I feel so spritely!

When I think of yellow, I think of you!
Under the yellow sun and daffodils growing,
And the buzz of the fuzzy bees,
Oh Jeez, would you like some yellow cheese?
Pamela Conriquez, Grade 5

High Merit Poems – Grades 4, 5, and 6

Dogs
Dog
Kind and loyal
Scratching, barking, staying
As a girl's best friend
Golden Retriever.
Maddison Edwards, Grade 5

Recital
I dance
It puts you in a trance
I stretch my feet into the ground
And what I have found
Is that dancing is like my romance
Paige Fincher, Grade 6

Snowboarding
Snowboarding
fast and light,
flying, grinding, riding
amazed, peaceful, adrenaline,
flipping.
Travis Benson, Grade 5

Mercury Planet
Mercury
Small, dangerous
Revolving, fiery, rotating
A flaming flaring orb
Planet
Bryan Cox, Grade 5

Hero
Hero
Strong, brave
Working, training, saving
Pager sends them out
Fire Fighters
Gannon Getz, Grade 5

Narwhals
Narwhals
Smooth, majestic
Sparkling, fishing, loving
Narwhals love to fish
Whale
Rudolfo Johnston, Grade 5

Flowers
Beautiful, sweet
Growing, blooming, dancing
Vibrant splash of color
Treasures!
Rameeka Wajid, Grade 6

Home
Home is with my family,
My family is everywhere,
with my parents or grandparents

I have my family to love,
I treasure them,
look up to them and,
always do activities with them.

These people always have things to do
play, relax, swim,
is what we love to do

Mom, Dad, Brother,
they protect me always.
Cheering me up when I am lonely, having surprises, tricking me, loving me

We play, we relax, we watch movies
We are a family that will always be a family.

I treasure my home, this home I will have forever.
My home is the best home, I could ever have.

Without this home I would not be alive,
my home loves me and
I shall always remember
that my home will be with me forever.
Kirra Newsome, Grade 4

Sewn with Memories
A soft and cuddly blanket, thick and warm with memories
Stitches made of comfort and fabric sewn with love
Covered in both her hugs and her tears
There are no worries on her mind with a teddy bear clasped in her arms

Love lies inside these precious possessions
Though simple, they are reassuring
Holding many memories
To the little girl they come alive

And then come those tough days
Her favorite teddy bear rips
Her beloved blanket is misplaced...
All of the early days, the treasured times
Are lost forever

The little girl has vanished
One look in the mirror tells me my childhood has come to an end
Now there are choices I will have to make
Without my stuffed animals

There are always times when I wish
I could hold my favorite toys once more
And become the five-year-old little girl I used to be.
Megan Doucette, Grade 6

Graduation

G oodbye my fellow friends
R est in peace elementary school
A way from all my classmates, I will be sad
D iplomas will be given to us
U nforgetable memories
A fresh start
T oday is the day in which we are set free
I t's time to move on to high school
O n to your next adventure
N othing will stop you from tackling the world

Emmanuel Fata, Grade 6

The Beauty of Spring

Spring is sunny and fun,
Riding your bike around
The park in a sunny day.
I love spring break,
What about you?
There is actually too much to do.
A day on the beach is a great way of tanning,
And relaxing in the sand.
You can say goodbye to winter,
Here comes spring!

Kemil G. Nyateu, Grade 6

New Friend

The one I see, over there,
standing, staring,
at something bare,
I inch, inch, inch, closer and closer until,
she turns to me,
her face, trying to hold back the drip, drip, of her tears,
I look into her eyes, with a slight smile,
her eyes looking back at I,
an unsteady stare,
then she hugged me.

Isabella Sullivan, Grade 5

My Little Sister

My little sister is funny, my little sister's cute
But sometimes she thinks she's an Easter Bunny.
She likes dolls but doesn't like to play with balls.
She loves ducks but hates hockey pucks.
She loves to sing and really likes Spring
But when her diaper gets smelly
I call her jelly belly.

Rachel Robley, Grade 4

Hitler

H is for his hatred of the Jews.
I is for the indented numbers scratched on the Jews.
T is for truly cruel to the Jews.
L is for lives Hitler has stolen.
E is for execution of the Jews.
R is for the rare survival of the Jews.

AJ West, Grade 6

Blue

Blue is cool
Blue looks like the sky, water,
And my lunchbox

Blue smells like blueberries, water, and blueprint paper
Blue sounds like a Bluebird chirping, a cry of joy, and a joke

Blue feels like water, a blue T-shirt, and a globe
Blue tastes like Blue raspberry and blueberry
Blue is my favorite color

Matthew Pelletier, Grade 4

Mother

Mother, you make me smile when I am sad
Mother, you make me laugh when I am mad
Mother you help me through the ups and downs
Mother you guide me all around
Mother, you are always there for me any time
Mother, you help me climb the highest mountains
One day I will miss your kisses because you are my best friend
And you will be there till the end
If I have to I will say it over and over again
I love you mother

Taylor Swope, Grade 6

Spring Activities

Spring is back, FLUFFY clouds are here,
Children catching butterflies,
And drinking lemonade.
Families riding bikes,
And exploring new places.
Friends are roasting marshmallows,
And having camping fun!
There's no time to be mad or sad,
So come on out and have some spring break
FUN!

Louisa Lieu, Grade 4

Lost in Thought

My dad said to write something from the heart
so here it goes; past the valves, through the veins
then it made it to the brain.
there it is and there it stays,
caught in thoughts from yesterday.
This is why my poems blocked,
and I hope you give this one lots of thought.

Owen Hunter, Grade 6

Blue

Blue looks like blue skies and the ocean
Blue smells like mint gum not out of the package
Blue sounds like blue waves crashing on the beach
Blue feels like sticky, sugary, cotton candy
Blue tastes like blue cotton candy and mint blue gum
Blue is Peace

Natalie Alldred, Grade 4

High Merit Poems – Grades 4, 5, and 6

Walking Along the Sidewalk
There we were,
Walking along the sidewalk.
Holding hands with bounce in our step,
For we thought we were safe,
Walking along the sidewalk.
Father reached down and picked me up,
He swung me through the air,
I leaned against his shoulder,
As he handed me a teddy bear,
I clutched it close to my heart,
I would never let it go,
Walking along the sidewalk.
A man dressed in fancy attire,
Dad whispered, "Oh no! He's a squire!"
Walking along the sidewalk.
My dad yelled, "Alise run, run, far away!"
"He will never catch you!"
Sprinting down the sidewalk.
I haven't seen my dad; they probably took him away,
The only thing I have to remember him by is that teddy bear,
That has been close to my heart since that very day.
Shannon Seidel, Grade 6

The Blanket
The fire crackled as the sparks
Danced high the warmth and
The light felt good on the cool and cloudy evening.
The clouds got angry and the
Wind picked up the beautiful sparks
Lost there light the crackling of the
fire got drowned by the roaring thunder.
The thunder roared the lighting
Flashed the rain poured down on the
Wetting fire and our marshmallow
Were ruined by the threatening rain.
An idea came to someone's mind
"Let's build a blanket house." We brought
A blanket along with a wagon we
Draped it over the wagon and the swing.
The sparks danced high once again
We were having fun in our
Blanket house which protected us from the pouring rain.
I wasn't there a scene but in my
Eyes I see the hand of God that is the blanket
He protects us from the horror of this world.
Adelheid Waldner, Grade 6

The Dolphin
The grey smooth dolphin jumping out of the water
the sun shining on the water,
the dolphins dark beady eyes looking in the ocean,
then dives back into the shining water.
Every bit of shining water starts to go dark it is now night
and now the dolphin will go to sleep
until the shark has awaken the midnight sea.
Abbie Rasmussen, Grade 5

Family for Now
My home
is your home, for now.
Other Dogs have been here before you two.

I remember the first day you two came here,
both of you recognized the dog next door.
A week later, I figured out
that the dog next door was your sister.

You two didn't have names at first.
My Dad named you,
the one with white socked paws, Chloe
I named you,
the one with long white booted paws, Hachi,
after I watched the True Story Of Hachiko.
Now,
you two are my family for now.
Natisha Avalak, Grade 6

The Owl and the Sun
I am an owl,
I wonder how far I can soar,
I hear myself cooing a soft song,
I see the sun rising in the horizon,
I am the sun,
I pretend that I am as bright as I think I am,
I feel extremely warm,
I touch a small heart on Earth,
I worry that no one will take my place when I go,
I cry that someday I will not be seen,
I am the Owl and the Sun,
I understand that the Sun will rise and the Owl will leave,
I say not to leave I am your friend,
I dream that the Sun and I could live in harmony,
I try to convince the Owl to stay,
I hope to one day live together,
I am the Owl and the Sun.
Alexia Baines, Grade 6

Halloween
The festival that's fun
The festival that's funny
It's Halloween everybody, the festival of scares

People dressing up in different costumes
Who's who we don't know
A bucket full of candy
A bucket full of scares
It's Halloween everybody, the festival of nightmares

Ring the doorbell, say trick or treat
Get some candy then go eat
Go to every house in the town
Dress up as I don't know maybe a clown
It's Halloween everybody, the festival of scares
Saniya Khanna, Grade 6

June

June is warm
June is hot
In June you show your father you care
Because in June, Father's Day is near
June is when kids want to play
June is when you put loads of sunscreen on
June is summer
June is when the sun shines bright
June is when you stuff your face with ice cream
June is when the rain says goodbye
And the sun says hello
June is when homework is thrown away
And parties come in the way
You can hear June when the children laugh
June is in the middle of the year
June is when vacation starts,
School stops
And kids go off on ferry rides
Most of all June is when fun arises
And everyone has a smile on their face!
Baneesh Khosa, Grade 5

A Place to Play

A place to play is not in the stars
It is no deeper than the ocean
A place to play is in your heart's desire

I can think of many places
But only in my imagination
A place to play is somewhere safe
Where you feel at home and not in another place

A place to play is somewhere unique
A place to play has to be in your own style
As long as you don't go beyond the stars
You're safe and sound

A place to play is in our hearts
Where we can imagine everything we see and hear
Where we feel nothing can stop us
Where no one can tell us NO!
Where we choose our destiny
A place to play is all of that.
Emily Zylstra, Grade 6

Visions

I have visions of the future
Visions of my teachers telling kids to turn in their homework
Visions of my friends laughing and doing activities
Visions of people I don't even know
Visions of my family on holidays
Thoughts I have are of me being famous
Thoughts I have are of me curing diseases
Thoughts I have are me saving the poor
Hopefully my visions and thoughts will happen
Ennui Knapick, Grade 6

Storm of a Hurricane

I am the storm
I wonder why I am feared
I hear worried children, shivering like they're made of ice
I see them hiding
I want to be nice,
But I am under no one's control
I pretend I am a hurricane
But I feel very small
I touch the sky and reach for the ground
I worry of my oh so little powers
I cry my tears of rain drops
I am a small storm who yearns to be big
I understand my potential
I say I can be better
I try I try I try
I hope some storms smaller, don't survive my storm
I am a small storm, who's now a hurricane.
Lewie Lawrence, Grade 6

Summer

Summer is almost here.
I can smell it in the air.

It's my favorite time of year.
Am I going on vacation? I don't know where.

All the time in the pool
just as cool as going to school.

Fourth of July
It's super fun; I will not lie.

The rest of the summer is also fun.
I don't ever want it to be done.

Bye, bye summer
What a bummer!
Noel Kowalkowski, Grade 5

So So Bored

I am water brushing against the
rocks.
I see fish every
day.
Fish
   fish
      fish
It gets really boring.
I wish I was a flower like the ones up the hills so I could be
pink or yellow not dark blue.
I wish I could be on top of
Mount Everest.
I wish I could travel to a desert so I could be hot.
I am water brushing against the rock bored every day,
nothing to do.
Danielle Martin, Grade 4

Water Lilies
Such a relaxing flow while the water lilies blow.
Deep under the blue water, seeing the beautiful green glow.
Beautiful reflection of the sun shining
on the bright blue water.
Pink and purple water lilies gloom,
While they bloom.
Bright green lilies shine on the pond.
At the same time as they bond.
Yet they go together so well.
Isn't that swell.

Sofia Gidaro, Grade 5

The Death March
They walked all day, they walked all night,
Every one of them filled with fright.
If they stumbled or walked too slow,
That innocent person would have to go.
When the people got a chance to rest,
Some thought it would be best.
But before they knew it, most people were gone,
The rest had to leave them and go move on.
Only some of them stayed alive,
But most of them could not survive.

Alexis Doherty, Grade 6

Crazy Colors
Some days I am Ripe Tangerine
All Hyped up
And Energetic,
Like I just had an espresso.
Other Days I am Burnt Spice.
Crabby and Cranky,
Careless and sleepy,
Ready to destroy the world with attitude.
But Today,
I am Frosted Coral; Ready to fill peoples buckets.

Cadence Tripp, Grade 6

Mikayla
Nice, funny, silly and crazy
Sibling of Ocean, Daylin, Abigail
Lover of dance, friends and family
Who fears fires and tornados
Who needs love and friends
Who gives a lot of love and kindness to people who need it
Who would like to see her aunt who died
DeBusschere.

Mikayla Debusschere, Grade 5

Star
Star star
You shine so bright
Shimmer shimmer
Please come out tonight
So everyone can see you shine so very bright

Ciera Oliver-Dares, Grade 5

The Ongoing Circus
The ongoing circus
the ongoing circus
has no destination
or pinpoint location
and certainly no hesitation
as the trapeze artists do flips and tricks
under the big top where they jump and land with a whump
and the crowds they laugh out loud
and they get amazed and praise the man who can
lift a 1,000 pound minivan
oh, that huge man
and at the end of the show
there are always mounds of clowns
after they fool around
the ongoing circus
the ongoing circus
has no destination
or pinpoint location

Pavel Hamill and Aaron Alexander, Grade 5

Winter
Snowflake falling down
      down
           down
all the birds have migrated
the snow covering the branches like little blankets
snowmen scattered everywhere
kids sledding down the hill with graceful swoops
snowflake falling down
      down
           down
boots thumping in the white snow
snowballs flying through the cold, frosty air
hot chocolate brewing on the stove
children ice skating on the slick ice
snowflake falling down
      down
           down
winter is my favorite time of year!

Elle Deith, Grade 5

Lego Set
Opening the box to the new Lego smell
Soon finding out there are two instruction books inside four bags
Seems like a million pieces, but nearly a thousand are inside
"Easier than it looks" you say to yourself
Opening to the first page
4 steps
One piece on another for forever

Hours have past
Fingers aching from such small pieces
Like the world's most complex jigsaw puzzle.
But still knowing what an accomplishment you have completed
Proud of paying for that Lego set.

Alex Cain, Grade 6

Growing Up

Mitten, hat, smile,
Happy times,
Remember those times when you were young,
Not a care in the world,
No right, no wrong.
Just a happy song,
Princesses and Pirate Ships: Fairies and mermaids,
Magic all around.

Remember those times,
Never forget,
Hold them in you heart FOREVER!

A fun filled day, with joy and play,
Heavy eyes and a dream.

Now think back to now,
You are older and brighter,
Capable of so much more,
Responsibility, and obligations
Growing, growing, growing, each day, of every year,
Taller and taller, above the world,
Sometimes we consume ourselves in the wonders of today,
As we continue to grow we tend to forget, those happy, happy days.

Sidney Barbier, Grade 6

That One Morning

That one morning
Is the day I realized I would fall in love with no warning
I ran into a teenager with a kind smile
And I knew that we would be friends, for a while

His eyes reflected my own
And a loving shimmer showed
I loved the way his eyes twinkled in the light
And he just seemed right

The smile he wore
Was not much of a chore
To know that there was kindness
And I was so lucky to be a witness

That one morning, changed my life
Little did I know that I would be his wife
Of course there were moments that were grim
I am still glad I ran into him

Our love is bright
Even at night
I am glad I found my love
That one on morning

Rebekah Garrido, Grade 4

The Holocaust

I can't sleep.
All I hear are the cries of children starvation.
They are as thin as paper and as fragile as glass.
People got beaten, killed, and gassed.
Everyone's hearts were shattered.
Everyone loved each other and cared, but a cruel
Man named Adolf Hitler didn't care.
Hitler had hate but WE had hope.

Dreanna Simmons, Grade 6

I Wish, I Try, and I Dream, Also Love

I wish I knew how to be a professional jumper.
I wish I could become famous.
I dream that I have a lot of friends.
I dream that I would have the biggest horse in the world.
I try to do my best in school.
I try to be good with my friends.
I love my crazy life.
I love that I wish, I try, and I dream.

Caydes Aronow, Grade 5

Holocaust

Were you an outsider?
Only if you had blonde hair and blue eyes.
You would survive.
You are one of the many that don't have either.
You have to hide but you are not fast enough.
You will be sent to a concentration camp.
Later you were killed.
You were only thirteen.

Nathan Bogar, Grade 6

Snow

I wake up in the morning to see the sparkling snow
Grab my boots and hat and out the door I go.

Build a snowman, snowball fight; we play games all day long
Hot cocoa by the fireplace, signing Christmas songs.

Put on cozy PJ's, snuggle up in bed
Dreams of snowy, fun filled days floating in my head.

Zoë Mahrlig, Grade 5

Again

A gain everyone has left
G oing somewhere else
A gain to forget I'm still here
I nside my small self
N owhere to go, nowhere to hide
S tanding still, all alone
T ill I find myself lost, again

Alyvia Scutt, Carena Colo, and Alicia Goldenziel, Grade 6

Darkness

In all darkness there is some light.
But the only way to get complete darkness
is to turn that light off.
You are that light.
If you let it burn your feelings, it will also burn your soul.
If the earth were totally dark,
you should be the person to find that small candle to light the way.
You should be that person.
You can't get light from darkness.
The new light would burn,
for once destroyed, light can
never be put back together the way it was before.

Claudia Sachs, Grade 6

Hello Spring!

Hello spring!
I love to take vacation in spring,
To see the flowers and trees blooming
To enjoy the warm weather,
I wish if I can go to the beach too and
to make sandcastles and to drink my favorite tasty lemonade.
I feel happy in the springtime,
to invite my friends over,
to go to the park and to play Soccer
to watch my kitten running in the grass
with the players.
Welcome Back SPRING

Adam Yamak, Grade 4

Friends

My friends are kind, loving and smart
Some of them enjoy doing art
They notice when I'm feeling down
They cheer me up to get rid of my frown
My friends make me smile
Every day for a while
We can be a little tough
But our friendship is a diamond in the rough
My friends are caring
They always have things that they are sharing
Together we are fun, fabulous, and funny
Our friendship is worth millions in money

Allison Carley, Grade 6

A Single Stroke of Color

A swirl, a line, a stroke of color
sinks deep within the canvas
My brush, though smeared with several coats of color
is just what makes this painting happen

I smear, I dab, I shade it all
until it's as marvelous as can be
and just then I realize that
a single stroke of color
is just as beautiful

Estelle Eppolito, Grade 6

Words

Simple scribbles scrawled out on a page
Or typed neatly in a line
Appearing so meaningless and futile
Under a deceiving mask

For it requires the insightful eye
Of a true imaginer
To see through the deluded disguise,
To find the virtue within

Under the sheet of deception
Lays a mystery much more potent
Than that of those
Forced from the lips

For even the thoughts cemented the deepest
Of despondency, acrimony, and overwhelming joy
Come bubbling up and retreat from their imprisonment
All just by placing the tip of the pen on its destination

If one day this power is incapable to describe
Our unfathomable life in its simplicity
But convoluted all the same
My soul would shatter like a sheet of glass

For I cannot imagine a world lost of words.

Kera Nelson, Grade 6

In the Mirror

I once looked in the mirror
I saw a girl wearing ragged clothes in a stormy world
Her face was teary
Her deep brown eyes bleary

She would look at me
and I would look at her
Both in our own worlds
We stared at each other in wonder

She tilted her head and so did I.
I smiled,
She smiled
I laughed,
She laughed
We laughed until we couldn't stop

She now stood in a field of flowers
A little cottage in the distance
The grass swaying in the sun

What could she see?
A soap dish, toothpaste and a towel?
Who knows.

"Coming Mom!"

Pranavi Doodala, Grade 5

Clock

Oh, that clock
Smooth as a polished
Stone, Although, loud
As a honked horn
Ticking and tocking
As fast as a
Running jackrabbit
The children
As happy as
Dogs reunited
With their
Owners after
Weeks when
The clock
Turns to
3 o'clock.
Jack Reed, Grade 4

Patch of Flowers

In a patch of flowers,
a secret lies.
In the dark earth,
Lies a piece of the sky.
And inside this piece
lies a whole new world.
There is no darkness to fight
No trace of war,
But what would you do
in that piece of sky,
Just lying on your back,
Watching clouds go by?
What would you do
without that edge of life?
What is the point
of paradise?
Eliana Feistner, Grade 6

What Happens in Spring

In spring we play,
We drink lemonade.
Outside, dandelions blow.
We have some allergies,
Well, after all,
It's the season of allergies.
But, just let it go,
No more snow,
No more coldness,
Just the sun.
Maybe there is rain,
But it causes no pain,
it's no big deal,
We are active in spring,
We don't sleep that much,
It's just forty winks.
Louis Lieu, Grade 5

Patriotic Flag

I am a flag
I am a flag that has a meaning
I am known as the land of the free
I am a flag that says we will not back down
I am a flag that promises bravery
I have 50 friends that are united as one
I

a

m

a

f
l
a
g.
Kyle Lenz, Grade 4

Boston

Sometimes happy things
happen during depressing times
the day of the bombing
we found a heavenly angel
a tiny gray kitten
named Boston
with her beady,
pussy, green eyes
green as emerald
purring and meowing
her scratchy, scuffy meow
but in a split second
the thing you love most
is gone forever
never to be seen again
in a blink of a pussy green eye
Maitlyn Poduszlo, Grade 6

Hero Sword

Used by heroes
generation by generation
An unbreakable force
handled carefully

Presented by magic
clinging, clashing
pinging, bashing
now being welded

By a green gloved figure
sneaking and whacking
A horned moon giving it a blue shine
Not sitting around always up and running
Always safe
from the forces of evil
Blake Hagan, Grade 4

Jet World

I am a jet
I wonder when the war ends
I hear nothing but loud bangs
I see cars and buildings on fire
I want it to stop
I am so scared and sad
I pretend nothing's happening
I feel like a hawk
I touched the sky when I took off
I worry if I hurt the wrong people
I cry for help
I am fast
I understand why we do this
I say we do it for our country
I dream of peace of all lands
I try to imagine being in a big cloud
I hope it ends
I am a jet
Preston Garrison, Grade 6

Spring Is Almost Here

It's almost time for spring to come,
The winter is leaving.
The time for the snow is done,
It is all melting.

The animals are waking up,
From their long hibernation.
The birds are all coming back up,
From the south, back to their nations.

The grass is growing,
The trees are aging,
The flowers are blooming,
And the leaves are sprouting.

It's almost time for spring to come,
The winter is leaving,
Another cycle is done.
Baron-Yuhao Liang, Grade 5

Tomorrow

Tomorrow is tomorrow
It is another day
Passing time
Pulling time forward
Try to stay in the moment
   if you can
Try so hard
Keep a hold
or you fall, fall, fall
Keep moving
Keep going
Time buzzing by
Tomorrow
Kaleb Oliver, Grade 5

I Am Morgan

I am a sad and creative girl.
I wonder if my grandma can see me trying my best in school.
I hear that she is done for.
I see her with me all of the time.
I want to hear her say "I love you" one last time.
I am a sad and creative girl.

I pretend that people know that she has existed.
I feel like she is with me when I'm down.
I touch her hand every day when I'm sad.
I worry that someone else in my family is going to die.
I cry because I think that it's my fault.
I am a sad and creative girl.

I understand that she is gone forever.
I say she is still here.
I dream about her every night.
I try not to cry.
I hope she believes in me.
I am a sad and creative girl.

Morgan Hill, Grade 6

Stars

I could just stare
as we shoot to the sky

and we'd drift to all those planets far far away
as we'd go near

back to home
we'd be lost

And we'd have each other
as we'd do it again

But then the dark side comes
every light shines beautiful

but has a terrorized ending
and every star must explode
and die
and not shine anymore
so stars are friends

Shiloh Robinson, Grade 5

I Have to Say

I have to say my life's been exciting.
I have gone to see a Monster Truck show.
I went to see the Terrier's hockey playoff game.
I have gone to the beach and a pool.
I have gone to Tinker Town and rode the roller coaster.
I have ridden a dirt bike very fast.
I went sliding down Rogers Hill on a tube.
I have done all those things, tell me true,
Have you?

Adrian Waldner, Grade 4

Canadian Icicles

Drip,
Drip, Drip,
The cold water fell,
our caps wet and cold,
we move away,
only to get hit again and again,
We look up towards the tall buildings,
hanging as if it were teeth,
the giant obelisks full of cold,
send drops of ice cold water,
Standing like a crowd of the dead,
we watched the gray clouds in boredom,
For months and months we dreaded that way,
until the day when the spring had ran away,
the icicles had disappeared,
After months we finally smiled,
but now the memory as clear as ice,
and the thought daunting, that only months away
the 72 icicles come by.

Soumya Thapa, Grade 6

Moose

He is close,
I am still.
A blue jay sings a morning lullaby,
As moose cries to the song
and walks to me,

The grass waves hello to the sky.
His hard smooth antlers are scarce
to many, but guards the gentle giant inside.
As his soft brushy fur runs forth over
his thick skin,
his cold breath makes waves
of happy smoke,
the grass brushing his hooves bows hello,

the say of the sweet pine holds the
blue jay singing,
in its palms choirs of birds dance through the morning.
Who is this gentle giant, moose

MarySue Smith, Grade 4

Video Games

I love video games
I play them a lot
I play them more than you know
But video games
Don't have recess, or math
Not the ones I play

They have building in it
Sometimes it involves science and social studies and reading
I know it does involve super-heroes and sometimes bad guys
It also has missions and challenges.

Daniel Love, Grade 4

The Wind
Through the lush forest
The wind will softly whistle
Out into the day
Thomas Lipscomb, Grade 6

Easter
Let's find Easter eggs
The Easter bunny's coming
The best time of year
Taylor Sherry, Grade 5

Butterflies
Flows with friendly breeze,
Gracefully gliding around,
Nature's miracle.
Megan Steinbach, Grade 4

A Spring Day
Unguided rain falls...
The most beautiful droplets
Bouncing off the ground!
Timothy Peralta, Grade 5

Crystal Water
Heavy snow falling
Sits beautifully untouched
Glares in the moon light...
Jonathan Caldino, Grade 5

Waterfalls
Hitting the rocks hard.
Water shining in the sun.
Elegant aqua.
Rachel Hamler, Grade 4

Pugs
Lazy, chubby pugs
Fast asleep on the green grass...
Playing in the field!
Emmanuel Garcia, Grade 5

The Fisherman and the Willows
A man is fishing
The willows are growing tall
Snow on the mountain
Justin Mclain, Grade 4

Spring
A cool spring breeze
Flowers swaying side to side
In the meadow
Ernesto Calderon, Grade 4

Home Is My Kingdom of Imagination
Home is my kingdom of imagination,
Home is my magical traveler it will take me anywhere I want
One moment I would be fighting pirates in the Caribbean
The next I could be swinging from vine to vine in the Amazon
My home is a place to relax, a place after school, a place during vacation.
My home and I go on many magical adventures.
Once I save a wizard from a fierce dragon.
Whenever I want to travel, my home takes me there,
When I feel like being a pirate, we go to the time of pirates
When I feel like riding a horse, we go to the old west
At the end of our adventures go back to our normal setting
Every time I'm At home I feel safe.
Home feeds me,
Home protects me,
Home gives me water
There is no place I'd rather be
When I'm at home
Home.
Olinmazatemictli Reyes, Grade 4

Hope
I am a word of wisdom
I wonder how I affect people
I hear people talking about me
I see how I influence people
I want to stay around forever
I am a word of wisdom
I pretend I am the solution to everything
I feel the happiness in the air
I touch people's hearts like the clouds touch the sky
I worry my meaning might be misjudged
I cry when people take me for granted
I am a word of wisdom
I understand that I don't always help
I say I am the cure to tragedies
I dream that I ring around the world like bells ring on Sunday morning
I try to be the best in the worst of times
I hope for nothing more than I already have
I am hope
Katie Prevette, Grade 6

Colorful Cars
Colorful cars, there are so many colorful cars,
like green and aquamarine, too.

Some colorful cars are red, orange, yellow, green,
blue, and purple, too.

So many colorful cars, I have to say.

Some cars are white, some cars are black like the night sky.

Some cars are baby blue like the sky, or white like puffy clouds.

Colorful cars can be so many colors like tickle-me-pink and rosy red.
Payton Michaels, Grade 4

Basements

Basements are creepy,
some with creaks, others with leaks.

Down the stairs,
you know there is nothing to fear
but you also know you're scared

Something grabs your leg,
you scream, kick, punch
but it's just a cord.
You see a creepy shadow,
but it's just the reflection off the mirror

Then, you think you hear your name,
your heart starts beating a mile a minute
you book it up the stairs screaming,
Skipping 3 steps at a time
you think, will I get to the top in time?

When you get to the top of the stairs,
you look down into your basement
then think you have nothing to fear,

Until you tiptoe back down the stairs,
and your fears start creeping back up your spine
and the process of your creeps starts all over again.

Terra Leiber, Grade 6

Home Is Being Loved

Home is being loved
a place where I feel safe
and near the people who care for me the most
home is where I feel guarded, protected, and secure
it's where I feel safe,
and know I'm shielded from any danger

its also a place where I can be alone, by myself,
with no one else around me

I know my home is familiar to me
and I know where everything's place is

but yet I could lose myself and I could show my emotions
alone or with a crowd
I can let my heart out by playing the music,
that speaks to me the most

Home is close to my family,
especially my sister
where together we could play for hours outside in the tire swing

when my sister's somewhere else
I go outside by the swing and wish she was there
to be with me, close to me, and love me
so I could love her back

Madeline Pennell, Grade 5

The Voice Inside

It whispers in your head all silently and smooth
Its words are all part of a self-conscious ruse
It tells you lies
Changes your view
Sometimes worries form from it too
If you let it in it will scream and shout
And you'll want it out! Out! Out!
It has power and cruelness
It makes you feel small
Just believe in yourself and stand up real tall
Don't let it hurt you
Do you know what to do?
Don't let it control what you think of you
We all have our secrets, something to hide
But don't let it be that you are self-conscious inside
Believe in who you are
Be the best you can be
Block it out of your head and listen to me
The voice is inside you
You can take control
Or else the words will take their toll

Kalie Holford, Grade 6

A Person That I Would Like to Be

There once was a person
Who could change the seasons.
He made summer appear,
Saw beautiful apple trees,
Heard the buzz of the bees.
He went into a pool
And thought it was cool.
Then, he made autumn appear,
He saw lots of pretty leaves
That were red and yellow in the trees.
He replaced autumn for winter,
He saw the snow glitter.
He then made spring.
He went on a swing,
Saw flowers bloom
And he thought, "Soon, I will have to make a special season.
A season where you can go into cool pools,
See trees and bees
And colourful leaves.
See the snow on the go and see flowers bloom."
This is the kind of person I would like to be.

Chloé Champredon, Grade 5

A Friend

A friend is someone who cares
A friend is someone who is not mean to you
A friend is someone who is there when you need help
A friend is someone who doesn't push you
A friend is someone who makes you happy
A friend is someone who does not call you mean names
A friend is someone who loves you

Michelle Reich, Grade 4

The Season We Love

Flowers buds grow up on the trees
Pine cones appear on evergreens
And don't forget the buzzing bees
This is just how beautiful nature can be
Beautiful kites flown in the blue sky
Luxurious gust of humid summer wind
Feels as if butterflies are skimming your skin
Now let's remember
The great qualities of fall
No season is like it
Not even at all
Outstanding colors of the fire red leaves
Fall to the ground leaving nothing
But bare trees
The on and off weather of chilly and warm
Sends the bees away in one big swarm
We mustn't forget the mysterious winter
When the snow comes down like a glazed feather
As the seasons pass and change and grow
Nature is the one to thank you know

Hailey Danielson, Grade 5

Life

Life is tough and life is great
But you should know the day will come.

From when you are just born
God has given you love, life, family and a home
So give thanks to Christ.

No one person is alike in any way (unless you are twin)
No one is perfect.
And to be honest with you,
Perfect is not real.

If I were you, I wouldn't say
"I want to die" because that is not good!

So just remember God loves you
No matter what!

Give thanks to your God!

Isabella Ortiz, Grade 4

Saving Grace

Through many dangers I may fear,
My saving grace is right here.
No matter where I go to play,
My saving grace is here to stay.
When I am far from home astray,
Even then my saving grace is here from day to day.
I love my saving grace so much,
I say it's perfect — God is such!
God's my saving grace today,
And no matter what — He's here to stay!

Isabella Morales, Grade 4

Overpowering Obstacles

Sometimes, nothing makes sense
After trying and trying to make the best of your tense
When you're fishing for walls of relief
Or falling down with pain when you thought it would be brief

Sometimes, life runs in circles
Goals, action, and then obstacles
Many trials and tribulations
Often feeling stronger than many nations

Sometimes, you need to have grit
Take a deep breath, and say it
"I can do it! I'm making progress!"
Motivate yourself for an overflowing success

Sometimes, when these obstacles hit you,
Know yourself and be true
If you try your best,
You know the rest

Other times, things may not work the way you wanted
Just know you didn't do this all for granted

Don't weep in sorrow, because there is a tomorrow
You tried your best, now take a rest

Wake up, and try again!

Samuella Aduboahen, Grade 6

The Doorway

The most important place in the world is home
A place where you can enjoy literacy tomes

Forget the outside with is numerous puzzles
It's a whole new world inside
You have freedom in your home
The choices are yours and yours to decide

The door is tempting you
to enjoy life at home
It is the only place
that one can really own

One step past the door
Is like fueling you with food
It may be a little step with your foot
But it's certainly a giant leap in mood

Out in that frightening world
Oh! The monsters you will meet!
But past the doorway you will see
all the treasures you will keep

Everything past the doorway is someone's home
Past your doorway, there's always something you own

Davis Lu, Grade 6

I Am Gentle, But Strong.

I wonder if I will always be able to remain standing.
I hear the scales of dragons clicking as they entangle themselves on the canvas.
I see sweeping ball gowns dance with poise as the ink flows over the paper.
I want to help, but I, myself, render hopeless.
I am gentle, but strong.
I pretend not to care but, shockingly, I do.
I feel myself crash and burn, but the strong arms of my father, mother, and brother keep me on my feet.
I touch the matted fur of the feral and the soft wing beats of the tame as they flow at the tip of my paintbrush.
I worry too much.
I cry too often.
I am gentle, but strong.
I understand how, but will never understand why.
I say nothing, because sometimes it's better to listen.
I dream in color.
I try too hard.
I hope for the best, but prepare for the worst.
I am gentle, but strong.

Grace Schwartzer, Grade 6

Deer Season

I love deer season, the snow is falling and piling up.
I get to take off school two days to go hunting.
We go driving for deer and see lots of deer running through the woods with snow covered backs.
They're scared and running away from us while we are shooting at them.
It is very cold out and snowing.
The snow on the trees is falling down on your head.
Slipping and falling over the hidden rocks that are snow covered.
Walking to the top is tiring.
When you get to the top you're huffing and puffing.
The wind is howling on the top of the mountain, your face is frozen, and your feet are sweating from walking up the side.
You get up to the top and you are waiting to start the drive.
You are sitting on a log and you're freezing from sweating.

Colson Fike, Grade 6

When One Is Born

Finally, it's spring and I'm alive,
I have been waiting and waiting.
All the green grass is around me,
And it's beautiful.
All my friends around me are enjoying this time too,
I am laying down and looking at the blue sky.
Spring is my favorite time,
It's the time I can be real.
My friend the tree,
Is growing brand new leaves.
I love to look at children,
Dancing,
Playing,
Swimming.
The animals are so happy,
But I like to stay where I am and watch people pass by.
What am I?

Acile Jammoul, Grade 4

Couch Potato

Lazy bones
couch, Cheetos
sluffing, laying, sitting
laughing, sleeping; lacrosse, playing
sweating, working, running
active, awesome
Athletic

Mathias Openshaw, Grade 6

Pig and Warthog

Pig
Pink, Cute
Grunting, Loving, Cuddling
Clean, Smart, Dirty, Smelly
Snorting, Hurting, Running
Black, Ugly
Warthog

Grace Tennant, Grade 4

Polar Bear

Polar Bears are white, smart and cuddly
Polar Bears are big and furry
Polar Bears can catch food, swim and dive
Polar Bears can lie and roll in the snow
While cold winds howl and blizzards blow
Polar Bears can roar, scratch and growl
Polar Bears have heavy coats that keeps them warm
So after dark in the night
No one cares to go after Polar Bear
Angie Paul, Grade 6

Holocaust

H itler was a cruel man.
O ne man started all the pain and suffering.
L ives taken, living in fear,
O ver eleven million Jewish people were killed.
C hildren's cries filled the night skies.
A lways remember the lives that were lost.
U nderstand the mistakes of our past.
S urvivors share the horrors they endured.
T he Holocaust will never be forgotten.
Courtney Paulson, Grade 6

Children

They run around all day long
They also sometimes know what is wrong.
When they have to go to bed they cry.
They also hide, when they go to sleep, they are like angels.
In the morning they ask you to play.
If they don't get their way they will be mad all day.
Look on the bright side, they make you smile.
They are at your side all the time.
They are also there even when you need a shoulder to cry on.
Kevin DiAmico, Grade 6

Shoveling

S now falls on the ground
H ail quickly whirls around
O ur driveway is covered in ice
V ictor's driveway looks very nice
E veryone is having lots of fun
L ifting the ice, not stopping till they are done
I finally finish my work of art
N ever even miss a part
G reat! Now I can play
Leonard Carey, Grade 5

Blue

Blue is a bright smile
Blue looks like the sea waves on a hot summer day
Blue smells like flowers swaying in the wind
Blue tastes like sweet cotton candy
Blue feels like fluffy bright fur
Blue sounds like the chirping of a Blue Bird
Blue is my best friend
Aidan Schneider, Grade 4

The World Seemed Ever So Perfect

The trees are towering extra high
The sun is smiling extra hard
The snow is showing off its glittering coat
The world seemed ever so perfect.
My joy was ready to erupt
My heart was pounding like a drum
My face was hurting from the smiles
The world seemed ever so perfect.
I'm going to build a snowman, I'm going to built a fort
I'm going to build my own world. The world seemed ever so perfect.
Hoping to find a good spot
Hoping for a good chance
Hoping for a great time
The world seemed ever so perfect
Running out our the door into my imaginary world
Running out to our yard, running to the snow
The world seemed ever so perfect.
Staring with great big eyes that are ready to pop
Staring with disappointment
Staring at the worthless snow
The world did not seem perfect.
Natalya Waldner, Grade 6

Summer

My favorite season is summer
Because it is not a bummer
And summer is so really cool
Because it is the best time to go the pool
Summer is the time when kids rule
Because there is no school
And once we've put our stuff in the locker
We can go and start a long game of soccer
And once that guy finishes with his daydream
We can go and buy some 3-scoop ice-cream
In summer you can't sit
Because we're playing tag and you're it
On sunny…hot days some birds come your way
Once it is night
Just light a night-light
You couldn't sleep all night long
Because of somebody's song
You woke up and looked at the skies
And you couldn't believe your eyes
There was an eagle
Chasing a fast seagull.
Tejanpreet Parmar, Grade 5

Bee and Wasp

Bee
Fat, fast
Drinking, biting, eating
Bees sting and die and wasps sting but do not die
Pollinating, swallowing, stinging
Long, yellow
Wasp
Sierra Woodley, Grade 4

Spring Secrets
The waterfall;
Whispering the secrets
Of how to move forward.

The tree;
Stating the secrets
Of how to stand tall.

The flower;
Giggling the secrets
Of how to love.

The deer;
Walking the secrets
Of how to be young.

The wind;
Singing the secrets
Of saying what you mean.

The sun;
Speaking the secrets
Of moving to new horizons.

The spring;
Announcing the secret
Of how to live new.
Kelsey Hertz, Grade 4

Christmas Anticipation
When are they coming?
I'm fairly bursting!
I can't wait to see them —
My bursting is worsening!

Are they dressed in gold or silver,
With boxes with bows,
Or dressed in many layers
To keep warm when it snows?

The phone! It's them!
What? TENNESSEE!
Only 5 hours?
How can this be?

The Christmas tree's up,
The table is set,
My presents are wrapped —
Are they here yet?

However, whenever,
I don't really care.
Just get us together,
Somehow and somewhere.
Brenna Peterman, Grade 6

I Am Me…
I am me, I like to see,
All the birds, and all the trees.

Curious as a Weddle Seal,
Eyeing humans visiting Antarctica.

An inquisitive sponge,
Ready to soak in knowledge.

The gears in my head turn as fast
As the cars in the Indy 500.

I'm considered to be short,
And soccer is my favorite sport.
Even though I'm just four foot eight,
I really think I'm pretty great!

A small, smart and smiley thinker!
And a happy, handy, hard worker!

Striving to be successful as Lionel Messi,
A cheetah on the soccer field.

I am a broom,
Hoping to sweet the competition!

I am me,
And as you see,
I'm as happy as can be!
Mikey DeAngelis, Grade 6

If I Was Only One Inch Tall
If I was only one inch tall,
Poplar fluff would make a lovely shawl,

I'd catch a ride upon a mouse,
My home would be a girl's doll house,

A predator would be a cat,
An acorn cap would be my hat,

A leaf would make the perfect boat,
Moss would be my winter coat,

A moth would be my airplane,
A drink would be a drop of rain,

I'd hope people wouldn't step on me,
French fries would be a pair of skis,

A crumb of bread would be my lunch,
Served with a thimble full of fruit punch,

I'd probably have no friends at all,
If I was only one inch tall.
Annalisa Ellingson, Grade 5

A Red Ribbon!
It tells you how you've done
You win it, because you earned it
You ignored all the trash-talk
You know you've done well
You're the symbol for first
You are hung where everyone can see you
You bring joy to the people who won you
Charlee Nichifor, Grade 5

Sun/Moon
Sun
Shining, warm
Pretty, yellow, round
Flaming, big, ball, craters
White, changing, hard
Bright, beautiful
Moon
Abygail Denie, Grade 4

Horses vs Ponies
Horses
Beautiful, graceful
Running, jumping, flowing
Braids, saddles, whips, spurs,
Bucking, fighting, resisting,
Resentful, stubby
Ponies
Hannah Wismer, Grade 6

Winter Game and Spring Soccer
Hockey
Ice, skates
Checking, passing, scoring
Winter game, spring soccer
Saving, winning, kicking
Grass, nets
Cleats
Treyton Chrispen, Grade 6

Turtles/Dogs
Turtles
quiet, inactive
swimming, sneaking, climbing
legs, shells; claws, jaws
barking, yelping, pawing
loud, obnoxious
Dogs
Nathan Seamons, Grade 6

Grandma
Bright November day
We got a call from your work
that you had passed away
we cried until we couldn't cry
then we packed and drove away
Faith Cranmer, Grade 6

Ode to Volleyball
Oh, how you tire me!
With my sprinting every which way
You make me fall asleep early every day
You take my breath away
But I always wish that I could stay.

Your repulsive sweaty stench.
Every time I play, you make me smell like a rotting fish
You are very troublesome, yet,
Fun like making a wish.

You are colorful and round.
Playing you makes my heart pound.
Oh, volleyball you fill me
But my arms they kill me.
Jacqueline Robinson, Grade 6

School
I am a school
You know me for the education I provide.
My mother is the head of education
My father is the principal.
I was born in a small neighborhood.
I live with hundreds of pupils and professors.
My best friend is the clock,
Because we celebrate when he says it's time to go.
My enemies are the trouble makers,
Because they never follow rules and hate to learn.
I fear graduation,
Because I'll miss the ones that were good to me.
I love summer vacation,
Because I get a break after an exhausting year.
I hope everyone would come to visit me again one day.
Mohamed Hammad, Grade 6

Loss
Take 2 loving people,
Put them in a bowl.
Add 2 cups of sorrow,
2 cups of sadness,
1 1/2 cups of pain.
Mix them with a machine,
Until you get really emotional.
Pour in some regret.
Bake it in a oven,
At 400 degree Fahrenheit for about 45-50 minutes.
You know it is done, when you are on the edge of tears.
Sprinkle them with grief.
It tastes like the loved one you lost.
You know you made it just right,
If you have tears flowing down like a waterfall.
Alexis Zhou, Grade 6

Rain
Rain,
Is blue like the ocean,
It pours fast like lightning striking.
Each drop looks like ice-cream cones melting,
When it rains I feel like playing soccer in it.
Davor Buric, Grade 5

Asian Paper Wasp
W asps, the murderers of the bug world.
A nd they sting your hand.
S welling bigger and bigger is your hand.
P oison rushing through your veins, you try to get it out.
Josh Sobiech, Grade 6

When I Used To
I remember the days when I kneaded dough
The days when I used to sew
I remember the days when I knew where to go
The days when I made friends with my foes
Rameen Khan, Grade 6

The Holocaust
F ear the German Nazis.
E veryone hide, the Nazis are coming, said the Jews.
A ll fear the German leader, Adolf Hitler.
R un, run, called the Jews as they ran in fear.
Kyle Nguyen, Grade 6

Hate
H is for Hitler, who wanted to kill all Jews.
A is for the Jews who were not asked to be in concentration camps.
T is for true love, which Hitler did not have.
E is for earnest people who wanted to be free.
Kylie Kostenbader, Grade 6

Wind
Wind is howling
The sky is turning black
Leaves and trees moving
As the wind takes it along

Thunder booming
Light so bright it blinds
Nowhere to go
Stay in the house for shelter

Wind dies down
You're able to see
No more noise
Birds chirp as the storm is over

Heaven shines its light
Light breeze calms the seas
Damage has been done
But nothing has been hurt
Gabriela Lopez, Grade 5

Writing

Writing brings out all the words people can't say.
Writing brings out all the colors stuck inside.
Writing explains your heartaches, your heartbreaks,
It explains math problems, theories, definitions, even colors.
Writing explains all that people can't say.
It makes books have words.
It gives voices to the speechless.
Writing let's you pour your heart onto it.
It lets you write!

Jazmin Padilla, Grade 4

Aly Raisman

Aly Raisman is a famous gymnast
She won two gold medals at the 2012 London Olympics
She began gymnastics at age two,
In mommy and me classes, "How about you?"

With brown eyes and brown hair
She's a true gymnast
People know her everywhere
I hope you meet Raisman somewhere.

Heidi Gresh, Grade 5

Treehouse

T he tree is strong to hold the house part up.
R eally great for an indoor hammock
E veryone has lots of fun
E verywhere you look there's bark
H igh from the ground
O utings with friends
U seful for a meeting place in case of a fire
S eeing everything below from the window
E ntirely made of wood

Elijah Rodriguez, Grade 6

Spring Is Here Now

The snow is gone and the birds are flying
The flowers and trees are growing and climbing
The bees are making honey
To add to my tea.

Spiders are eating bugs
And baby bears are giving hugs
Canada Geese are coming back
They are waiting for the ice to crack!

Jerome Claux, Grade 4

Eagles vs Redskins

Eagles
Awesome, Best
Hitting, Winning, Running
There are big rivalries between these two football teams
Screaming, Losing, Catching
Terrible, Worst
Redskins

Zayd Meziati, Grade 4

A Secret Child

An indigo child, rare, fresh, beautiful.
No one understands,
their feelings, love,
mind.

It looks about to not understand.
So much goes on where people cannot see
Alone.
Drawing late at night not using a pencil nor pen.

What will happen? Was the only thought.
Where will things go? Anxiety.
Depression.
This world, is going nowhere
to a place of nothing.

Its eyes a mimicking blue or evergreen secret.
Oh this indigo child is like a gem. No one sees this,
no one hears or thinks this. The child is alone and dark.

She is alone with her secret, mimicking green eyes,
she needs someone.
But no one's there...

Patti Love, Grade 6

Pictures

The pictures on the wall are staring at me.
There's a monster looking, terribly.

There's a bear picture over there,
but I wouldn't dare give it a glare.

There's a creepy picture of a guy in a chair.
There are freaky pictures everywhere.

There's one of a tree.
There's one of a bee.

Would you look at that, there's one of the sea.
Oh! There's even a picture of me!

A picture of a clock.
A picture of a lock.

Over there is a picture of hay
They have a picture of everything, don't they?

Do all these pictures want to play?
So many pictures; I want to stay.

Alex Ricci, Grade 5

Blue

Blue is the sky and the way it moves
It is the rain that drips down.
Blue is the ocean and the water that you drink.

Isaiah Anderson, Grade 4

My Aunt Alex in the Army
she fights for our country
she trains for war and people
she goes over seas to fight
she rides in a Humvee for training
she stays at army camp overnight
she protects our country for safety
Samantha Frey, Grade 6

Blue
Blue is the blanket of mother earth,
The blanket called the sea.
Blue is a wave of calmness,
Sweeping over me.
Blue is the sky that's speckled,
With clouds as white as white can be.
Dakota Anderson, Grade 4

Darkness
Creeps into your skin
Through your soul
And out
Can see nothing
No light
No life
Dawn Brisco, Grade 4

Beaches
Come on
Sea shells shimmer
The crispy sun shining
Silky water all over me
Swimming
Akayjah Moses, Grade 5

Rain
I am as clear as glass.
I feel like water.
I'm round like a ball.
I'm sensitive to your eyes.
I am in the wavy clouds.
Adan Valtierra-Teran, Grade 4

Sledding
Sledding
Bumpy, cold
Falling, freezing, tumbling
This is so fun
Sliding
Sophia Nehr, Grade 5

Fire
Fire
Surrounded by rock
Flaming around the campsite
Burning bright and hot
Matt Fezenko, Grade 5

Books
Some people hate books
They think books are boring
Well, here is what I have to say to them.
Books are your best friend, your BFF.
The only thing in the world that will never leave you.
A book will be with you during hard times and easy times it will never leave you.
A book is an adventure waiting to happen.
A book is your BFF, it will never leave you no matter what.
When you open the first page you are sucked in by a portal.
That portal will lead you somewhere amazing.
A book, your BFF, portal and much more.
Sometimes you are running to get a thief.
In a book you might be with a talking mouse
telling you how to get a diamond.
Book is your BFF
A portal, a book is amazing in other words.
If you do not read books because you like movies.
A book is much better than a movie, it has details, it is the real things.
A movie is your BFF a portal it is better than movies.
In other words a books are AMAZING.
That was what I had to say to people about who hate books.
Amardeep Bains, Grade 5

The Children's March*
Water stings my back
and blows me down the street
Like a sheet of paper
No place to hide
No place to be safe
No one will help
I hear "Freedom" sung over
and over again
Water hits me like a boulder
As I'm swept, like paper, into the street once more
I'm jerked up by my shirt collar
Someone spits in my face
CLANG!!!
Behind bars
This is how I must get Freedom
I'm only 15
and off to jail

All Because I'm Black
Mara Anderson-Skelly, Grade 6
In honor of the brave children who marched in Birmingham for Freedom

Best Friends
Everyone has that very special person in their life they are always there for
You when you need them, best friends don't always get along, they're just like a
Family member, when you're sad or down they're all ways there to cheer you up, best
Friends don't have to be just girls... guys can be best friends, best friends
Are AMAZING! A best friend is someone who you can tell anyone or anything
About, best friends do everything together, best friends make the dumbest mistakes
Everyone has that "sister or bro" in their lives, no matter what happens they will
Always be there, now that is what I call a real best friend
Jade Smith, Grade 6

High Merit Poems – Grades 4, 5, and 6

Rainbows
Rainbows look like neon laser
Lights shooting across the sky.
Rainbows taste like sweet and
Sour candy. Rainbows are colorful
Like a fresh bloomed flower.
Rainbows feel like soft clouds
Disappearing from my sight.
So there I am sliding down a
Rainbow eating colorful candy
And I fall into a big pot of gold.
Ariyana Warner, Grade 5

The Forest
He has been for centuries.
Mountain wiser than all, cares for all.

Tree recalls bursting out of the hard soil.
Feeling the heat of the beating sun on his body.
Tree wishes that the wind would not blow through his hair,
For only to get the needles crushed under a cars feet.

Mountain has seen you grow,
Now you must follow his steps to success.
Aidan McCloud, Grade 4

Rose
The petals of the rose dance when they fall.
The luscious red, white, and pink petals show
Peace, love, and tranquility.
The lively stem holds the entire amazing flower together
The sharp thorns protect the beautiful rose like a
Mom and Dad protect their children.
The amazing rose grows in big, lively bushes
Like a big, loving family.
Rose, you are warm and kind to others
Like they are your own family.
Andrew Bebko, Grade 6

Flowers
I sit in a vase waiting at home.
I get picked for bouquets and else.
I get smashed and stooped kicked.
I get smelled and seen for my beauty.
I sprout and grow during the spring.
When winter comes I go and freeze.
I'll be back next spring but for now I'll stay underground.
Danny Wright, Grade 6

Math Book
I am a math book.
Every day students learn from me.
I help them learn subtraction, addition, and much more.
I have many numbers, as you can imagine. I can,
Travel anywhere and anyway. When they close me,
I'm sad because they can't learn from me.
Janet Garduño Mendez, Grade 4

What Is in California's Backyard?
What is in California's backyard?
A California Grizzly picking off berries
A Redwood Tree looking down on skyscrapers
A Golden Poppy just making you smile
A California Quail perched on a branch
A Bighorn Sheep climbing and climbing
A Desert Cottontail sitting in shade
A Joshua Tree so amazing to look at
A Sea Lion joyfully swimming
A world so beautiful and unique
Sierra Jones, Grade 5

Rainy Day
I put on my rain boots and walk outside.
I splash in puddles, what a wild ride.
Here I come with my umbrella.
I dance in the rain like Cinderella.
My rain coat as a dress and boots as slippers.
Now I'm underwater with goggles and flippers.
I'm inside now cause I was too cold.
I look through my window and see the rainbow.
The colors so pretty, ROY G. BIV.
The rain has stopped and I'm saying have a RAINY DAY!
Ashley Karn, Grade 6

I Am a Cushion
You know me for my softness.
I live on top of your rough and filthy sofa.
My best friend is my warm case,
because it protects me when you fling me around.
My enemies are "the humans,"
because they throw me on the floor and then jump on me!
I fear the rough carpet,
because it scratches me.
I wish I was a soft and cozy sofa.
I am a cushion!
Nadir Khan, Grade 6

Fall Nature
The big hill of leaves is forming an ocean wave
The rough tree against me is hugging me like it's my friend
Wind is whispering trying to tell me a secret that winter is coming
The powerful free wind is knocking over plants in pot
The bird that keeps mocking me is like my sister
Vines trying to escape the evil green tree
Fall is calling all through the kingdom of nature.
Kara Conner, Grade 5

The Hike
Mountains remind me of a fantastic hike with family
Seeing the horizon skies
Almost FALLING!
Getting to the top just to realize it wasn't the top
Seeing rocks fall from the mountain
Seeing wild animals roam!!
Rowan Moore, Grade 4

Deep Blue
The water glistens as I gaze out
Looking at the deep blue
Wonders of Standley Lake

A wave of envy
Washes over me
As a fish jumps

The lights
Shining, reflecting
Off the smooth water

The stars
As bright as
The center of the sun

The lights
Shining, reflecting
Off the smooth water

Standing on
The still dock
In the silent night

The lights
Shining, reflecting
Off the smooth water
Rachel Kaiser, Grade 4

Home
My Hideout,

A Home needs a family,
it needs kind and friendly neighbors,
and playful, funny friends

My Home has many memories,
some happy,
some funny, and some sad

A Home cannot be made
With only inanimate objects,
but it is made with
the people and the feelings,
inside of it

A home cannot become a true Home,
with only happiness,
but it also needs hard times,
to go through,
sad days to overcome,
and then a home becomes a Home

Home is the best place to just
CHILL
Chiraag Sachdev, Grade 5

Rain
The sky begins to thunder
Lightning strikes the ground
I am here inside
All safe and sound

Rain splatters on the sidewalk
Right into a huge mud puddle
I am here inside
With my cats to cuddle

The rain falls harder
It's raining cats and dogs!
I am here inside
Not floating on the logs

Now the sun is shining
There's a rainbow in the sky
I am here outside
Gotta go! Good-bye!
Suchita Hadimani, Grade 5

The Rusted Iron Dagger
The news hits me
As it comes and goes
Like a smarting crack
On a face of my soul

Completely unexplained
Completely unexpected
I feel no pain yet—
Until the words sink in

The tears that I did not
Call for to flow
Drip anyway
Uselessly down my face

The bitter sting of reality
Has dented me beyond repair
To heaven and beyond,
I do assume.
Richa Mahajan, Grade 6

The Holocaust
The Holocaust story is told,
It attacked the young and the old.
There were victims that passed,
They died they were gassed.
The Kristallnacht night of broken glass,
All the horrors they will face,
In their minds it will never pass.
The night of broken glass.
Hitler was cold, he was like mold.
He killed the very young and the very old,
That is how the story was told.
Arianna Casner, Grade 6

A Wooden Piece of Gold
Such a little thing
worth so much
a small treasure worth its weight in gold
we hunt and keep hold of it
yet we lose it so often
when we find it again we treasure it
it's such a little thing
worth so much
Bode Flanigan, Grade 6

Football
F ast feet
O ne yard line
O ur amazing throws
T ouch down
B all is thrown
A ccurate
L ine backer
L iving large
Christopher Bungay, Grade 5

March
Children coming out to play
Flowers waiting for the day
Where they can pop out of the ground
You can hear barking from the hound
Days are starting to turn long
Birds chirping their peaceful song
Bees coming out in a swarm
Just starting to get warm
Ellie Billings, Grade 5

Why I Love Hamsters
Hamsters can be fluffy or well groomed
They can be small or a bit bigger
They can be hyper or calm and tame
They are fragile but sometimes tough
They are so adorable to me
They can also be goofy
They calm me down
I love Hamsters
Haley Keesee, Grade 6

Football
Football, football, football…
What a great sport it is!
Score a touchdown — do a dance
Try not to get a penalty!
Practice, practice, practice
To get better so you can win
Every game and championship
then see every person grin!
Orlando Watson, Grade 4

High Merit Poems – Grades 4, 5, and 6

Hot and Cold
Hot
Fiery, sunny
Boiling, sweating, dehydrated
Steamy, bright, chilly, frozen
Sleeting, snowing, blowing
Cloudy, icy
Cold
Evan Fedora, Grade 5

Up and Down
fly
high, sky
playing, laughing, floating.
in the trees, something bound then swatted
down, I frown
I'm gonna
fall
Dylan Esplin, Grade 6

Pirates
P lundering
I ncredible
R eally smelly
A t sea
T reasure stealing
E vil
S washbucklers with swords
Kyle Bennett, Grade 5

The Dog
There was a dog,
Who liked to jog,
And saw a hog,
In the fog,
On a log.
Michael Halstead, Grade 4

Soccer
Soccer is fun
Ball, kick, score, goal, field
Hard working team
Ashlyn Brtalik, Grade 4

Animals
Animals are cute
Nice, cute, fluffy, awesome, mean
You need animals
Marisa Ramsey, Grade 4

Dreams
Every night my dreams summon me.
They tire me, whisper to me
summoning me to another world where my thoughts lay.
In the other world is where I met him,
the lord that rules the night.
The lord is strong and powerful,
his emotions thwart my thoughts,
changing and shaping them to his convenience.
When morning comes and the lord is weak,
I pull free from his grasp.
And during the day
he lay in my mind tugging at me,
waiting for night to come.
And when night has come,
I resist once more,
trying to prevent him from wreaking my thoughts.
To no prevail,
I fall once more in his grasp.
In this never ending cycle,
where I start the day and end it.
Bridget Kim, Grade 6

Grades K-1-2-3 High Merit Poems

Canada
Canada is my native country
A freedom country
A multicultural country
Best place to be
Wonderful people in Canada
Gurshawn S. Bhullar, Grade 3

Kitten
kitten
cute, fluffy
jumping, climbing, biting
growing to be fat
cat
Quinn Riley, Grade 2

Spring Is Blooming
Spring is blooming
and people are planting flowers.
Then when rain passes by,
little green sprouts
pop out of the dark soil.
Henry Wright, Grade 2

Puppy
Puppy
So cute
Play outside together
Fetching a tennis ball
Friend
Sierra Symanoskie, Grade 2

Seed
seed
tiny oval
sprouting, growing, blooming
being a beautiful plant
flower
Luca Pickeral, Grade 2

Spring
The animals, the animals
Swim, fly or walk
When the sun shines
The flowers, the trees love it
The snow transforms into the rain!
Morgane Chaveron, Grade 2

Jesus
Jesus
Loves us
Carried a cross
Dying for our sins
Savior
Ella Matthis, Grade 2

Star
S hiny stars are bright
T iny stars are red
A constellation in the sky
R eally pretty starfish in the sea
Si Jiao Lam, Grade 2

Birds
Colourful, amazing
Flying, singing, migrating
Canada Geese are going north
Beautiful!
Marie Gagnon, Grade 3

Rain
Rainbows are full of colour
A drop of rain falls on my umbrella
I like to play in puddles
Nature likes rain
Kayla Lombardo, Grade 2

Owls
Huge, wise
Eating, flying, sleeping
Hunting for wild mice
Feathers!
Massimiliano Baron, Grade 3

Vacation
Vacation is happy
Swim in the ocean
I lay in the sand
Don't forget the suntan lotion!
Maksim Levin, Kindergarten

Lion
L ions are scary
I t has good eyesight
O ne dangerous animal
N ever eats plants
Adam Sellami, Grade 2

Summer
Sunny, beautiful
Playing, sweating, swimming
No more school
Vacation
Emanuelle Lambert, Grade 3

Leaves
Leaves falling on the ground.
Bump, Bump, Bump
Look, more trees growing.
That means more leaves to come around.
Jordyn Robinette, Grade 3

I Scream for Ice-Cream
I ce
C ream
E verywhere

S undaes
C reamy
R ockin
E verywhere
A wesome
M any flavors!
Stephen Elliker, Grade 3

Sports in the Springtime
No more ice and snow.
It's spring!
No more hockey!
It's time for soccer!
No more skates,
It is all about running shoes.
We will have fun in spring,
We will have fun playing soccer.
I love spring,
But I love soccer even more!
Christian Anguelov, Grade 3

A Little About Me
My name is Morgan,
but I am not an organ.
I play guitar,
but I don't drive a car.
I play with legos
and eat potatoes.
Cool blue eyes I have
and play soccer with the guys.
That's a little about me
so I hope you like what you see.
Morgan Silber, Grade 1

Dog
I'm a dog.
I love to eat.
Sometimes I take long naps.
Chasing cars is fun to do.
I love to play with my,
Owners.
I see a lot of people,
In the park.
I love my family,
A lot.
Marlene Trillo, Grade 3

The Polar Bears
The cuddly polar bears
Like to play in the soft snow
During the day.
Ella Khan, Grade 2

Lovely Nature
Fresh, green luscious leaves
All nature spirits dancing.
Beautiful nature.
Mischa Markovic, Grade 3

Northern Lights
Frosty Northern Lights
Northern Lights are colorful
The lights are famous.
Nathan Barnard, Grade 3

Beautiful Sunset
Beautiful sunset.
Red and orange, you are blazing.
I love your bright shine.
David Goldapper, Grade 3

Dogs
Dogs are very fun!
They are cute, sweet, and fluffy.
I love dogs so much.
Ariel Reichler, Grade 3

Lovely Hawaii
The glass rainbow waves,
Ombre pink, orange, purple sky.
Graceful palm trees sway.
Sydney Wagner, Grade 3

A Bear
There is a small bear
In a beautiful forest
That was eating meat
Nini Li, Grade 3

Emperor Penguins
Emperor penguins
Lay one egg at a time
In a rookery
Kayla Friesen, Grade 2

The Owl
The snowy owl
Made angels on the ground
In the winter time.
Amrit Bains, Grade 2

Polar Bears
The cold polar bears
Roam freely in the cold Arctic
When the sun goes down
Dylan Kong, Grade 2

Grey
Grey is thunder
Grey is a cloud
Grey is a scooter
But not a cow
Grey is a bike
And grey is jail
Grey is dust
And grey is smooth
Grey is everything, except for some
Grey are rocks
And grey is a car.
Grey are lamps
And some are not
Grey is clay
And grey is hippopotamus
And grey is elephants
And mice
Grey is pavement
Jana Alnakeeb, Grade 2

Harmony Bobowski
H allway stomper
A pple eater
R eally cool bedroom
M akes hurricanes
O n a bicycle
N ever too young
Y OUR TOUNGE IS BLUE!!

B londe hair
O n another adventure
B umping stuff
O h, she likes *Frozen*
W AKE UP!!!
S ings O Canada !
K ind and funny
I s really awesome!!!
Magenta Bobowski, Grade 3

Cake
Chocolate, vanilla icing on top
Bowls, whisks and measuring cups
Bakers and families like to dress me up
Sometimes I can be sweet
I can be the perfect treat
I am scared of the oven
Please don't treat me like a muffin
Children gather around my flames
Chanting and singing different names
I am made into different shapes
I wear fondant as a cape
I spend my time in a baking pan
Guess who I am?
Liam Griese, Grade 2

Math
Math
fun, great
exciting, counting, learning
adding coins is easy
Numbers
Elikem Fumey, Kindergarten

Flowers
Flowers
Pretty, colorful
Drinking, picking, watering
They make me happy
Plants
Giada Pernicello, Kindergarten

Cheetahs
Cheetahs
fast, cool
eating, running, hunting
Faster than other animals
Predators
Olivia Gatewood, Kindergarten

Dogs
Dogs
Funny, playful
Jumping, running, fetching
Dogs are really cute!
Friendly
Adam DiBattista, Kindergarten

Spring
Spring is here
everyone gives some cheer!
flowers bloom, plants develop
flowers grow for hours
bees buzz, say hooray spring is today!
Gurshawn Bhullar, Grade 3

Birds
B ig as an owl
I nteresting like a peacock
R ed feathers like a cardinal
D otted like a woodpecker
S pecial flying skills
Giulia Sicoli, Grade 2

Springtime Cheer
It's the perfect time to swim,
You can pick beautiful flowers.
You can hear the lovely birds sing.
Birds are laying eggs in their nests.
Rabbits hopping about.
Majida Frida Sleiman, Grade 3

Sports
Exciting, fun
Jogging, swimming, winning
Sports are really fun!
Soccer
Michael Ly, Grade 2

Teachers
Teachers are nice,
They teach me.
I love them!
Teachers
Ava Rainero, Grade 2

Snow
Snow is my favourite
Now it's snowing
Over the mountains it's snowing
Wind is blowing too
Gaurav Sidhu, Grade 3

Wind
When it's going to rain
It is very strong
No one can see it
Dancing leaves
Aurora Richards, Kindergarten

Sports
Awesome, exciting
Playing, winning, trying
Hockey is super fun!
Goooal!!
Joseph Jartidian, Grade 2

A Raindrop
A raindrop on my face.
A raindrop in a race.
A race with all of the other drops
To see who goes kerplop!
David Abercrombie, Grade 3

Winter
Snowflakes, windy
Icy, snowy, sprinkling, snow
freezing, snow glides through the air
Cold
Addison Glace, Grade 3

Owls
O wls soar up in the sky
W ise old birds
L oud and noisy at night
S leep during the day
Emma Elisabeth Luis, Grade 2

Dogs
D ogs are noisy
O beys its master
G ray, brown, spotted
S mells its food
Frederique Clement, Grade 2

Warm Weather
Gently blowing
Flowers swaying
Playing
Mowing the lawn
Ella Wood, Grade 2

Play Outside
Playing outside is fun!
I play with my sister outside.
When I play outside,
I see butterflies fly and bumblebees buzz!
Aubrie Harmon, Grade 2

Snowflakes
Peaceful falling
Cold beautiful
Ice crystals
Falling from the sky.
Abigail Gabbard, Grade 2

Raindrops
Raindrops falling down
Falling so peacefully
Like a leaf so quiet
Falling like bubbles on your head
Julian Sepulveda, Grade 3

Volcanoes
Volcanoes have lava that blows up
There are rocks too
You can climb up them
But be careful if you do!
Liam Zwanch, Kindergarten

Snowflakes
Snowflakes cover trees
Snowflakes falling from the sky
So quietly down
Keaton Ort, Grade 3

Hedgehog
Look, a hedgehog den.
They are prickly like cacti
Watch them eat some fruit.
Ani Lahser, Grade 3

Danny
D anny is a good pal
A s awesome as me
N icely helping
N ow amazing
Y ou are the best
Noah Drisner, Grade 3

Spring Sights
I'm seeing birds
And cars on the street
People walking
And very tall trees
Growing leaves
Tim Ghanem, Kindergarten

Heart
H ugs and kisses
E mail kind messages
A lways the shape of a strawberry
R ed and lovely
T iny little heart!
Axel Belanger, Grade 2

Books
B eautiful stories
O riginal pictures
O pen the pages
K eep reading
S mart you'll be!
Vinh Quoc Dam, Grade 2

A Little Turtle
There once was a little turtle,
who lived in a log.
He loved to go visit the pond
and play.
He always had fun!
Alessandra Santarelli, Kindergarten

Summer Time
Hot sun
Colourful flowers
Blue sky
Air breeze
Light rain
Faris Elkanzi, Grade 2

Flowers
Flowers
pretty, smelly
growing, planting, picking
they have green leaves
Garden
Savanna Barton, Kindergarten

Me
My name is Leah
And I like first grade
I like to read books
Sometimes in the shade
I like sports
Like soccer and swim
I have lots of cousins
And one is named Tim.
Leah Burke, Grade 1

All About Me
I like to sing
and jewelry is my thing.
Pink is the color for me
and some friends call me G.
I really like to skate on the ice
and my favorite food is fried rice.
I have two brothers, they are fun
and we like to run.
Gianna Lentini, Grade 1

Things About Me
I like to be happy, not to be sad.
I like to play ball with my Mom and Dad.
I like to swim and have lots of fun
playing in the sand under the sun.
My eyes are blue like the seas
and sometimes green like the trees.
My bike is fun to ride down the street
I go very fast and my heart starts to beat.
Megan Irvine, Grade 1

Puppy
I'm a puppy.
I love when people,
Tickle my stomach.
If they drop me,
I will feel sad.
I run when they throw the ball.
I feel happy when,
I chase cats.
Alondra Hernandez, Grade 3

Feelings
I feel happy when I get Xbox
But I am sad when I am sick.
I feel excited when it is my birthday
But I feel mad when I get pushed.
Sometimes I feel cool
When I score a goal
But happy is the feeling
That I feel most of all.
Isaiah Rushton, Grade 2

I Love Sports!
Summer brings grass
It's time to swim
Fall brings flowers
Winter brings snow
It's time to ski
And spring brings leaves
It's time to play
Soccer, karate, roller skating
Yassine Febri, Grade 1

Earth
Home sweet home
Earth is worth
Millions of dollars
Stars are far away and beautiful
Earth is the third planet
From the sun
From space
It looks mostly blue
Nola Stenstrom Moser, Grade 3

Families
Praying
Eating
Reading
Watching
Chasing
Tickling
Gaming
Families
Jayella Funk, Grade 1

Blossoms Are Growing
Blossoms are growing
I am so glad!
Look at those insects,
I am excited to see the pollen,
Even though I am allergic.
Wow! The dog is running,
On the green grass.
I love spring so much!!!
Julia Bourgeois-Matus, Grade 3

Gymnastics
Hanging
Jumping
Falling
Twirling
Hopping
Flopping
Balancing
Gymnastics
Emily Allen, Grade 1

Spring Time
Spring is ringing to have some fun.
It is time for the sun to come out.
The grass is lime color.
Put on your glasses.
Trees have pretty flowers.
   Flowers are tall in
   SPRING
Darshpreet Brar, Grade 3

All About the Teddy Bear
Teddy bear
Fluffy, cuddly
Smiling, sitting, growling
Sitting on your bed
Moving, playing, sleeping
Fuzzy, pal
Stuffed animal
Brennen Lucia, Grade 3

Life and Death
Life
Sunny, lovely
Shining, singing, playing
Beauty, brightness, fear, coldness
Screaming, clawing, chasing
Dark, hateful
Death
Hannah May, Grade 3

Teacher/Student
Teacher
Clever, nice
Teaching, writing, working
Markers, books, pencils, crayons
Studying, reading, drawing
Young, smart
Student
Samantha Edwards, Grade 3

Moon and Sun
Sun
Big, bright
Burning, rising, shining
Star, center, Armstrong, craters
Shining, glowing, setting
Dark, small
Moon
Seamus Marshall, Grade 2

Games
Bingo numbers
Monopoly dice
Heads Up animals
Scrabble letters
Twister fall
Vanessa Beldi, Grade 2

Snowman
Frosty, icy
Frosting, warming, cooling
Warm to the heart
snow pal
Emma Girod, Grade 3

Snow
Cold, white
Falling, icing, crisping
Funny, happy, wonderful, soft
Slush
Abby Davis, Grade 3

Snow
Cold winter
Hockey, skiing, snowboarding
Exciting, wonderful, cool, blurry
Snowing
Caroline Adams, Grade 3

Ants
A nts work in a team
N ature is their home
T errific builders
S uper force to lift a leaf
Matheo Piccinin, Grade 2

Vinh
V inh is a little boy
I like to play with him
N obody is kinder than Vinh
H e's a great friend
Maxence Lavigne, Grade 2

Fall
Fall down, fall down
All over the place
Leaves fall down
Low on the ground
Harveer Kaur Chahal, Grade 3

Lily
Lily is my best friend.
I like her so much.
She lives so close to me.
Yippee we are friends!
Supriya Kaur Randhawa, Grade 3

Snow
S nowy days are past
N ow snow is melting
O h! The warm days are here
W e'll have fun this spring
Joanna Lian, Grade 2

Arriana
A wesome
R eally nice
R eally helpful
I nterested in books
A lways looks pretty
N ever is unhappy
A lways runs fast
Arriana Rodriguez, Grade 2

Friends
F un
R espectful
I ncredible
E xciting
N ice
D ifferent
S weet
Melody Lehtiniemi, Grade 3

Spongebob and Squidward
Spongebob
Dumb, likes everybody
Loving, screaming, running
Friendly, helpful, mean angry
Lying, kicking, talking
Weak, tall
Squidward
Nykeem Abu-Zebiba, Grade 2

Dog
I am a dog.
I chase deer and birds.
I have friends.
I eat with my friends.
My friends play with me.
We play in the pool.
We play ball.
Laila Valtierra Alonza, Grade 2

Fame
Fame takes people away from life.
At a level of pressure you can't control.
My theory is fame is bad,
No time for family
No time for play
Empty life is where you're at…
in a life of FAME.
Leia Culbert, Grade 3

Egg
egg
still, white
cracking, breaking, squeaking
breathing a lot of fire
dragon
Henry Scallorns, Grade 2

Wall
They,
Hang stuff on me.
I don't know why.
I see the children,
Coming in with their
Weird eyes and I am scared,
When people put staples on me,
I bleed. But, I hold it in.
They put nails in me.
Please, stop, I am begging you.
Casandra Barajas Ibarra, Grade 3

Dog
I am a dog.
I love to eat dog food.
I play with people.
I like chasing squirrels.
Also I would be friendly.
I would not run away.
I jump over ropes.
I also get happy.
I am a dog.
Lizbeth Martinez Higareda, Grade 3

Poems
Poems are nice
Every time I read
A poem
I think about
What it is saying
What ideas it gives me
Makes me wonder
What are the pictures telling?
What the poem is saying.
Thomas John Cullen, Grade 2

God Is
God is as big as the universe
And as small as a grain of sand.
He is as strong as a bulldozer
And as gentle as a bunny.
God is as far as the clouds
And as close as a hug.
He is as wild as a tiger
And as calm as a still lake.
God is amazing.
William McVittie, Grade 2

Spring Activities
I swim in the water
Play soccer in the field
Basketball in the garden
And hockey in the rink
But my favorite of all is
Tennis on the court
Alejandro Trenado, Grade 1

Summer/Winter
Summer
Bright, beautiful
Walking, playing, swimming
Birds, sun, coats, ice
Skiing, snowboarding, sledding
Cold, windy
Winter
Elizabeth Zelinsky, Grade 3

The Taste of Spring
Springtime is my favorite because…
the vacationing rain returns
to give the earth a drink.
The apple tree blooms
and a butterfly lands on a blossom
tasting the sweet taste
of spring.
Emily Hume, Grade 2

Ferrari
F astest car ever
E ver fast
R acing cars
R ampaging
A lways fast
R eally awesome
I s the best car ever
Jonah Marshall, Grade 3

Dogs
Dogs
Fast, fun
Running, playing, swimming
Leash, fur, collars, bed
Jumping, playing, sleeping
Cute, awesome
Puppies
Callie Snow, Grade 1

Books
Books
Interesting, awesome
Reading, looking, listening
Characters, nonfiction, fiction, words
Imagining, whispering, writing
Smooth, thin
Pages
Brady Kunkle, Grade 1

Deer
Deer
Brown, furry
Fast, skittish, jumping
They get scared easily
Doe
Connor Hagy, Grade 2

Puppy
I am a puppy.
I like to run around,
And play with my owners.
I love to play,
Around outside.
It's scary when people,
Pick me up.
I drink milk and eat puppy food.
When people are sad,
I play with them,
And they could pet me.
After a long day,
I take a long nap at night.
Then it starts all over again,
In the morning.
I love you.
Melissa Torres, Grade 3

Puppy
I am pretty,
Soft. People like,
To pet me, Since,
I am so friendly.
I am bright and,
White, like a cloud,
In the sky. I like,
To eat good food. I like to,
Lay down in the window, so,
I could feel the shining sun.
Sometimes I ask my owners for,
Food, but, they say no, it's,
Bad for me.
Brianna Estrada, Grade 3

Championship
There are lots of things you could do
Like;
Dance,
Play soccer,
Play basketball,
Gymnastics.
You could win with your group or team.
But there are something's you have to do
To win;
Teamwork,
Friendship
Honor
And that is called championship.
Sarah Holder, Grade 2

Spring
Cool, fun
Melting, blowing, growing
Taffy on snow
Sweet!
Erika Cao, Grade 3

Rain
Freezing cold
Playing, jumping, splashing
I love splashing puddles
Storm
Aaron Peters, Grade 3

Cats
C are
A sk for food
T ravel on feet
S oft
Alexandra Kosgei, Kindergarten

Tigers
Stripy, cool
Hiding, springing, pouncing
Running, killing, ripping, eating
Luring
Mackenna Berg, Grade 3

Dogs
D ive
O pen gates
G o run
S wim
Sam Wiersema, Kindergarten

Dogs
D o tricks
O ur pet
G et you
S pecial
Jillian Wiersema, Kindergarten

Cars
C rash
A ccidents
R ough
S ome do stunts
Santiago Valle, Kindergarten

Cats
C lever
A mazing
T ough
S leep
Keely Semtner, Kindergarten

Baby Bunnies, Little Bunnies
Baby bunnies can be found
They are all around in the springtime
I want one for my self
Baby bunnies, little bunnies
Meena Madhavan, Grade 2

Sounds of Spring
When I look out my window
Cars are beeping
People walking
Look up and see birds
Birds flying in a triangle
Sarah Sharif, Kindergarten

Nature Fun
Leaves are green
Flowers grow
Play with friends
See squirrels go!
It is Spring!
Haroun Ben-Mansour, Kindergarten

Marie
M arvelous at gymnastics
A wesome friend
R ight-handed
I go to Klein Elementary
E ntertaining
Kayleigh Kosko, Grade 2

Golden Yellow
Summer pyramids
Made of triangles
Glued with sand
Big and tall
Golden yellow
Andrew Matar, Kindergarten

Nature Me
Look at me!
I am as small as a bee.
There's my hive in the tree.
Oh what fun this could be
Playing up in the tree!
Lyla Thurman, Grade 1

The Doll with a Fall
The doll that had a ball.
Went to the mall.
And got a call,
Then she ran back home in the tall hall,
And had a fall.
Khushi Kaur Cheena, Grade 3

Water
W ater evaporates from rain
A quariums with dolphins swimming
T errific beluga whales
E arth is mostly covered by water
R ain is part of the water cycle
Luca Matteo, Grade 2

Spring
Springtime
the birds whistle
the trees sway
smell the spring air all day.
Enjoy the breeze and the smell of rain.
Spring is here, shout hooray!
Nicholas Crawford, Grade 2

Easter
Easter looks like colorful eggs.
Easter sounds like the quiet Easter Bunny.
Easter feels like soft stuffing in the basket.
Easter smells like yummy candy.
Easter tastes like sweet peeps.
Easter is very nice!
Bianca Ruiz, Grade 3

Spring
After spring comes fall,
And God is special.
He makes spring.
I love the spring.
In spring the sun shines,
And I play with my brown cat.
Isaac Gross, Grade 2

Things About Me
My name is Braedin and I like to play
and I go to school every day.
I have blue eyes and light brown hair
and my Mom tells me not to stare.
I wear glasses so I can see
and I like when dad builds legos with me.
Braedin Deardorff, Grade 1

Shark
I am a shark.
I smell blood all around the ocean.
I eat fish every day.
So I can't get hungry.
I travel all around the world,
Swimming.
Kirby Adrian Diaz, Grade 3

I Am a Puppy
I am a puppy,
I like to run all around.
I like to chase my toys.
I am a puppy.
I am so soft.
I am a friendly puppy.
Ashly Tovar Cabral, Grade 2

The Four Seasons
Winter is cold,
Spring has flowers,
Summer is very hot,
Fall has colorful leaves,
I love the seasons,
What season do you love?
Amaya Rico, Grade 2

Pumpkin
Orange, round
Spinning, rolling, carving
Pie, soup, seeds, pumpkins
Falling, eating, picking
Green, brown
Gourd
Andrew Michael, Grade 3

Spring
S pring is a season
P lay at the sun
R ain will come and go
I t is so colourful
N ext season is summer
G o outside and play
Anand Gill, Grade 3

Fall
Yellow, brown
Rushing, hunting, pouncing
Squirrels, apple cider, apples, hay rides
Picking, hiding, keeping
Windy, cold
Autumn
Sasha Konitzer, Grade 3

Spring
S pring is here!
P lants are growing!
R ain drops are falling!
I have spring!
N ever go away!
G o play outside!
Benita Jaswal, Grade 3

Spring
S pring is a break
P eople play games and relax
R ain falls and people play
I t is going to be a colourful spring
N ow you have a
G reat spring break
Gurjeet Singh Gill, Grade 3

Chocolate Labs

Chocolate labs are silly with no care,
They also have some beautiful long hair.
Chocolate labs are the best,
Also with food they're really obsessed.

My chocolate lab is three years old,
Now he's gotten so big his fat rolls fold.
Sometimes he sees a squirrel he likes to chase,
When I'm riding my bike, he likes to race.

Cam's favorite toy is his big red ball,
Sometimes when we play, he trips and falls.
When I'm sad Cam cheers me up,
He is a crazy, lovely pup.

Elise Missigman, Grade 3

Thoughts of a Caterpillar

I love to read and play in the sunlight.
It is quiet and fun.
I love to eat leaves.
I never get sad or mad or excited.
I'm always in between.
What makes me happy is a quiet, nice friend.
What makes me sad is when a nice friend leaves me.
What makes me angry is very rarely,
You'll see me yelling at those annoying bees.
What would change my life and always make me happy
Is a nice little house for me to sleep.
What I would say to my owner,
"Hello, can you see me?"

Andrew Devoe, Grade 3

Grandma's Llama

There once was a grandma
Who had a pet llama.
The llama ran away
So she looked every day.
While looking she saw a bee
And jumped into a tree.
The llama came by
And said a big, "HI!"
She jumped on his head
And said, "Help or we're dead!"
The llama ran fast
And they got home at last.
So they had cake and went back to bed.

Miss Stonehouse's 2nd Grade Class

Summer

Summer looks like kids playing in the pool.
Summer sounds like water splashing at the water park.
Summer feels as hot as hot cocoa.
Summer smells like sunscreen at the beach.
Summer taste like ice cream in the parlor.
Summer is my favorite season.

Ayden Zazulak, Grade 3

Owls

I love owls because they are fun.
They come out when the day is done.
Owls can turn their heads all the way around.
But they only make one loud hooting sound.
I love owls because they are cute and funny.
They make me feel like every day is sunny.
Owls can fly extremely well.
Owls are active at night and are very swell.
They use their talons to catch their prey.
Owls make sure that their prey doesn't get away.
Owls are interesting and very smart.
They will always be in my heart.

Lillian Arnold, Grade 3

Ice Cream

Oh, you're delightful, creamy, tasty
So yummy, so good
I want to eat you forever
I wish I could
You look just like whipped cream
What I put on strawberries
Well I put something on my ice cream
It is called cherries
I love the way it looks
If feels so milky in my mouth
I wonder where it's made
Well I think the ice cream is invented in the south

Anushka Sai Tankala, Grade 3

Nellie

I have a dog named Nellie
When she eats she has a big belly
She likes to play every day with her neighbor Ohey
He is her good friend
Nellie and Ohey will play to the end
When I give her a treat
She knocks me off my feet
She grunts when she can't hunt
She barks at the people that park
She hunts well because she has a good sense of smell
Nellie is my special pet
A better dog I have not met

Noah Frye, Grade 2

Hello Spring, Goodbye Winter

Hello to flowers such as roses and tulips
Goodbye to snow that covered the ground
Hello to birds that fly in the sky
Goodbye to polar bears that like the winter cold
Hello to butterflies that liked the warm weather
Goodbye to hot chocolate warming us in the winter
Hello to the blue sky that we see
Goodbye to gray clouds that fill the sky
Hello to rainbows after rainfall
Goodbye to snow storms that kept us inside

Ivy Tian, Grade 3

Running
R unning
U nder
N eed
N ever Stopping
I nto
N oise
G round
Andrew Nelson, Grade 2

Springtime is Here
What a beautiful day!
Warmer weather,
rain falls from the sky.
Blooming flowers,
oh flowers, oh flowers.
Birds tweet their beautiful songs.
Springtime is here!
Susana Pantoja, Grade 2

Crop Dusters
Crop dusters flying low to the ground
spraying chemicals over the fields.
Up and down,
over and over again.
When dusters are done
they fly up up up and away
to another field.
James Galdean, Grade 2

Wolf
I am a wolf. I like,
To chase moose, deer, and raccoons,
Because I eat them. I run with my pack
I live with them.
All my kind live in Asia and North America.
My kind are good hunters.
We are never vegetarians.
Miguel Leyva Quiterio, Grade 3

School
S tudy spelling words.
C ut out art projects.
H unt for clues.
O rganize your desk.
O pen your mind.
L earn new things.
Chris Strain, Grade 3

Spring
S uch good weather
P lants grow tall
R ain brings out the worms
I nside ants build their homes
N ice big trees
G reen grass
Kushal Shome, Grade 2

Strawberries
Strawberry ice cream
Strawberry milkshakes
Strawberry yogurt
Strawberry doughnuts
Strawberry pie
Strawberry jelly
Strawberry cupcakes
Strawberry cake
Strawberries
Harper Robinette, Grade 2

Ocean
Life is an ocean
Love is in the air
The ocean is peaceful as can be
Bees fly in the air
Birds fly peacefully in the air
Life is an ocean
I hear the ocean sand
Life is an ocean
The ocean is great as can be
Emmanuel White, Grade 3

Things Around Me
I love the things around me
like…

My house
My family
My games
My world

I for sure love the things around me.
Joshua Wiest, Grade 3

Spaghetti
Slimy and slippery
Your swirly strings
Makes a sound as I slurp it
You are such a yummy thing
Your tomato sauce is so delicious
And yummy
The tomatoes are so juicy and sweet
So good for my tummy
Sriya Tanguturi, Grade 2

The Teacher Gets A
I look forward to your class
When I come to school.
You're an awesome teacher;
I think you're very cool.
You're smart and fair and friendly;
You're helping all of us.
And if I got to grade you,
From me you'd get A!
Avery Forney, Grade 3

Favorite Thing
My favorite thing to do is read.
like the Cat in the Hat,
which is fun to read.
So help me read
and I will help
you to if you'd
like me to.
Tristan Bonilla, Grade 2

The Savior
Jesus
Gentle, peaceful
Loving, teaching, leading
He loves every person
Saving, sacrificing, suffering
Faithful, hopeful
Christ
Matthew Kaatz, Grade 3

Dog and Cat
Dog
Lovable, sweet
Chewing, growling, wagging
Collar, bones, yarn ball, bells
Crawling, meowing, purring,
Cuddly, soft
Cat
Kinga Malinowski, Grade 3

Fire and Ice
Fire
Soft, bright
Smoking, burning, cooking
Stove, lighter, skates, blizzards
Slipping, cracking, melting
Shiny, hard
Ice
Brayden Rivera, Grade 3

Fire and Water
Fire
Bright, hot
Burning, lighting, scorching
Flames, stove glaciers, steam
Freezing, boiling, flowing
Icy, snowy
Water
Chance Joyner, Grade 3

Anna
A nand is a child
N ot a man
A nand studies
N ever went to another school
D oesn't play a lot
Anand Singh Gill, Grade 3

Spring
S pring is here!
P lants are growing!
R ain drops are falling pretty as crystals
I love
N ice flowers
G rowing in my garden
Lovleen Brar, Grade 3

Sharks
S ome are different sizes
H ammerhead sharks are super cool
A wesome sharks eat meat
R azor sharp teeth are for sharks
K iller sharks eat people
S harks that are giant eat a lot of food
Daniel Gonzalez, Grade 3

School
S uccessful
C ommunication
H elpful
O ne, two, three
O n the computer
L earning
Mark Litwiler, Grade 2

Tigers
T ough to beat
I s in cat family
G ood hunter
E ats meat
R oars loud
S peedy cat
Vinayak Prasannakumar, Grade 3

Dhivya
D hivya likes cupcakes
H onest person
I ntelligent girl
V alentina is her friend
Y es, she loves ice cream
A wesome personality
Dhivya Jooravan, Grade 3

Summer
S hade trees keep you cool
U sually I play outside
M eals are yummy
M aking flower necklaces
E agles flying high in the sky
R ainbows come when it rains
Sophia Schlieman, Grade 1

Bullying
Bullying is bad
It can cause a lot of problems
If you are the person that is getting bullied
Then you may feel sad
But don't you worry tell an adult
And an adult can make it stop for sure
And you will feel happier than before
Ravleen Padda, Grade 3

Kitten and Puppy
Kitten
cute, fluffy
meowing, running, jumping
sly, camouflage, outside, cry
barking, annoying, following
light brown, eats a lot, want more
puppy
Parker Snyder, Grade 2

Dog and Cat
Dog
Furry, loud
Catching, running, barking
Leash, dog park, toys, cat nip
Purring, cleaning, sleeping
Lovable, soft
Cat
Grayson Vollmer, Grade 2

Easter Colours
Green is for palm branches
Red is for His blood
Purple is for his robe
Black is for death
Yellow is for heaven
White is for him cleaning us white as snow
Pink is for new life
Emma Norval, Grade 1

Flowers
Flowers bloom.
They grow and bloom.
Flowers blow in the wind.
Winter is cold and summer is hot.
Fall is chilly and spring is warm, just warm.
I like spring and I like summer.
I like winter but I like fall better.
Jerzie Kotelnikoff, Grade 2

Serpents
Serpent
In sea
Wiggles in water
Crazy swimming toward food
Snake
Sarah Willey, Grade 2

Baymax
Big, cute
Hugging, snuggling, helping
Baymax is so awesome
Adorable
Brielle Abramoff, Grade 3

Vacation
Hot, sunny
Swimming, playing, running
Going to the airport
Traveling!
Matteo Carmosino, Grade 3

Spring
Windy, cloudy
Playing, planting, growing
Cycling outside after school
Perfect!
Nathan Fortin, Grade 3

Vacations
Enjoyable, hot
Jogging, playing, swimming
Beautiful sandy beach
Excited!
Alessandro Buccione, Grade 3

Sports
Fun, hard
Tricking, scoring, celebrating
Trying to beat your opponents
Challenging!
Elliot Charbonneau-Provost, Grade 3

Spring
Beautiful, colourful
Enjoying, playing, jogging
Picking flowers from your garden
Perfect!
Cristina Sacco, Grade 3

Sports
Fun, sweaty
Playing, running, swimming
Great for your body
Healthy!
Gianni Rossi, Grade 3

Basketball
Fun, fantastic
Shooting, dunking, scoring
Using teamwork for winning
Great!
Michael-Ryan Ricci, Grade 3

Dad
D ad's silly
A wesome
D elightful
Makel Sanjines, Kindergarten

Frog
I am a frog. I am all wet. I want to stay dry
from the rain. I see a leaf
I am going to grab it to stay dry.
Lilly Smith, Grade 1

Trees
The trees are greener than the grass.
The birds are making noisy sounds.
The bark feels rough on my skin.
Izzy Foster, Grade 1

Squirrels
Squirrels are so cute
Stuffing their faces full of nuts
They are very smart
Kiersten Nienhuis, Grade 3

Deer
Deer run in the woods
They eat leaves and bounce by trees
They stick together
Rachel Bonebrake, Grade 3

School
School is very fun.
I am in grade 3. School will
Never be boring.
Denalyn Coziahr, Grade 3

Sun
In the sky
The sun shines light
In the morning.
Skylar Gerbrandt, Grade 3

Race Car
Racing on the track
Faster it goes on the track
Wind blows through her hair
Hannah Glass, Grade 3

Snow
Snow falls from the sky
It's chilly outside my house
A coat keeps me warm
Caleb Wright, Grade 2

Creepy Creatures…
The creepy creatures come for you at night,
It can also scare you and give you a big fright.
Sometimes at night I have a bad dream, but that is just a spine tingling theme.
I see them by my antique dresser,
But then I feel really bad pressure.
If you want to see the ghost of Mary,
Just to warn you… she is very scary.
If she hits you in your gut,
Then she is going to give you really bad luck.
I see them on my green moldy wall,
And then start to shake and fall.
I see them in my long dark hallway,
Then I start to walk away.
My dog sees them in the dark,
Then he starts to let out a vicious bark.
When I hear a frightening green witch, I start to cry and twitch.
Then I hear a rare vicious zombie dog,
I wish I could turn into a bloody grumpy frog.
I think I see Washington's ghost, I hope I'm not being a bad host.
My fingers turn to freezing ice when I see green, moldy mice.
Then my body instantly freezes, because I feel a couple cold blooded breezes.
Isaiah Tolbert, Grade 3

Spring Is Here
Spring is here for everyone let's go outside and join the fun.
The flowers, oh, the flowers they are tall as towers.
The birds fly away while I play.
Rabbits hop while I drink pop.
Trees grow like never before.
You'll never stay inside because of the sunshine outside.
When I think of bows a rainbow appears.
I hope spring does not end, so I could play with my friends.
Everyday the way I play, I bother the flies to go away.
So, I say, "Hooray!!"
Spring when you are saying "Bye," you let your friend Summer to say "Hi."
Khushbir Kaur Basra, Grade 3

Summer
In summer it's always hot and never stops.
Summer is nice and cool and rainy too!
It's never cold and there are a lot of pretty things like flowers.
I can feel the breeze blowing on me.
I can feel the sun looking right at me.
In summer we ride our bikes up and down the hill and play at the park.
We carry my dog and he barks and we play all day in the hot sun.
Rihanna Davis, Grade 3

Summer
Summer looks like hot.
Summer sounds like a person jumping in a pool making a big splash.
Summer feels like dry grass.
Summer smells like a hot fire.
Summer tastes like hot sauce.
Summer is the best season ever.
Ryan Ballantine, Grade 3

Love

How do I love you?
Let me count the ways.
I love you as a kid
Likes to play.

How do I love you?
Let me tell you how.
I love you as a cat
Likes to meow.

How do I love you?
Look and you will see.
I love you as deep
As the sea.

How do I love you?
I want the world to know.
I love you more than a cat
With a bow.
Nathan Van Agteren, Grade 2

Grass

There are many types of grass.
Grass is green
Grass can sway in the wind
Grass can be many sizes
It can be many shapes too
Grass smells good
Sometimes it smells like rain
Grass is fun to tumble in
Grass can even be yellowish and brownish.
Grass feels good on hot summer days.
Bugs like to be in the grass.
Weeds are related to grass.
Plants and trees are too.
I like grass.
I would not like to eat grass.
Grass is fun to play in.
I feel grass.
There is a lot of grass.
I planted grass in school.
Charlotte Calhoun, Grade 2

Mikayla Ann

M ariska's sister
I ce cream lover
K eeper of her phone
A good friend
Y oung lady
L oves her phone
A good sister

A lmost a teenager
N ever gives up
N ever wants to give up
Mariska Habursky, Grade 2

I Am

I am a dog
furry, hairy, with a tail,
walking in the house.

I am a dog
big, medium, small,
eating dog food.

I am a dog
eyed, eared, nosed,
playing in the grass.
Nicholas Taylor, Grade 2

I Am

I am Alex Ovechkin
Shooting, never passing
On the Ice.

I am Alex Ovechkin
Skating, sliding, gliding
Very fast.

I am Alex Ovechkin,
Fierce to other teams
And getting hat tricks.
Caiden Hofstedt, Grade 2

Hello Spring, Goodbye Winter

Hello to the shining sun
Goodbye to the snow

Hello to the glittering flowers
Goodbye, Old Man Winter

Hello to rain that falls
Goodbye slippery ice

Hello chirping birds
Goodbye whirling blizzards
Colby Frey, Grade 3

I Am

I am Kamal
Who is a son of Jib and Maya
Who likes chips
Who dislikes onions
Who thinks about a puppy
Who wishes about money
Who loves a puppy
Who wonders about friends
Who dreams about hair
Who wants to be a millionaire
Khanal
Kamal Khanal, Grade 3

Poems

Poems can be fun,
Poems can be bad.
But between all the poems,
There is always gold in them!
Tosh Thompson, Grade 2

Kids

K ind to friends
I nteresting ideas
D o listen
S pecial people
Nicolas Saoumaa Garcia, Grade 2

Snow

Snow is white!
Near my house.
On the grass.
Winter has snow.
Harneet Kaur Gill, Grade 3

Sweet Treat

Yummy, delicious
Hopping, eating, skipping
Finding many chocolate surprises
Candy
Victoria Nacked Cabral, Grade 3

Good Fish, Bad Fish

My fish swim peacefully
My fish fight
My fish play
My fish chase each other
Noah Broglio, Grade 2

Bats

Bats are not scary
And these winged creatures
Aren't much fun
So bats are friendly
Hari Rakeshkumar Patel, Grade 3

Wolves in the Moonlight

Wolves in the forest
and they are howling to communicate.
They are also howling to the
sparkling moon.
Emily Lilienthal, Grade 2

Snow

S hiny and white
N ice and fluffy
O utrageously fun times
W et and watery
Kassandra Lombardo, Grade 2

Ninja Sports
Kung Fu
Karate chops
Punching in the air
Ninjas sneaking
Quietly walking
Jumping in the air
Rudy Kanao, Kindergarten

Winter
W hite snow
I cy ground
N ice winter days
T iny snowflakes
E veryone plays outside
R ecess in the snow
Mia Di Caprio, Grade 2

Winter
W hen it is cold
I n the snow
N ever stops snowing
T eams of shovelers
E xtravagant use of salt
R acing on sleds
Jack Hafer, Grade 3

Spring Break
Take a break
Sleep on a chair
At the beach
Or anywhere!
Because it's sunny
Because it's spring!
Megan Lopes Toroyan, Kindergarten

Winter
W inter is cold
I nteresting sometimes
N ot fun driving
T housands of accidents
E ntertaining in the snow
R ain making ice
Laura Sokso, Grade 3

Spring Life
Flowers bloom
Green trees
Flying bugs
Stinging bees
Muddy ground
Swinging swings
Anaelle Chaveron, Kindergarten

Wishes
I wish I was a cheetah
And I could run all day.
I wish I was a turtle
And roll a long way.
I wish I was a bear
And I could sleep all day.
I wish I was a big bee
And I could sting all the way.
Xavier Ledoux, Grade 2

I Wish
I wish I was a shark
And I would swim in the bay.
I wish I was a horse
And I could run all day.
I wish I was a pig
And I would roll in the muck.
I wish I was a whale
And I would eat a duck.
Zachary Radoux, Grade 2

A Storm
A storm was on last night.
It had thunder
Bam, boom, screeech!
It went like this
Bang, boom, bam!
My dog Billy was there.
I was not scared.
I finally fell asleep.
Samara Desjardine, Grade 2

Neon Deon
My name is Deon.
It rhymes with neon.
I like to run,
Out in the sun.
I live in this state,
I will be eight.
When I grow up I'll be a vet,
So that I am able to help your pet.
Deon Carter, Grade 1

Dog
I am a dog.
One thing I like to do is chase my tail.
I can't climb, but I can run fast.
I like to chase cats and cars.
I eat dog food.
If I be good, I get treats.
I play with other dogs, toys, and my friends.
I like to sleep.
Jonathan Villa Ortiz, Grade 2

Rabbit
R abbits jump and jump
A lways being cuddly
B aby bunnies are cute
B ut they could be funny
I n spring when
T hey eat your carrots
Emma Langlois, Grade 2

White
White
It tastes like snow
It smells like warm cauliflower
It looks like the clouds
It sounds like wiggling paper
It feels like a white board
R. Brayden Wright, Grade 2

Spring
S pring is coming
P eople like flowers
R acing on a bike
I am waiting for green trees
N ature is beautiful
G od, thank you!
Eloi Abran, Grade 2

Flower
F lowers smell wonderful
L ook at them so pretty
O rchids are purple
W ater for the plant
E ven in the summer they grow
R eplant more flowers all the time
Évelyne Crowe, Grade 2

Emma
Emma
Artsy, happy, sweet, loving
Lily
Cupcakes
Desi
Green
Emma Amodeo, Grade 1

My Canoe
My canoe is nice and deep,
I dream about it in my sleep.
In the winter so, so, long,
My canoe is my heart song.
And when it breaks, my heart breaks too,
It will never be just me and you.
Grace Ruth Evelyn Farmer, Grade 2

The Storm
S plashing puddles
T hunder cracking
O bservation towers
R ain dropping
M ud jumping
S unshine glowing!
Victoria Dimitrova, Grade 2

Hot Pink
Hot pink
Tastes like pink peaches
Smells like nail polish
Looks like pink cotton candy
Sounds like screaming girls
Feels beautiful
Alex Moore, Grade 2

Going Buggy
The bugs are strange!
Scorpions are poisonous
Flies scavenge
Praying mantis' camouflage
Bees go buzzing
What's strange about bugs?
Nakki Della Cioppa, Grade 1

Larsen
L oves pets
A dog lover
R eads a lot
S ings
E ntertaining
N ice to others
Kyrsten Larsen, Grade 2

Snug
I am snug,
Snug as a bug.
Then my mom comes to give me a hug!
Now I want milk in a mug,
Now I am snug as a bug.
Then my mom brings me a rug!
Ameira Pettitt, Grade 2

Spring
Flowers grow in the spring
Rain falls from the sky
The sky is beautiful
And sunny
It gets windy
And the grass is muddy!
Adam Dia, Grade 1

Baby
B eautiful
A wesome
B oring
Y ou feed them
Isabella Gil, Kindergarten

Fish
F ins
I n a tank
S pecial
H appy
Augie Biviano, Kindergarten

Summer
Sunny, tropical
Jumping, splashing, swimming
Going to water parks
Refreshing!
Shubhreet Kaur Padda, Grade 3

Sports
Action, hot
Running, skating, scoring
Giving your best shot
Sweaty!
Denis Malyugin, Grade 3

Snow
S now is falling
N icely at night
O nce a year
W onder winter wonder land.
Farren Stevenson-Akapew, Grade 3

Easter
Delicious, colourful
Painting, hiding, eating
Finding eggs and having fun
Amazing!
Émerik Leclair, Grade 3

Cats
C lever
A re lazy
T icklish
S oft
Emily Sanford, Kindergarten

Animals
Small, beautiful
Petting, playing, feeding
Baby bunnies, kittens, puppies
Cute!
Annie Linna Qu, Grade 3

I Love to Dance
I love to dance,
Dancing is fun.
How do we dance?
We can dance how we want!
Dancing makes me crazy!
I can even dance like a bee.
Amrita Singh, Grade 1

Plants
P lants are part of nature
L eaves need water
A ir and soil are important
N ight time flowers sleep
T rees need sunshine
S unflowers grow in fields
Lydia Sun, Grade 2

Spring
S pring is fun
P lants growing tall
R ed or pink buds will wake from sleep
I nside we're spring cleaning
N eatly planting seeds
G ardening on the green grass
Hope Ashley Smith, Grade 2

Spring Vision
I see a tree
And a rainbow too.
I see a ladybug
And flowers too.
I love bugs
and the butterflies too.
Ryme Bouazzaoui, Grade 1

Commotion in the Ocean
Humpback whale,
Hungry shark,
Swimming in the sea.
Electric eel,
Barracuda,
All swim with me!
Marcos Alvarez Caporale, Grade 1

My Dog
My dog
My dog jumps
My dog jumps up
My dog jumps up in
My dog jumps up in my
My dog jumps up in my face!
Ryan Fish, Grade 2

Winter

The feeling of winter is so much more than I can say.
In winter you build snowmen, snow forts and you play.

We all know winter is cold and chilly.
It feels good to be home, where you are allowed to be silly.

When you sit next to a fire, you feel warm and cozy.
When there's a blizzard, in your book you can be nosey.

In the winter the temperature drops.
All the plants go into hibernation, including the crops.

When you step on snow, you here a cracking sound.
Make sure that you are not stepping on ice instead of the ground.

Enjoy winter while it is still here
Because the season is only once a year!

Ashley Close, Grade 3

Wonderful Dolphins

Dolphins shoot glowing blue water up in the air,
They do it with a whole bunch of care,
Dolphins eat squid and colorful fish,
They have a delicious gigantic dish.

In the water dolphins have so much fun,
Sometimes they get burned by the steaming hot sun.
They have a great time flipping,
It's like they are really slipping.

Dolphins have a light gray fin,
If they aren't careful, they'll get a sharp pin.
Dolphins play in the water and have a blast,
Man, dolphins are so extremely fast.

Abigail Hatfield, Grade 3

Nature

I love to take long walks in the woods, magical and green,
Beautiful animals can be seen.
Swimming in a dark blue lake,
In the hot sun an arrow I will make.
In the sky I see a beautiful eagle,
Running across the field is my silly beagle.
My favorite red roses attract the honey bees,
My favorite flower won't ever beat my most favorite trees.
Sometimes I get burned by the golden sun,
But I am having so much fun.
In the blue lake I see pretty goldfish,
They are really colorful and a bold fish.
Sometimes in the wild field I see a cute furry bunny,
I love being in nature because it is really funny.

Kayleigh Napier, Grade 3

What I Like to Do in Season

When I was four I knew how to ice skate.
Now that I am seven I want to learn to roller-skate.
Mom and I like to hike.
When it is warm I like to ride my bike.
More than math I like to play in the park
and then I go to sleep when it is dark.

Alessandra Marengo, Grade 1

Me and My Family

My name is Ryan, I have brown hair and eyes.
I like to play basketball, which is good exercise.
I like playing on the computer, but not most of all.
I like to go golfing with my Dad, but sometimes I hit it over the wall.
Wolves, tigers, and rhinos really make me smile.
I love my family, Mommy, Daddy, Adam and Kyle!

Ryan Swallow, Grade 1

Canada

C anada is where I live.
A country where you want peace and nature
N ot every country is the same as Canada.
A person who comes to Canada will be so excited and surprised.
D ay and night there is peace.
A ll the stuff you see in Canada is different and amazing

Amol K. Bhallar, Grade 3

Soccer

S occer is cool
O ne goal everybody goes wild
C ourage from everybody goes to the players
C oolest sport ever
E veryone loves it
R un players run!!!

Sukhvir S. Jheout, Grade 3

Spring Is Here!

Now it is spring and winter is not here
A beautiful spring has come along with us
From winter to spring, a beautiful shine is here
A swan is there in the pond
Rain is going to come for jumping in puddles
Enough of winter, we all need spring for fun and cheer!

Chloe Youwakim, Grade 2

Spring

S pring is here.
P lants are growing and the birds are chirping.
R ain is dripping from the clouds.
I love spring.
N ew plants and new flowers are growing.
G reen leaves are growing more.

Kirat Kaur Purba, Grade 3

High Merit Poems – Grades K, 1, 2, and 3

God Is
God is as big as the solar system
And as small as a mouse.
He is as strong as a gorilla
And as gentle as a kitten.
God is as far as the desert
And as close as the wall.
He is a wild as a tiger
And as calm as the wind.
God is love.
Savannah Heller, Grade 2

Praise
God is as big as an elephant
And as small as an ant.
He is as strong as Goliath
And as gentle as a cute cat.
God is as far as New York City
And as close as a white cloth.
He is as wild as a horse
And as calm as a bird.
God is our father.
Jade Everett, Grade 2

God Is
God is as big as the universe
And as small as a tiny rock.
He is as strong as 10,000,000 men
And as gentle as 1 kid.
God is as far as 270,000,000 skyscrapers
And as close as 1 spider.
He is as wild as a lion
And as calm as a mouse.
God is great.
Wyatt Lane, Grade 2

I Am
I am a dolphin
Swimming, playing and splashing
in the zoo.
I am a dolphin
eating fish and shrimp
in the pool.
I am a dolphin
Sleeping, sleeping and sleeping
in the pool.
Chantel Barnes, Grade 2

Water and Lava
Water
Wet, clear
Dripping, running, flowing
Pool, waterfall, volcano, Hawaii
Blowing, flowing, slowing
Hot, red
Lava
Amber Mezzacapo, Grade 2

Space Is Amazing
Space
Pretty, amazing
Floating, spinning, twinkling
Air, planets, gravity, stars
Falling, exploding, burning
Big, dark
Meteors
Caitlin Dodds, Grade 1

Sneakers
Sneakers is fluffy, cute,
Like to play,
It looks like he is wearing shoes,
Purring loudly,
He is sometimes lazy,
He is fat and does not scratch.
Sneakers is the best cat in the world.
Nicola Norval, Grade 3

Animals
A nimals are athletic
N arwhals splash water
I guanas climb trees
M onkeys climb
A wesome animals
L ions are awesome
S eals are great
Annie Rieben, Grade 1

Friends
F riends support you
R emembering you every day
I know that my friends care for me a lot
E ven though I am angry at them
N ever leave your friends
D ay by day they get more happy
S ometimes they just act funny
Harjas Kaur Panag, Grade 3

Demon/Angel
Demon
Mean, evil
Killing, fighting, attacking
Fire, horns, halo
Helping, singing, watching
Good, thankful
Angel
Chase Whaley, Grade 3

Shane's Crane Accident
There once was a boy named Shane.
Who wanted to drive a crane.
It fell on his head,
Then he went in his bed,
I hope he has no bruise on his brain.
Alex Waldner, Grade 3

A Deer's Life
When deer run
Their feet beat the ground
As they play and run and jump around.
The mother and father
Take care always
And watch their children play.
The mom and dad
Take care of their baby fawns.
They run along the grass
In the beautiful
Evergreen forest!
Nancy Harris, Grade 3

Dolphin
I do tricks in the water.
I love to eat fish. I love,
The water, I am friendly,
Because I love seeing people,
Next to me.
I like people,
Touching me. I like to swim,
In the water, I am happy,
Because people freed me.
I like my babies, they are so cute.
They are small and look like me.
Ingrid Ledezma, Grade 3

Jade Unterschute
Jade
Daughter of Jaylene and Ryan
Who likes cake
Who dislikes mean people
Who thinks I'm beautiful
Who wishes to have 10,000 friends
Who loves her friends and B.F.F's
Who wonders if she is awesome
Who dreams to be a soccer star
Who wants to be an artist
Unterschute
Jade Unterschute, Grade 3

I Am
I am a dog
brown, big, cute
with a big tail.

I am a dog
wagging my tail
running across the field.

I am a dog
flapping my ears
fetching the ball.
Payton Ogden, Grade 2

Winter
Fluffy polar bears,
Crawling around when flakes fall
On all the icebergs.
Jeneya Boone, Grade 3

Summer
It is very hot.
Tripping and splashing in pool.
I like winter more.
Aidan De Bie, Grade 3

Winter Time
Winter jingle bells,
Snowflakes fall down to the grass.
Santa in his sleigh.
Sophia Rogers, Grade 3

Sunset
I sit on a hill,
I see a burning red dot,
Of course, the sunset.
Carter Leitgeb, Grade 3

Taipan
The deadly taipan,
Slithering in the darkness,
Deadliest poison.
Ryan Guthrie, Grade 3

Grand Canyon
Very breathtaking.
Lots of very cool colors.
Please don't fall off now!
Brandon Chiles, Grade 3

Flowers
Beautiful flowers.
Gorgeous colors of all kinds.
Flowers in the grass.
Alexis Pena, Grade 3

Monkeys
Monkeys have big eyes.
Monkeys are tan, brown, and white.
They are cute and soft.
Taylor Stacy, Grade 3

Butterflies!
Butterflies are cool.
I see them when I walk home.
Wings are fluttering.
Savannah Peterson, Grade 3

Electricity
E lectrical power is the same as electricity
L ove electricity is what people do
E verybody's phone, tablets anything like that is powered by electricity
C omputers run by electricity
T V's are electric too
R oads are lit by electricity at night
I like electricity
C ities bright at night
I have gone camping without it
T errific to have
Y ou use it to do many things.
Durriyah Khondoker, Grade 3

I Am an American Girl
I like my American Girl dolls and right now I have three,
I have Isabelle, Saige, and Julie.
I'm hoping to get Grace this Easter and some of her clothes too,
But right now any American Girl thing would do.
I dress them up, fix their hair, play school and read to them when I can,
To my American Girl dolls I am their biggest fan.
I have ten little Mini American Girl dolls in a shelf on display,
But I take them out often when I use them to play.
Some girls don't bother with the American Girl dolls like I do, and that is okay,
But as for me I enjoy going home to mine each and every day.
Emma Treber, Grade 1

Spring Season
Hooray, it's the first day of spring!
It is the first day of spring!
It's the season when birds come back from the south and make new nests on the trees.
Bears wake up from their hibernation and go fish some fresh fish to eat.
Squirrels leave the hole of theirs trees.
Frogs jump on water Lilies: SPLOUCH! SPLACH! SPLICH!
Families go to the park and play games with bliss.
Sometimes, they just take a walk to have some fresh air and be attacked by bees.
Talking about spring made me eager to go see the sea.
Hamza Febri, Grade 3

Me
Alexis
Pretty, cheerful, sweet, funny
Sibling of Mya and Bryce
Lover of kittens, dogs, and reading
Who feels like summer vacation is too short, my dog is too short, and I grow up too quickly
Who fears spiders, snakes, and lightning
Who would like to see Little Italy, Egypt, and Germany
Jenkins
Alexis Jenkins, Grade 2

In the Spring
In the spring there might be some pretty flowers or some green grass
or some leaves on some trees and some fresh air and a blue sky the
sun might be out it might smell sweet and cool there might be
birds chirping or building their nest and the flowers might bloom and
they might be different colors.
Claire Schultz, Grade 1

Dogs
Dogs are fluffy, cuddly, cute, big, tiny, mean and hyper.
Dogs are also hungry, thirsty, playful, slobbery, and sometimes nice.
Dogs are fast, rough, growling, and loud.
If I were a dog I'd be nice.
Jacob Whitt, Grade 2

Storms
I see tornadoes and tornadoes and tornadoes
But the worst are storms! Storms! Storms!
Bam! Boom! Bang!
This is a very scary day!
Llyr Redweik-Leung, Grade 1

A Purpose
I know I have a purpose.

I just don't know what it is,
something important, I hope.
Or something normal.

What is my purpose in the world?

And how do I make it?

By going down the tracks of life I hope.

Will I be the ringmaster?
Or will I be a person in the crowd?

What is my purpose in the world?

To help people or the planet?
To help animals or us?
Will I be rich or poor?

What is my purpose in the world?

I don't know what it will be, but
I know it will be good.

I know I have a good purpose in the world!
James Rath, Grade 3

Snow Tumbling
The snow is tumbling down,
it is as bright as a ghost on a post.
Should I go in the snow to make a show?
Should I go in the bright white snow?
Yes, I should go in the bright white snow!
The snow is so cold I just want to go.
The snow keeps on falling.
I wish I was gone far, far from the snow!!!
I wish I was, I wish I was
but I am not.
I will go in with a grin when I get in.
Chase Clarke, Grade 1

Spring
Spring, spring, winter's gone
Now you'll need to mow your lawn
Green grass springs from the ground
No more fall wind that howls like a hound
Everything is alive
Even the bees from their hive
When the trees grow their leaves again
I will be ten
In April it's Earth Day
Then you can go strolling on the bay
Earth Day is all about going green
You don't have to be a teen
Earth day is done
Now go have some fun
April showers
Brings May flowers
Now that it's May
That wraps up spring days
Summer pushes spring out with a fling
Now spring's gone 'til next year
Daniella Idrovo, Grade 3

Twister
Twisting and twirling,
Spinning and whirring,
The clouds are getting darker,
I hope it's not a twister.
Throwing stuff around,
Roaring very wildly,
The twister is getting
Very close.
I get into my truck,
I see it,
Spinning up —
my door.
Whirling very close —
and more.
Then suddenly the spinning —
giant stops,
I run up to it super close,
Taking pictures of its hose,
Anything that I can do,
The swirling giant has been doomed.
Viraj Kamath, Grade 2

My Kite Is Stuck
My
kite is
stuck
in that tree
over there!
Will you please,
help me get
that kite
up there!
Meghan McKenna, Grade 2

Orange

Orange
Orange is the color of my favorite socks.
Orange feels like wind blowing in the breeze.
Orange taste sweet.
Orange sounds like Fireworks.
I like Orange.

Alessia Sattler, Grade 1

Spring

S pring is beautiful like roses
P eople and animals come out and enjoy the great weather
R ain drops fall as flowers start to bloom
I like to see colorful rainbows in the sky
N ight and day people and animals want spring to be here
G reen as grass is spring

Amol Bhullar, Grade 3

Keerat

K eerat is my name
E veryone in my class is friendly
E ven they have friends like me
R unning is what my teacher teaches me in PE
A nd I have lots of friends
T eachers are very very very nice

Keerat Kaur Brar, Grade 3

My Eyes

My eyes help me see the beauty of the sea.
My eyes also help me see the beauty of every single thing.
My eyes help me read when I can't go to sleep.
My eyes help me see the ball on the field.
My eyes are the beauty of me.
My eyes, my wonderful, wonderful eyes.

Mira Witwer, Grade 3

Riding

Riding is so fun to do!
It feels bumpy when you trot.
My horse feels like a pillow when I pet her.
I feel free when I ride my horse.
The more I ride I am less nervous and I feel better.

Kallyn Odom, Grade 2

Spring

In spring, everyone knows me by my colors.
In the morning hours I bloom my flowers.
My afternoon cool weather makes me feel like a butterfly.
The green trees make me feel like a red bird.
My cool night makes me feel like an owl hooting at night.

Trinity Youssef, Grade 3

Horses

Horses are great because you can have them as pets
and you can ride them too. Horses are great.
They have been around for a really long time.

Laurel Hagan, Grade 1

My Hair

I love my hair because I can braid it!
I love my hair because I can dye it!
I love my hair because it is soft!
I love my hair because it is fun to play with!
I love hair because my friends like to play with it!

Ellery Pietzsch, Grade 3

Sunlight Moonlight

Sunlight, moonlight shines like a bright light.
The moon shines bright and the sun shines so bright.
The sun shines in the day and the moon shines in the night.
What a bright light the sun and the moon make,
They are so bright.

Reneem Farhan, Grade 3

Erie Nature Trail

There is a lot of grass.
A lot of leaves,
Pinery of the trees.
The colors around me are green, brown and yellow.
There are lots of sticks and there is fresh air.

Logan Hosmer, Grade 2

Birds and Stars

The stars shine among us
throughout the night sky,
and in the morning the larks sing and fly,
As the stars watch over us beneath moonlight,
The larks sing with wonderful delight!

Myla Sexton, Grade 3

Books

The books are tired from opening.
The books are happy because there are lots of words.
The books are sad because they are bored.
The books are also mad from writing words.
The books are excited to see new places that they have never seen.

Thuran Ranjan, Grade 3

Valentine's Day

Valentine's Day sounds like love in the air.
Valentine's Day feels like warm hugs.
Valentine's Day smells like yummy chocolate.
Valentine's Day taste like sweet candy hearts.
Valentine's Day is love.

Kate Spindler, Grade 3

Cow

There once was a cow
It was a sow
She was fat
Because she had a baby named Matt
It was different but happened, the baby kept saying meow.

Lydia Johnson, Grade 3

Candy
It tastes good when it's in my mouth
Looks yummy
Chocolate and delicious
Tasty when it goes in my tummy
Sometimes maple is in it
When I squeeze it chocolate comes out
But the part I like is the middle
When I eat it, I shout!
Chocolate milk reminds me of it
But when I eat it, it's tasty
There are lots of flavours
When some people eat candy, they eat hasty
Lara El-Ghalayini, Grade 3

Mila Beerson
M akes stuff
I s smart
L oves Labor Day
A wesome

B est student ever in second grade
E arth lover
E lectric guitar
R eads magazines
S ad sometimes
O utside
N eptune is my favorite planet
Mila Beerson, Grade 2

Gelato
It's cold like ice cream
But very yummy
But it's not jello
And it is good to have it in my tummy
It is multiflavoured
Sometimes it's coloured yellow
That flavour is pineapple
But you should never ever let it mellow
It is Italian
Gelato is tasty
Definitely fruity
But eat it quickly, don't be hasty
Liam Petersen, Grade 3

Spring Dance
Dancing, dancing, dancing
Dancing on vacation
Dancing in the rain
Dancing in the sun!
Dancing in the show
Dancing on the trees
Dancing everywhere!
Dancing in the swings
Dancing on the slide
Dancing in the breeze!
Jessica Elisma, Grade 1

Star Wars
My Star Wars game is very cool
You have a crew
Jedi Counsels fight
With all their might

Then clones are bad
And they're very mad
And it was very sad
And I was glad
Julian Sosa, Grade 3

Ice Cream
I ce cream is good
C reamy vanilla ice cream
E veryone likes it

C old and sweet
R evels are like ice cream
E specially good on hot days
A wesome in a cone
M ountains of ice cream
Emily Letkeman, Grade 3

Hockey Showdown
The teams are tied at 91 points
Canadians, Ducks, Predators
The teams are tied at 90 points
Lightning, Blues
Red Wings or Capitals?
Which one will win?
They'll be in the playoffs and we will see!
Who is the champion?
Who will it be?
Ahmed Adam Zghal, Grade 1

Gummy Bear
I am a Gummy Bear
Squished all the time
I don't want to get eaten
What would I do?
Help me
Can you let me free?
Please?
Please?
Please?
Isaac Bradley, Grade 3

Farmers Are...
Farmers are drilling wheat,
Farmers are hoeing weeds,
Farmers are watering and fertilizing,
Farmers are out of water,
drought hits.
Farmers are...
Sad!
Cody Malone, Grade 2

Star, Star
Star, star
oh so bright
Fills the night
with its beautiful light
It is quite a sight
Black and white
is the color of the night
Brennan Oliver, Grade 2

Bedtime
I see an apple pie.
I see my doll.
I see a lime.
I see a mouse in the hall.
It makes me say eek!
Mom says, "please"
Madeleine. Go to sleep…
Madeleine Kaatz, Grade 1

Beach
I love the nice beach.
The ocean water and sand.
The beach is so fun.

You can play at shore.
The beach has lots of sand.
I love the sweet beach.
Jacob DesRosiers, Grade 3

Spring
Frogs in the pond
Roses starting to bloom
Pine trees on the ground
Butterflies going out of a cocoon
Burning logs from the campfire
Raindrops falling in the air
Splashing puddles on the ground
Bree March, Grade 3

Rainbows
Red like a firefighter
Pink like a crayon
Black like pants
Green like the grass
Gray like a pencil
Blue like our beads
Big, big rainbows are all in spring!
Maryssa Addeh, Kindergarten

Wolves
Wolves
Hunting animals
Chasing down prey
The pack is full
Hunters
Brandon Bevins, Grade 2

Marker
I am a marker.
I write on the board every day.
When blue, I smell like blueberries.
I smell good.
People like to hold me.
When I get wasted, they buy another marker.
That smells like strawberry.
Now I write on the board every day.
Gerardo Bustamante, Grade 2

All About Me, Ellie
My name is Elliana but my family calls me Ellie.
My favorite food for lunch is peanut butter and jelly.
I like to play with Barbie dolls,
At soccer I run and kick the balls.
My Dad says I talk a lot,
But I think not.
When I grow up I want to be a teacher.
I am a really loud SCREECHER!
Elliana Bauer, Grade 1

Sports and Sebastian
Hey, my name is Sebastian.
My life is all about action.
I love to play sports with a ball,
so I'll try to name them all.
Hockey is my favorite along with soccer,
but in football my coaches say I'm a good blocker.
I really like playing on teams.
It's really as fun as it seems.
Sebastian Angelo, Grade 1

Spring
In spring the flowers bloom.
The birds comeback from the south.
There is action all about.
The birds lay their eggs.
The Rosebud river causes a flood at the dairy barn.
When spring begins the snow starts to melt
Causing big puddles for us to jump around and make ourselves wet,
Spring is my best season.
Jesse Gross, Grade 3

Nature
The birds are chirping, the light breeze is at the right amount.
The sweet smell of plants fills the air.
Some seeds have been transplanted.
Pine needles cover the ground.
New blossoms are on bushes, trees and flowers.
Some cobwebs come too.
N-A-T-U-R-E.
Nature is awesome.
Brianna Romero, Grade 2

Leading the Way
I lead the way every day.
I see the sun lead the day
It shines so bright
I can save the day!
I help myself lead the way too!
So help yourself lead the way.
I'm almost home about to be there.
So let me lead the way, so it can be safe for all.
Israel Slonglo, Grade 3

Rainbows Are a Girl's Best Friend
Red is the color of fire in the night.
Orange is when the sun is setting.
Yellow sun will burn your nose.
Green are the leaves of spring.
Blue eyes of a baby make grown-ups smile.
Purple is the color of fireworks glittering in the sky.
Pink is how I am when I am embarrassed.
What are your favorite colors?
Lily Wallace, Grade 3

Isabella Walker
Isabella
Caring, loves music, smart
Daughter of Jenelle and John
Lover of cats, spiders, and fish
Who feels friendly, scared, and mad
Who fears claws, snakes, and black bears
Who would like to see New York, Australia, and Egypt
Walker
Isabella Walker, Grade 2

Spring
Spring is in the air
Spring I wish was here
The sun shines so bright at day and sleeps at night
I love the long days full of light
Flowers bloom, trees will bud
All the rain makes lots of mud
We play outside, we splash and splish
Days like this are a come true wish
Ethan Moody, Grade 2

Blaine
Blaine
Good, funny, cool, awesome
Sibling of Reagan and Banks
Lover of dogs, reading, and spending time with my family
Who feels that winter is too long, more summer and skip spring
Who fears bats, bees, and death
Who would like to see Myrtle Beach, South Carolina, and Florida
Oler
Blaine Oler, Grade 2

Dogs

There are big dogs
There are little dogs
There are furry and fluffy dogs
Like a fluffy cloud
They are fun and they do tricks
They do backflips and front flips on walls and bricks
They are part of our family
She licks me like my mom kisses me.
My dog is my favorite pet in the whole world!

Tysean Kempf, Grade 3

Christmas

C hristmas, o Christmas
H ow wonderful can you be
R ising as the sun, beautiful like a star
I can get everything thanks to you
S inging above the world Christmas, o Christmas
T rees lighting up in a window of a star
M erry Christmas presents are finally here
A long the sky, here comes Santa Claus
S uper and greatest day I can wish for

Khushvir K. Birk, Grade 3

Wind

Wind —
Tingles my hair,
rides a cloud through the air
Sings a sweet song,
as it rides along
Wind can be happy or mad,
but wind can never be sad
Birds can see wind as it flies through the sky,
Bye wind, Bye

Sarah Henry, Grade 3

Sports in the Spring

Welcome back Spring!
Because of you, I get to do sports!
I love to jog and run around the park.
Spring, you get to watch little kids play sports.
The birds sing songs and breathe fresh air.
You grow us green grass for sports and fun!
In Spring, swimming is my favorite sport.
Welcome back Spring!
I love you a lot!

Angelina Phan, Grade 2

My Teacher

My teacher is nice, cool, kind, and funny.
She makes me laugh every day.
Sometimes she is nice and sometimes she is strict.
Sometimes she is happy and sometimes she is mad.
But even though you are sometimes mean
You will always be the best teacher
Mrs. Menon

Maneet Kaur Bhullar, Grade 3

St. Patrick's Day

I love St. Patrick's Day because it's really fun,
When the day is over, the pinching is done.
When you go to school. you must wear green,
Somebody might pinch you, but they're not trying to be mean.

The leprechaun goes down the rainbow to find a pot of gold.
He may be small, but he's very bold.
Someday I might find a four-leaf clover,
When the sun sets St. Patrick's Day is over.

The leprechaun comes to give you a wish,
You might ask him for a colorful fish.
St. Patrick's Day is so much fun.
It makes me sad when the day is done.

Makayla Valentine, Grade 3

Dogs

Dogs can be brown and very round,
I don't want to see any in the pound.
Dogs may bite, and they love to hike,
Dogs may chase you while on a bike.

Beagles and coon dogs love to hunt,
The deer they chase may give a grunt.
They love to run around the yard and play,
When I get home they jump on me each and every day.

My coon dogs sleep with me every night,
When I see them running toward me, it is a beautiful sight.
When the dogs try to get the deer, they run all day,
And the only time they see them is a trail far away.

Jadon Howe, Grade 3

Puppies

My big black and brown German Shepherd is getting massive,
But I wouldn't say that she is passive,
The other night she delivered eleven adorable babies,
Good thing the mother does not have dangerous rabies.
The babies are playful and all so lovely,
They are mischievous and extremely clumsy.
The dad does not like people when they're touching his puppies.
I wish that they could all get along and be buddies.
The sweet puppies like to run around the house,
While inside our home, they will even try to catch a mouse.
The bark of the trees the puppies have peeled,
We also allow them to run in a large green field,
They are fluffy and will lick your face,
I couldn't imagine them living any other place.

Steven Rapids, Grade 3

Summer

Summer is fun, summer is warm.
Every day in summer the sun shines on everything.
Summer is the best time of the year.
Summer is awesome.

Hailey Robinson, Grade 3

Penguins
Penguins
Funny, cuddly
Belly sliding, swimming, waddling
Live in cold places
Bird
Charlie Fricker, Grade 3

SpongeBob SquarePants!
SpongeBob
Square, yellow
Jellyfishing, laughing, playing
Works at the Krusty Crab
Cartoon
Sean Rocco, Grade 3

Awesome Kyson
K yson is kind
Y es, he is
S ometimes silly
O ctopus lover
N ever weird.
Kyson Gawryluk, Grade 2

Orange
Orange looks like a marker
Orange smells like a crayon
Orange feels like a soft kitten
Orange tastes like Jell-O
Orange sounds like a cat
Samuel Chubak, Grade 2

Creepy
Legs run
Eyes stare
Ears listen
Claws stab
A big cheetah
Elijah Peters, Grade 2

Baseball
Baseball
Dirty, loud
Cheering, running, hitting
Pitching the ball
Sport
Nicholas Sobolewski, Grade 3

James Bond
James Bond
Handsome, British
Spying, chasing, running
Gets out of any situation
MI6 Agent
James Callas, Grade 3

Happy Sad
Happy
Glad, joyful
Exciting, delighting, smiling
Hugs, love, tears, depression
Boo-hooing, crying, drowning
Miserable, upset
Sad
Kaila O'Connor, Grade 3

Sun and Moon
Sun
Sunny, bright
Shining, shimmering, burning
Gasses, fire, rock, craters
Sleeping, lighting, smiling
Glistening, big
Moon
Amaya Heffelfinger, Grade 3

November
No grass, No Cultus Lake,
No basketball practice, No worms,
No vacation, No birds,
No trees, No butterflies,
No ice, No light,
No Canadian geese, No bears,
November!
Zavier Anwar, Grade 2

Life/Death
Life
Heavenly, goodness
Living, breathing, seeing
God, Heaven, devil, fire
Worsening, burning, suffering
Horrible, terrible
Death
Zachary Barna, Grade 3

God/Devil
God
Light, beautiful
Loving, caring, smiling
Heaven, angel, demon, underground,
Screaming, tempting, yelling
Scary, horrible
Devil
Ashlynn Miller, Grade 3

Water
W ater is very important
A nimals, people, and plants use water
T iny drops make clouds
E arth has lots of water
R ain is water
Albi Cullhaj, Grade 2

Koala
K ind, cute animal
O nly cuddly bear
A nimal with gray fur
L ots of koalas eat leaves
A ustralia is where they live
Jade Beauséjour, Grade 2

Rainbows
I see colors
in the sky
it is beautiful
I don't know why
I love rainbows
Liliana Hathaway, Grade 1

Zach's Hands
Hands they help me farm in the barn.
Hands help me bake a cake for my mom.
Hands help me throw my football far.
Hands help me pick up a cup.
Hands help me hit.
Zach Dorch, Grade 3

Dogs
Dogs
Playful, jumpy
Jumping, running, walking
Like eating food all day and night
Hungry
Maggie Lucas, Grade 3

My Dog
My dog has sharp claws.
My dog has a lot of sharp teeth.
My dog can jump really high.
My dog loves me.
And I love him too!
Keegan Olson, Grade 2

Skate
S o fun
K ids like skating
A lways be safe
T ie your skates
E veryone falls when they skate
Lometh Jayawardhana, Grade 3

Spring
Stormy clouds roll in,
heavier, heavier, and heavier.
Raindrops fall,
flowers bloom,
spring.
Conner McDonald, Grade 2

Computer
C oding
O utstanding
M ath
P rinting
U nderstanding
T echnology
E ducating
R eading
Alton Zimmerman, Grade 2

I Love Summer!
We go to the beach
To have some fun
Sunscreen on my shoulders
It's time to have fun
Summer is my favorite season
Summer days we play on the beach
People say that summer is for fun
But for me, summer is to have sun!
Logan O'Doherty, Grade 2

Last Year's Christmas
It was last year's Christmas…
It was fun.
I opened presents before it was done
I was happy
Until the last one…

CLOTHES!?!?
Now it's done!!
Dylan King, Grade 3

Car
I am a car. I go fast.
My color is red.
They feed me all the time.
I get muddy. Sometimes they,
Throw things in me. Sometimes,
I do not have gas, but they,
Put a lot in me. They sit in me.
They take me places.
Jazmin Dominguez Montiel, Grade 2

Panda
I like
To eat a lot of bamboo. I love
Being a happy friend. I like to
Live in the jungle. I like to
Play in the grass. I love
Being funny. I like
People seeing me.
I am black and white
Cindy Contreras, Grade 3

Family
Family, family, family
Noisy family, silly family
Singing, dancing, swimming family
Last of all, best of all,
My Family!
Liesel Nelson, Grade 1

Cat
There once was a cat named Pat
Who liked to sit on a mat
He was orange and black
And had his own plaque
And liked to eat rats
Elizabeth Wiens, Grade 3

Family
Family, family, family
Quiet family, crazy family,
Tickling, laughing, praying family
Last of all, best of all,
My family
Nicole Nielsen, Grade 1

Family
Family, family, family
Crazy family, loud family
Yelling, chasing, singing family
Last of all, best of all
My Family!
Corianne Matthies, Grade 1

Family
Laughing
Sharing
Crying
Snuggling
Family
Nathanael Merke, Grade 1

Family
Families, families, families
Large families, small families
Teasing, chasing, laughing families
Last of all, best of all.
My Family!
Jack Lane, Grade 1

Video Games
Fun and cool.
Very hard games.
Playing for an hour.
On an iPad, Wii U, PS4, Xbox 360.
Playing with a friend.
Elijah Zhao, Grade 3

Colours of Easter
Green is for palm branches
Brown is for the cross
Black is for sin
Red is for the blood
Yellow is for heaven
Jerica Coziahr, Grade 1

Jeeps
J ump hills
E xcellent
E normous
P ut things in it
S trong
Edy Aron, Kindergarten

World
W onderful place for plants to grow
O ver the water the sky is bright
R ivers give us water
L ittering is bad to it
D ifferent from all the planets
Adam Yesnik, Grade 3

Easter Fun
Happy, peaceful
Exciting, searching, running
Painting beautiful eggs
Interesting!
Marianne Simard, Grade 3

Nature
Important, pretty
Enjoying, blooming, living
Feeling the light wind
Interesting!
Sarah Vianou, Grade 3

Hockey
Fun, cool
Skating, scoring, winning
Teamwork and fair play
Challenging!
Thomas Svoiski, Grade 3

Easter
Funny, yummy
Finding, tasting, collecting
Looking for chocolate eggs
Fantasy!
Nina Gu, Grade 3

Butterfly Wonderland
They are breathtaking.
I love watching butterflies.
It's so magical.
Caden Zitar, Grade 3

In Spring
Farmers start sowing,
Crops start growing.
Storms come rolling,
Wind is howling,
Thunder is booming,
Lightning is striking,
Rain is falling.
Sun is shining,
Grass starts growing,
Dad is mowing,
in spring.
Colby Batterton, Grade 2

The Thunderous Machine
Yes, I am Thunderous,
Lucmenderus made me,
He's a crazy scientist.
I am a machine
Used to create lightning storms.
Lucmenderus makes me
Do lightning storms for evil.
When Lucmenderus comes by,
I,
Thunderous,
Outta teach him a lesson.
Isaac Cervantes Garcia, Grade 3

Summer
The greetings of summer
are hot and long…
From beaches and pools
they swim to have fun.
They splash and they play
oh what a blast of fun.
They play outdoors to enjoy
the outdoors.
So much fun to be had
Oh a ton of fun!
Joshua Purington, Grade 3

Me
Addy
Pretty, cooking, baking, singing
Sibling of Colin and Rowan
Lover of animals, family and friends
Who feels happy, mad, and important
Who gives love and kindness
Who fears the dark
Who would like to see Selena Gomez
Resident of Marysville
Graupensperger
Addison Graupensperger, Grade 3

I Am
I am a Boston Terrier
black, brown and white,
sitting on the couch.

I am a Boston Terrier
playful, funny, happy
showing off.

I am a Boston Terrier
smart and likes to go for walks
and chase balls.
Sophia Botelho, Grade 2

Grass
A warm summer day in a grassy field.

Sitting…
Listening to a bird's song.
A deer in prone.
The gnats are flying all around me.
My silent cousin next to me.
I feel him breathe on me.

On a grassy field…
On a warm summer day.
Aidyn Gushue, Grade 3

Summertime
What do I do on a summertime day?
I usually get up to go out and play.

Sometimes I swim, sometimes I run,
Sometimes I like to lay in the sun.

Don't have to rush, don't have to hurry,
Not any homework to cause me a worry.

And when it feels really hot,
I like to get Dippin' Dots.
Katelyn Smout, Grade 3

I Am
I am a hockey player
sharing the puck,
scoring a hat trick.

I am a hockey player
skating, stretching, racing
taking a shot.

I am a hockey player
winning the Stanley Cup
and getting medals.
Calvin Bright, Grade 2

Sport Check
Tennis is the best,
In tennis you hit hard.
Swimming you go fast,
But skating makes your feet warm
Hockey is fun,
But football is hard.
Racing is fast,
But karate makes you ready.
Adam Jaafar, Grade 1

Thanksgiving Dinner
We all give
Thanks
For everything
We have.
Then we all
Say that
We love our
Things!
McKayla Hettler, Grade 2

Gymnastics
Rolling
Jumping
Hopping
Falling
Running
Rolling
Flopping
Gymnastics
Clive Scott, Grade 1

Spring Sports
Inside or outside
Spring is the best season to do sports
Jogging next to beautiful flowers
Playing tennis on green grass
Soccer on sunny days
Zoomba next to trees
All on pretty spring days
I love spring sports!
Joannie Normand Plante, Grade 2

The Eagle
I am so fast,
I fish,
I fly
Attack at night,
Fish at noon.
I am the knight,
So strong,
So quick.
Tameem Awad, Grade 1

The Snowy Owl
The white snowy owl
Travels around the Arctic
Looking for juicy food.
Emma Bergen, Grade 2

Roadrunner
I love roadrunners.
They run fast in the desert.
They are very fast.
Lina Tan, Grade 3

Birds
Watch all kinds of birds
It is fun to watch them fly
See them as they go
Bradley Miller, Grade 2

Puppies
Puppies are so soft
They are adorable
Puppies feel like silk
Taylor Schneider, Grade 3

Lilies by the Lake
Gentle white petals
Float by lakes pretty and smooth
Lily pads are near
Catherine Smith, Grade 3

Soccer
Soccer is the best.
It's a sport to kick all day
It is a fun sport
Yonathan Landa, Grade 2

Wolves
Wolves eat lots of meat
Every day wolves hunt for prey
Wolves don't like people
Jonas Lor, Grade 2

Natural Disasters
Volcanoes, earthquakes
Many disastrous storms
All around the world
Matthew Chachkin, Grade 3

Happy
I am happy every day,
I am happy in every way,
I play all day in every way!
Lindsay Newman, Grade 2

Ancient Greece
Ancient Greece looks like a country with a lot of olive trees and the Parthenon.
Ancient Greece smells like baklava from the bakery.
Ancient Greece tastes like the ash of volcanoes.
Ancient Greece feels like the Greek Gods are right next to me.
Ancient Greece sounds like people shouting at the person they want to win in the Olympics.
I love Ancient Greece.
Emerson Uphoff, Grade 3

Fall
Fall looks like orange, brown, and yellow leaves.
Fall feels like dried up flowers.
Fall smells like fresh green grass.
Fall tastes like the freshest honey from the beehive.
Fall is a great season.
Carolyn Keim, Grade 3

Fire
F irst a spark
I n an instant the fire unleashes chaos
R acing fire engines rush to put out the flame.
E ating everything in sight now, the fire engines don't stand a chance.
Samuel Merke, Grade 3

School!
I like school,
It is very cool!
American history,
Is a great experience for me!
I like painting art,
But I try to think smart.
When I'm in math,
I have to follow the path.
When you're in P.E.,
Drink water to stay healthy!
When you socialize,
You might have a friend to surprise.
School!
Cheyenne Harris, Grade 3

Spring Is Back!
Spring is back, finally!
The bunnies come out.
The birds come out too.
The bears come out of their dark,
Scary, scary caves.
The bees start to work.
The deer don't hide anymore.
Squirrels are no longer hiding.
The foxes start to hunt for fish.
The kids come out and play.
Spring is back!
And I am glad!
Lucia Trenado, Grade 3

Pickles
I really like pickles
In my mouth they tickle
I like the way they crunch
But they prickle
The pickles are bumpy
Slippery smooth and rough
I like the way they feel
But they're really tough
I like the way they slip
And I like how they taste
Pickles are very good
And you shouldn't waste
Imaan Kanda, Grade 3

Spring Sky
The blue sky so high
Birds singing in their nests
The rain is falling
The sun is shining
The sea is shimmery blue
The air is fresh
Animals come out
Flowers bloom colors
The trees have apples too
Sunshine everywhere
I love spring!
I love you too!
Polina Polyanskaya, Grade 2

A Celebration of Poets Grades K-6 – Spring 2015

I Love Books

I love mystery books,
Especially the ones with crooks.
I've read fiction that makes me happy,
The characters can be mean and snappy.

I don't mind reading a boring book,
I even read a colossal book while I cook.
My fluffy cat meows while I read in the hot sun,
I think about the book I will read as I run.

I go to my lovely garden to read,
While I plant a cute little seed.
I go on vacation and may read a joke,
And the waiter kindly offers me a coke.

My mom said I couldn't fit all these books in my backpack,
So I hesitated and tossed a stack of books in the old shack.
My mom called me for lunch, but I wanted to stay and read,
The necklace around my neck stands for my love of books
And it is made of a single red bead.
I hurried inside, ate lunch, and read an entire book,
I really like the book called The Fish on the Hook.

Jasmine Price, Grade 3

United We Stand

United we stand, and united we stay.
United we are in some sort of way.

We agree on the law, we agree on the land.
We want peace and not war — united we stand.

... And united we stay.
United we are in some sort of way.

The government stands through peace and through war.
They love our country from the air to the floor.

United we stand, and united we stay.
United we are in some sort of way.

Our country shall stand through peril and rain.
The president will treat us all the same.

United we stand, and united we stay.
United we are in some sort of way.

Nate Lyons, Grade 2

Spring

In spring the flowers turn red, yellow, and blue.
The snow melts in big puddles
And the boys and girls play in them.
The creek flows everywhere.
The men are busily working,
And the cats have their nice, cute kittens.
My spring was excellent.

Cornel Gross, Grade 3

Love*

How do I love you?
Let me count the ways?
I love you as bright as the sun
Can blaze.

How do I love you?
Let me tell you how.
I love you as much as a cat
Can meow.

How do I love you?
Look and you will see.
I love as free as an animal
Can be.

How do I love you?
I want the world to know.
I love you more than a fire
Can glow.

Mycah Olson, Grade 2
Inspired by "How Do I Love Thee" by Elizabeth Barrett Browning.

Hello Spring, Goodbye Winter

Hello to rain drops that fall from the sky
Goodbye to snow as white as new paper.

Hello to warm cozy weather
Goodbye to cold bad weather.

Hello to surfing days that brighten my day
Goodbye to wintery days that make my legs cold.

Hello to flowers that are so delightful
Goodbye to snow man's that you make yourself.

Hello to green fresh grass
Goodbye to white, old snow.

Hello to the summer sun that really warms my day
Goodbye to really bad and cold days.

Valentina Bastidas Garcia, Grade 3

Horses

Horses running like the wind across the field,
When I am hiding from them I am concealed.
When the white beautiful horses prance,
It makes me feel like I want to dance.
Each and every day I feed the horses hay,
Then I may travel to the crystal blue bay.
When I ride the silky horses through the pink flowers,
I hope the day is not spoiled with lightning showers.
My beautiful horses like to follow the sun,
The only way they do it is when they run.
I ride the horses at the deep blue lake,
And may even play with them while I bake.

Emily Jenkins, Grade 3

I See Sweet Snowflakes
Snowflakes are just ice crystals in clouds.
Clouds are just like houses.
Blue crystals, blue crystals, I love blue crystals!
I like sweet snowflakes!
Ice crystals are just like the moon in the sky at night.
I see snow crystals on the moon in the morning.
I see the sun.
I see the star's light shine bright like a kite.
You should see the bright lights.
I hope you like snowflakes too!
Do you see the stars in the sky?
I know they are pretty, right?

Chan'ae Sims-Hawkins, Grade 3

Clock
I am a clock. I have two hands that move.
I have numbers 1012. I also count by 5's. When teachers,
Parents and kids, see what time,
It is, I get a little bit scared,
Because what if I am moving the hands wrong.
I can have all kinds of sizes; big, medium, and small.
When I am hanging on the wall,
I see people, tables, and desks.
I make a sound,
That sounds kind of like a tic-tock sound.
I have different kinds of colors.

Maday Sarai Valtierra Leon, Grade 2

Lily Weber
Lily
Daughter of Jason Weber and Tricia-Ulmer
Who likes her family
Who dislikes mean and annoying people
Who thinks about her dog and cat.
Who wishes for another baby cousin
Who loves Albert Einstein
Who wonders about anything really
Who dreams about pickles
Who wants to be a gold miner or diamond miner
Weber

Lily Weber, Grade 3

Peaceful World
Peaceful world, so bright and dawn.
So many beautiful things to see in this beautiful world.
You can see so many beautiful flowers.
What a peaceful world!
So many beautiful houses to see in this beautiful world.
So many beautiful cars in this peaceful world
So many peaceful people in this world.
What a peaceful world!
You can see so many corner stores.
This is just an awesome world!

Etoria Sellie, Grade 3

Spring
I go outside
And spring is here!
What joy and cheer,
Spring is here!
My friends Mya and Kya and I say "Happy Spring!"
Flowers and warmth this season brings.
What joy and cheer!
Spring is here!

Savannah Jackson, Grade 2

Summer
Summer is when you play a lot
Summer is when it is hot
Summer is when you plant flowers
Summer is when you go out without a jacket
Summer is when you get off the TV and your games
Summer is when kids get outside
Summer is when you have a lot of stuff to do
SUMMER ROCKS!

Michael Marshall, Grade 3

The Thankful Velociraptor
I am a velociraptor and I am thankful for
Being one of the smartest dinosaur!
I have sharp teeth and claws to catch prey,
But when it comes to T-Rex, I stay away!
I am thankful for Mongolia, where I live outside,
And for the big sand hills for me to hide.
I have feathers, but I don't soar,
I live in packs, I am a carnivore!

David Deacle, Grade 1

Waiting for April Showers
When you look out your window
at your drooping garden,
you wish there was just one drop of rain.
Then you hear it...
The pitter-patter of tapping rain on the window
telling you that your thirsty garden is getting a drink.
The sun comes out and you run outside
and see your rising garden.

Jamie Hume, Grade 2

Spring Season
Dear spring
It's raining
Kids splashing the puddles
The pool is fresh
Spring is a season for sports
In spring, we play soccer, basketball and billiards
Spring is my favorite season of all.
Oh! I love spring!

Hatem Alamri, Grade 2

Wonderful Rainbows

Wonderful rainbows
Rainbows colorful, colorful rainbows
Ah! Oh the blue! The purple! And turquoise too!
I love rainbows so much!
Now how are they made?
But how are they made?
Oh! I know! With rain and sunshine!

Aaliyah Benzakour, Grade 2

Soldier

S oldiers saved our country because they wanted to save us,
O r else we would be ruled.
L oving the soldiers who saved us is the greatest respect.
D on't ever make fun of them.
I am so proud of those soldiers.
E ven if you're dead, I will remember you.
R emember you forever.

Harshvir Singh Shergill, Grade 3

God Is Good

The angels are in Heaven.
God's the one that died for us.
He's wonderfully beautiful.
He loves us so much…
All of us and everyone even people that are sick and
People that have problems with their bodies, too.
God is good.

Joel Kline, Grade 3

Nature

Nature the beautiful spell
With the flowers coming out all different colors
The grass shiny green
The trees all different colors
Wow! Wow! Wow!
Water making muddy puddles!
Splash! Splash! Splash!

Simona Melchionno, Grade 2

My Kitten

I play with my kitten.
She has white paws and fat, black fur.
My kitten is always hungry.
She likes me when I feed her.
The leaves fall off the trees green, yellow, and red.
I like to play with my kitten in the leaves.

Jacobie Gross, Grade 2

My Wishful Life

I wish that life was more simple.
I wish that life was more fun.
I wish all that life was playing out in the sun.
But because my life is OK.
But because my life is fine.
I am glad I'm living because my life is mine.

Eleanor Hudson, Grade 3

A Light Shade of Blue

A light shade of blue,
A sweet juicy blueberry,
A cold, windy breeze.

The rain on a cold day,
The sky with clouds passing by,
The salty smell of the ocean.

A blue flower with a sweet smell,
A shade of blue could be anything in the world.

Scarlett Eppolito, Grade 3

Let's Celebrate Winter

Christmas is a wonderful celebration;
All the children are excited for Santa to grant their wishes;
The elves are bustling in their workshops;

Winter is a very festive season;
Brightly coloured lights adorn the streets;
Children are building snowmen and having snowball fights;

Winter is a cool season;
So let's celebrate!

Prashik Juta, Grade 3

Supermom

Supermom flies so high that the sky said hi!
I said Ooh my!
I don't want to say bye.
Supermom leads the crime.
The criminal took a dime.
All I want to do is rhyme.
I know you are mine!
I want the sun to shine.
Thank you Super Mom!

Dashawn Brown-Williams, Grade 3

Nature

The water, the seas, the ocean breeze
There are so many flowers too!
Animals big and small and
There is something different about them all.
Trees are ginormous!
There are many kinds like,
Elm trees and Oak trees, so pretty!
I like nature and I hope you
Like it too

Adetola Ade-Oyetayo, Grade 3

Messi

Messi is the best, he is even better than Rolaldo and Rooney.
Some people think that Ronaldo is better than Messi,
So Messi challenged Ronaldo and Messi won.
In the whole wide world there is no one born to beat Messi
But there is one person and he is the legend he is Ronaldinho.

Eakampreet S. Jaswal, Grade 3

Home Sweet Home
Homes people love
Like flying through the air like a dove
Me and You need a true home.
Back in the old times we lived in domes
I think we all need houses.
But not one filled with mouses!
I think we all need homes.
But I say, Home Sweet Homes.
Grace Sayon, Grade 3

Families
Building
Reading
Watching
Teasing
Fighting
Playing
Eating
Families
Lincoln Abramoff, Grade 1

What Shall I Be?
What shall I be?
Maybe a teacher?
Or a wildlife biologist.
Oh what shall I be?
Should I be a climber?
And climb the Himalayan Mountains?
I don't know yet
What I shall be.
Kylei MacArthur, Grade 2

What I Could Be
There are lots
Of things I could
Do or be.
Like a cop
Or a construction worker
Or a mechanic.
Are examples of
Three.
Nicholas Baldwin, Grade 2

Fashion Forward
Flowered tank tops,
Ruffled scarf,
Bird printed skirts.
Flip flops and
Sun dresses.
Sweaters away!
Yah!
Lila Tyrer, Grade 1

Family
F amily is the best thing ever.
A family takes care of you.
M y family is so nice.
I love them a lot.
L ove your family too.
Y ou are the best family ever.
Kirat K. Purba, Grade 3

Spring
S pring is awesome
P lants grow
R eed loves Spring
I have allergies in Spring
N ow plants grow
G row little plants, grow
Reed Robinson, Grade 1

Spring
S uper warm
P erfect blue sky
R eally nice flowers
I ncredible weather
N o more snow
G reat fun times
Alexandre Bussières, Grade 2

Beautiful Flowers
Beautiful flowers
are glistening in the sun.
Dazzling colors
growing high to the sky.
Spring always comes back to
beautiful flowers.
Melissa Rangel, Grade 2

Flowers
Flowers
Very beautiful
Swaying in wind
Sparkles in the light
Dazzling
Lydia Biviano, Grade 2

Seed
seed
round acorns
sprouting, rooting, growing
buds turning into leaves
tree
Anna Sanford, Grade 2

The Lonely Penguin
In the Antarctic
there was a lonely penguin
sitting on a rock.
Sarah Kim, Grade 2

Rhyming Rocks
I like to roller blade,
and watch the show "How it's made"
I'd like to rhyme this day away
and play my games every day
My name is Abby
but don't worry, I won't get crabby
Abigail Bennett, Grade 1

Beautiful Flowers
A colorful rainbow of flowers
blooming in the spring.
Yellow, purple, red,
orange, blue, and green.
The prettiest colors ever seen.
A beautiful sight to be enjoyed by all.
Maribel Carrillo, Grade 2

May
May is my favorite month
Swimming in the pool
Playing in the park
Eating picnics
and riding my bike!
May is the best!
Emma Youwakim, Kindergarten

Nuts About Spring
I see squirrels
Black eyes
Soft fur
He can climb up the trees
Holding a nut
Ready for lunch
Mehdi Jaber, Kindergarten

Spring Imagination!
Sunshine everywhere
Pools are fresh
Ooey gooey adventures
Relaxing in the air
Too much fun
Super cool
Jonathan Lorcy, Grade 2

Spring
S pring is a great season.
P erfect for everyone.
R oses bloom every day
I n spring the sun always shines.
N o heavy jackets, no rain.
G ood season to play outside.
Harshvir Shergill, Grade 3

Me and My Husky

I'm Ryan and I love my husky,
My beautiful, fluffy dog's name is Musky.
On the majestic high mountain top he likes to race,
But he likes to win and always gets first place.
When we go to the shady green park,
At a big fierce cat he always will wildly bark.
When we go to my enormous home,
His nice, cute, big doggy friends are all alone.
And when we are at the huge, gigantic store,
To my sweet dog, it's always a bore.
And when we go to the sunny beach,
He's back with his friends and playing with each.

Ryan Sweeney, Grade 3

Fishing

I really like fishing for humongous catfish,
Or maybe even a big, fat, scary blob fish.
I think fishing is the best and absolutely awesome,
But I really don't want to fish next to a possum.
My feet dangle in the water while I cast my line,
A day spent fishing feels just fine.
I take a wiggly worm and place it on my hook,
I may even fish while reading a book.
My dad is my favorite fishing bud,
But everyone knows you can't fish in the mud.
The best part of a fishing day is eating the fried fish,
Fishing with my dad is all that I wish.

Kel Shifflett, Grade 3

Aidan Froh

Aidan
Son of Rachel and John
Who likes his friends
Who dislikes his friends
Who dislikes chores
Who thinks about his dogs
Who wishes he was a man
Who loves his family
Who wonders about how the first tools were made
Who dreams to be a doctor
Who wants to be a doctor
Froh

Aidan Froh, Grade 3

Hello Spring Goodbye Winter

Hello to flowers pink, red and yellow
Goodbye to dirty snow
Hello to swimming in the pool
Goodbye to skating on the rink
Hello to spring break fun
Goodbye to getting up early (I will not miss getting up early)
Hello to sun shining on my body
Goodbye to coldness on my body
Hello to wearing T-shirts
Goodbye to wearing warm sweaters

Maggie Allenspach, Grade 3

Dogs

Dogs are a man's best friend.
They are your friend 'til the end.
When my dog sees me sad, he comes and makes me glad.
When I am mad, my dog comes to cheer me up.
He is my favorite pup!
He's like a brother to me.
When he goes outside, he runs to us!
This is why dogs are a man's best friend.

Saamir Dade, Grade 3

Stars

Stars are yellow,
They shine so bright!
Today I sit outside and count how many I see,
One, two, three!
And you can do all of this,
Read some books and you can study them too!
Stay inside if it rains,
But look out your window and you can still see!

Aiden Blessing, Grade 2

Fall

When I see the leaves fall
They are brown, green, and red leaves.
When it falls
I jump into a pile of leaves.
I am happy it's fall.
New seeds come when it's spring.
I like fall and it's one of the best things that could happen!

Eli Jones, Grade 3

Dear Spring

You are my favorite season
It's my birthday
A little cold
And we can play sports
Animals hibernate in winter but wake up in spring
There are more things about spring
Do you know more about spring?

Jason Elisma, Grade 2

Flowers

Flowers are skinny, short, tall, fat.
Different colored but still flowers.
Curls, twirls, swirls in the meadow, waiting to be picked.
Pretty, ugly treated same.
Do things different in many ways but still the same in many ways.
Love, care, and share always flowers, no matter what others say.
Just like people!

Julia Walsh, Grade 3

Leo the Constellation

L eo, Leo where are you
E ast, south, west, or north
O ver I look there you are hiding in the night time sky

Navpreet K. Gosal, Grade 3

Katy Seidler
Katy
Pretty, friendly, shy, hard working
Daughter of Julie and Stephen
Loves dogs, reading, spending time with my family
Who feels summer goes by so fast, enjoys playing outside every day, feels like summer break is only 60 days
Who fears the death of loved ones, getting stung by a bee, and getting in a car crash
Who would like to see Hawaii, Texas, and North Carolina
Seidler

Kaitlyn Seidler, Grade 2

Me
Angie
Loving, caring, hard worker, funny
Daughter of Christie and Craig
Lover of dogs, reading, and fruit
Who feels that summer is too short, there's too much snow in Erie, and Mrs. Brown is the best
Who fears spiders, ghosts, and vampires
Who would like to see Hawaii, Italy, and Australia
Anderson

Angela Anderson, Grade 2

The Best Part of Me
These help me play board games on holidays with family
These help me hold a water bottle, Gatorade, and hold a cup if I need a drink
These help me eat Chicken Lombardy
These help me hold and turn the pages of a book
These help me write handwriting in cursive beautifully,
   writing on scrap paper before on homework, writing letters to people saying how I missed them

Alisa Wright, Grade 3

One with the Snow
Snow, snow it falls on my nose and glows.
It falls on my nose.
I love snow day and night am I right?
I will make a snowman and play with him.
I like to watch the snow fall on the roof and drink apple juice.
Most of all I love to watch the snow!

Lesedi Anyika, Grade 3

Fall
Fall looks like leaves on the ground.
Fall sounds like boo! Witches, ghosts, and other scary things.
Fall feels like the fresh air and breeze.
Fall smells like a candle burning.
Fall tastes like homemade pumpkin pie.
Fall is a fun, awesome, amazing season.

Gabby Ottaviano, Grade 3

Summer
Summer looks like bloomed flowers
Summer sounds like water splashing.
Summer feels like a Popsicle dripping on my hand.

Summer smells like fresh cut grass.
Summer tastes like a cool cream soda.
Summer is very hot

Alexus Streeper, Grade 3

Growing Flowers
Flowers are blooming,
Bees pollinate the flowers,
Here spring comes with bees.

Lincoln Hastings, Grade 2

Ocean
O ver the waves
C overing the fish
E ating the fish
A water wonderland
N o littering the ocean

Aidan Edwin Robinson, Grade 3

Winter Seasons
Jingles everywhere
leaves on the trees falling off
and snow on the ground.

Christopher Towne, Grade 3

My Favorite Season
Fall, Thanksgiving, leaves
Halloween, leaves fall down, cool
Pumpkin, apple pie
Alexandra Martinez, Grade 1

Icicles
Icicles are cold
Dripping, dropping to the ground
Hanging from a cave
Christian Sorells, Grade 3

The Golden Gate Bridge
Red, humongous, long
Durable, gigantic, cool
The Golden Gate Bridge.
Kyle DesRosiers, Grade 3

Snowflakes
Snowflakes everywhere
Falling from the dark blue sky
In all different shapes
Alden Kyes, Grade 3

Nature
Snowflakes fall from the sky
Raindrops make puddles of water
Icicles hang off caves
Elliot Lindsay, Grade 3

The Weather
Clouds rain in the fall
It snows when it is winter
Sun shines in summer
Naurgol Rafaat, Grade 1

Tree
A bird in a tree
is looking for butterflies.
It's waiting for them.
Jade Bonito, Grade 3

Smiling
Smiling is like a rainbow
spreading through a sunset
over the beach.
Demetria Magnini, Grade 3

Waves
The salty waves splashing around me
And smears the coral reef
Out in the deep
The big waves push me over

I feel my feet sink in the warm sand
Twisted waves
I feel like I rule the sea

Smashes against the sand
Ups and downs
Splashing loud waves
It is music to my ears
Madison Brown, Grade 3

Index by Author

Abdi, Khadro 88
Abercrombie, David 148
Abou Nader, Alexia 50
Abramoff, Brielle 155
Abramoff, Lincoln 175
Abran, Eloi 158
Abran, Maíra 45
Abu-Zebiba, Nykeem 150
Achenbach, Matthew 81
Adamow, Maria 55
Adams, Caroline 150
Adams, Elisabeth "Elise" 102
Addeh, Maryssa 165
Addona, Adam 49
Ade-Oyetayo, Adetola 174
Aduboahen, Samuella 134
Agayev, Ammiela 24
Aguilar, Ruben 64
Al-haddad, Isabel 96
Alamri, Hatem 173
Alexander, Aaron 127
Alldred, Natalie 124
Allegrini, Daniela 23
Allen, Amber 87
Allen, Emily 149
Allenspach, Maggie 176
Allison, Nicholas 93
Allman, Haley 19
Alnakeeb, Jana 147
Alomar, Karim 55
Alvarez Caporale, Marcos 159
Amir, Ebar 77
Amodeo, Emma 158
Amoroso, Nicole 80
Amoroso, Vanessa 78
Anderson, Angela 177
Anderson, Dakota 140
Anderson, Isaiah 139
Anderson, Jameel 43
Anderson, Porter 56
Anderson, Raena 34
Anderson-Skelly, Mara 140
Andres, Samantha 63
Andrews, Emma 34
Andrews, Jessica 57
Angelo, Sebastian 166
Angleberger, Charles Henry 36
Anguelov, Christian 146
Anwar, Zavier 168
Anyika, Lesedi 177
App, Nickales 32
Araiza, Jessica 74

Archer, Tyan 59
Arellano, Bailey 60
Argiro, Mark 119
Argoth, Jesus 97
Arias, Ivan 16
Arneaud, Kasi 86
Arnold, Lillian 153
Aron, Edy 169
Aronow, Caydes 128
Arriaga, Jenner 29
Atkins, Scottie 115
Avalak, Natisha 125
Awad, Tameem 170
Ayala, Giselle 26
Baines, Alexia 125
Bains, Amardeep 140
Bains, Amrit 147
Bajwa, Onkar Singh 98
Baker, Ava 50
Baker, Victoria 18
Baldwin, Nicholas 175
Baldwin, Rylie 121
Ballantine, Ryan 156
Balliet, Soph 64
Baltodano, Vanderley 51
Balzer, Levi 40
Bang, Savanah 114
Banks, Lily 109
Barajas Ibarra, Casandra 150
Barbier, Sidney 128
Barker, Jerron 120
Barkley, Robert 91
Barna, Zachary 168
Barnard, Nathan 147
Barnes, Chantel 161
Barney, Oakley 91
Baron, Massimiliano 146
Barrett, Jaron 82
Barron, Julie 120
Barrow, Nyia 44
Barrus, Madeleine 50
Barton, Savanna 148
Bartsch, Ella 24
Basra, Khushbir Kaur 156
Bastidas Garcia, Valentina 172
Batterton, Colby 170
Bauder, Selena 110
Bauer, Elliana 166
Bauerle, Jaclyn 121
Beach, Ayden 80
Beauséjour, Jade 168
Bebko, Andrew 141

Beebe, Nicholas 91
Beerson, Mila 165
Behm, Carter 58
Belanger, Axel 148
Beldi, Vanessa 149
Ben-Mansour, Haroun 152
Bennett, Abigail 175
Bennett, Barrett 37
Bennett, Jayne 45
Bennett, Kyle 143
Bennett-Manke, Zoe 75
Bennie, Patrick 84
Benson, Travis 123
Bentancor, Vittoria 24
Bentzinger, Austin 93
Benzakour, Aaliyah 174
Berg, Mackenna 151
Bergen, Emma 171
Berish, Alexandra 17
Berish, Samantha 33
Bernard, Benita 77
Bernhardt, Lainee 18
Berry, Katie 65
Bessey, Emma 117
Betcher, Sophie 37
Betts, Nora 111
Betzner, Thomas 17
Bevins, Brandon 165
Bhallar, Amol K. 160
Bhullar, Amol 164
Bhullar, Gurshawn 147
Bhullar, Gurshawn S. 146
Bickel, Lucy 29
Bidwell, Evan 24
Bielawski, Sarah 104
Bier, Hannah 31
Biffle, Caitlyn 47
Billett, Gavin Michael 32
Billings, Ellie 142
Birch, Alexis 47
Birk, Khushvir K. 167
Birkenkamp, Maya 49
Biviano, Augie 159
Biviano, Lydia 175
Bjornstad, Sarah 74
Blessing, Aiden 176
Bobowski, Magenta 147
Bogar, Nathan 128
Bonanno, Isabella 91
Bonebrake, Rachel 156
Bonilla, Mario 39
Bonilla, Tristan 154

Bonito, Jade	178	
Bonomo, Nathaniel	48	
Boone, Jeneya	162	
Booth, Nicholas	27	
Borsato, Benjamin	51	
Botelho, Sophia	170	
Bouazzaoui, Ryme	159	
Bourgeois-Matus, Julia	149	
Bousserghine, Andre	70	
Bowman, Kiana	38	
Boyd, Marty	35	
Bradley, Isaac	165	
Bradley, Jacob	25	
Bradnam, Ryland	28	
Brar, Darshpreet	149	
Brar, Keerat Kaur	164	
Brar, Lovleen	155	
Brasson, Madison	33	
Brewer, Evan	22	
Bright, Calvin	170	
Brinkert, Sagan	31	
Brisco, Dawn	140	
Briscoe, Samuel	62	
Brocklehurst, Tristan	55	
Broglio, Noah	157	
Brooks, Sarah	34	
Brown, Catherine Noelle	76	
Brown, Ella	24	
Brown, Madison	178	
Brown-Williams, Dashawn	174	
Brtalik, Ashlyn	143	
Brubaker, Ella	91	
Bruce, Owen	44	
Bubash, Kaiden	59	
Buccione, Alessandro	155	
Bugarin, Jasmine	52	
Buhaly, Madison	96	
Bui, Reagan	88	
Bungay, Christopher	142	
Burford, Sa'Renity	27	
Burgwin, Edrea	86	
Buric, Davor	138	
Burke, Leah	149	
Burns, Neely	107	
Busciacco, Sophia	104	
Buskirk, Amber	60	
Bussières, Alexandre	175	
Bustamante, Gerardo	166	
Bustos, Joshua	27	
Butkovic, Riley	36	
Byes, Alayna	77	
Byrne, Chloé	27	
Cady, Avery	103	
Cahill, Bridget	46	
Cahill, Reilly	107	
Cain, Alex	127	
Cake, Samantha	67	
Calderon, Ernesto	132	
Caldino, Jonathan	132	
Caldwell, Quincy	80	
Caleca, Sophia	108	
Calhoun, Charlotte	157	
Calixto Rodriguez, Karina	86	
Callas, James	168	
Camacho, Daphne	80	
Cameron, Carter	112	
Campa, Jessie	109	
Campbell, Ailsa	24	
Campbell, Tydan	89	
Cao, Erika	151	
Cardenas, Natalie	83	
Cardona-Torres, Allen	39	
Carey, Leonard	136	
Carley, Allison	129	
Carmody, Carleigh	54	
Carmosino, Matteo	155	
Caron, Jordan	114	
Carpenter, Samantha	103	
Carrera, Damien	88	
Carrillo, Maribel	175	
Carter, Deon	158	
Carter, Shelby	108	
Case, Seth	121	
Casey, Luna	29	
Casner, Arianna	142	
Castagnero, Annie	122	
Castleman, Nico	88	
Celestino, Uriah	32	
Cendejas, Emmanuel	109	
Ceres, Cordelia-Marie	22	
Cervantes Garcia, Isaac	170	
Chachkin, Matthew	171	
Champredon, Chloé	133	
Chang, Isabelle	30	
Chapman, Ella	61	
Charbonneau-Provost, Elliot	155	
Chaveron, Anaelle	158	
Chaveron, Morgane	146	
Chavez, Lesly	33	
Cheena, Khushi Kaur	152	
Chen, Angela	71	
Chen, Eileen	107	
Chestnut, Hannah	70	
Chiles, Brandon	162	
Chintalan, Christopher	37	
Chitambar, Lilianna	89	
Choromanski, Megan	25	
Chow, Carissa	51	
Chrispen, Treyton	137	
Christensen, Cassandra	78	
Christensen, Isaac	44	
Christiansen, Tenesha	8	
Chubak, Kaylee	30	
Chubak, Samuel	168	
Chung, Angela	67	
Church, Alex	49	
Cintron Berdeja, Brayan	40	
Claggett, Chaziyah	77	
Clarke, Caleb	56	
Clarke, Chase	163	
Claux, Jerome	139	
Claytemple, Richard	115	
Clement, Frederique	148	
Close, Ashley	160	
Colbert, Emily	70	
Coleto, Alicia	24	
Coletta, Joseph	43	
Collison, Ian	82	
Colo, Carena	128	
Combs, Jackson	48	
Conner, Brody	63	
Conner, Kara	141	
Connors, Emma	63	
Conriquez, Pamela	122	
Contreras, Cindy	169	
Contreraz, Torri	39	
Cooke, Jada	46	
Corkery, Maura	19	
Corson, Hayley	68	
Costlow, James	84	
Côté, Chanel	98	
Coutts, Elizabeth	42	
Cox, Bryan	123	
Cox, Jacob	34	
Coyne, Rylan	20	
Coziahr, Denalyn	156	
Coziahr, Jerica	169	
Cranmer, Faith	137	
Craw, Abby	68	
Crawford, Martha	47	
Crawford, Nicholas	152	
Crawley, Lilyana	102	
Crockett, Emmylee	122	
Crowe, Évelyne	158	
Crowe, Marianne	68	
Cruddas, 5th Grade Class	29	
Cruz, Parker	79	
Culbert, Leia	150	
Cullen, Thomas John	150	
Cullhaj, Albi	168	
Currie, Olivia	89	
Currimbhoy, Anna	16	
Curry, Anna	110	
Curzon, Natasha	54	
Czekaj, Jessica	23	
D'Ambrosio, Abby	26	
D'Amico, Kaylee	25	
Dade, Saamir	176	
Dalsis, Brick	50	
Dalton, Katie	99	
Daly, Sean	82	
Dam, Vinh Quoc	148	
Daniel, Alec	17	
Danielson, Hailey	134	
Danquah, Jada	18	
Dardanis, Thea	24	
DaRosa, Alexandra	49	

Index by Author

Dash, Colton 58
Davie, Anika 17
Davis, Abby 150
Davis, Caroline 115
Davis, Kai 18
Davis, Rihanna 156
De Bie, Aidan 162
de la Zerda, Leticia 59
Deacle, David 173
DeAngelis, Mikey 137
Deardorff, Braedin 152
Debusschere, Mikayla 127
Deems, Zoe 100
Deems-Warnick, Brendon 21
Deetlefs, Carla 44
DeFelice, Christian 48
DeFranco, Sydney 82
Deith, Elle 127
Della Cioppa, Nakki 159
Delorme, Mathieu 95
DeMarco, Alyson 65
Demill, Kaleb 56
Dempsey, Naoise 17
Denie, Abygail 137
Deorsay, Evander 119
Deschenes, Samuel 27
Desjardine, Samara 158
DesRosiers, Jacob 165
DesRosiers, Kyle 178
Devoe, Andrew 153
Di Caprio, Mia 158
Dia, Adam 159
DiAmico, Kevin 136
Diarra, Cherif 88
Diaz, Kirby Adrian 152
DiBattista, Adam 147
Dick, Vanessa 71
Dimitrova, Victoria 159
Dinesh, Diya 52
Dingwell, Lexi 111
Dinh Vien Duong, Vincent 81
Djordjevic, Matthew 37
Dobich, Haley 89
Dobson, Alexandria 18
Dockter, Leyna 103
Dodds, Caitlin 161
Doherty, Alexis 127
Doherty, Branden 54
Dolan, Nicholas 19
Dominguez, Ariana 119
Dominguez Montiel, Jazmin 169
Donaghy, Liam 41
Donchez, Margeaux 106
Doodala, Pranavi 129
Dorch, Zach 168
Dorko, Olivia 20
Doucette, Megan 123
Dougherty, Patrick 16
Douglas, Alaina 109

Douglas, Dana 119
Drisner, Noah 148
Du, Kaden 80
Dudak, Timothy 20
Duetsch, Sarah 20
Dunbar, Breck 57
Duncan, Lily 103
Durrett, Ryann 26
Duvall, Cole 21
Dzurenda, Ava 30
Eberly, Natalie 82
Edwards, Maddison 123
Edwards, Paige 112
Edwards, Rivers 101
Edwards, Samantha 149
Ehrlich, Lila 49
El-Ghalayini, Lara 165
Elie, Chloe 76
Elisma, Jason 176
Elisma, Jessica 165
Elitz, Luke 104
Elkanzi, Faris 148
Ellefson, Tilda 28
Elliker, Stephen 146
Ellingson, Annalisa 137
Ellison, Michael 94
Endrizzi, Mikey 57
Englebreth, Ryan 69
Eppolito, Estelle 129
Eppolito, Scarlett 174
Eppolito, Wyatt 89
Epstein, Rose 50
Erlandsen, Quinn 45
Eskanos, Jazlyn 45
Esplin, Dylan 143
Essler, Isabella 22
Estes, Gillian 55
Estrada, Brianna 151
Evans, Eden 33
Everett, Jade 161
Ewert, Brooklyn 99
Eyzaguirre, Ryan 52
Fahey, Emma 94
Fales, Tyler 112
Farhan, Reneem 164
Farina, Tegan 43
Farmer, Grace Ruth Evelyn 158
Farnell, Ella 55
Fata, Emmanuel 124
Fatebene, Adam 65
Faudoa, Jenni 97
Fauht, Carley 47
Fedora, Evan 143
Fehri, Hamza 162
Fehri, Yassine 149
Feistner, Eliana 130
Felsmann, Meg 26
Fenwick, Anneliese 26
Ferguson, Emma 55

Ferrari, Marisa 23
Ferreira, Trevor 79
Ferstl, Brandon 27
Fezenko, Matt 140
Figueroa, Xavior 71
Fike, Colson 135
Filler, Isac 120
Fincher, Paige 123
Fischer, Cassidy 77
Fish, Ryan 159
Fisher, Max 36
Flanigan, Bode 142
Fletcher, Shameka 55
Fletcher, Wesley 78
Flores, Faith 88
Flores, Francie 52
Foose, Zoë 38
Forney, Avery 154
Forry, Seth 73
Fortin, Nathan 155
Foster, Izzy 156
Foster, Karsten 21
Fox, Trent 37
Frank, Madison 113
Frank, Sophia 16
Franklin, Gracie 34
French, Jenna 19
Frey, Colby 157
Frey, Samantha 140
Frezza, Lucia 85
Fricker, Charlie 168
Friday, Destiny 85
Friesen, Kayla 147
Fritsche, Luke 63
Froh, Aidan 176
Frye, Noah 153
Fumey, Elikem 147
Funk, Jayella 149
Furmanek, Bayla 106
Gabbard, Abigail 148
Gaddam, Medha 83
Gaglioti, Joey 38
Gagné, Keira 47
Gagnon, Marie 146
Galdean, James 154
Gamboa, Mariana 37
Ganguli, Rajnandini 26
Garcia, Emmanuel 132
Garcia, Jose 97
Garduño Mendez, Janet 141
Garner, Jade 50
Garrett Vasquez, Hannah 26
Garrido, Rebekah 128
Garrison, Preston 130
Gatewood, Olivia 147
Gawryluk, Kyson 168
Gawryluk, Makara 58
Gaydos, Tyler 49
Gerbrandt, Skylar 156

Gerritsen, Jeremy ... 23	Gunther, Claire ... 16	Hernandez, Katherine ... 36
Gerz, Madeleine ... 36	Gushue, Aidyn ... 170	Hernandez-Ramirez, Jovany ... 52
Gesler, Naomi ... 69	Guthoff, Stevie ... 60	Hertz, Kelsey ... 137
Getz, Gannon ... 123	Guthrie, Ryan ... 162	Hess, Sara ... 59
Ghanem, Tim ... 148	Ha, Anthony ... 85	Hesser, Dustin ... 105
Gibson, Kennedy ... 52	Habursky, Mariska ... 157	Hettler, McKayla ... 170
Gibson, Lena ... 18	Hache, Olivia ... 75	Hickey, Emma ... 106
Gidaro, Sofia ... 127	Haddad, Ian ... 106	Hicks, Claudia ... 116
Gil, Isabella ... 159	Hadimani, Suchita ... 142	Higinbotham, Ronald ... 47
Giles, Briona ... 19	Hafer, Jack ... 158	Hildebrant, Nathan ... 26
Gill, Anand ... 152	Hagan, Blake ... 130	Hill, Morgan ... 131
Gill, Anand Singh ... 154	Hagan, Laurel ... 164	Hilyard, Austin ... 101
Gillespie, Aiden ... 19	Haggerty, Shane ... 55	Hilyard, Selah ... 68
Gilmartin, Hannah ... 84	Hagy, Connor ... 151	Hirschland, Quinn ... 54
Ginsberg, Mara ... 40	Hahn, Melanie ... 120	Hitchens, Alexis ... 78
Giordina, Gracie ... 114	Hailey, Sam ... 23	Hoben, Riley ... 96
Gira, Tara ... 42	Hall, Logan ... 122	Hoffman, Tyler ... 45
Girod, Emma ... 150	Halstead, Michael ... 143	Hofstedt, Caiden ... 157
Givner, Dayana ... 49	Hamill, Pavel ... 127	Hogarty, Kelli ... 23
Glace, Addison ... 148	Hamler, Rachel ... 132	Holder, Sarah ... 151
Glass, Hannah ... 156	Hammad, Mohamed ... 138	Holford, Kalie ... 133
Glockner, Austin ... 85	Hampton, Madalyn ... 49	Holland, Madelyn ... 84
Glover, Abra ... 55	Hanscom, Maddie ... 69	Holt, Charley ... 106
Goldapper, David ... 147	Hansen, Mykela ... 32	Holt, Gwendolyn ... 60
Goldenziel, Alicia ... 128	Hardgrove, Eric ... 94	Hong, Alice ... 86
Gonzalez, Briana Rose ... 44	Harmon, Aubrie ... 148	Hons, Xavier John Django ... 21
Gonzalez, Daniel ... 155	Harmston, Miranda ... 78	Horn, Alex ... 80
Gonzalez, Kenneth ... 42	Harrington, Alexandra ... 22	Hornsby, Mags ... 90
Good, Erin ... 91	Harris, Cheyenne ... 171	Hosmer, Logan ... 164
Goodwin, Presleigh ... 78	Harris, Emma ... 19	Houtz, Rayvin ... 98
Gosal, Navpreet K. ... 176	Harris, Megan ... 46	Howard, Alexandre ... 56
Goudy, Sophia ... 40	Harris, Nancy ... 161	Howe, Jadon ... 167
Graham, Brooke ... 72	Harrison, William ... 111	Howell, Trevor ... 107
Graham, Morgan ... 19	Hartley, Andie ... 51	Hoyt, Clare ... 27
Grambau, Aidan ... 94	Hartman, Natalie ... 85	Huang, Susan ... 27
Graupensperger, Addison ... 170	Hasan, Lilly ... 35	Hubley, Arianna ... 89
Green, Abby ... 43	Hastings, Lincoln ... 177	Huckaby, Hayden ... 31
Greenland, Kamryn ... 113	Hatfield, Abigail ... 160	Huddleston, Brinley ... 85
Greenwald, Carolyn L. ... 25	Hatfield, Madalyn ... 47	Hudgins, Bailey ... 17
Grégoire, Benjamin ... 42	Hathaway, Emma ... 16	Hudson, Eleanor ... 174
Gresh, Heidi ... 139	Hathaway, Liliana ... 168	Hudson, Trevor ... 95
Griese, Liam ... 147	Haugen, Jared ... 35	Hulmes, Colin ... 38
Grondin, Nicolas ... 95	Haun, Olivia ... 40	Hume, Emily ... 151
Gross, Cornel ... 172	Hause, Alexandria ... 56	Hume, Jamie ... 173
Gross, Isaac ... 152	Hayden, Kayne ... 118	Humphreys, Caitlin ... 46
Gross, Jacobie ... 174	Hays, Alex ... 37	Humphreys, Gracie ... 46
Gross, Jesse ... 166	Healey, Corinna ... 61	Hunt, David ... 69
Gross, Johanna ... 71	Hedlund, Molly ... 98	Hunter, Owen ... 124
Gross, Leah ... 118	Heffelfinger, Amaya ... 168	Iatesta, Ava ... 82
Gross, Susan ... 71	Heffner, Matthew ... 23	Idrovo, Daniella ... 163
Gross, Tim ... 94	Heitmann, Katie ... 97	Iorio, Olivia ... 56
Gross, Zach ... 41	Heller, Savannah ... 161	Ipock, Josh ... 42
Grosser, Emilie ... 79	Helton, Kaylee ... 85	Iraheta, Tiffany ... 56
Groves, Jordan ... 58	Hendry, Ryder ... 92	Irvin, Mikayla ... 58
Gu, Nina ... 169	Henry, Sarah ... 167	Irvine, Megan ... 149
Gudla, Reshma ... 35	Henry, Sophia ... 41	Jaafar, Adam ... 170
Guerin, Sabrina ... 21	Herbott, Heather ... 28	Jaafar, Dalia ... 56
Guiffre, Jasmyn ... 31	Hernandez, Alondra ... 149	Jaber, Mehdi ... 175
Gunther, Cameron ... 72	Hernandez, Elise ... 77	Jackman, Britnee ... 82

Index by Author

Jackson, Savannah 173	Kaur Randhawa, Supriya 150	Lalonde, Devyn 45
Jacobs, Sarah 25	Keating, Bryce 97	Lam, Brandon 53
Jacobs, Valerie 32	Keating, Julia 54	Lam, Si Jiao 146
Jacobson, Cenya 103	Keenan, Kelsey 100	Lambert, Emanuelle 146
Jaime, Victoria 94	Keener, Myra 35	Lanagan-Blanc, Logan 77
Jain, Toshan 48	Keesee, Haley 142	Landa, Yonathan 171
Jama, Mahad 24	Keim, Carolyn 171	Landis, Reilly 93
Jammoul, Acile 135	Keirl, Maya 57	Lane, Jack 169
Janowicz, Christina 38	Keith, Lillian 89	Lane, Marshall 30
Jaramillo, Mariana 84	Kellar, Taylor 33	Lane, Wyatt 161
Jartidian, Joseph 148	Kelly, Mary Grace 46	Langevin, Bryan 86
Jaswal, Benita 152	Kelly, Maureen 27	Langlois, Emma 158
Jaswal, Eakampreet S. 174	Kempf, Tysean 167	Langlois, Juliane 36
Jayaraman, Simren 108	Kennedy, Julia 53	Langston, Allison 44
Jayawardhana, Lometh 168	Kerber, Will 39	Lapointe, Samantha 25
Jenkins, Alexis 162	Kerns, Madison 76	Lapp, Sarah 73
Jenkins, Emily 172	Khan, Ella 146	Larsen, Kyrsten 159
Jennings, Walker 68	Khan, Nadir 141	Lau, Angus 85
Jensen, Alex 26	Khan, Rameen 138	Lauck, Allie 97
Jewell, Kennedy 111	Khanal, Kamal 157	Lavigne, Maxence 150
Jheout, Sukhvir S. 160	Khanna, Saniya 125	Law, Zoë 95
Jiang, Frank 49	Khatib, Talia 59	Law-Jackson, Hermasia 87
Johnsen, Shaylee 92	Khondoker, Durriyah 162	Lawrence, Lewie 126
Johnson, Adam 80	Khosa, Baneesh 126	Lawson, Mikie 72
Johnson, Alicia 49	Kim, Bridget 143	Lazar, Ava 35
Johnson, Jack 63	Kim, Sarah 175	Leach, Caleb 111
Johnson, Lydia 164	Kim, Sean 122	LeBaron, Ruby 26
Johnson, Mackenzie 17	Kim, Yvonne 105	Leclair, Émerik 159
Johnson, Nick 33	Kines, Amira 116	LeCuyer, Ethan 84
Johnson, Timea 89	King, Dylan 169	Ledezma, Ingrid 161
Johnston, Rudolfo 123	King, Gracie 73	Ledoux, Xavier 158
Johnston, Trevor 62	Kingsley, Mackenna 46	Lee, Aiden 24
Jones, Eli 176	Kinnison, Sage 110	Lee, Isabella 76
Jones, Miranda 101	Klein, Jonathan 51	Lee, Peter 25
Jones, Riley 67	Kline, Joel 174	Lee, Rosa 23
Jones, Sierra 141	Klopp, Jillian 69	Leevy, Kylonna 115
Jones, Zoey 114	Knapick, Ennui 126	Lefever, Kate 71
Jooravan, Dhivya 155	Knize, Reiley Bell 72	LeGendre, Savannah 31
Joy, Setia 31	Koester, Eve 84	Lehtiniemi, Melody 150
Joyner, Chance 154	Kohli, Eshi 41	Leiber, Terra 133
Julseth, Autumn 47	Kokish, Cole 48	Leitgeb, Carter 162
Juta, Prashik 174	Kong, Dylan 147	Lema, Maria-José 57
Kaatz, Christopher 20	Kong, Jonathan 51	Lentini, Gianna 149
Kaatz, Madeleine 165	Konitzer, Sasha 152	Lentz, Sophie 34
Kaatz, Matthew 154	Kosgei, Alexandra 151	Lenz, Kyle 130
Kaiser, Rachel 142	Kosko, Kayleigh 152	Letkeman, Emily 165
Kamath, Viraj 163	Kostenbader, Kylie 138	Levin, Maksim 146
Kamenitz, Jordana 99	Kotelnikoff, Jerzie 155	Levison, Elise 70
Kanao, Rudy 158	Kowalkowski, Noel 126	Levy, Brooklynn 63
Kanda, Imaan 171	Kozlov-Shishkina, Marie-Hélène 60	Ley, Samuel 89
Kane, Brianna 107	Kozlova, Marie-Helene 45	Leyva Quiterio, Miguel 154
Karafilis, Brandon 74	Krady, Leilani 71	Li, Max Yue 18
Karn, Ashley 141	Krehmeyer, Amber 42	Li, Nini 147
Karnis, Genevieve 26	Kruslicky, Chloe 120	Lian, Joanna 150
Kash, Anna 102	Kunkle, Brady 151	Liang, Baron-Yuhao 130
Kaufman, Audrey 16	Kyes, Alden 178	Lieu, Louis 130
Kaur Bhullar, Maneet 167	Lafleur, Alexa 20	Lieu, Louisa 124
Kaur Chahal, Harveer 150	Lago Quijano, Juan David 50	Liles-Crayton, Ayla 122
Kaur Gill, Harneet 157	Lahser, Ani 148	Lilienthal, Emily 157

Linberger, Antonio ... 96	Marshall, Dakota ... 86	Milani, Isabelle ... 92
Lindsay, Elliot ... 178	Marshall, Jonah ... 151	Miller, Ashlynn ... 168
Linkow, Shira ... 87	Marshall, Michael ... 173	Miller, Bradley ... 171
Lipscomb, Thomas ... 132	Marshall, Seamus ... 149	Miller, Emily ... 30
Little, Ashley ... 89	Martens, Michelle ... 74	Miltier, Jenna ... 35
Litwiler, Mark ... 155	Martin, Danielle ... 126	Misavage, Paige ... 19
Lockwood, Avery ... 55	Martinez, Alexandra ... 178	Mishoe, Sophia ... 20
Lombardo, Kassandra ... 157	Martinez, Isabella ... 38	Mishoe II, Chaka ... 59
Lombardo, Kayla ... 146	Martinez, Steven ... 85	Missigman, Elise ... 153
Long, Grace ... 75	Martinez Higareda, Lizbeth ... 150	Mohammed, Suhana ... 47
Long, Korben ... 57	Martiny, Kaleb ... 25	Mohanathasan, Mahishajini ... 31
Loop, Emma ... 96	Marwaha, Rahul ... 81	Mohney, Reyna ... 46
Lopes Toroyan, Megan ... 158	Masiak, Carolina ... 76	Moody, Ethan ... 166
Lopez, Gabriela ... 138	Mastrangelo, Maggie ... 101	Moore, Alex ... 159
Lopez, Juan ... 32	Matar, Andrew ... 152	Moore, Rowan ... 141
Lor, Jonas ... 171	Matteo, Luca ... 152	Morales, Isabella ... 134
Lorcy, Jonathan ... 175	Matthies, Corianne ... 169	Morgan, Abbie ... 113
Los, Madison ... 73	Matthis, Ella ... 146	Morgan, Dale ... 29
Louis, Sam ... 28	Mattson, Dallis ... 46	Morris, Kyle ... 66
Love, Daniel ... 131	Maurer, Nadiah ... 97	Morrow, Oliver ... 89
Love, Patti ... 139	Maximo, Aliyah ... 64	Moses, Akayjah ... 140
Lu, Davis ... 134	Maxson, Elijah ... 104	Mote, Liam ... 23
Lucas, Maggie ... 168	May, Hannah ... 149	Motichka, Carter ... 32
Lucia, Brennen ... 149	McCalips, Devon ... 32	Mucchetti, Emily ... 39
Lucio, Vanessa ... 78	McCloud, Aidan ... 141	Muirhead, Leah ... 33
Luffman, Haley ... 91	McDonald, Conner ... 168	Muller, Alexis ... 99
Luis, Emma Elisabeth ... 148	McDonald, Jiana ... 33	Munion, Mackey ... 56
Lunsford, Gabriel ... 94	McFarland, Jenna ... 34	Murevesi, Onai ... 81
Ly, Brian ... 111	McFarland, Lane ... 26	Murphy, Mikayla ... 34
Ly, Jessica ... 37	McFarland, Leevi ... 44	Murriell, Danielle ... 106
Ly, Michael ... 148	McGaughran, Connor ... 82	Myers, Emma ... 84
Lynch, Daniel ... 33	McGee, John Cole ... 29	Nabozniak, Alyson ... 78
Lynch, Julia ... 64	McGowan, Faith ... 84	Nacked Cabral, Victoria ... 157
Lyons, Nate ... 172	McGrath, Kelsey ... 115	Nair, Devika ... 39
M., Carmen ... 81	McHugh, Morgan ... 37	Napier, Kayleigh ... 160
MacAdams, Abigail ... 36	McKay, Sage ... 41	Nauffts, Rylee ... 20
MacArthur, Kylei ... 175	McKenna, Meghan ... 163	Neba, Ma'a ... 81
Macdonald, Hudson ... 83	McKittrick, Mac ... 79	Nehr, Sophia ... 140
Mack, Kyle ... 59	Mclain, Justin ... 132	Neiport, Maleah ... 57
MacKenzie, Sarah Jane ... 120	McLaughlin, Brennan ... 87	Nelson, Andrew ... 154
MacLean, Ashley ... 79	McPherson, Addison ... 44	Nelson, Kate ... 117
Macri, Lucabella ... 103	McVittie, William ... 150	Nelson, Kera ... 129
Madhavan, Meena ... 151	McVoy, Beckett ... 23	Nelson, Liesel ... 169
Madison, Yakeir ... 102	Mehlmann, Timothy ... 75	Newman, Lindsay ... 171
Madrid Jr., Mario ... 97	Mei, Eric ... 95	Newsome, Kellen ... 87
Magnini, Demetria ... 178	Mejalli, Gabrielle ... 30	Newsome, Kirra ... 123
Mahajan, Richa ... 142	Mejia, Marco ... 39	Newton, Alyssa ... 83
Mahmde, Jada ... 28	Mejia, Paul Alexandre ... 97	Nguyen, Kyle ... 138
Mahrlig, Zoë ... 128	Melchionno, Simona ... 174	Nguyen, Lilly ... 36
Maines, Sheridan ... 57	Mendez, Karen ... 21	Nguyen, Melanie ... 70
Malak, Nadine ... 29	Mendonca, Carson ... 41	Nichifor, Charlee ... 137
Malinowski, Kinga ... 154	Merke, Nathanael ... 169	Nichols, Krysta ... 98
Malone, Cody ... 165	Merke, Samuel ... 171	Nichols, Maya ... 83
Malyugin, Denis ... 159	Messick, Nicky ... 99	Nicholson, Elaina ... 102
Mannrique, Cristal ... 32	Metzel, Tyler ... 38	Nielsen, Nicholas ... 33
Mansfield, Becky ... 30	Meziati, Zayd ... 139	Nielsen, Nicole ... 169
March, Bree ... 165	Mezzacapo, Amber ... 161	Nienhuis, Kiersten ... 156
Marengo, Alessandra ... 160	Michael, Andrew ... 152	Nizar, Aya ... 26
Markovic, Mischa ... 147	Michaels, Payton ... 132	Nolan, Maura ... 117

Index by Author

Normand Plante, Joannie 170
Normandy, Luc 99
Norval, Emma 155
Norval, Nicola 161
Nyateu, Kemil G. 124
O'Brien, Bridget 63
O'Brien, Colin 50
O'Brien-Turner, Aidan 112
O'Connor, Kaila 168
O'Doherty, Logan 169
O'Leary, Tragar 24
Occena, Louisse 119
Odom, Kallyn 164
Oduok, Ariana 31
Ogden, Payton 161
Oler, Blaine 166
Oliver, Brennan 165
Oliver, Kaleb 130
Oliver-Dares, Ciera 127
Olson, Keegan 168
Olson, Mycah 172
Openshaw, Mathias 135
Orlando, Marcus 98
Ormsbee, Joshua 109
Orr, Holden 40
Ort, Keaton 148
Ortiz, Isabella 134
Ortiz, Jayden 42
Osborn, Philip 99
Osborne, Noah 53
Ottaviano, Gabby 177
P., Tori 51
Packer, Tatum 99
Padda, Ravleen 155
Padda, Shubhreet Kaur 159
Padgett, Kimberly 98
Padilla, Jazmin 139
Paige, Dalton 121
Panag, Harjas Kaur 161
Pandher, Armaan 77
Pantoja, Susana 154
Pardee, Lauryn 75
Park, Lily 56
Park, So-Won 120
Parks, Marielle 117
Parmar, Tejanpreet 136
Pasternak, Brianna 81
Pastor, Riley 85
Patel, Hari Rakeshkumar 157
Patterson, Ashleigh 111
Patterson, Hunter 33
Paul, Angie 136
Paulsen, Nevaeha 39
Paulson, Courtney 136
Payne, Myah 29
Pechersky, Ruth 96
Pedroza, Katharine 20
Pelletier, Matthew 124
Pellot, Maryleeana 38

Pena, Alexis 162
Pennell, Madeline 133
Peralta, Timothy 132
Perez-Ricaurte, Monica 40
Perlow, Dylan 104
Pernicello, Giada 147
Perrigo, Sara 21
Peterman, Brenna 137
Peters, Aaron 151
Peters, Elijah 168
Petersen, Liam 165
Peterson, Olivia 88
Peterson, Savannah 162
Petrakis, Nyah 98
Pettinger, Joey 65
Pettitt, Ameira 159
Phan, Angelina 167
Phan, Kevin 96
Phillips, Laya 97
Piccinin, Matheo 150
Pickeral, Luca 146
Pieper, Brandon 71
Pierson, Mackenna 117
Pietzsch, Ellery 164
Pilon, Marc-Olivier 21
Pinel, Benjamin 24
Pirtle, Reese 25
Pittarelli-Papadeas, Melina 111
Pitzer, Preston 106
Pjetrushi, Melissa 34
Plaitis-Levesque, Alexi 28
Pliley, Dacey 85
Poduszlo, Maitlyn 130
Podwats, Elle 47
Poltorak, Lauren 34
Polyanskaya, Polina 171
Porras, Brian 42
Poschner, Madison 25
Posey-Risberg, Jezebel 108
Poulson, Ella 109
Pozderka, Luca 79
Poziviak, Maya 118
Prakash, Aagam 62
Prasai, Arohan 86
Prasannakumar, Vinayak 155
Praveen, Jivitesh 51
Prentice, Madison 30
Prevette, Katie 132
Price, Jasmine 172
Prince, Kaylee 70
Prince, Sawyer 87
Pruim, Douglas 72
Puc, Kasia 113
Pugh, Payton 28
Purba, Kirat K. 175
Purba, Kirat Kaur 160
Purington, Joshua 170
Purtle, Sara 101
Puscher, Ethan 40

Qasim, Syed 46
Qazi, Sarah 44
Qu, Annie Linna 159
Quezada, Raymundo Garfio 109
Quillen, Haley 103
Quinones, Lucia 43
Quinteros, Bryan 88
R., Trinity 18
Rabeau, Mackenzie 63
Radoux, Zachary 158
Rafaat, Naurgol 178
Rai, Jasmeen 24
Rainero, Ava 148
Rainier, Vanessa 16
Raitano, Carl 83
Ramey, Alexandra 63
Ramey, Lydia 53
Ramisetty, NagaSriya 21
Ramsey, Marisa 143
Rangel, Melissa 175
Ranjan, Thuran 164
Rao, Ananya 108
Rapids, Steven 167
Rasmussen, Abbie 125
Rasmussen, Becky 114
Rath, James 163
Raymond, Paige 99
Raza, Abbas 65
Reardon, Emily Jean 43
Reccord, Cassie 47
Rechkemmer, Payton 104
Redweik-Leung, Llyr 163
Reed, Jack 71
Reed, Jack 130
Regenhard, Annie 114
Reich, Michelle 133
Reichler, Ariel 147
Rensberger, Norine 63
Ress, Victoria 98
Reyes, Olinmazatemictli 132
Reyna, Maria 105
Rhoads, Jenna 71
Rhoads, Raquel 96
Rhodes, Hope 40
Ricci, Alex 139
Ricci, Michael-Ryan 155
Richards, Ashleigh 85
Richards, Aurora 148
Richardson, Joseph 54
Richer, Elizabeth 36
Rico, Amaya 152
Rieben, Annie 161
Riehl, Paige 25
Righetti, Alison 51
Riley, Aidan 32
Riley, Quinn 146
Riordan, Ryan 73
Rivera, Brayden 154
Roberts, Jayden 50

Name	Page
Roberts, Liam	23
Robertson, Joshua	109
Robinette, Harper	154
Robinette, Jordyn	146
Robinson, Aidan Edwin	177
Robinson, Alexis	94
Robinson, Clara	102
Robinson, Hailey	167
Robinson, Jacqueline	138
Robinson, Reed	175
Robinson, Shiloh	131
Robison, Madison	32
Robley, Rachel	124
Rocco, Sean	168
Roccograndi, Sam	81
Rodger, Emilly	80
Rodriguez, Arriana	150
Rodriguez, Elijah	139
Rodriguez, Xavier	42
Roe, Annie	60
Rogers, Caitlin	30
Rogers, Camryn	84
Rogers, Janet	95
Rogers, Sophia	162
Rohrer, Shaye	98
Rojas, Destiny	44
Romero, Brianna	166
Roschat, Olivia	75
Rosenblatt, Elizabeth	56
Rosenboom, Stefan	79
Rosio, Emily	25
Ross, Donny	59
Rossi, Gianni	155
Rossman, Adrianne	41
Rostami, Mehrbod	98
Rovnanik, Sarah	82
Rowe, Hailey	117
Ruby, Caleb	56
Ruiz, Bianca	152
Rushton, Isaiah	149
Ryan, Evelyn	104
Sacco, Cristina	155
Sachdev, Chiraag	142
Sachs, Claudia	129
Salankey, Brayden	88
Salayandia Moran, Adrian	80
Salloum, Eliana	65
Salvin, Annabelle	105
Sanborn, Grace	19
Sanderson, Kade	105
Sanford, Anna	175
Sanford, Emily	159
Sanjines, Makel	156
Santarelli, Alessandra	148
Santise, Lucas	26
Santoro-Hernandez, Claudia	70
Saoumaa Garcia, Nicolas	157
Sattler, Alessia	164
Saw, Maika	56
Saxena, Parnika	100
Sayon, Grace	175
Scallorns, Henry	150
Schaeffer, Drake	116
Schatz, Jillian	43
Schlieman, Sophia	155
Schlieper, Maximus	52
Schlingemann, Froukje	43
Schmidt, Nathan	113
Schneider, Aidan	136
Schneider, Taylor	171
Schultz, Claire	162
Schultz, Emma	17
Schwartzer, Grace	135
Scott, Clive	170
Scott, Kenza Amaris	86
Scott, Norah	108
Scutt, Alyvia	128
Seamons, Nathan	137
Seidel, Shannon	125
Seidler, Kaitlyn	177
Seigel, Jordan	64
Sellami, Adam	146
Sellie, Etoria	173
Semtner, Brady	17
Semtner, Ella	86
Semtner, Keely	151
Sepulveda, Julian	148
Serna, Daniel	109
Sexton, Myla	164
Shackelford, Matthew	119
Shade, Trent	68
Shand, Katelyn	74
Sharif, Sarah	152
Shaver, Amber	109
Shea, Mckenzie	63
Shearn, Nathan	53
Sheehan, Kaley	45
Shelp, Shevelle L.	77
Shergill, Harshvir	175
Shergill, Harshvir Singh	174
Sherry, Taylor	132
Shetty, Simone	48
Shewchuk, Catherine	94
Shifflett, Kel	176
Shilling, Leesha	74
Shome, Kamilia	74
Shome, Kushal	154
Shorinde, Joanna	38
Shott, Leilani	32
Sicoli, Giulia	147
Sicoli, Marco Luigi	21
Sidhu, Gaurav	148
Siebrands, Lexys	85
Siemens, Toby	107
Silber, Morgan	146
Simard, Marianne	169
Simmons, Dreanna	128
Simpson, Julia	77
Sims-Hawkins, Chan'ae	173
Singh, Amrita	159
Singh Gill, Gurjeet	152
Singh Jabbal, Damandeep	82
Sivia, Livjot	36
Skandan, Neha	105
Skov, Posy	59
Sleiman, Majida Frida	147
Sloan, Colin	96
Slonglo, Israel	166
Sluka, Ava	92
Smiley, Ava	120
Smith, Catherine	171
Smith, Eden	72
Smith, Hope Ashley	159
Smith, Jade	140
Smith, Jeffrey	23
Smith, Kaiden	39
Smith, Lilly	156
Smith, Maddy	62
Smith, MarySue	131
Smith, Thomas	84
Smout, Katelyn	170
Snow, Callie	151
Snyder, Parker	155
Sobiech, Jake	98
Sobiech, Josh	138
Sobolewski, Nicholas	168
Sokso, Laura	158
Sorbello, Angela	40
Sorells, Christian	178
Sosa, Julian	165
Soto, Mariana	48
Southam, Audrey	16
Spath, Emma	97
Speed, Falisity	31
Spindler, Kate	164
Sprenger, Jaime	38
Sprister, Reese	53
Sprouse, Miranda	116
Stacy, Taylor	162
Stampone, Elizabeth	62
Stapley, Brinly	44
Starosta, Hubert	25
Steckbeck, Sarah	41
Steel, Malia	75
Steele, Rusel	111
Steinbach, Megan	132
Steinbach, Nicole	121
Stenstrom Moser, Nola	149
Stephens, Drew	27
Stephenson, Trent	58
Stevens, Delia	31
Stevenson-Akapew, Farren	159
Stewart, Hunter	70
Stillio, Bella	53
Stillwell, Michaela	40
Stoddard, Patrick	43
Stoica, Maya	82

Index by Author

Stonehouse, 2nd Grade Class 153
Story, Hannah 110
Strain, Chris 154
Strauch, Patrick 109
Strazdins, A'nya 112
Streeper, Alexus 177
Streeter, Ethan 120
Stricker, Nolan 96
Stuckey, Aubrey 41
Stutzman, Riley 45
Suit, Morgan 99
Sullivan, Isabella 124
Sumerlin, Austin 60
Sun, Lydia 159
Sutton, Luke 43
Svidron, Carson 115
Svoiski, Thomas 169
Swain, Rachel 42
Swallow, Ryan 160
Swarr, Declan 24
Sweeney, Maddie 118
Sweeney, Ryan 176
Sweeny, Rachel 68
Swope, Taylor 124
Symanoskie, Sierra 146
Tabor, Sawyer 37
Tafoya, Tommy 99
Tammaro, Nicholas 35
Tan, Lina 171
Tangora, Austin 44
Tanguturi, Sriya 154
Tankala, Anushka Sai 153
Taylor, Blake 57
Taylor, Nicholas 157
Teague, Kloie 118
Telili, Ibrahim 63
Temple, Bryonna 42
Templeton, Trent 39
Temuujin, Khulan 37
Tenan, Skylar 18
Tennant, Grace 135
Terpstra, Lily 95
Texter, Kayleigh 79
Thai, Kristie 16
Thapa, Soumya 131
Thatte, Ketaki 73
Thibault, Zachary 38
Thomas, Jacob 106
Thomas, Regan 106
Thompson, Kailee 55
Thompson, Tosh 157
Thurman, Lyla 152
Tian, Ivy 153
Tiger, Joey 49
Tobo, Mari 114
Todd, Abigail 89
Tolbert, Isaiah 156
Toledo, Anahi 42
Tolujo, Eunice 74

Tom, Victoria Rose 31
Topoleski, Sydney 16
Torres, Jorge 85
Torres, Melissa 151
Torres, Pearl Elizabeth Jean 49
Tovar Cabral, Ashly 152
Towne, Christopher 177
Tran, Ryan 80
Tran, Vivian 53
Treber, Emma 162
Tremblay, Zachary 24
Trenado, Alejandro 150
Trenado, Lucia 171
Trillo, Marlene 146
Tripi, Elliott 75
Tripp, Cadence 127
Trout, Jersey 32
Trunzo, Matt 27
Truong, Gabrielle 94
Truscott, Charlotta 83
Trzaska, Amber 80
Tsang, Tiffany 23
Turgeon, Audrey 43
Turman, Chloe 34
Tyree, Janie 104
Tyrer, Lila 175
Ukisu, Norielle 70
Unterschute, Jade 161
Uphoff, Emerson 171
Urias, Alicia 39
Valentine, Makayla 167
Valle, Santiago 151
Valtierra Alonza, Laila 150
Valtierra Leon, Maday Sarai 173
Valtierra-Teran, Adan 140
Valverde, Bryan 51
Van Agteren, Nathan 157
Van Agteren, Samuel 86
Van Berkel, Sophie 29
Van Hise, MeiLi 116
VanCamp, Nikkole 30
Vaught, Addison 67
Veinotte, Sam 29
Veitch, Makena 28
Velazquez, Antonio 39
Verhage, Isabella 109
Vianou, Sarah 169
Vidil, Halle 112
Villa Ortiz, Jonathan 158
Vining, Mina 118
Vollmer, Grayson 155
Vorobey, Alyssa 108
Waehner, Madison 121
Wagner, Maisie 17
Wagner, Sydney 147
Wajid, Rameeka 123
Walden, Ca'Mari 108
Waldner, Adelheid 125
Waldner, Adrian 131

Waldner, Alex 161
Waldner, Jesse 95
Waldner, Megan 58
Waldner, Natalya 136
Waldner, Tamar 83
Walker, Grant 114
Walker, Isabella 166
Walker, Trinity 58
Wallace, Lily 166
Walsh, Julia 176
Warburton, Caitlin 43
Warner, Ariyana 141
Watson, Jennifer 88
Watson, Orlando 142
Weaver, Alayna 47
Weaver, Edward 55
Weaverling, Bailey 52
Weber, Lily 173
Weeks, Ruthie 50
Weld, Cheyenne 45
Wenhold, Gregg 40
Wernsman, Machenzie 67
West, AJ 124
Westcott, Clara 48
Whalen, Lanazia 76
Whaley, Chase 161
White, Emmanuel 154
White, Michaela 88
Whitt, Jacob 163
Wiens, Elizabeth 169
Wiersema, Jillian 151
Wiersema, Sam 151
Wiest, Joshua 154
Wilbekaitis, Julia 45
Wilhelm, Sophie 102
Willey, Sarah 155
Williams, Stephanie 116
Williamson, Larissa 35
Wilson, Irving 48
Wilson, Jacob 110
Windrem, Matthew 31
Wipf, Renae 20
Wismer, Hannah 137
Wissler, Madison 80
Witwer, Mira 164
Wolstenholme, Jason 58
Wong, Desiree 90
Wong-Fortin, Maya 26
Wood, Ella 148
Wood, Robbie 99
Wood, Skyler A. 88
Woodley, Sierra 136
Woolley, Samuel 66
Worrall, Francesca 26
Wright, Alisa 177
Wright, Caleb 156
Wright, Danny 141
Wright, Henry 146
Wright, Jaida 48

Name	Page
Wright, Miles	48
Wright, R. Brayden	158
Wright, Scott	51
Wyatt, Jake	28
Xiao, Sara	97
Yalamanchili, Keertana	69
Yamak, Adam	129
Yao, Tony	56
Yeager, Emma	47
Yesnik, Adam	169
Yoder, Brandon	111
Yohannes, Abigail	49
Youssef, Trinity	164
Youwakim, Chloe	160
Youwakim, Emma	175
Yu, Angela	78
Yu, James	62
Zajac, Jessica	106
Zalevsky, Alexis	83
Zazulak, Ayden	153
Zehr, Haley	110
Zelinsky, Elizabeth	151
Zeng, Yu Qi	43
Zerfoss, Noah	47
Zern, Mark	20
Zghal, Ahmed Adam	165
Zhang, Albert	40
Zhao, Elijah	169
Zhou, Alexis	138
Zielinski, Caitlin	103
Zimmerman, Alton	169
Zitar, Caden	169
Zwanch, Liam	148
Zylstra, Emily	126

Index by School

A J McLellan Elementary School
Surrey, BC
- Zavier Anwar ... 168
- Amrit Bains ... 147
- Chantel Barnes ... 161
- Emma Bergen ... 171
- Sophia Botelho ... 170
- Calvin Bright ... 170
- Kayla Friesen ... 147
- Caiden Hofstedt ... 157
- Ella Khan ... 146
- Sarah Kim ... 175
- Dylan Kong ... 147
- Payton Ogden ... 161
- Nicholas Taylor ... 157

Abbotsford School of Integrated Arts - North Poplar
Abbotsford, BC
- Nola Stenstrom Moser ... 149

Adlai Stevenson Elementary School
Pittsburgh, PA
- Ava Baker ... 50
- Ethan LeCuyer ... 84
- Samuel Ley ... 89
- Faith McGowan ... 84
- Maya Nichols ... 83
- Carl Raitano ... 83
- Camryn Rogers ... 84
- Carson Svidron ... 115
- Alexis Zalevsky ... 83

Alexander Adaire School
Philadelphia, PA
- Yakeir Madison ... 102

Annieville Elementary School
Delta, BC
- Emma Andrews ... 34
- Benjamin Borsato ... 51
- Carley Fauht ... 47
- Karsten Foster ... 21
- Adam Johnson ... 80
- Zoey Jones ... 114
- Aiden Lee ... 24
- Brooklynn Levy ... 63
- Addison McPherson ... 44
- Carson Mendonca ... 41
- Angie Paul ... 136
- Madison Poschner ... 25
- Jasmeen Rai ... 24
- Olivia Roschat ... 75

Arrowwood Elementary School
Littleton, CO
- Julia Keating ... 54
- Terra Leiber ... 133
- Lilly Nguyen ... 36
- Kaylee Prince ... 70
- Mari Tobo ... 114

Aurora Quest K-8 School
Aurora, CO
- Vivian Tran ... 53

Baker Central School
Fort Morgan, CO
- Khadro Abdi ... 88
- Jesus Argoth ... 97
- Mario Bonilla ... 39
- Owen Bruce ... 44
- Jonathan Caldino ... 132
- Jessie Campa ... 109
- Allen Cardona-Torres ... 39
- Damien Carrera ... 88
- Uriah Celestino ... 32
- Emmanuel Cendejas ... 109
- Lesly Chavez ... 33
- Torri Contreraz ... 39
- Jenni Faudoa ... 97
- Faith Flores ... 88
- Emmanuel Garcia ... 132
- Jose Garcia ... 97
- Briana Rose Gonzalez ... 44
- Kenneth Gonzalez ... 42
- Anthony Ha ... 85
- Kaylee Helton ... 85
- Sarah Jacobs ... 25
- Amber Krehmeyer ... 42
- Allie Lauck ... 97
- Juan Lopez ... 32
- Mario Madrid Jr. ... 97
- Cristal Mannrique ... 32
- Steven Martinez ... 85
- Nadiah Maurer ... 97
- Leevi McFarland ... 44
- Marco Mejia ... 39
- Karen Mendez ... 21
- Joshua Ormsbee ... 109
- Nevaeha Paulsen ... 39
- Timothy Peralta ... 132
- Dacey Pliley ... 85
- Brian Porras ... 42
- Arohan Prasai ... 86
- Raymundo Garfio Quezada ... 109
- Bryan Quinteros ... 88
- Joshua Robertson ... 109
- Madison Robison ... 32
- Destiny Rojas ... 44
- Daniel Serna ... 109
- Amber Shaver ... 109
- Leilani Shott ... 32
- Lexys Siebrands ... 85
- Kaiden Smith ... 39
- Patrick Strauch ... 109
- Bryonna Temple ... 42
- Trent Templeton ... 39
- Anahi Toledo ... 42
- Jorge Torres ... 85
- Jersey Trout ... 32
- Alicia Urias ... 39
- Antonio Velazquez ... 39
- Jennifer Watson ... 88
- Skyler A. Wood ... 88

Bakersfield Public School
Thornhill, ON
- Desiree Wong ... 90

Barclay Elementary School
Warrington, PA
- Samuella Aduboahen ... 134

Barratt Elementary School
American Fork, UT
- Porter Anderson ... 56
- Madeleine Barrus ... 50
- Cole Duvall ... 21
- Lena Gibson ... 18
- Claire Gunther ... 16
- Britnee Jackman ... 82
- Caleb Leach ... 111
- Abbie Rasmussen ... 125
- Jillian Schatz ... 43
- Audrey Southam ... 16
- Patrick Stoddard ... 43
- Ethan Streeter ... 120

BASIS Mesa
Mesa, AZ
- Devika Nair ... 39

Bensley Elementary School
Richmond, VA
- Julian Sosa ... 165

Blacksburg New School
Blacksburg, VA
- Charles Henry Angleberger ... 36
- Ava Lazar ... 35
- Elise Levison ... 70
- John Cole McGee ... 29
- Joey Pettinger ... 65
- Norine Rensberger ... 63
- Grant Walker ... 114

Boyce Middle School
Upper St Clair, PA
- Alaina Douglas ... 109
- Reshma Gudla ... 35
- Sara Hess ... 59
- Bryce Keating ... 97

Lucabella Macri ... 103
Richa Mahajan ... 142
Vanessa Rainier ... 16

Bright Beginnings School
Chandler, AZ
Alexandra DaRosa ... 49
Emma Loop ... 96
Emma Myers ... 84

Broadview Avenue Public School
Ottawa, ON
Jana Alnakeeb ... 147
Vanessa Beldi ... 149
Isaac Bradley ... 165
Isaac Cervantes Garcia ... 170
Andrew Devoe ... 153
Lara El-Ghalayini ... 165
Faris Elkanzi ... 148
Liam Griese ... 147
Imaan Kanda ... 171
Melody Lehtiniemi ... 150
Liam Petersen ... 165
Thuran Ranjan ... 164
Sriya Tanguturi ... 154
Anushka Sai Tankala ... 153

Buckingham Elementary School
Buckingham, PA
Carter Behm ... 58
Abby D'Ambrosio ... 26
Carolyn L. Greenwald ... 25
Jordan Groves ... 58
Walker Jennings ... 68
Nyah Petrakis ... 98
Annie Regenhard ... 114
Grace Schwartzer ... 135

Burgundy Farm Country Day School
Alexandria, VA
James Rath ... 163

California Middle School
Coal Center, PA
Elisabeth "Elise" Adams ... 102
Sarah Bielawski ... 104
Brody Conner ... 63
Brendon Deems-Warnick ... 21
Isac Filler ... 120
Shameka Fletcher ... 55
Aiden Gillespie ... 19
Ronald Higinbotham ... 47
Elaina Nicholson ... 102
Raquel Rhoads ... 96
Alison Righetti ... 51
Donny Ross ... 59
Caleb Ruby ... 56
Jaime Sprenger ... 38
Jacob Thomas ... 106
Pearl Elizabeth Jean Torres ... 49
Matt Trunzo ... 27
Ca'Mari Walden ... 108
Cheyenne Weld ... 45
Jacob Wilson ... 110
Jaida Wright ... 48

Center for Creative Education
Cottonwood, AZ
Miranda Jones ... 101

Central Public School
Guelph, ON
Jessica Andrews ... 57
Hannah Bier ... 31
Nick Johnson ... 33
Setia Joy ... 31
Sophie Wilhelm ... 102

Cheswick Christian Academy
Cheswick, PA
Nathaniel Bonomo ... 48
Noel Kowalkowski ... 126
Sam Louis ... 28
Reyna Mohney ... 46
Alex Ricci ... 139
Emily Rosio ... 25
Maximus Schlieper ... 52

Chickahominy Middle School
Mechanicsville, VA
Ashley Karn ... 141
Brenna Peterman ... 137
Sawyer Tabor ... 37
Ruthie Weeks ... 50

Christiansburg Elementary School
Christiansburg, VA
Alexis Robinson ... 94

Colby Village Elementary School
Dartmouth, NS
Tristan Brocklehurst ... 55
Christopher Bungay ... 142
Leonard Carey ... 136
Mr. Cruddas' 5th Grade Class ... 29
Kaleb Demill ... 56
Lexi Dingwell ... 111
Madalyn Hatfield ... 47
Emma Hickey ... 106
Zoë Law ... 95
Sarah Jane MacKenzie ... 120
Akayjah Moses ... 140
Leah Muirhead ... 33
Rylee Nauffts ... 20
Ciera Oliver-Dares ... 127
Myah Payne ... 29
Michelle Reich ... 133
Rachel Robley ... 124
Katelyn Shand ... 74
Hunter Stewart ... 70
Zachary Thibault ... 38
Sophie Van Berkel ... 29
Sam Veinotte ... 29
Haley Zehr ... 110

Collegiate School
Richmond, VA
Isabella Lee ... 76

Colorado Connections Academy
Englewood, CO
Sage Kinnison ... 110
Dakota Marshall ... 86

Colwyn Elementary School
Colwyn, PA
Adetola Ade-Oyetayo ... 174
Lesedi Anyika ... 177
Dashawn Brown-Williams ... 174
Saamir Dade ... 176
Rihanna Davis ... 156
Reneem Farhan ... 164
Nancy Harris ... 161
Eli Jones ... 176
Tysean Kempf ... 167
Grace Sayon ... 175
Etoria Sellie ... 173
Chan'ae Sims-Hawkins ... 173
Israel Slonglo ... 166
Emmanuel White ... 154

Commodore Perry Elementary School
Hadley, PA
Avery Lockwood ... 55

Community Bible Fellowship Christian School
Swan River, MB
Annalisa Ellingson ... 137
Sophia Goudy ... 40
Michelle Martens ... 74
Delia Stevens ... 31

Copper Beech Elementary School
Glenside, PA
Evan Bidwell ... 24
Sagan Brinkert ... 31
Mara Ginsberg ... 40
Dayana Givner ... 49
Abigail MacAdams ... 36
Ariana Oduok ... 31
Khulan Temuujin ... 37
Caitlin Zielinski ... 103

Crestview Elementary School
Carlisle, PA
Rebekah Garrido ... 128

Culpeper County Middle School
Culpeper, VA
Catherine Noelle Brown ... 76

Decker Colony School
Decker, MB
Adelheid Waldner ... 125
Natalya Waldner ... 136
Tamar Waldner ... 83
Renae Wipf ... 20

Denver Jewish Day School
Denver, CO
Shira Linkow ... 87

Eagleview Middle School
Colorado Springs, CO
Kate Nelson ... 117
Kera Nelson ... 129

East Stroudsburg Elementary School
East Stroudsburg, PA
Kasi Arneaud ... 86
Ayden Beach ... 80

Index by School

Christopher Chintalan 37
Elizabeth Coutts 42
Rylan Coyne 20
Cherif Diarra 88
Michael Halstead 143
Justin Mclain 132
Jayden Ortiz 42
Maryleeana Pellot 38
Lucia Quinones 43
Xavier Rodriguez 42
Austin Tangora 44
Noah Zerfoss 47
Mark Zern 20

Eastern Lebanon County Intermediate School
Myerstown, PA
Lucy Bickel 29
Jillian Klopp 69

Ecole elementaire Des Sentiers
Orleans, ON
Chloé Byrne 27
Samuel Deschenes 27
Emilie Grosser 79
Alexandre Howard 56
Mahad Jama 24
Timea Johnson 89
Alexa Lafleur 20
Aya Nizar 26
Maya Wong-Fortin 26

Ecole elementaire Renaissance
Burlington, ON
Ryland Bradnam 28
Chloé Champredon 133
Chanel Côté 98
Mathieu Delorme 95
Matthew Djordjevic 37
Brandon Ferstl 27
Nicolas Grondin 95
Genevieve Karnis 26
Julia Kennedy 53
Hudson Macdonald 83
Ashley MacLean 79
Morgan McHugh 37
Zayd Meziati 139
Mackenzie Rabeau 63
Mehrbod Rostami 98
Nathan Shearn 53
Colin Sloan 96
Ibrahim Telili 63
Grace Tennant 135
Sierra Woodley 136

École Montessori de Montréal
LaSalle, QC
Eloi Abran 158
Maíra Abran 45
Adam Addona 49
Massimiliano Baron 146
Jade Beauséjour 168
Axel Belanger 148

Alessandro Buccione 155
Alexandre Bussières 175
Ailsa Campbell 24
Erika Cao 151
Matteo Carmosino 155
Elliot Charbonneau-Provost 155
Jerome Claux 139
Frederique Clement 148
Joseph Coletta 43
Marianne Crowe 68
Évelyne Crowe 158
Albi Cullhaj 168
Kaylee D'Amico 25
Vinh Quoc Dam 148
Mia Di Caprio 158
Emmanuel Fata 124
Nathan Fortin 155
Marie Gagnon 146
Benjamin Grégoire 42
Nina Gu 169
Sabrina Guerin 21
Frank Jiang 49
Marie-Hélène Kozlov-Shishkina 60
Marie-Helene Kozlova 45
Si Jiao Lam 146
Emanuelle Lambert 146
Bryan Langevin 86
Emma Langlois 158
Juliane Langlois 36
Maxence Lavigne 150
Émerik Leclair 159
Joanna Lian 150
Kassandra Lombardo 157
Kayla Lombardo 146
Emma Elisabeth Luis 148
Denis Malyugin 159
Luca Matteo 152
Paul Alexandre Mejia 97
Victoria Nacked Cabral 157
Shubhreet Kaur Padda 159
Matheo Piccinin 150
Marc-Olivier Pilon 21
Melina Pittarelli-Papadeas 111
Annie Linna Qu 159
Michael-Ryan Ricci 155
Gianni Rossi 155
Cristina Sacco 155
Nicolas Saoumaa Garcia 157
Maika Saw 56
Adam Sellami 146
Kamilia Shome 74
Kushal Shome 154
Giulia Sicoli 147
Marco Luigi Sicoli 21
Marianne Simard 169
Livjot Sivia 36
Hope Ashley Smith 159
Maya Stoica 82
Lydia Sun 159

Thomas Svoiski 169
Kristie Thai 16
Audrey Turgeon 43
Sarah Vianou 169
Abigail Yohannes 49

Ecole Montessori International Montreal
Montreal, QC
Alexia Abou Nader 50
Maryssa Addeh 165
Isabel Al-haddad 96
Hatem Alamri 173
Marcos Alvarez Caporale 159
Christian Anguelov 146
Tameem Awad 170
Haroun Ben-Mansour 152
Aaliyah Benzakour 174
Ryme Bouazzaoui 159
Julia Bourgeois-Matus 149
Anaelle Chaveron 158
Morgane Chaveron 146
Nakki Della Cioppa 159
Adam Dia 159
Victoria Dimitrova 159
Vincent Dinh Vien Duong 81
Jason Elisma 176
Jessica Elisma 165
Hamza Fehri 162
Yassine Fehri 149
Tim Ghanem 148
Adam Jaafar 170
Dalia Jaafar 56
Mehdi Jaber 175
Acile Jammoul 135
Joseph Jartidian 148
Rudy Kanao 158
Juan David Lago Quijano 50
Baron-Yuhao Liang 130
Louis Lieu 130
Louisa Lieu 124
Megan Lopes Toroyan 158
Jonathan Lorcy 175
Brian Ly 111
Michael Ly 148
Nadine Malak 29
Andrew Matar 152
Simona Melchionno 174
Joannie Normand Plante 170
Kemil G. Nyateu 124
Logan O'Doherty 169
Angelina Phan 167
Kevin Phan 96
Polina Polyanskaya 171
Llyr Redweik-Leung 163
Elizabeth Richer 36
Eliana Salloum 65
Sarah Sharif 152
Amrita Singh 159
Majida Frida Sleiman 147

Ryan Tran 80
Alejandro Trenado 150
Lucia Trenado 171
Lila Tyrer 175
Adam Yamak 129
Chloe Youwakim 160
Emma Youwakim 175
Yu Qi Zeng 43
Ahmed Adam Zghal 165

Edith Bowen Lab School
Logan, UT
Megan Harris 46

Emily Carr Public School
Oakville, ON
Joanna Shorinde 38

Enfield Elementary School
Oreland, PA
Savanna Barton 148
Adam DiBattista 147
Elikem Fumey 147
Olivia Gatewood 147
Giada Pernicello 147
Alessandra Santarelli 148

Enon Elementary School
Chester, VA
Chase Clarke 163

Erie Elementary School
Erie, CO
Robert Barkley 91
Charlotte Calhoun 157
Nicholas Crawford 152
Izzy Foster 156
Luke Fritsche 63
Presleigh Goodwin 78
Blake Hagan 130
Laurel Hagan 164
Logan Hosmer 164
Mackenna Pierson 117
Ashleigh Richards 85
Brianna Romero 166
Claire Schultz 162
Lilly Smith 156

Evergreen Elementary School
Drayton Valley, AB
Amber Trzaska 80
Makena Veitch 28

Falk Laboratory School
Pittsburgh, PA
Froukje Schlingemann 43

Falmouth Elementary School
Fredericksburg, VA
Kloie Teague 118

Fern Hill School
Burlington, ON
Prashik Juta 174

Fireside Elementary School
Phoenix, AZ
NagaSriya Ramisetty 21

Fishing Creek Elementary School
Lewisberry, PA
Ashlyn Brtalik 143
Abby Craw 68
Marisa Ramsey 143
Gregg Wenhold 40

Foothill Elementary School
Boulder, CO
Aaron Alexander 127
Caydes Aronow 128
Ella Bartsch 24
Barrett Bennett 37
Lilianna Chitambar 89
Anika Davie 17
Elle Deith 127
Evander Deorsay 119
Max Fisher 36
Pavel Hamill 127
Beckett McVoy 23
Tragar O'Leary 24
Ruth Pechersky 96
Caitlin Rogers 30
Mckenzie Shea 63
Isabella Sullivan 124

Forest Hill School - Senior Campus
St Lazare, QC
Keira Gagné 47
Samantha Lapointe 25
Maya Keirl 57
Emilly Rodger 80
Kaley Sheehan 45
Nicholas Booth 27
Jordan Caron 114
Alicia Coleto 24
Sofia Gidaro 127
Aliyah Maximo 64
Charlee Nichifor 137
Alexi Plaitis-Levesque 28
Cassie Reccord 47
Zachary Tremblay 24
Francesca Worrall 26

Francis Asbury Elementary School
Hampton, VA
Suhana Mohammed 47

French Creek Elementary School
Pottstown, PA
Natalie Alldred 124
Ella Brown 24
Madelyn Holland 84
Matthew Pelletier 124
Liam Roberts 23
Lucas Santise 26
Aidan Schneider 136
Riley Stutzman 45

George Washington Academy
Saint George, UT
Savanah Bang 114
Isaac Christensen 44
Faith Cranmer 137

Dylan Esplin 143
Emma Ferguson 55
Mykela Hansen 32
Olivia Haun 40
Ryder Hendry 92
Charley Holt 106
Cenya Jacobson 103
Riley Jones 67
Mac McKittrick 79
Hunter Patterson 33
Janet Rogers 95
Brinly Stapley 44
Cadence Tripp 127
Charlotta Truscott 83
Samuel Woolley 66

Glenmore Christian Academy
Calgary, AB
Tara Gira 42

Gordon A Brown Middle School
Toronto, ON
Abbas Raza 65

Green Acres School
Ogden, UT
Jerron Barker 120
Kiana Bowman 38
Pamela Conriquez 122
Jeremy Gerritsen 23
Corinna Healey 61
Brinley Huddleston 85
Sierra Jones 141
Kailee Thompson 55

Greenbriar West Elementary School
Fairfax, VA
Pranavi Doodala 129
Medha Gaddam 83
Eshi Kohli 41
Keertana Yalamanchili 69

Greystone Heights School
Saskatoon, SK
Maggie Allenspach 176
Valentina Bastidas Garcia .. 172
Colby Frey 157
Aidan Froh 176
Lometh Jayawardhana 168
Dhivya Jooravan 155
Kamal Khanal 157
Durriyah Khondoker 162
Emily Letkeman 165
Nini Li 147
Vinayak Prasannakumar ... 155
Ivy Tian 153
Jade Unterschute 161
Lily Weber 173

Haine Middle School
Cranberry Township, PA
Annie Castagnero 122
Simren Jayaraman 108
Ashleigh Patterson 111
Ananya Rao 108

Index by School

Harrisburg Academy
Wormleysburg, PA
- Zach Dorch 168
- Emma Hathaway 16
- Liliana Hathaway 168
- Sarah Henry 167
- Daniella Idrovo 163
- Ellery Pietzsch 164
- Mira Witwer 164
- Alisa Wright 177

Harrison Road Elementary School
Fredericksburg, VA
- Ivan Arias 16
- Victoria Baker 18
- Vittoria Bentancor 24
- Jacob Bradley 25
- Sarah Brooks 34
- Briona Giles 19
- Trevor Hudson 95
- Amira Kines 116
- Daniel Love 131
- Holden Orr 40
- Isabella Ortiz 134
- Jeffrey Smith 23

Hawthorne Elementary School
Salt Lake City, UT
- Yvonne Kim 105

Heritage Christian Online School
Kelowna, BC
- Carla Deetlefs 44

Higher Vibration Academy
Pleasant Unity, PA
- Estelle Eppolito 129
- Scarlett Eppolito 174
- Wyatt Eppolito 89

Hillcrest Elementary School
Holland, PA
- Julie Barron 120
- Nicholas Dolan 19
- Alexandria Hause 56
- Ava Iatesta 82
- Joey Tiger 49
- Stephanie Williams 116

Hollymead Elementary School
Charlottesville, VA
- Nate Lyons 172

Holy Rosary School
Duryea, PA
- Patrick Bennie 84
- Gracie Giordina 114
- Carmen M. 81

Homeschool
Fort Collins, CO
- Reese Sprister 53

Fleetwood, PA
- Isabella Morales 134

Hunters Glen Elementary School
Thornton, CO
- Gillian Estes 55
- Austin Hilyard 101
- Isabelle Milani 92

Huntington Hills Elementary School
Calgary, AB
- Vanderley Baltodano 51
- Cassandra Christensen 78
- Vanessa Dick 71
- Abra Glover 55
- Sean Kim 122
- Jessica Ly 37
- Eric Mei 95
- Alyson Nabozniak 78
- Norielle Ukisu 70
- Matthew Windrem 31

Interboro GATE Program
Prospect Park, PA
- David Deacle 173

Isle of Wight Academy
Isle Of Wight, VA
- Jenna Miltier 35

J G Hening Elementary School
Richmond, VA
- Samantha Cake 67

Jack Hulland Elementary School
Whitehorse, YT
- Natisha Avalak 125
- Tenesha Christiansen 8
- Naoise Dempsey 17
- Angus Lau 85
- Annabelle Salvin 105

Jefferson Middle School
Pittsburgh, PA
- Zoe Deems 100

Jenkintown Elementary School
Jenkintown, PA
- Ryan Ballantine 156
- James Callas 168
- Matthew Chachkin 171
- Charlie Fricker 168
- Carolyn Keim 171
- Gabby Ottaviano 177
- Sean Rocco 168
- Bianca Ruiz 152
- Catherine Smith 171
- Nicholas Sobolewski 168
- Kate Spindler 164
- Alexus Streeper 177
- Julia Walsh 176
- Ayden Zazulak 153

John McCrae Public School
Guelph, ON
- Raena Anderson 34

Khalsa Montessori Elementary School
Phoenix, AZ
- Samantha Andres 63
- Jenner Arriaga 29
- Soph Balliet 64
- Lily Banks 109
- Jayne Bennett 45
- Ian Collison 82
- Ariana Dominguez 119
- Tyler Fales 112
- Davis Lu 134
- Jiana McDonald 33
- Kellen Newsome 87
- Kirra Newsome 123
- Madeline Pennell 133
- Aagam Prakash 62
- Olinmazatemictli Reyes 132
- Maria Reyna 105
- Chiraag Sachdev 142
- Ava Smiley 120
- Hannah Story 110
- Lily Terpstra 95
- Mina Vining 118

Khalsa School - Old Yale Road Campus
Surrey, BC
- Amardeep Bains 140
- Onkar Singh Bajwa 98
- Khushbir Kaur Basra 156
- Amol K. Bhallar 160
- Amol Bhullar 164
- Gurshawn Bhullar 147
- Gurshawn S. Bhullar 146
- Khushvir K. Birk 167
- Darshpreet Brar 149
- Keerat Kaur Brar 164
- Lovleen Brar 155
- Khushi Kaur Cheena 152
- Anand Gill 152
- Anand Singh Gill 154
- Navpreet K. Gosal 176
- Benita Jaswal 152
- Eakampreet S. Jaswal 174
- Sukhvir S. Jheout 160
- Maneet Kaur Bhullar 167
- Harveer Kaur Chahal 150
- Harneet Kaur Gill 157
- Supriya Kaur Randhawa 150
- Baneesh Khosa 126
- Ravleen Padda 155
- Harjas Kaur Panag 161
- Tejanpreet Parmar 136
- Hari Rakeshkumar Patel 157
- Kirat K. Purba 175
- Kirat Kaur Purba 160
- Harshvir Shergill 175
- Harshvir Singh Shergill 174
- Gaurav Sidhu 148
- Gurjeet Singh Gill 152
- Damandeep Singh Jabbal 82

Klein Elementary School
Erie, PA
- Nykeem Abu-Zebiba 150
- Angela Anderson 177
- Mila Beerson 165
- Mariska Habursky 157

Alexis Jenkins ... 162
Kayleigh Kosko ... 152
Kyrsten Larsen ... 159
Seamus Marshall ... 149
Amber Mezzacapo ... 161
Ethan Moody ... 166
Alex Moore ... 159
Blaine Oler ... 166
Arriana Rodriguez ... 150
Kaitlyn Seidler ... 177
Parker Snyder ... 155
Grayson Vollmer ... 155
Isabella Walker ... 166
Caleb Wright ... 156
R. Brayden Wright ... 158

Lake Ridge Middle School
Woodbridge, VA
Bridget Kim ... 143

Lancaster Mennonite School - Locust Grove
Lancaster, PA
Matthew Achenbach ... 81
Ella Brubaker ... 91
Carter Cameron ... 112
Chloe Elie ... 76
Xavior Figueroa ... 71
Wesley Fletcher ... 78
Seth Forry ... 73
Madeleine Gerz ... 36
Erin Good ... 91
Aidan Grambau ... 94
Tiffany Iraheta ... 56
Valerie Jacobs ... 32
Jonathan Klein ... 51
Leilani Krady ... 71
Sarah Lapp ... 73
Kate Lefever ... 71
Gabriela Lopez ... 138
Kaleb Martiny ... 25
Paige Riehl ... 25
Elijah Rodriguez ... 139
Sarah Steckbeck ... 41
Regan Thomas ... 106
Hannah Wismer ... 137
Madison Wissler ... 80

Lava Ridge Intermediate School
Santa Clara, UT
Shaylee Johnsen ... 92

Learning Foundation and Performing Arts Charter School-Warner
Gilbert, AZ
Kylonna Leevy ... 115

Learning Foundations
Gilbert, AZ
David Hunt ... 69

Lewistown Middle School
Lewistown, PA
Devon McCalips ... 32

Lfpa Charter School-Warner
Gilbert, AZ
Scottie Atkins ... 115
Natalie Cardenas ... 83
Chaziyah Claggett ... 77
Richard Claytemple ... 115
Tilda Ellefson ... 28
Hannah Gilmartin ... 84
Katie Heitmann ... 97
Elise Hernandez ... 77
Morgan Hill ... 131
Selah Hilyard ... 68
Jacqueline Robinson ... 138
Ava Sluka ... 92
Jake Wyatt ... 28

Lightfoot Elementary School
Unionville, VA
Lillian Arnold ... 153
Abigail Hatfield ... 160
Jadon Howe ... 167
Emily Jenkins ... 172
Elise Missigman ... 153
Kayleigh Napier ... 160
Jasmine Price ... 172
Steven Rapids ... 167
Kel Shifflett ... 176
Ryan Sweeney ... 176
Isaiah Tolbert ... 156
Makayla Valentine ... 167

Lincoln Elementary School
Pittsburgh, PA
Caroline Adams ... 150
Abby Davis ... 150
Emma Girod ... 150
Addison Glace ... 148
Sasha Konitzer ... 152
Andrew Michael ... 152

Line Mountain Middle School
Herndon, PA
Abbie Morgan ... 113

Lititz Elementary School
Lititz, PA
Melanie Hahn ... 120
Paige Misavage ... 19
Jack Reed ... 71
Norah Scott ... 108
Declan Swarr ... 24

Lookout Mountain School
Phoenix, AZ
Sophie Betcher ... 37
Evan Brewer ... 22
Neely Burns ... 107
Isabella Essler ... 22
Hannah Garrett Vasquez ... 26
Jared Haugen ... 35
Shaye Rohrer ... 98

Loudoun Country Day School
Leesburg, VA
Caitlin Dodds ... 161
Brady Kunkle ... 151
Alexandra Martinez ... 178
Naurgol Rafaat ... 178
Annie Rieben ... 161
Reed Robinson ... 175
Sophia Schlieman ... 155
Callie Snow ... 151

Louise Archer Elementary School
Vienna, VA
Jonathan Kong ... 51

Luther Memorial Academy
Erie, PA
Ammiela Agayev ... 24
Jameel Anderson ... 43
Rylie Baldwin ... 121
Andrew Bebko ... 141
Shelby Carter ... 108
Treyton Chrispen ... 137
Marielle Parks ... 117
Ethan Puscher ... 40
Lydia Ramey ... 53
Trinity Walker ... 58

Luther Memorial Learning Center
Erie, PA
Noah Osborne ... 53

Manor Elementary School
Levittown, PA
Sam Roccograndi ... 81

Mantua Elementary School
Fairfax, VA
Suchita Hadimani ... 142

Marguerite F Christian Elementary School
Colonial Heights, VA
Caleb Clarke ... 56

Mary Blair Elementary School
Loveland, CO
Tyan Archer ... 59
Bailey Arellano ... 60
Caitlyn Biffle ... 47
Alexis Birch ... 47
Joshua Bustos ... 27
Alexandria Dobson ... 18
Ryann Durrett ... 26
Lila Ehrlich ... 49
Brooklyn Ewert ... 99
Sam Hailey ... 23
Kayne Hayden ... 118
Arianna Hubley ... 89
Kennedy Jewell ... 111
Anna Kash ... 102
Kyle Lenz ... 130
Danielle Martin ... 126
Aidan McCloud ... 141
Rowan Moore ... 141
Payton Rechkemmer ... 104
Jayden Roberts ... 50
MarySue Smith ... 131
Trent Stephenson ... 58
Nolan Stricker ... 96

Index by School

Morgan Suit 99
Elliott Tripi 75

Mary Ellen Henderson Middle School
Falls Church, VA
Becky Rasmussen 114

Mary Walter Elementary School
Bealeton, VA
Ernesto Calderon 132
Noah Frye 153
Connor Hagy 151
Cheyenne Harris 171
Kallyn Odom 164
Taylor Sherry 132
Chris Strain 154
Jacob Whitt 163

McDowell Mountain Elementary School
Fountain Hills, AZ
David Abercrombie 148
Nathan Barnard 147
Jade Bonito 178
Jeneya Boone 162
Brandon Chiles 162
Aidan De Bie 162
Jacob DesRosiers 165
Kyle DesRosiers 178
Avery Forney 154
David Goldapper 147
Daniel Gonzalez 155
Ryan Guthrie 162
Alden Kyes 178
Ani Lahser 148
Carter Leitgeb 162
Elliot Lindsay 178
Maggie Lucas 168
Bree March 165
Mischa Markovic 147
Keaton Ort 148
Alexis Pena 162
Savannah Peterson 162
Ariel Reichler 147
Hailey Robinson 167
Sophia Rogers 162
Julian Sepulveda 148
Katelyn Smout 170
Christian Sorells 178
Taylor Stacy 162
Lina Tan 171
Christopher Towne 177
Emerson Uphoff 171
Sydney Wagner 147
Trinity Youssef 164
Caden Zitar 169

McNair Elementary School
Herndon, VA
Diya Dinesh 52
Sarah Qazi 44

Mercer Middle School
Aldie, VA
Parnika Saxena 100

Mifflin County Middle School
Lewistown, PA
Nicholas Allison 93
Hayley Corson 68
Anna Curry 110
Colson Fike 135
Samantha Frey 140
Madalyn Hampton 49
Dustin Hesser 105
Mackenzie Johnson 17
Emily Miller 30
Dale Morgan 29
Dalton Paige 121
Jenna Rhoads 71
Hope Rhodes 40
Adrianne Rossman 41
Drake Schaeffer 116
Trent Shade 68
Leesha Shilling 74
Jade Smith 140
Maddie Sweeney 118
Taylor Swope 124
Emma Yeager 47
Emily Zylstra 126

Mon Yough Catholic School
White Oak, PA
Thomas Betzner 17
Madison Buhaly 96
Edrea Burgwin 86
Ava Dzurenda 30
Anneliese Fenwick 26
Tyler Gaydos 49
Gabrielle Mejalli 30
Payton Michaels 132
Luc Normandy 99
Philip Osborn 99
Brianna Pasternak 81
Maya Poziviak 118
Bella Stillio 53
Luke Sutton 43
Victoria Rose Tom 31
Halle Vidil 112
Orlando Watson 142

Monelison Middle School
Madison Heights, VA
Nyia Barrow 44
Reagan Bui 88
Sa'Renity Burford 27
Jada Cooke 46
Caitlin Humphreys 46
Gracie Humphreys 46
Haley Keesee 142
Thomas Lipscomb 132
Sheridan Maines 57
Kimberly Padgett 98
Miranda Sprouse 116
Michaela White 88

Montessori Development Center
Furlong, PA
Maksim Levin 146

Aurora Richards 148
Alessia Sattler 164
Liam Zwanch 148

Moravian Academy Middle School
Bethlehem, PA
Angela Chen 71
Caroline Davis 115
Margeaux Donchez 106
Sophia Frank 16
Krysta Nichols 98
Grace Sanborn 19
Claudia Santoro-Hernandez 70
Neha Skandan 105
Jake Sobiech 98
Josh Sobiech 138
Sara Xiao 97

Mosby Woods Elementary School
Fairfax, VA
Jivitesh Praveen 51

Mount Nittany Middle School
State College, PA
Mara Anderson-Skelly 140
Mark Argiro 119
Nicholas Beebe 91
Gavin Michael Billett 32
Tydan Campbell 89
Cordelia-Marie Ceres 22
Angela Chung 67
Colton Dash 58
Megan Doucette 123
Paige Edwards 112
Meg Felsmann 26
Bayla Furmanek 106
Stevie Guthoff 60
Lilly Hasan 35
Xavier John Django Hons 21
Rayvin Houtz 98
Mikayla Irvin 58
Will Kerber 39
Nicky Messick 99
Tyler Metzel 38
Maitlyn Poduszlo 130
Paige Raymond 99
Evelyn Ryan 104
Kade Sanderson 105
Soumya Thapa 131
Bailey Weaverling 52
Brandon Yoder 111
Jessica Zajac 106
Albert Zhang 40

Mountain View Elementary School
Broomfield, CO
Samantha Carpenter 103
Alex Church 49
Leyna Dockter 103
Haley Quillen 103
Malia Steel 75
Tommy Tafoya 99
Larissa Williamson 35

Nazareth Area Intermediate School
Nazareth, PA
- Amber Allen ... 87
- Austin Bentzinger ... 93
- Nathan Bogar ... 128
- Amber Buskirk ... 60
- Arianna Casner ... 142
- Sean Daly ... 82
- Sydney DeFranco ... 82
- Alyson DeMarco ... 65
- Alexis Doherty ... 127
- Branden Doherty ... 54
- Olivia Dorko ... 20
- Natalie Eberly ... 82
- Rivers Edwards ... 101
- Adam Fatebene ... 65
- Nathan Hildebrant ... 26
- Trevor Howell ... 107
- Mackenna Kingsley ... 46
- Kylie Kostenbader ... 138
- Julia Lynch ... 64
- Connor McGaughran ... 82
- Kyle Morris ... 66
- Kyle Nguyen ... 138
- Armaan Pandher ... 77
- Courtney Paulson ... 136
- Brandon Pieper ... 71
- Benjamin Pinel ... 24
- Elle Podwats ... 47
- Sara Purtle ... 101
- Nathan Schmidt ... 113
- Shannon Seidel ... 125
- Dreanna Simmons ... 128
- MeiLi Van Hise ... 116
- Alayna Weaver ... 47
- AJ West ... 124
- Scott Wright ... 51

Nederland Elementary School
Nederland, CO
- Brennan Oliver ... 165
- Kaleb Oliver ... 130

Nevin Platt Middle School
Boulder, CO
- Maya Birkenkamp ... 49
- Kaden Du ... 80
- Breck Dunbar ... 57
- Eliana Feistner ... 130
- Trevor Ferreira ... 79
- Paige Fincher ... 123
- Maddie Hanscom ... 69
- Molly Hedlund ... 98
- Quinn Hirschland ... 54
- Owen Hunter ... 124
- Audrey Kaufman ... 16
- Grace Long ... 75
- Aidan O'Brien-Turner ... 112
- Marcus Orlando ... 98
- Trinity R. ... 18
- Emily Jean Reardon ... 43
- Stefan Rosenboom ... 79
- Miles Wright ... 48

New Kent Elementary School
New Kent, VA
- Dana Douglas ... 119

Norquay Colony School
Portage La Prairie, MB
- Adrian Waldner ... 131
- Alex Waldner ... 161
- Jesse Waldner ... 95
- Megan Waldner ... 58

North Pocono Middle School
Moscow, PA
- Haley Allman ... 19
- Isabella Bonanno ... 91
- Hannah Chestnut ... 70
- Carena Colo ... 128
- Lilyana Crawley ... 102
- Kennedy Gibson ... 52
- Alicia Goldenziel ... 128
- Sarah Rovnanik ... 82
- Alyvia Scutt ... 128

North Salem Elementary School
Dover, PA
- Savannah Jackson ... 173

North West Central School
Plenty, SK
- Mikayla Debusschere ... 127
- Autumn Julseth ... 47
- Louisse Occena ... 119

Nottingham Elementary School
Arlington, VA
- Kyle Bennett ... 143
- Ellie Billings ... 142
- Nico Castleman ... 88
- Emily Colbert ... 70
- Zoë Foose ... 38
- Ian Haddad ... 106
- Natalie Hartman ... 85
- Alex Horn ... 80
- Lillian Keith ... 89
- Elizabeth Rosenblatt ... 56
- Austin Sumerlin ... 60

Oak Ridge Elementary School
Harleysville, PA
- Madison Brown ... 178

Oswayo Valley Elementary School
Shinglehouse, PA
- Nickales App ... 32
- Alex Hays ... 37
- Laya Phillips ... 97
- Sawyer Prince ... 87
- Shevelle L. Shelp ... 77

Our Lady of Mount Carmel School
Doylestown, PA
- Maria Adamow ... 55
- Alexandra Berish ... 17
- Samantha Berish ... 33
- Bridget Cahill ... 46
- Reilly Cahill ... 107
- Megan Choromanski ... 25
- Mikey DeAngelis ... 137
- Ryan Englebreth ... 69
- Rachel Hamler ... 132
- Isabella Martinez ... 38
- Timothy Mehlmann ... 75
- Liam Mote ... 23
- Megan Steinbach ... 132
- Nicole Steinbach ... 121
- Nikkole VanCamp ... 30
- Jason Wolstenholme ... 58

Panther Valley Elementary School
Nesquehoning, PA
- Selena Bauder ... 110
- Riley Hoben ... 96
- Chloe Kruslicky ... 120
- Ashley Little ... 89
- Haley Luffman ... 91

Paul L Dunbar Middle School for Innovation
Lynchburg, VA
- Jovany Hernandez-Ramirez ... 52
- Hermasia Law-Jackson ... 87
- Elijah Maxson ... 104
- Danielle Murriell ... 106
- Preston Pitzer ... 106
- Falisity Speed ... 31
- Janie Tyree ... 104

Peasley Middle School
Gloucester, VA
- Alexia Baines ... 125
- Samuel Briscoe ... 62
- Avery Cady ... 103
- Seth Case ... 121
- Emmylee Crockett ... 122
- Alec Daniel ... 17
- Lily Duncan ... 103
- Trent Fox ... 37
- Preston Garrison ... 130
- Austin Glockner ... 85
- Cameron Gunther ... 72
- Logan Hall ... 122
- Andie Hartley ... 51
- Bailey Hudgins ... 17
- Josh Ipock ... 42
- Trevor Johnston ... 62
- Myra Keener ... 35
- Gracie King ... 73
- Lewie Lawrence ... 126
- Mikie Lawson ... 72
- Ayla Liles-Crayton ... 122
- Madison Los ... 73
- Carolina Masiak ... 76
- Colin O'Brien ... 50
- Ella Poulson ... 109
- Katie Prevette ... 132
- Douglas Pruim ... 72
- Ryan Riordan ... 73

Index by School

Matthew Shackelford 119
Eden Smith 72
A'nya Strazdins 112
Rachel Swain 42
Skylar Tenan 18
Lanazia Whalen 76

Penn-Kidder Campus
Albrightsville, PA
Nicholas Baldwin 175
Zachary Barna 168
Travis Benson 123
Tristan Bonilla 154
Daphne Camacho 80
Emma Connors 63
James Costlow 84
Bryan Cox 123
Thomas John Cullen 150
Christian DeFelice 48
Timothy Dudak 20
Maddison Edwards 123
Samantha Edwards 149
Eden Evans 33
Ella Farnell 55
Evan Fedora 143
Matt Fezenko 140
Destiny Friday 85
Gannon Getz 123
Shane Haggerty 55
Eric Hardgrove 94
Amaya Heffelfinger 168
Heather Herbott 28
McKayla Hettler 170
Kelli Hogarty 23
Sarah Holder 151
Victoria Jaime 94
Mariana Jaramillo 84
Rudolfo Johnston 123
Chance Joyner 154
Taylor Kellar 33
Kylei MacArthur 175
Meena Madhavan 151
Jada Mahmde 28
Kinga Malinowski 154
Hannah May 149
Meghan McKenna 163
Ashlynn Miller 168
Kaila O'Connor 168
Riley Pastor 85
Katharine Pedroza 20
Alexandra Ramey 63
Victoria Ress 98
Brayden Rivera 154
Thomas Smith 84
Emma Spath 97
Isabella Verhage 109
Edward Weaver 55
Chase Whaley 161
Elizabeth Zelinsky 151

Pine Lane Intermediate School
Parker, CO
Hayden Huckaby 31
Eve Koester 84

Platte Valley Middle School
Kersey, CO
Lainee Bernhardt 18
Gracie Franklin 34

Poplar Tree Elementary School
Chantilly, VA
Eleanor Hudson 174

Pottsgrove Middle School
Pottstown, PA
Kayleigh Texter 79

Prairie Waters Elementary School
Cherstermere, AB
Myla Sexton 164

Promontory Heights Community Elementary School
Chilliwack, BC
Kalie Holford 133

Providence Hall Elementary School
Herriman, UT
Mikey Endrizzi 57
Ruby LeBaron 26
Savannah LeGendre 31
Becky Mansfield 30
Alyssa Newton 83
Tatum Packer 99
Blake Taylor 57

Queen of All Saints Elementary School
Coquitlam, BC
Daniela Allegrini 23
Nicole Amoroso 80
Vanessa Amoroso 78
Jessica Araiza 74
Davor Buric 138
Sophia Caleca 108
Carissa Chow 51
Mariana Gamboa 37
Olivia Iorio 56
Devyn Lalonde 45
Onai Murevesi 81
So-Won Park 120
Monica Perez-Ricaurte 40
Simone Shetty 48
Hubert Starosta 25
Tiffany Tsang 23
Ariyana Warner 141

Ray E Kilmer Elementary School
Colorado Springs, CO
Olivia Peterson 88

Renaissance Academy
Phoenixville, PA
Maggie Mastrangelo 101
Mackey Munion 56
Lauren Poltorak 34

Ringgold School
Monongahela, PA
Kaiden Bubash 59

River Bend Middle School
Sterling, VA
Jacob Cox 34
Leticia de la Zerda 59
Talia Khatib 59
Maria-José Lema 57

Riverdale Elementary School
Thornton, CO
Jonas Lor 171
Bradley Miller 171
Taylor Schneider 171

Robeson Elementary Center
Birdsboro, PA
Leia Culbert 150
Stephen Elliker 146
Aidyn Gushue 170
Jack Hafer 158
Dylan King 169
Joel Kline 174
Michael Marshall 173
Joshua Purington 170
Jordyn Robinette 146
Laura Sokso 158
Joshua Wiest 154

Rocky Heights Middle School
Highlands Ranch, CO
Jazlyn Eskanos 45
Rosa Lee 23

Roosevelt Edison Charter School
Colorado Springs, CO
Casandra Barajas Ibarra 150
Gerardo Bustamante 166
Karina Calixto Rodriguez 86
Brayan Cintron Berdeja 40
Cindy Contreras 169
Kirby Adrian Diaz 152
Jazmin Dominguez Montiel 169
Brianna Estrada 151
Janet Garduño Mendez 141
Alondra Hernandez 149
Ingrid Ledezma 161
Miguel Leyva Quiterio 154
Lizbeth Martinez Higareda 150
Adrian Salayandia Moran 80
Melissa Torres 151
Ashly Tovar Cabral 152
Marlene Trillo 146
Laila Valtierra Alonza 150
Maday Sarai Valtierra Leon 173
Adan Valtierra-Teran 140
Bryan Valverde 51
Jonathan Villa Ortiz 158

Roosevelt Middle School
Roosevelt, UT
Oakley Barney 91
Jade Garner 50
Miranda Harmston 78
Vanessa Lucio 78

Rosebud River School
Strathmore, AB
- Cornel Gross ... 172
- Isaac Gross ... 152
- Jacobie Gross ... 174
- Jesse Gross ... 166
- Johanna Gross ... 71
- Leah Gross ... 118
- Susan Gross ... 71
- Tim Gross ... 94
- Zach Gross ... 41

Rosemont Forest Elementary School
Virginia Beach, VA
- Jasmine Bugarin ... 52
- Jada Danquah ... 18
- Kai Davis ... 18
- Peter Lee ... 25
- Kyle Mack ... 59
- Chaka Mishoe II ... 59
- Gabrielle Truong ... 94
- Robbie Wood ... 99

Ross Montessori School
Carbondale, CO
- Cole Kokish ... 48

Rumbaugh Elementary School
Mount Pleasant, PA
- Emma Treber ... 162

Russell Byers Charter School
Philadelphia, PA
- Maureen Kelly ... 27

Sagewood Middle School
Parker, CO
- Carter Motichka ... 32

Saint Anne's School
Bristol, VA
- Harper Robinette ... 154

Saskatoon Christian School
Saskatoon, SK
- Brielle Abramoff ... 155
- Lincoln Abramoff ... 175
- Emily Allen ... 149
- Ebar Amir ... 77
- Levi Balzer ... 40
- Mackenna Berg ... 151
- Magenta Bobowski ... 147
- Kaylee Chubak ... 30
- Samuel Chubak ... 168
- Denalyn Coziahr ... 156
- Jerica Coziahr ... 169
- Anna Currimbhoy ... 16
- Abygail Denie ... 137
- Samara Desjardine ... 158
- Noah Drisner ... 148
- Jade Everett ... 161
- Jayella Funk ... 149
- Kyson Gawryluk ... 168
- Makara Gawryluk ... 58
- Skylar Gerbrandt ... 156
- Hannah Glass ... 156
- Olivia Hache ... 75
- Savannah Heller ... 161
- Lydia Johnson ... 164
- Jerzie Kotelnikoff ... 155
- Yonathan Landa ... 171
- Jack Lane ... 169
- Marshall Lane ... 30
- Wyatt Lane ... 161
- Xavier Ledoux ... 158
- Jonah Marshall ... 151
- Corianne Matthies ... 169
- William McVittie ... 150
- Nathanael Merke ... 169
- Samuel Merke ... 171
- Liesel Nelson ... 169
- Nicole Nielsen ... 169
- Kiersten Nienhuis ... 156
- Emma Norval ... 155
- Nicola Norval ... 161
- Mycah Olson ... 172
- Aaron Peters ... 151
- Elijah Peters ... 168
- Zachary Radoux ... 158
- Aidan Edwin Robinson ... 177
- Isaiah Rushton ... 149
- Clive Scott ... 170
- Toby Siemens ... 107
- Farren Stevenson-Akapew ... 159
- Miss Stonehouse's 2nd Grade Class ... 153
- Nathan Van Agteren ... 157
- Samuel Van Agteren ... 86
- Elizabeth Wiens ... 169
- Adam Yesnik ... 169
- Elijah Zhao ... 169

Sewickley Academy
Sewickley, PA
- Ashley Close ... 160

Silver Creek Elementary School
Thornton, CO
- Rachel Kaiser ... 142
- Kelsey Keenan ... 100

Silver Stream Public School
Richmond Hill, ON
- Alyssa Vorobey ... 108

Sol Feinstone Elementary School
Newtown, PA
- Jackson Combs ... 48
- Jessica Czekaj ... 23
- Patrick Dougherty ... 16
- Quinn Erlandsen ... 45
- Marisa Ferrari ... 23
- Jenna French ... 19
- Abby Green ... 43
- Susan Huang ... 27
- Jordana Kamenitz ... 99
- Brandon Lam ... 53
- Sophie Lentz ... 34
- Max Yue Li ... 18
- Daniel Lynch ... 33
- Kelsey McGrath ... 115
- Alexis Muller ... 99
- Sara Perrigo ... 21
- Nicholas Tammaro ... 35

South Valley Middle School
Platteville, CO
- Machenzie Wernsman ... 67

Springhouse Middle School
Allentown, PA
- Rameen Khan ... 138

St Anne's School
Bristol, VA
- Aiden Blessing ... 176
- Noah Broglio ... 157
- Ryan Fish ... 159
- Aubrie Harmon ... 148
- Lindsay Newman ... 171
- Keegan Olson ... 168
- Ameira Pettitt ... 159
- Ava Rainero ... 148
- Tosh Thompson ... 157
- Ella Wood ... 148

St Jerome Elementary School
Philadelphia, PA
- Ruben Aguilar ... 64
- Jaclyn Bauerle ... 121
- Riley Butkovic ... 36
- Allison Carley ... 129
- Maura Corkery ... 19
- Kevin DiAmico ... 136
- Liam Donaghy ... 41
- Luke Elitz ... 104
- Emma Fahey ... 94
- Brooke Graham ... 72
- Tyler Hoffman ... 45
- Colin Hulmes ... 38
- Brianna Kane ... 107
- Madison Kerns ... 76
- Sage McKay ... 41
- Mikayla Murphy ... 34
- Ma'a Neba ... 81
- Melissa Pjetrushi ... 34
- Payton Pugh ... 28
- Joseph Richardson ... 54
- Emma Schultz ... 17
- Angela Sorbello ... 40
- Elizabeth Stampone ... 62
- Caitlin Warburton ... 43
- Julia Wilbekaitis ... 45

St Joan of Arc School
Hershey, PA
- Sebastian Angelo ... 166
- Elliana Bauer ... 166
- Abigail Bennett ... 175
- Leah Burke ... 149
- Deon Carter ... 158
- Braedin Deardorff ... 152
- Megan Irvine ... 149

Index by School

Gianna Lentini 149
Alessandra Marengo 160
Morgan Silber 146
Ryan Swallow 160

St John Bosco Academy
Pittsburgh, PA
Brandon Karafilis 74
Ennui Knapick 126
Maleah Neiport 57

St. John Neumann Academy
Blacksburg, VA

St John Neumann Academy
Blacksburg, VA
Emma Amodeo 158
Edy Aron 169
Brandon Bevins 165
Augie Biviano 159
Lydia Biviano 175
Andre Bousserghine 70
Martha Crawford 47
Sarah Duetsch 20
Isabella Gil 159
William Harrison 111
Alice Hong 86
Christopher Kaatz 20
Madeleine Kaatz 165
Matthew Kaatz 154
Alexandra Kosgei 151
Brennen Lucia 149
Gabriel Lunsford 94
Demetria Magnini 178
Ella Matthis 146
Sophia Mishoe 20
Bridget O'Brien 63
Luca Pickeral 146
Aidan Riley 32
Quinn Riley 146
Anna Sanford 175
Emily Sanford 159
Makel Sanjines 156
Henry Scallorns 150
Brady Semtner 17
Ella Semtner 86
Keely Semtner 151
Catherine Shewchuk 94
Mariana Soto 48
Rusel Steele 111
Sierra Symanoskie 146
Lyla Thurman 152
Santiago Valle 151
Addison Vaught 67
Lily Wallace 166
Clara Westcott 48
Jillian Wiersema 151
Sam Wiersema 151
Sarah Willey 155

St Mary Star of the Sea School
Hampton, VA
Parker Cruz 79

St Mary's Roman Catholic Separate School
Sexsmith, AB
Brennan McLaughlin 87

St Peter Cathedral School
Erie, PA
Katie Berry 65
Alayna Byes 77
Lucia Frezza 85
Mary Grace Kelly 46
Logan Lanagan-Blanc 77
Nicholas Nielsen 33
Julia Simpson 77
Aubrey Stuckey 41

St Sebastian Elementary School
Pittsburgh, PA
Rachel Sweeny 68

St Thomas the Apostle School
Phoenix, AZ
Michael Ellison 94

State Street Elementary School
Baden, PA
Haley Dobich 89
Katherine Hernandez 36
Alexis Hitchens 78
Jenna McFarland 34
Lily Park 56
Madison Prentice 30
Maddy Smith 62

Steamboat Springs Middle School
Steamboat Springs, CO
Sidney Barbier 128
Zoe Bennett-Manke 75
Emma Bessey 117
Marty Boyd 35
Luna Casey 29
Ella Chapman 61
Natasha Curzon 54
Brick Dalsis 50
Thea Dardanis 24
Rose Epstein 50
Bode Flanigan 142
Morgan Graham 19
Kamryn Greenland 113
Emma Harris 19
Patti Love 139
Posy Skov 59
Maisie Wagner 17

Stem Launch K-8 School
Thornton, CO
Mags Hornsby 90

Stem Magnet Lab School
Northglenn, CO
Abigail Gabbard 148
Lincoln Hastings 177
Emily Lilienthal 157
Mark Litwiler 155
Andrew Nelson 154
Amaya Rico 152
Alton Zimmerman 169

Summit Middle School
Frisco, CO
Alex Cain 127
Sophia Henry 41
Claudia Hicks 116
Korben Long 57
Dylan Perlow 104
Kasia Puc 113

Susquenita Elementary School
Duncannon, PA
Grace Ruth Evelyn Farmer 158
Addison Graupensperger 170

Swanson Middle School
Arlington, VA
Emily Mucchetti 39

Taylor Canyon Elementary School
Ogden, UT
Annie Roe 60

Teller Elementary School
Denver, CO
Jaron Barrett 82
Clare Hoyt 27
Reilly Landis 93
Jezebel Posey-Risberg 108
Jack Reed 130
Brayden Salankey 88
Irving Wilson 48

The Lutheran Academy Scranton
Scranton, PA
Nora Betts 111
Sarah Bjornstad 74
Rachel Bonebrake 156

The Valleys Senior Public School
Mississauga, ON
Karim Alomar 55
Eileen Chen 107
Ryan Eyzaguirre 52
Rajnandini Ganguli 26
Mohamed Hammad 138
Toshan Jain 48
Nadir Khan 141
Rahul Marwaha 81
Mahishajini Mohanathasan 31
Melanie Nguyen 70
Luca Pozderka 79
Syed Qasim 46
Ketaki Thatte 73
Eunice Tolujo 74
Rameeka Wajid 123
Alexis Zhou 138

Thomas Edison Charter School - South
Nibley, UT
Giselle Ayala 26

Timpanogos Intermediate School
Heber City, UT
Clara Robinson 102

Tuckahoe Middle School
Richmond, VA
Claudia Sachs 129

Tyee Elementary School
Vancouver, BC
    Isabelle Chang 30

Vernfield Elementary School
Telford, PA
    Carleigh Carmody 54
    Kara Conner 141
    Katie Dalton 99
    Hailey Danielson 134
    Tegan Farina 43
    Francie Flores 52
    Matthew Heffner 23
    Reiley Bell Knize 72
    Antonio Linberger 96
    Reese Pirtle 25
    Drew Stephens 27
    Madison Waehner 121

Verrado Middle School
Buckeye, AZ
    Kenza Amaris Scott 86

Villa Maria Academy Lower School
Immaculata, PA
    Benita Bernard 77
    Sophia Busciacco 104
    Olivia Currie 89
    Cassidy Fischer 77
    Madison Frank 113
    Joey Gaglioti 38
    Heidi Gresh 139
    Alexandra Harrington 22
    Christina Janowicz 38
    Zoë Mahrlig 128
    Sophia Nehr 140
    Maura Nolan 117
    Tori P. 51
    Abigail Todd 89

Waller Mill Fine Arts Magnet School
Williamsburg, VA
    Dakota Anderson 140
    Isaiah Anderson 139
    Dawn Brisco 140
    Naomi Gesler 69
    Jasmyn Guiffre 31
    Gwendolyn Holt 60
    Alicia Johnson 49
    Jack Johnson 63
    Lane McFarland 26
    Jazmin Padilla 139
    Lauryn Pardee 75

Walsh Elementary School
Walsh, CO
    Colby Batterton 170
    Maribel Carrillo 175
    James Galdean 154
    Emily Hume 151
    Jamie Hume 173
    Cody Malone 165
    Conner McDonald 168
    Susana Pantoja 154
    Melissa Rangel 175
    Henry Wright 146

Waples Mill Elementary School
Oakton, VA
    Viraj Kamath 163

Watauga Elementary School
Abingdon, VA
    Hailey Rowe 117
    Chloe Turman 34

Werner Elementary School
Fort Collins, CO
    Shiloh Robinson 131

Westbriar Elementary School
Vienna, VA
    Kelsey Hertz 137
    Jordan Seigel 64
    Sydney Topoleski 16

Westside Academy
Prince George, BC
    Madison Brasson 33
    Oliver Morrow 89
    Michaela Stillwell 40

White Pine Middle School
Richmond, UT
    Quincy Caldwell 80
    Alex Jensen 26
    Allison Langston 44
    Dallis Mattson 46
    Mathias Openshaw 135
    Nathan Seamons 137
    Danny Wright 141

William Berczy Public School
Unionville, ON
    Tony Yao 56

William Cook Elementary School
Richmond, BC
    Angela Yu 78
    James Yu 62

Wismer Public School
Markham, ON
    Saniya Khanna 125

Author Autograph Page

Author Autograph Page

Author Autograph Page

Author Autograph Page